Classical Mythology

Elizabeth Vandiver, Ph.D.

THE
GREAT
COURSES

PUBLISHED BY:

THE GREAT COURSES
Corporate Headquarters
4840 Westfields Boulevard, Suite 500
Chantilly, Virginia 20151-2299
Phone: 1-800-832-2412
Fax: 703-378-3819
www.thegreatcourses.com

Elizabeth Vandiver, Ph.D.

Visiting Assistant Professor of Classics
Whitman College

Professor Elizabeth Vandiver did her undergraduate work at Shimer College, Mt. Carroll, Illinois, where she matriculated in 1972 as a sixteen-year-old "early entrant." After receiving her B.A. in 1975, she spent several years working as a librarian before deciding to pursue graduate work in Classics at the University of Texas at Austin. She received her M.A. in 1984 and her Ph.D. in 1990.

In addition to teaching at the University of Maryland, Professor Vandiver has held visiting professorships at Northwestern University, where she taught from 1996 to 1999; the University of Georgia; The Intercollegiate Center for Classical Studies in Rome, Italy; Loyola University, New Orleans; and Utah State University. Her course on Classical Mythology has been particularly successful.

In 1998, Dr. Vandiver received the American Philological Association's Excellence in Teaching Award, the most prestigious teaching award available to American classicists. Other awards include the Northwestern University Department of Classics Excellence in Teaching award for 1998 and the University of Georgia's Outstanding Honors Professor award in 1993 and 1994.

Dr. Vandiver has published a book, *Heroes in Herodotus: The Interaction of Myth and History*, and several articles, as well as delivering numerous papers at national and international conferences. She is currently working on a second book that examines the influence of the classical tradition on the British poets of World War I. Her previous Teaching Company courses include *The Iliad of Homer*, *The Odyssey of Homer*, and *Virgil's Aeneid.*

Dr. Vandiver is married to Franklin J. Hildy, Ph.D., Professor and Chair of the Department of Theatre at the University of Maryland. ∎

Table of Contents

Table of Contents

Table of Contents

Classical Mythology

Scope:

This set of 24 lectures introduces the student to the primary characters and most important stories of classical Greek and Roman mythology and surveys some of the leading theoretical approaches to understanding myth in general and classical myth in particular.

The first lecture introduces students to the overall plan of the lectures and identifies key issues of definition and terminology. This lecture begins a discussion of the definition of "myth" that will continue through the next two lectures. The lecture also discusses some of the problems inherent in studying classical mythology, which is preserved in literary form.

Lectures 2 and 3 examine some of the most influential 19th- and 20th-century theories about myth's nature and function. Lecture 2 discusses the theories of Müller, Lang, Frazer, Harrison, and Malinowski; Lecture 3 looks at the psychological theories of Freud and Jung; the structuralist methodologies of Propp, Lévi-Strauss, and Burkert; and the metaphysical approach of Campbell.

Lectures 4 through 6 concentrate on the account of the creation of the world given in Hesiod's *Theogony* and in the much later Roman author Ovid's *Metamorphoses*. Lecture 4 examines the three-generation struggle for power in *Theogony*, which ends with Zeus's rise to power as the ruling god. This lecture discusses the implications of a creation story in which the gods are not transcendent but are part of the physical universe and come into being with it. The lecture ends by briefly comparing Ovid's creation story to Hesiod's. Lecture 5 continues the discussion of Zeus, focusing on his role as the protector of abstract concepts (such as justice) that concern the orderly functioning of human society. The lecture also examines Zeus's early marriages and the birth of Athena from his head and suggests possible interpretations of these episodes. Lecture 6 looks at Hesiod's depiction of humans in the myth of Prometheus and Pandora. We consider the implications of this myth for the Greek view of society and particularly of women and gender roles. The lecture then discusses the nature of the gods, as reflected in *Theogony*, and delineates the essential differences between gods and humans.

Lectures 7 through 11 focus on individual gods and their interactions with human beings. Lecture 7 examines the crucial myth of Demeter, Persephone, and Hades as it is recounted in the *Homeric Hymn to Demeter*. The lecture discusses the myth's implications for the Greek view of life and death, marriage, and gender roles. Lecture 8 continues our discussion of Demeter by examining the Eleusinian Mysteries, one of the most important ancient religious cults, which honored her and promised a happy afterlife to initiates. The lecture then compares the afterlife implied by the Eleusinian Mysteries with contrasting views of the afterlife found elsewhere in Greek myth and religion. Lecture 9 discusses Apollo and Artemis and examines their characteristic functions and associations, including Apollo's famous oracle at Delphi. Lecture 10 examines Zeus's two youngest sons, Hermes and Dionysos, and offers interpretations of the very disparate areas of influence of each of these gods. In Lecture 11, we examine Aphrodite, the goddess of sexual passion. The lecture focuses on the account in the *Homeric Hymn to Aphrodite* of her affair with the human Anchises and discusses the implications of that affair for our understanding of the Greek view of sexual passion and the relationship between the sexes.

Lecture 12 turns to the cultural and historical background of Greek myth. We examine the similarities between Hesiod's creation account and Mesopotamian myth; then we look at the two great prehistoric cultures of Greece, the Minoans and the Mycenaeans, and discuss the origins of classical mythology in those two cultures. The lecture takes the modern theory of a prehistoric "great mother goddess" as a test case for the difficulties of reconstructing prehistoric religious beliefs.

In Lectures 13 through 21, we shift our focus from the gods to the heroes. Lecture 13 discusses Hesiod's story of the Five Ages or Races of human beings (in *Works and Days*) and contrasts it with Ovid's reworking of the same myth. The main difference is that Hesiod includes a Race of Heroes; the lecture examines what is meant by the term "hero" in Greek myth and discusses the possibility that the heroes reflect memories of the Mycenaean

Age. Lecture 14 gives a detailed synopsis of the adventures of one such hero, the Athenian Theseus. We pay special attention to his adventure with the Minotaur, his marriage to an Amazon, and his killing of his son Hippolytos. Lecture 15 continues our examination of Theseus by discussing possible theoretical interpretations of his adventure with the Minotaur, then looks at the possibility that this myth is based in memories of Minoan civilization. In Lecture 16, we consider the greatest and most complicated hero of all, Heracles. We see how this hero embodies contradictions. We discuss Hera's special hatred for Heracles, consider Heracles's tendency toward excess, and examine his famous twelve labors. The lecture describes Heracles's death and subsequent immortality and concludes by discussing some of the implications of this hero's many contradictory characteristics.

Lecture 17 summarizes the most famous event of classical myth, the Trojan War. The Trojan War is the most frequently drawn on by authors in various genres, possibly because it functioned as the dividing line between the heroic age and the age of normal human history. The lecture includes a brief summary of the basic story of the Trojan War, from its beginnings in the marriage of Peleus and Thetis through the ill-fated sack of Troy. Lecture 18 moves from the Trojan War to one of the primary families involved in it, the House of Atreus. The lecture discusses the hereditary curse of that unhappy family and considers the implications of that curse for the concepts of fate and individual responsibility. Lecture 19 continues our examination of the cursed House of Atreus by looking closely at the use Aeschylus made of that myth in his great trilogy *The Oresteia*. The lecture discusses Aeschylus's shaping of the myth to focus on issues of justice and considers the difficulty of separating the myth itself from the literary treatment of the myth. Lecture 20 addresses similar issues in its examination of Sophocles's *Oedipus the King*. The lecture briefly reviews Freud's and Lévi-Strauss's readings of the myth, considers the standard interpretation that the play's main focus is the conflict between fate and free will, and discusses another reading that sees Oedipus as a paradigm of the 5th-century Athenian rationalist. The lecture ends by examining the difficulties of discussing this myth apart from Sophocles's play. Lecture 21 pulls together several threads of earlier lectures by examining the threatening women and female monsters that many heroes must face. The lecture concentrates on the Amazons and Medea and includes a brief discussion of such monsters as Medusa and the Sphinx.

Lectures 22 and 23 focus on specifically Roman uses of classical myth. In Lecture 22, we consider the Roman appropriation of the Greek story of the Trojan War and see how the Romans shaped the story to serve as their own foundation myth. We also discuss the purely Roman legend of Romulus and Remus. Lecture 23 sets Ovid's *Metamorphoses* in context by examining the cultural milieu in which Ovid wrote; the lecture also considers the difficulties of trying to recover "myth" from Ovid's very literary, ironic retelling of it.

Finally, Lecture 24 concludes the course by examining the influence of Ovid in particular and classical myth in general on later European, English, and American culture. The lecture suggests that the narrative sequences, images, and characters of classical myth are still very much alive in modern culture. ■

Introduction
Lecture 1

Now these three categories of traditional tales, these subdivisions into myth, legend and folktale, are useful; they can sometimes be very helpful in determining what kind of a story we are dealing with. But at least in classical mythology, these categories overlap to such an extent that the distinctions seem rather artificial.

This introductory lecture has three main objects. The lecture begins by defining the terms "classical" and "mythology." The second section of the lecture considers some of the difficulties inherent in the study of classical mythology. The third section outlines the approach and format of the course.

What is meant by "classical mythology"? "Classical" in this context refers to the cultures of ancient Greece and Rome. Ancient Greek culture's highpoint occurred in Athens in the 5th century B.C. Roman culture reached its zenith in the 1st centuries B.C. and A.D. These two cultures shared the bulk of their mythology, because Rome simply adapted Greek mythology wholesale. In this course, I will use the terms "classical" and "Greek" mythology interchangeably.

"Mythology" is an ambiguous term. Strictly speaking, the "-ology" ending means "the study of"; thus, "mythology" means "the study of myth." However, the word "mythology" is frequently used to mean "a culture's body of myths." "Myth" is a notoriously difficult concept to define, as we will see in the next two lectures. For this lecture, we need a basic, working definition to start with. I define myth as "traditional stories a society tells itself that encode or represent the world-view, beliefs, principles, and often fears of that society." We will look at definitions in much more detail in the next two lectures, but this definition is sufficient for now.

Many scholars subdivide traditional tales into three categories: myth, legend, and folktale. In this scheme, myth refers only to stories that concern the gods and their rites. It is closely connected with religious ritual. Legend refs to traditional stories rooted in historical fact, describing the (greatly exaggerated) adventures of people who actually lived, such as Robin Hood or George Washington. Folktale refers to stories that are primarily entertaining and that often involve animals or ordinary but clever humans, such as Little Red Riding Hood or Goldilocks. This course will cover traditional stories that would count as "legend" according to this division; we will even see a few examples of "folktale."

If myths are traditional tales that a society tells itself about itself, then the next question must be: which societies use myth, and why? All societies have myths; however, myth is most important in preliterate cultures. Modern, literate cultures have many different forms of explanation available to them, including theology, psychology, philosophy, ethics, history, and so on. All these depend on a sophisticated and long-lived literate tradition. In a preliterate culture, myth is the only means available to explain and discuss a whole range of phenomena and concepts. This idea is important for the question of what *myth* really means. Modern Western culture makes a distinction between fact and fiction, true and false, actual and imaginary. When myth is the only available form of explanation, these distinctions cannot be so clear cut. The question "What does it really mean?" is anything but simple. In Greek myth, Gaia (Earth) and Ouranos (Sky) are good examples of this. As anthropomorphized deities, they are also physical "realities"—our usual distinction between metaphorical and literal doesn't apply.

Greek mythology, like most other mythologies, developed in a preliterate culture. Trying to study Greek mythology, thus, is somewhat paradoxical, because literature is our main source of access to that mythology. Many modern scholars of myth work with living cultures. This anthropological approach means that scholars of living cultures can observe myth in its "native habitat." In studying classical mythology, we are, in effect, trying to "do" anthropology backward in time, on a culture without living representatives. Our sources for this are literature and archaeological artifacts. Both present formidable problems.

Even in as well-documented and well-studied a society as classical Greece, the written versions of myths present difficulties for scholars. Written versions of myths are "frozen," as in the case of Oedipus, whose final fate was described differently by Sophocles and Homer. Because myths were the "givens" of the society, literary works frequently refer to myths without giving a full synopsis of them. Only a fraction of ancient Greek literature has survived, and it often does not tell us what we would most like to know about people's religious beliefs and practices, daily lives, and so on. One book that we will use a great deal in this course is *The Library of Greek Mythology*, by Apollodorus (who probably lived in the 1st or 2nd century AD), which gives summaries of most of the myths we will discuss. The archaeological record and the literature can sometimes shed light on one another. Archaeological remains, such as buildings and artwork, are even more difficult to interpret than literature is. References in literature can mislead us into thinking that we know what an object or building was for when we don't.

We cannot recover all the nuances of the myths' functions in their original society, any more than we can recover all their variants.

What are the implications for our study of classical mythology? We are studying only particular variants of the myths. Sometimes we can reconstruct a fairly full version of the myth as it underlies the written variants and as it must have existed in the living culture of ancient Greece. Many times we cannot; references remain tantalizingly obscure. Occasionally a work of art will preserve what is clearly a very different version from the ones preserved in literature, which reminds us that living myth is not fixed. We cannot recover all the nuances of the myths' functions in their original society, any more than we can recover all their variants. Within these limitations, however, we can use what we know about the society to shed light on the myths and what we know about the myths to shed light on the society.

These lectures will concentrate on several of the most famous and important myths of Greco-Roman culture. The course has three main points: First, the lectures will familiarize students with the primary classical myths that are covered by the course. Most lectures will include some synopsis of the relevant myth's storyline. We will frequently address the surviving variants of the myths and the implications of these variants for our understanding. The "Essential Readings" will usually be taken from classical literature, especially Apollodorus. Second, the lectures will discuss the cultural aspects of the myths under consideration *within* their formative culture (i.e., ancient Greece). Finally, we will consider how well (or poorly) these myths "match" various theories about myth and will discuss the usefulness of these theoretical approaches for our understanding of classical myth. ∎

Supplementary Reading

Bascom, "Forms of Folklore."

Kirk, "On Defining Myths."

Questions to Consider

1. Do you think the division of traditional tales into myth, legend, and folktale is useful? Why or why not? How would you categorize Santa Claus (whose name derives from Saint Nicholas) under this system?

2. One problem of reconstructing Greek myth is that we have only a small amount of ancient Greek literature. Would the problem be solved if we had everything the Greeks ever wrote? Put another way, can we ever reconstruct the belief system of a society solely from its literature?

Introduction
Lecture 1—Transcript

Hello and welcome to this course on classical mythology. My name is Elizabeth Vandiver; I teach Classics, that is, Latin and Greek language, culture, history and literature, at the University of Maryland. In these 24 lectures, I am going to be talking to you about the mythology of classical society.

In this introductory lecture, there are three main things I want to accomplish. I want to start by defining some terms: "classical," "mythology," and most importantly and most difficultly, "myth" itself. Then, I want to look at some of the problems and difficulties inherent in studying classical mythology, and finally, briefly at the end of the lecture, I want to describe the approach I am going to take to the course, what I am going to do with these lectures as we look at classical mythology.

So, to start with definitions. What do we mean by "classical mythology?" The term "classical" in this context refers to the cultures of ancient Greece and Rome. Now, those are two separate cultures, separated from one another not only by location—Italy and Greece—and by language—the Romans spoke Latin, the Greeks spoke Greek—but also separated from one another by time in regards to their high points. Greek culture reached its high point in Athens in the fifth century B.C. Roman culture hit its zenith in the first centuries B.C. and A.D. So, there is a gap of several hundred years between the high points of these two civilizations, and yet we talk about their mythology as a single unit—classical mythology.

We can do that because while they are two separate cultures, there is a strong relationship between the two in their literature, their art, and particularly, in their mythology. Roman culture borrowed (or perhaps "adapted" would be a better term) a great deal of its mythology wholesale from Greek culture. Therefore, the myths that developed in ancient Greece were taken over by the ancient Romans. This makes it possible to discuss not just Greek mythology or Roman mythology, but classical mythology as a unified whole. In this course, I will probably find myself using the terms Greek myth and classical myth more or less interchangeably, simply because the myths did originate in Greece and were later adapted by the Romans. In the lectures at the end of the course, we will look specifically at what the Romans did with Greek myth when they adapted it.

So much for "classical." What about "mythology?" The term mythology is actually rather ambiguous. Strictly speaking, it ought to mean the study of myth. The "-ology" ending means study of—just as biology is the study of life, psychology is the study of the mind, geology is the study of the earth— mythology ought to mean the study of myth. In fact, some scholars do use it that way. Properly speaking, that is what it ought to mean. Yet, in common usage, mythology tends to mean the whole body of myths told by a particular culture; if someone says to you, "I've been reading a lot of Norse mythology lately," you don't assume that mean they have been reading theoretical statements about the myths of Norse culture, or that they have been reading examinations of those myths. You tend to believe that they have been reading an anthology of Norse myths.

Mythology has these two separate meanings: the study of myth, and simply the whole body of myth developed within any particular culture. I will use the term both ways in these lectures. We are doing mythology in the first sense: we are studying myth. I will also frequently refer to classical mythology or Greek mythology, meaning the body of myths developed in those cultures.

If mythology is the study of myth or the whole body of myth developed by a culture, what is "myth?" That is a question that has no easy or obvious answer; the attempt to define myth is very difficult. Myth is a notoriously hard concept to define, as we will see in detail in the next two lectures where we look at several theories about myth. For this lecture, I want to give you a basic working definition to start with, a definition I have worked out over years of teaching classical mythology to college students. I define myth—as a working definition to start with—as "traditional stories a society tells itself that encode or represent the world view, beliefs, principles, and often the fears of that society." Every single term in that definition could be argued with. There are scholars who would disagree with every one of them. Just as a working definition to start with, it is, I think, useful.

Myths, in my definition, are traditional stories or tales. Right away, that needs a little fine-tuning. Many scholars subdivide traditional tales, in any society, into three subcategories: myth, legend and folktale. In that division, myth—"myth proper" as it is sometimes called—would refer only to stories that have to do directly with the gods. A story about Zeus's rise to power would be a myth in this three-fold division; a story about Oedipus, Odysseus, or Achilles would not be, because they are humans and not gods.

In this three-fold division, "legend" would refer to traditional stories rooted in historical fact, describing adventures of people who once actually lived, but whose adventures have been greatly exaggerated through the passage of time. Robin Hood would be an example of a legend. Taking a more recent example closer to home, George Washington is starting to accrue all sorts of legendary stories around him. There is no doubt that there was an actual George Washington, and yet many of the stories we tell about him—such as chopping down the cherry tree, throwing a silver dollar across the river—those sorts of exploits have more to do with the symbolic function that we want George Washington to fulfill in our society, than with anything that the historical man George Washington actually did. Given enough centuries, he could become purely legendary.

The third division, "folktale," would refer to stories that are primarily entertaining, and that often involve animals (very frequently talking animals) or clever human beings, but not exceptional human beings—common people who are particularly clever in one way or another. Folktale is also referred to as "fairy tale," though that is often a misleading term because these stories do not often have anything to do with fairies whatsoever. An example of folktale would be "Little Red Riding Hood," "Goldilocks and the Three Bears," that kind of thing.

Now these three categories of traditional tales, these subdivisions into myth, legend and folktale, are useful; they can sometimes be very helpful in determining what kind of a story we are dealing with. But at least in classical mythology, these categories overlap to such an extent that the distinctions seem rather artificial. We have stories in classical mythology that combine elements of all three, myth, legend and folktale. Some of the most famous works of classical literature—for instance, *The Iliad* and the *Odyssey*—are impossible to categorize in this system as either myth or legend, because they partake of elements of both. In this course, we will be looking at traditional stories that would count as legend according to this scheme, and we will even see several examples of at least folktale elements within the traditional stories that we look at. I tend to use myth as a wider category to account for all three types of traditional stories.

If myths are traditional tales or stories that a society tells itself about itself, then the next question must be: Which societies use myth and why do they use it? All societies have myths. They seem to be a given of human culture. I don't think there has ever been a society that did not have some sort of traditional stories, traditional tales. But myth has an importance in preliterate cultures that it has lost in modern, highly literate, highly technological Western culture. I say "preliterate" rather than "illiterate," because "illiterate" always sounds pejorative to me. It sounds like the culture ought to be able to read and write and is just too lazy to have managed that technology yet. "Preliterate" seems more accurate, because it indicates more precisely the status of the culture. The culture may be very sophisticated but has not yet developed writing.

In a preliterate culture, myth has an importance that it does not have in a literate culture. The reason for that, I think, is that in a literate culture, we have all sorts of different forms of explanation, of analysis—different windows for looking at the world and human experience that have developed after the invention of writing. For instance, we have: psychology, theology, history, science. We have a whole cornucopia of approaches, if we want to ask ourselves questions such as: "Why does the world work as it works? Why are physical entities as they are? How can human beings get along better together? Why are there two sexes? Why do the two sexes have so much trouble getting along with one another?" Those sorts of questions we can approach through any one of a number of avenues.

Take that last one. In our culture, we ask ourselves, "Why is it that men and women have such a hard time getting along together?" We can turn to psychology. We can turn to biology, to science. We can, if we like, turn to theology. We have all sorts of avenues of looking at, exploring, discussing, analyzing that question. But, in a preliterate society, what means do they have for discussing such issues? If they do not have a sophisticated, long-lived, literate tradition out of which these different disciplines can grow, what do they have? The answer is they have traditional tales—or, if you like, myth.

In other words, in a preliterate society, all the functions that these different "-ologies" and "-osophies" that I have just talked about have to fulfill must be fulfilled, in a preliterate society, only by traditional tales. Students often look very surprised when I say that, but if you think about it for a minute, I think you will see that it is so. How can a culture that does not have writing pass down its belief system, its values, its traditions, its history, its view of the world, its view about the gods, about humans? The only open means is traditional, word-of-mouth, repeated knowledge handed down from one generation to the next, and that knowledge is almost always put in the form of stories—probably for ease of remembering it and thinking about it.

Now, this has important implications for the question I am frequently asked in the classroom, "What does myth really mean?" In modern Western—or at least modern American—culture, we tend to make a very strong distinction between fact and fiction, true and false, real and imaginary, literal and metaphorical. That is, in fact, one of the main analytical tools we use for thinking about anything. That is one of the first things we ask of any story. (Most of our stories come to us now—to most of us—through television and movies rather than through books; that does not matter.) One of the first things we ask about any story is, "Is this true or is it fiction? Is this biography or is it a novel?" One of the reasons that so many people were uncomfortable with the recent movie *Titanic*, I think, is that it blended fact and fiction in a way that we found uncomfortable. It was a very detailed factual reenactment of the sinking of the Titanic, but it incorporated into that factual reenactment a completely fictional story. We are uncomfortable with that. We don't know how to deal with that sort of story.

In a culture in which traditional tales are the only available form of explanation, analysis, thinking about reality—if you want to put it that way—these distinctions can't be anything like so clear cut. The questions "What does this myth really mean? What does this story really mean?" become anything but simple. Let me give you an example of that from Greek mythology itself. In Lecture Four, we will start talking about the creation story of the Greeks as told by an author named Hesiod. And, in that story, we will encounter two entities named Gaia and Ouranos. Gaia is a goddess; Ouranos is a god. They have volition, they have desires, they have speech. They can mate with one another, produce children. They are anthropomorphized human-like entities, female and male.

And yet, *Gaia* is simply a word that means Earth. *Ouranos* is simply a word that means sky. Gaia is the earth. If you go out and stamp your foot on the ground, you are stamping on Gaia. Ouranos is the sky. All you have to do to see him is go out and look up. Students in my classes will very frequently raise their hands and say, "Which is Gaia, really? Is she really the Earth, or is she really a goddess with arms legs, mind, speech, etc.?" And I answer— it infuriates them, but I answer—"Yes," because that is the only possible answer. She is really both of those things. The distinction we tend to make between metaphorical and literal simply is not there.

A side point: We do sometimes tend to speak in metaphor. Several years ago, I was watching a television program about protestors who were protesting logging in the redwood forests in the West—and I remember one protestor (who was chained to a redwood tree) saying, "We have abused Mother Nature shamelessly, and she will take her revenge." That sounds on the surface like the same sort of thing that you see with Gaia in Greek myth. Yet, I think all of us recognize that as a metaphor. We don't think there is actually an entity called Mother Nature out there who is looking at human beings and saying, "I'm going to get those little creeps for what they've done to me." We recognize this as a metaphorical way of saying that we have damaged our own environment, and we will suffer for it. The metaphor still has much more emotive value than the purely literal statement, but we recognize it as a metaphor. It would be a mistake to assume that Hesiod and his audience— when Hesiod talks about Gaia and Ouranos—felt it as a metaphor in the same way. I am quite sure they did not. Gaia was a goddess at the same time that she was the Earth.

Greek mythology, like other mythologies, developed in a preliterate culture. This means that if we set out to study Greek mythology or classical mythology, we are setting for ourselves a very paradoxical task. It developed in a preliterate culture, but how do we know about it? What do we study when we study Greek myth? We study it through literature. We have to. That is our only access to it, or our main access to it, is through literature. Modern scholars of myth very frequently turn to modern, preliterate societies to try to figure out what myth is and how it works. The anthropological approach to myth is one of the most fruitful ones in the modern field of theoretical myth study.

In the anthropological approach, scholars go in to live in cultures, talk to living representatives of those cultures, write down what representatives tell them about their myths, get a sense of how myth works in its native habitat. They can study myth as a living element of a living culture. When we talk about classical myth—when we want to look at the myth of the ancient Greeks and Romans—in effect, we are trying to do anthropology backwards in time. We are trying to do anthropological observation on a culture that has no living representatives. This is a very frustrating and very difficult task. Obviously, I think it is worth undertaking, but there are some difficulties and problems inherent in it that we need to bear in mind throughout this course.

What are our sources for doing this "backwards in time" anthropology? Most obviously, literature—the literary works that have survived from Greece and Rome that recount the myths of those cultures. And, to supplement literature, archaeology comes into the picture. We can supplement archaeological artifacts—remnants of buildings, artwork. Both of these things, literature and archaeology, present formidable problems for trying to reconstruct what Greek and Roman myths were in their living environment.

First, let's think about literature. Even in as well-documented and well-studied a society as classical Greece, the written versions of myths involve several problems for a scholar of myth. First of all, written myths are frozen. By that I mean once a version of a myth is written down, it is fixed. There it is. And we, as literate people, have a strong tendency to assume that that means that version is somehow *the* myth—the real myth—the only way the myth was ever told. But that is not how traditional tales work in any oral setting. If I asked every one of you watching this lecture to tell me the story of "Little Red Riding Hood," I would get as many slightly different versions as there are people watching this lecture. That is how a living oral tradition works.

Once a story is written down, when our only access to it is through writing, we tend to assume that is the real story. I can give a very clear example of what I mean by this. Everyone knows the story of *Oedipus the King*—how he killed his father and married his mother without knowing who they were. When he discovered the terrible thing that he had done, after his mother hanged herself, Oedipus blinded himself, went into exile, never returned home to Thebes again. Right? Well, right, according to Sophocles who wrote the play *Oedipus the King*. In Homer, in the *Odyssey*, there is a very brief reference to Oedipus, which agrees that yes, he killed his father and married his mother. Yes, his mother killed herself after the truth came out, but Oedipus, said Homer, continued to rule at Thebes for many years thereafter. Which is the real version of the Oedipus myth? They both are. Sophocles's version dominates our understanding of the myth because it is such a marvelous play and so famous. This is the kind of thing we have to guard against. Often we have only one version of a myth. We have to remember that there probably were others.

Another problem in studying myth through literature is that myths were the givens of the society, were something that everybody knew; and so very frequently authors will make the briefest possible allusion to a myth without explaining what it means or who it is. I did this a few minutes ago when I referred to George Washington. I didn't have to tell you who George Washington was, tell you where he was born, where he died, what he did, whom he married—you know all that. He is a given of our society. A scholar 2500 years from now in the future—if all the references that scholar had to George Washington were equally elliptical as what I just said, it would be very difficult to reconstruct who George Washington was, what he did and why he was important. That is another difficulty in approaching myth through literature.

Another problem is that only a fraction of ancient Greek literature has survived. Most of what was written has been lost, and what has survived does not tell us what we would particularly like to know. They weren't written for us, so they don't give us the details that would be most helpful to us. One book we will use a great deal in this course is called *The Library of Greek Mythology*. It was written by a man named Apollodorus, about whom we know absolutely nothing except that he wrote this book. He lived in the first or second century A.D., probably. And he compiled brief summaries of all the myths he knew, at a time when some of those myths were starting to fragment or be forgotten. So that is very useful to us. We will use Apollodorus, but even there we have to remember that he is giving usually only one or two versions of myths; and that there may be myths he chose not to recount or did not know; and that there may be other versions of those he did recount.

So much for literature. What about archaeology? The archaeological record and literature can often shed light on one another, but archaeology is, if anything, even more difficult to use as a reconstruction of myth than literature is. An archaeological artifact, by itself, tells us little or nothing about a myth to which it may refer. A statue, a painting—if we do not already know the stories on which those are based, we cannot extrapolate the stories from the artifacts themselves. The same is true for buildings. If we know a building was a temple in honor of a particular god, we may be able to come up with some idea of what went on in that building, and how that particular god was honored. If we don't have external—and that, in the case of an ancient culture, means *written*—evidence to explain the archaeology, the archaeology itself can often be close to incomprehensible.

There is a joke among classical archaeologists that when an archaeologist has no idea what an object is for, he or she will say it is of "clear ritual significance." If we don't know what something was, it must have been used in a ritual. That really explains nothing, and that is a problem that we come up against in archaeology over and over again—not knowing what things were for, not knowing the stories behind images.

We can also be misled by references in literature to thinking we know what an archaeological building or artifact was for, when actually we don't. Let's imagine for a moment that we are archaeologists 2500 years in the future, excavating some great American city—Washington, D.C.—and that we have as remnants of English-language literature several novels of Dickens, two or three of Jane Austen's novels, *Huckleberry Finn* and eight volumes of the 1925 *Encyclopedia Britannica*, including the Volume G. As we excavate Washington, D.C., we come across all sorts of small buildings, each one laid out on the same plan, and each one with large, clearly ritually significant golden arches in front of it.

We have read our Dickens and our Jane Austen. We've got Volume G of the *Encyclopedia Britannica*. We know that gothic cathedrals and churches featured arches. It is a little bit disconcerting that our one American novel, *Huckleberry Finn,* doesn't say anything about these little gothic churches, but Mark Twain wasn't a very religious man perhaps, or he just wasn't interested in something everybody already knew. So, there you have it: McDonald's or gothic churches? Now, that is a silly example, perhaps, but I think it is also an illustrative example, because, very frequently, the written record is no closer a match to the archaeological record than that. We can *think* we know what we are looking at when, in actuality, we are looking at something entirely and completely different, but we have no way of knowing that.

So where does this leave us? Is this a hopeless endeavor? Should we just give up at this point and say there is no way we could possibly study classical mythology? Obviously, I don't think so. I think we need to bear these difficulties in mind as we start our survey of classical mythology. We need to remember that we are studying only particular variants of the myths. Sometimes, we can reconstruct a fairly full version of how the myth must have operated in its original society, when we have all sorts of variants to work from. Other times we can't. Other times we will have only one version of a myth and no others. Some references remain tantalizingly obscure. Sometimes we just don't know what a character's name or what a snippet of a story refers to.

Occasionally, a work of art preserves what is clearly a very different version from the ones known to us by literature. There is a beautiful classical Greek vase painting of a character who is quite clearly Jason. Jason got the Golden Fleece after his voyage on the Argo; the Golden Fleece is there on a tree behind Jason; the tree is guarded by a dragon. All of these elements point to the fact that this is very clearly Jason. Yet, in this painting, the dragon is either swallowing Jason or spitting him back out again. Jason is halfway out of the dragon's mouth. His arms and head are visible outside of the dragon's mouth. In no written version of Jason's story that has survived for us, does the dragon eat Jason or attempt to eat Jason. The whole point is that Jason is helped by Medea, who gives him a magic potion so that he can overcome the dragon without being eaten. If this vase painting had not survived, we would not know that there had ever been a variant in which Jason was eaten by the dragon. Because of the painting, we know this variant existed, but that is all we know about it. We have no written description of that version of Jason's story.

We can't recover all the versions of a myth. We also probably can't ever know all the nuances, all the resonances of that myth within its own society. Again, when I say George Washington, that brings up all sorts of associations in our mind: grade school, plays (I played George Washington when I was six years old in the grade school play), the Fourth of July, bands, John Phillip Souza marches. All of those things are there as free associations with the name George Washington. That kind of nuance, that kind of resonance is unrecoverable. We are not going to know that in all its detail about any culture, probably, other than our own. Within these limitations, we can use what we know about classical society to shed light on its mythology, and we can use what we know about the myths to shed light on the society.

What I want to conclude with in this lecture very briefly is what I am planning to do in the course, how I am planning to organize the lectures. There are three main points to the course. First of all, most simply, the lectures will provide you with familiarity with the primary classical myths that are covered by the course. This is by no means a survey of *all* classical myths, or even of all important classical myths. I've had to leave a very great deal out. What I have tried to do is to pick representative, important myths that will give you a good taste of classical mythology.

Of course, the course will familiarize you with at least some of the major characters, stories, themes of classical myth. So most of the lectures will include some synopsis of the relevant myth's story line. That will frequently mean discussing different versions, variants of the myth when we have them, and discussing the implications of those variants for our understanding of how the myths work. The essential reading for each lecture will normally be taken from classical literature, very frequently from Apollodorus's *The Library of Greek Mythology.*

Second, the lectures will discuss the cultural aspects of these myths, as they functioned in the culture that developed them. That is, we will look at the myths in the context of ancient Greek and ancient Roman culture, and I will talk about what the myths tell us about the belief systems of those cultures, what those cultures tell us about the meanings of the myth.

Finally, we will consider, in many of the lectures, how well or how poorly the myths we are looking at match various theories about myth as a category—about myth with a capital M. And we will discuss the usefulness of various theories and theoretical approaches for our understanding of classical mythology.

In this lecture, we have sketched out a working definition of what myth is. We have talked about some of the difficulties of studying classical mythology. And, in our next lecture, we will move on to continue our discussion of what myth is and how it works, by beginning our examination of several of the most influential theories about myth and its function.

What Is Myth?

Lecture 2

One useful distinction of categorizing is to say that "religion" refers to what people actually do to honor their gods—the rites, ceremonies, rituals and so forth that people enact in honor of their gods—whereas "myth" refers to the underlying narratives, the narratives that explain or justify or go along with those rites, rituals and ceremonies.

The question "What is myth?" has no easy or obvious answer. As used in popular speech, "myth" has several meanings that we can exclude right away. It is often used to mean a lie, a mistaken belief, or a misconception. These usages do not concern us here. Despite the difficulties of definition, most people have a sense that the category of myth exists and that they know it when they see it.

We can begin to supplement our working definition by identifying some characteristics of "myth":

- Myths are traditional tales or stories. Myths are presented in narrative form. Myths are handed down in a society from one generation to the next. It is usually impossible to say who first "invented" a particular myth. In this regard, they are unlike most other forms of narrative, such as poems, novels, and plays.

- Myths are set in the past. A myth recounts events of long ago (usually very long ago). Myths often reflect the assumption that in the far past, things were different in many ways.

> **It is usually impossible to say who first "invented" a particular myth.**

- Myths are ostensibly "true"; that is, they present themselves as giving an accurate narrative of "what really happened." A culture rarely recognizes its own mythology as mythology. Judged from *within* a culture, myths are true accounts of the way things really are.

- Myths often explain, justify, instruct, or warn. An *aetiological myth* may explain why things are as they are or how certain events, entities, or conditions came into existence. A *charter myth* may offer a justification for a certain rite or social institution. A myth may instruct its audience in how people ought or ought not to behave. Such instruction frequently takes the form of a warning by showing the consequences of misbehavior.

- Myths frequently concern gods and the supernatural. This area of myth overlaps with religion. Obviously, categorization of certain narratives about divinities as "myths" depends largely on whether the observer believes those narratives or not.

From antiquity onward, many scholars have come up with theories that attempt to define and explain myth. These theories fall into two main types, which could be called the "what" and the "why" types of theory. "What" theories attempt to explain myth by identifying it as a subcategory, derivative, or forerunner of something else (such as history, ritual, or philosophy). At their worst, such theories are excessively reductive; they tend to say that myth "is only" misunderstood history, or primitive science, or some other thing. For example, Euhemerus (c. 300 B.C.E.) suggested that myth was misremembered history; the gods of Greece had originally been great kings whose characteristics were exaggerated through time. Later versions of this theory are called *euhemerism*. Even at their best, such theories tend to ignore the distinctive qualities that make myth appealing; the theories can't explain why transformations into myth occur in the first place.

"Why" theories look for wider explanations to identify the impetus in the human mind or human culture that motivates myth-making. Psychological and structuralist theories fall under this heading. "Why" theories assume that myth is an extra- or transcultural phenomenon; the same narrative elements serve the same functions in different cultures. Some overlap exists, of course, between the two types of theories. As we shall see, "what" theories were more common in the 19th century and "why" theories, in the twentieth.

One very popular theory that has been resurrected over and over since antiquity is that myths are a form of allegory. Max Müller (1823–1900) developed the allegorical interpretation of myth into what is often called the "Solar Mythology" theory. Müller thought that myths were misunderstood statements about the battle between light (specifically sunlight) and darkness. In a phrase that has become infamous, Müller said that mythology is "a disease of language." He meant that as terms changed meaning, people misinterpreted them. Thus, the "maiden dawn" came to be seen, much later, as a female deity.

Andrew Lang (1844–1912) saw myth as primitive science: Myths were meant to explain the cause of things or how things came to be.

The primary challenge to Müller's theory was mounted by Andrew Lang (1844–1912), who saw explanation as the essential function of myth. Myth, he thought, was driven by the same impulse that would later develop into science; in fact, myths were "primitive" science. Thus, all myths were basically aetiological.

One of the most influential theorists was Sir James Frazer (1854–1941). For Frazer, myth was part of a continuum, running from magic through religion to science. He modified the idea of myth as explanation to argue that myth, in all societies, was specifically an explanation for ritual. In *The Golden Bough* (first published in 1890), Frazer presented evidence collected from around the world to demonstrate myth's origins in primordial religious beliefs common to most human societies. He argued that narratives of myth remain long after the rituals they are based on have disappeared. The most important strand of Frazer's argument was his claim about a "King of the Wood," who represented grain and who had to be killed by a younger successor. *The Golden Bough* was a pioneering work, but its methodology was flawed and few scholars today accept its premises. Frazer took examples out of context and claimed that details from myths in different societies performed the same function. Frazer's work inspired "The Cambridge School" of myth scholars, who saw ritual as the primary motivating force for myth.

The next important school of myth theory to arise after Frazer was Functionalism, pioneered by Bronislaw Malinowski (1884–1942). Malinowski studied myth as a living tradition among the Trobriand islanders and concluded that the defining characteristic of myth was its functionality. Myth contributes to society by helping to maintain the social system. Its origin is less important than its function. Malinowski rejected the idea that myth's primary purpose is to explain, rather than to help justify and maintain the social system. Myths do not, in fact, refer to any culture outside of their own. He called such justificatory myths "charters"; i.e., they provided validation for the social institutions they described. Malinowski also posited a hard and fast distinction between myth as "sacred" narrative and folktale as "entertainment," with a third category of historicizing legend in between these two poles.

Each of these theories has struck its critics as unsatisfactory in at least some regards. Some seem too restrictive. The "Solar Myth" hypothesis of the 19th century is perhaps the most obvious example, but other theories, too, fall short in this regard: If myths must be tied to rituals, then how do we account for stories that seem to have no ritual associations whatsoever? If myths must concern the gods, then the stories of Oedipus, Theseus, Perseus, and many others are excluded by definition. If myths must provide charters for social institutions, how do we explain those that seem to perform no such function?

The most obvious answer in each case is to say that those tales that do not fit the definition are not *myths* at all but some other type of traditional tale. This sort of narrowing of the definition to make the theory work is not very satisfactory. Another answer is to say that in each case, the myth has undergone change or corruption that has disguised its original character. But this is a form of special pleading, persuasive only to those who have already accepted the theory in question. It seems better to admit that, so far, no "monolithic" theory has completely defined or explained myth. ∎

Essential Reading

Kirk, *Nature of Greek Myths*, Ch. 1–3.

Supplementary Reading

Burkert, *Structure and History*, Ch. 1, sections 1–4, 6–8; Ch. 2.

Kirk, "Aetiology, Ritual, and Charter."

———, *Myth: Meaning and Function*, Ch. 1.

Powell, *Classical Myth*, Ch. 22.

Questions to Consider

1. Do you find any of the overarching theories about the nature of myth satisfactory? Why or why not?

2. Do you have a sense that you "know myth when you see it"? If so, can you form a satisfactory definition of myth?

What is Myth?

Lecture 2—Transcript

In our previous lecture, we began talking about the difficulty of defining exactly what myth is and how it functions. In this lecture and in Lecture Three, we are going to continue our discussion of what myth is and how it can be defined, and in particular, we are going to look at several of the most influential theories about myth that developed in the nineteenth and twentieth centuries.

As I said in the previous lecture, the question "What is myth?" has no easy or obvious answer. One thing that we can dispense with right away is the usage of the term "myth" in popular speech to mean a lie or a misconception or a mistaken belief. That does not concern us here. For instance, if someone says, "Love at first sight is just a myth," what they mean by that is something along the lines of "That is a mistaken belief, a misconception, it doesn't really happen." That is a very common usage of the term "myth," but clearly that is not what we are dealing with here.

Despite the fact that myth is so difficult to define precisely, most people seem to have a sense that there is such a category as myth—that we are not just chasing a chimera here—that there is such a category as myth and most people have the sense that they know it when they see it; that when they are told or read a story that is a myth, they somehow sense a difference in that from other kinds of stories that they may be told or may read.

We can begin to try to close in on what myth is, what that difference is between myth and other forms of story, how we know it when we see it, by identifying some characteristics of myth to supplement the working definition that I gave you in the previous lecture. If you remember, that definition started by saying that myths are traditional stories or tales that a society tells. Let's think about the implications of the term "traditional tales." Myths are tales, are stories. That may seem so obvious that it doesn't need to be said, but it is worth focusing on. There are many forms of human communication that are not stories; even if they follow a logical narrative, they are not stories. These lectures, for instance: I hope follow a logical narrative order, but they are not stories despite the fact that they are communication. Myth is story. If something is not a story, it is not a myth.

I would push that far enough to say that a representation of a myth in artwork is just that. This behind me is a representation of the birth of Venus (or Aphrodite in her Greek name); it is not a myth of the birth of Aphrodite. So, myths are stories, and they are traditional stories. I touched on that pretty thoroughly in the last lecture, but here it's worth pointing out one implication of that: stories handed down from generation to generation in a society normally cannot be attributed to any one author or any one originator. Put another way, it is usually impossible to tell who first thought up a story that becomes a myth. That means that one major difference between myths and other stories that we may be more familiar with—such as novels, plays, poems, that kind of thing—is that we don't know who invented a myth. It is traditional; it is changed over time, handed down through generations. Obviously, if you think about it logically, there must have been someone who first told any story that later becomes a myth. The point is, that "someone" is lost in time. We don't know who it was who invented a myth.

Going along with the idea that myths are traditional stories handed down through time is another characteristic that is very important in myth. Namely, it is that myths are stories dealing with the past. Myths do not deal with what is happening today or this week or even last year. We don't have myths about current time. Myths are set in the past, often in the very remote past— frequently in the time before the world was set in the way that it was going to be from there on out. As part of being set in the past, myths very frequently reflect a sense that in the remote past, things were quite different than they are now. Very frequently, the idea is that, in remote past, things were much better than they are now—that there is some kind of "golden age" that we have now lost. Almost invariably, things in myth are different than they are now. Gods and humans interact more freely. Things in the world are still changeable. People can still turn into trees from time to time. Myths deal with a time when the order of the world is a little bit different than it is now—or a great deal different than it is now—and that time is set in the remote past.

Another characteristic of myth that we touched on in the last lecture, that is worth bringing out in more detail, is that they are ostensibly true. They present themselves, within the society in which they develop, as factual accounts of how things actually happened in that remote past in which they are set. It would be very rare for any culture to recognize its own mythology as mythology. In fact, once a culture looks at its own traditional stories and says, "These are our myths," that culture no longer believes in those myths as a living entity. Another way of putting that—which is somewhat paradoxical but I think a valid statement—is that myth is a category that really only exists when you are outside a culture looking in. From within any culture, myths are accounts of the way things really are. It is only when we step outside the culture and look in that we can say "these stories are myths."

What do these stories do, these tales that people tell? Why do they tell them? Myths do many things. Among the most obvious functions they fulfill is, myths often explain, justify, instruct or warn. Explanatory myths are often called aetiological myths—that comes from the Greek word *aetion,* which means cause. Explanatory myths may explain why things are as they are, how certain events or entities came into being, why conditions of the world are as they are. Perhaps the most obvious and most famous aetiological myth of classical mythology is the story of Demeter, goddess of grain and the harvest, grieving for her lost daughter Persephone who had been kidnapped by Hades, king of the dead. When Persephone is in the Underworld with her husband Hades, Demeter grieves and no grain grows. When Persephone comes back to spend two-thirds of the year with her mother, Demeter is happy and the grain grows again. Very clearly, an aetiology for why there are seasons, why there is a time of the year when nothing grows. This myth gives an explanation for why that should be so.

Another function that myths fulfill is to offer a justification for a certain rite or social institution—a certain rite in honor of a goddess, a social institution such as marriage, etc. Myths that provide justification for social rites or institutions are very frequently called "charter myths." Myths may also instruct their audience in how the audience ought or—more frequently— ought not to behave. Myths very frequently instruct through presenting horrible warnings of what is likely to happen to people who transgress the boundaries of proper human behavior. Thus, myths provide instruction on how humans ought and ought not to behave. They don't do that apparently, very frequently. They don't come right out and say, "This is what you ought or ought not to do." Rather, through the narrative line of the story, the audience draws its own conclusions about proper behavior—very frequently through seeing improper behavior.

Obviously, myths very frequently concern gods and the supernatural. Though, drawing on my discussion of the division into myth, legend and folktale in the previous lecture, I do not say that myths *have to* involve gods and the supernatural, but certainly, very frequently, they involve gods and the supernatural. Here, we are in an area of myth that overlaps with religion, and it can be quite difficult to determine whether a particular narrative should be called a myth or should be studied as part of a religion. One useful distinction of categorizing is to say that "religion" refers to what people actually do to honor their gods—the rites, ceremonies, rituals and so forth that people enact in honor of their gods—whereas "myth" refers to the underlying narratives, the narratives that explain or justify or go along with those rites, rituals and ceremonies.

Now, here again, the categorization of certain narratives about gods or divinities as myths depends entirely upon the observer's stance with regard to the gods or divinities in question. Looked at from inside the religion, certain stories can be profound—in fact, crucial—religious truths. Looked at from outside the religion, those same stories would be characterized as myth. For example, from inside Christianity, the stories of the virgin birth of Christ and the resurrection of Christ are central narratives—all-important narratives—and within Christianity, those narratives are accepted as unquestionably true narratives. Looked at from outside, looked at from the point of view of a non-Christian, those stories are myths about the divinity Jesus Christ. It depends entirely on the audience member's stance with regard to the religion in question, whether a particular religious narrative is a true narrative or a myth. As I said before, myth is a category that only exists from the outside looking in.

From antiquity onwards, many scholars have come up with theories that attempt to define myth or explain how myth functions, why it functions as it does, what it is that myth is doing. As I was working on these lectures, it occurred to me that the most important theories of myth that developed in the nineteenth and twentieth centuries could be very broadly divided into two main types of theories, which for simplicity's sake, I am calling the "what" theories and the "why" theories.

This is a very broad categorization and there is overlap between the two types, but here is what I mean by that terminology. "What" theories attempt to explain myth by identifying it as a subcategory, a derivative or a forerunner of something else, such as history, ritual, philosophy, that kind of thing. At their worst, these theories are excessively reductive. "What" theories tend to say that myth "is only" misunderstood history, or "is only" primitive science, or "is only" the first attempt at philosophy or something else. These theories have a tendency to become overly reductive.

For example, there was a Greek thinker named Euhemerus who lived around 300 B.C., who suggested that all myths were originally mis-remembered history. The gods of Greece had actually been great kings who lived way back in prehistory, and whose characteristics had been greatly exaggerated through time. So, Zeus had been a very great king, according to Euhemerus, and his people recounted his stories through time, recounted his legend. They exaggerated his characteristics until he became Zeus, the great god— the primary Olympian who hurls the thunderbolt, father of gods and men.

Later versions of this theory (and this is one that has had a very long run for its money; it keeps popping up, even in the late twentieth century), that myth is basically misremembered history, are called "Euhemerism"—after Euhemerus, the first inventor of the theory. Even at its best, Euhemerism and other "what" theories tend to ignore the essential quality, whatever it is that makes us recognize myth as myth. In attempting to explain myth by saying it is nothing but misremembered history, Euhemerus really explains nothing at all.

Let's grant him for the moment that myth is only misremembered history, that Zeus was just a great king. Euhemerus has not told us why the story of that great king developed into the story of the numinous, awe-inspiring king who hurls the thunderbolt. Even if he is right that it did, that Zeus was only a king whose story developed into a story of a god, he hasn't explained why that should happen, what it is that makes that particular kind of story that appealing.

"Why" theories, as opposed to "what" theories, look for wider explanation—try to identify the impetus within the human mind or human culture that motivates myth-making. Psychological and structuralist theories fall under my heading of "why" theories. "Why" theories generally assume that myth is an extra-cultural or trans-cultural phenomenon. By that, I mean they tend to assume that the same narrative elements serve the same function in different cultures, so that a story about a snake is going to have the same resonance, the same meaning, the same function in different cultures, according to "why" theories. If "what" theories suffer from being over-reductionist, "why" theories tend to suffer from being overly general and overly vague, from saying that the same stories mean the same thing in all cultures at all times, and we don't need to demonstrate that, we can simply assume it. I'll talk more about "why" theories in the next lecture.

As I have already said, there is some overlap between the two types of theories. As we shall see, "what" theories were more common in the nineteenth century, mesmerized as it was by science and the scientific method. "Why" theories are much more common in the extremely psychologically-oriented twentieth century. That would come as a surprise to nobody.

One very popular "what" theory that has been resurrected over and over again since antiquity is the theory that myths are simply a form of allegory—that when a mythic narrative talks about Demeter and Persephone, it is really talking about something else. This overlaps with the idea of aetiological myths. But allegory, the allegorical theory of myth, says again that that is *all* that myths are—that they are always allegorical and they are purely allegorical. The most famous allegorical theory or interpretation of myth was developed in the nineteenth century by a scholar named Max Müller. Müller came up with what is often called the "Solar Mythology Theory." (According to Müller, not only were myths misunderstood allegories, they were misunderstood allegories about one particular thing—the battle between light, specifically sunlight, and darkness. Hence the name, the "Solar Mythology Theory.") Müller claimed that all classical myths were, in their origin, statements about the sun rising in the morning and putting the darkness to flight. Even so sophisticated and complex a narrative as the *Odyssey*, according to Müller, was at the heart a statement about the sun rising and chasing away the night. Odysseus's battles with gods and monsters, all his adventures, represented the sun overcoming darkness.

In a phrase that has become infamous, Müller said that mythology was actually a "disease of language." By that, he meant that as terms changed their meaning through time, the people within Greek culture lost sight of the original meanings of statements and started to misinterpret them as statements about anthropomorphic entities. An example will probably help to clarify what I mean here. Müller claimed that when, in the early stages of Greek society, someone made the statement, "Maiden dawn arose," the term "maiden" in that context simply meant "early." As the word changed its meaning through time and came to mean a young, unmarried, female entity, the statement, "Maiden dawn arose," was misinterpreted to mean "There is a young female entity called Dawn, and she got up, arose from her bed." According to Müller, all mythology is at heart a disease of language of that kind, and mythology is simply a statement about the sun and darkness.

Müller's theory was extremely influential in the nineteenth century, but nobody (and I think that is safe to say) believes it today. It is no longer taken as valid by any scholar of myth. The primary challenge to Müller's theory in the nineteenth century was mounted by another great and famous nineteenth-century scholar, Andrew Lang, who saw explanation as the essential function of myth, not allegory—not that myths were misunderstood statements of something else, but that myths were attempts at explaining phenomena that could not otherwise be explained.

Myth, Lang thought, was driven by the same impulse that would later develop into science. He said that myth was primitive science. So, as Euhemerus said myth was misremembered history, Lang said, "No, it's not history at all, it's science." It is primitive science—science that has not yet developed the scientific method. This means that all myths, according to Lang, were basically aetiological, explained causes of things and how things came to be as they were.

One of the most influential theorists of myth, and one of the most famous theorists of the late nineteenth and early twentieth centuries, was Sir James Frazer. Frazer modified the idea of myth as explanation to argue that myth in all societies was specifically an explanation for ritual. He though that, very frequently, myths were narratives about rituals written after the rituals had fallen into disuse. So that very frequently, one could not identify the ritual to which a myth had originally been attached—that the narratives were made after the rituals had been performed. He saw myth's original function as an explanation of ritual.

In all of these theories, I am simplifying to an extent that frightens me. In Frazer's case, in particular, his main work, *The Golden Bough,* is an extraordinarily complex work. Its first edition was two volumes. By the time he published the third edition, it had grown to eleven volumes, and trying to summarize the thesis of an eleven-volume work in about two minutes is very difficult. But Frazer's most important strand of argument was his claim about what he called a "King of the Wood;" a man, a human king, who supposedly represented or embodied the Vegetation God—the god who causes all things to grow, causes plant fertility, human fertility, animal fertility. Frazer's theory was that society originally had rituals in which an actual human man, called "The King"—for the year or so that he *was* king—embodied the god and was then killed by his successor. You can't have a god who then ages and grows old, particularly not a god of fertility—so he is killed each year by another young successor.

Frazer claimed to demonstrate the prevalence of this mythic pattern throughout human society by gathering examples from all sorts of different cultures. *The Golden Bough* was a pioneering work of scholarship. Frazer's methodology was grievously flawed; in particular, he collected examples from various cultures but ripped them entirely out of context. He assumed that the slightest resemblance of narrative detail must mean precisely similar ritual function, which is a very big assumption to make—that a narrative detail in one society must function precisely the same as another detail functions in another society. That is a very large assumption to make, and no scholar today would accept Frazer's theory in its entirety, although he was a pioneering scholar, and his work is fascinating as an element in the history of scholarship, and in particular scholarship on mythology.

Frazer's work was also the inspiration for a whole so-called "school" of myth theory, often referred to as the "Cambridge School" or the "Cambridge Ritualists." Centered in Cambridge, England, these scholars saw ritual as the primary motivating force for myth, though they disagreed with Frazer about which rituals were most important.

After Frazer, the next important school of myth theory was "Functionalism," which was pioneered by a scholar named Bronislaw Malinowski. Malinowski happened to be marooned on the Trobriand Islands during World War I. He couldn't get back to Europe until the war ended; so, while he was there, he decided to study the indigenous myths of the Trobriand Islanders in their native habitat. He learned the language, talked to the people and decided that the defining characteristic of myth was its functionalism, its functionality within a society. That is why his school of thought is called Functionalism.

He said that—far from trying to explain things or being allegories or necessarily being connected with ritual—myths were functional. In particular, myth contributes to society, according to Malinowski, by helping to maintain the social system. Its origin is less important than its function. In fact, Malinowski denied not only that myths' primary purpose is to explain. He even said that they had no meaning outside themselves, that they do not refer to anything outside themselves and the societies in which they function. Their main, primary, in fact, *only* function is to help justify and maintain the social system in which they arise. This is, in a way, almost opposite to Frazer's idea that the same narrative elements, cross-culturally and across time, indicate the same mythic impulse. Malinowski would say myth is purely limited to the culture in which it arises. It justifies, explains and provides a charter for the social system in which it originates. Charter myths, according to Malinowski, provide a validation for the social institutions they describe, and that is their main function.

It was Malinowski who also posited the hard and fast distinction between myth, legend, and folklore that I talked about before. Among the Trobriand Islanders, he found, the islanders themselves, the people who recounted their traditional tales to him, made this distinction between myth as stories about the gods, legend as stories about heroes or great men who once lived, and folktale as stories purely for entertainment. He thought that distinction was valid cross-culturally; that in all societies, we should categorize only stories about the gods as myth and other traditional tales as either legend or folktale. However, as I said in the first lecture, that distinction does not apply nearly so well to classical myth as it applies to its native home in the Trobriand Islands.

Each of these theories, which I have gone through, has struck its critics as unsatisfactory in at least some regards. Some of the theories seem way too restrictive. The most obvious example is the solar mythology theory of the nineteenth century; that one is easy even to make fun of because it is so restrictive. It seems obvious to us at the end of the twentieth century that whatever myth is doing, it is something more than saying, "The sun rises every morning and then goes away." But other theories, too, fall short in this regard. If myths must be tied to rituals, if Frazer and the Cambridge School are correct, and myth implies ritual, myth is simply the narrative that goes along with ritual—then what do we do with traditional stories that seem to have no ritual associations whatsoever?

In classical myth, for instance, the struggles of the gods for power—which we will talk about when we get to Hesiod's *Theogony* in Lecture Four—as far as we know have no connection with any ritual that ever happened. Are they, then, not myths? How do we account for stories that are not connected with rituals? If myths must concern the gods, how do we account for stories about Oedipus, Perseus, Theseus? Many of the most famous myths of Greek mythology deal directly with heroes and do not deal with gods. If myths must prove charters for social institutions—if Malinowski is correct in that regard—how do we explain myths that don't seem to perform any such function? Again, take the example of the birth of Aphrodite from the sea. What social institution finds its charter in that story? I can't think of one. Certainly there is no obvious answer to that.

With all of these objections, in each case, the theorist would probably say that any stories that don't fit the theory are by definition not myths at all, but some other type of story. This narrowing the definition to make the theory work is not very satisfactory to someone who has not already bought into the theory. I could, if I wanted to, for the purpose of this course, say I define myths as stories about entities whose names begin with "A." I could say if a story is not about a god whose name begins with "A," it is not a myth. I am only going to talk about Aphrodite, Artemis, Achilles, so forth. And, as I was trying to think of some way to limit this course to a manageable size, something like that was rather tempting. But, I could make that definition. It would not persuade anyone, and that is obviously an exaggeration, but any theory that says, "Any story that doesn't fit my theory is by definition not a myth," is really taking a very easy way out and is leaving something to be desired.

Another answer—and one that most theorists would say deserves more attention—is to say that in any case where there is no apparent match of the myth to the ritual, or the myth to the charter to justify some social institution, then the myth has undergone change or corruption, which has disguised its original character. Malinowski would probably answer my objection about the birth of Aphrodite by saying it did provide a charter for some social institution, we just don't know what it was. The Cambridge Ritualists would probably say about my objection to the story of the gods' struggles for power that there were rituals, to match those myths; we just no longer have any evidence to match those rituals.

This, again, is a form of special pleading, and it is persuasive only to those who have already accepted the theory in question. If we accept that all myths must be tied to ritual—if we take that as our first premise—then when we find a myth that does not seem to be tied to ritual, we have no recourse except to say we don't know what the ritual was. If we don't start with the first premise "myth must be tied to ritual," then it certainly looks as though many myths are not. These theories tend to require acceptance of the theory first, and some manipulation of the evidence second, to make the theory work, which is troubling to many scholars. It seems to me better to admit that so far no monolithic theory (the term "monolithic" is the scholar Geoffrey Kirk's) of myth so far has completely defined, nor explained, what myth is. Someone may yet come up with such a theory, but it has not been done yet.

In this lecture, we have continued trying to determine what myth is. We have surveyed a few important "what" theories. In our next lecture, we will move on to looking at some of the most important "why" theories of the twentieth century, specifically psychological and structuralist theories.

Why Is Myth?
Lecture 3

In our previous lecture, we began our examination of some of the most important theories about myth by looking at what I call "what" theories of myth. In this lecture, we are going to move on to the "why" theories of myth and look at the psychological theories of Freud and Jung, the structuralist approaches of Propp, Lévi-Strauss and Burkert. We will also discuss the work of the very popular theorist Joseph Campbell.

This century has seen the development of crucially important, extremely influential, and very complex "why" theories of myth, which assume that myths reflect the same underlying human realities in all cultures and, therefore, are somehow cross-cultural or transcultural. The most obvious instances of this type of theory are psychological. Sigmund Freud (1856–1939) proposed that myth reflects psychological forces present in the individual. His most famous theory for the study of myth was, of course, the Oedipus complex. The story of Oedipus, who killed his father and married his mother, reflected the repressed desires of all male children. According to Freud, myths are the collective dreams of the human race; myths use the same kind of imagery, condensation, and displacement that are found in an individual's dreams. This imagery is primarily sexual in nature. Carl Jung (1875–1961) saw myths as reflections of the "collective unconscious." In Jung's view, the collective unconscious contains archetypes, or recurrent images that exist cross-culturally and throughout time. Myths use these archetypes (such as the "Earth Mother" or the "Wise Old Man"). Because they reflect the collective unconscious and feature the archetypes, myths are crucially important.

Another "universal" approach to myth is Structuralism, "a system of definable relations between the parts or elements of a whole which admit predictable transformations," according to Walter Burkert (1931–). There are two primary varieties of structuralist theory. The first, often called the "Formalist" school, was developed by the Russian folklorist Vladimir Propp. It analyzes traditional tales based on their surface elements. In analyzing Russian folktales, Propp found one basic pattern, the "quest pattern," which he further analyzed into thirty-one separate "functions." Although not all of these functions are present in any given tale, they are constant elements in the tales, and they appear in fixed sequence. Thus, the sequence of functions creates (or defines) the tale; the characters who happen to appear in the tale are not its defining characteristic.

In Jung's view, the collective unconscious contains archetypes, or recurrent images that exist cross-culturally and throughout time.

The second main category of structuralism looks at the underlying structure of the myths, rather than at their surface narratives. Claude Lévi-Strauss developed this approach. Lévi-Strauss's theory claims that myth provides a mediation of contradictions, a way of dealing with binary oppositions that underlie the human mind. Myth is analogous to language; just as the individual components of language (phonemes) have no inherent meaning in themselves but gain meaning only in relationship to one another, so too are the components of myth (sometimes called "mythemes") significant only as part of a structure. Lévi-Strauss held that "a myth is made up of all its variants"; thus, even Freud's interpretation is part of the Oedipus myth.

The scholar Walter Burkert has developed a structuralist approach that differs from both Propp's and Lévi-Strauss's in assigning the basic impetus for certain myths to biological "programs of action." Burkert's theory resembles Propp's in that he isolates narrative elements that recur in different myths; an example of this is his description of "the girl's tragedy." Burkert's thesis that these narrative elements can be traced to early human or even pre-human biological necessities—from menarche to deflowering to bearing a first child—is controversial. Burkert also assigns great importance to ritual; thus, he is sometimes called a "neo-ritualist."

The best-known theorist of myth to appear in recent decades is Joseph Campbell (1904–1987). Though he is often called a Jungian, a better term to describe his approach to myth might be "metaphysical." Campbell takes as a given that all myth is the same cross-culturally. His method, like Frazer's, depends largely on gathering examples of narrative similarities from different cultures. Campbell assumes that myth is "true" in a metaphysical sense. He imputes a spiritual meaning to myth that he thinks is both constant across societies and crucial for individual psychological and spiritual health. He separates this meaning from the specific religious doctrines held by the societies that formed the particular myths.

Most scholars do not have a high opinion of Campbell's work. He never attempts to demonstrate the validity of his interpretations of myth; instead, he asserts his interpretation—for instance, that the human mind has a spiritual cast—as a given. He claims to be discussing narratives ("monomyths") that occur worldwide, but, in fact, he takes elements from many narratives to make a composite that does not actually occur anywhere. He assumes that the multiplication of examples amounts to proof of his interpretation. He assumes that similar narrative elements must have the same meanings in different cultures. But Amazons or snakes, for example, have different functions in different times and places.

These universalist "why" theories, no less than the "what" theories of the previous lecture, have struck many critics as unsatisfactory, mainly because they tend to rest on unproven and unprovable assumptions. The psychological theories of Freud and Jung both espouse the idea that myths are in some sense the "dreams of the people." This idea implies that a "people" or a society has a collective mind that is capable of dreaming. Freud further assumes that dreams have the same significance cross-culturally. But the interpretation of dream symbols changes according to time and place. Jung posits the "collective unconscious" as an entity and assumes that it produces the archetypes. Lévi-Strauss assumes that the mediation of oppositions is a driving force of all cultures. Burkert's assumption that myth is rooted in pre-cultural biological realities, while fascinating, can only be asserted, not demonstrated.

The best approach may be to recognize that myth is a varied but recognizable category that can include all these theories (and more). No one theory seems adequate to explain "myth" overall. Theories can be useful for elucidating individual myths. The theories we have discussed cannot be proven, but they cannot be disproven either; we will use these theories as tools when and where they are helpful.

Where does this leave us? My own working definition combines elements from several of these approaches. Again, I define myths as "traditional stories a society tells itself that encode or represent the world-view, beliefs, principles, and often fears of that society." As such, myths offer insight into what a specific culture thinks about the nature of the world in general and about key questions, such as: The nature and function of the gods Humans' relationship to the gods. What it means to be human. The two sexes' relationship to one another. I find the universalizing "why" theories of myth less useful than an approach that examines myth in the context of the culture that developed it. However, I will refer to the "why" theories at key points throughout these lectures. ∎

Essential Reading

Kirk, *Nature of Greek Myths*, Ch. 4.

Segal, "Joseph Campbell's Theory of Myth."

Supplementary Reading

Bremmer, "What Is a Greek Myth?"

Burkert, *Creation of the Sacred*, Ch. 3.

Caldwell, "Psychoanalytic Interpretation."

Jung, "Psychology of the Child Archetype."

Kirk, *Myth: Meaning and Function*, Ch. 2 and 6.

Leach, *Claude Lévi-Strauss*.

Lévi-Strauss, *The Raw and the Cooked.*

Propp, *Morphology of the Folktale.*

Segal, *Joseph Campbell.*

Wender, "The Myth of Washington."

Questions to Consider

1. Do you find specific ("what") theories or universalist ("why") theories of myth more helpful? What are some of the advantages and limitations of each approach?

2. It has sometimes been suggested that Jung, Campbell, and even Freud are closer to mystics whose doctrines are based on faith than to theorists whose arguments are based on demonstrable facts. Do you agree?

Why is Myth?

Lecture 3—Transcript

In our previous lecture, we began our examination of some of the most important theories about myth by looking at what I call "what" theories of myth. In this lecture, we are going to move on to the "why" theories of myth and look at the psychological theories of Freud and Jung, the structuralist approaches of Propp, Lévi-Strauss and Burkert. We will also discuss the work of the very popular theorist Joseph Campbell.

This century has seen the development of crucially important, extremely influential and very complex theories about myth, which fall under the category that I call "why" theories. Again, all I can do is scratch the barest surface of these theories, but we will begin with the psychological theories of Freud and Jung and then move on to structuralist theories. The thing that these "why" theories have in common is that they assume myth reflects the underlying human realities in all cultures; and that myth, therefore, is somehow cross-cultural or trans-cultural, rather than being specific to the individual culture in which it develops.

Let's begin with Sigmund Freud. Among his other contributions to modern thought, Freud proposed that myth reflects psychological forces present in the individual and, through the individual, present in society. Truly, his most important contribution to the study of myth was his interpretation of Sophocles's treatment of *Oedipus the King*, to develop his own theory of the Oedipus Complex. Freud developed the Oedipus Complex theory after he asked himself why it was that Sophocles's tragedy, *Oedipus the King*, was still so compelling, so electrifying to modern audiences.

Freud disagreed with the interpretation given by most critics of his time, which was that it was the interaction of fate and free will in that drama that made it so compelling—the fact that Oedipus, by trying to avoid his fate through the use of his free will, drives himself ever more inexorably into his fate. Freud said that can't explain its popularity, because there are other dramas written about the interaction of fate and free will that are not so compelling, that do not retain their popularity centuries or even decades after they are written. Therefore, he thought the appeal of the story of

Oedipus must lie not in the fate-free will issue, but in something specific to that narrative; in the details of that story rather than in its wider issues. And, of course, the details of the Oedipus story are that Oedipus is a man who killed his father and married his mother. Freud saw this as reflecting the desires of all male children to do away with their fathers and have access to their mothers.

According to Freud, not just the Oedipus myth, but myths in general, are in effect the collective dreams of the human race. By that, he meant that he thought myths utilized the same kind of imagery, condensation and displacement that we find in our own individual dreams. He thought that the imagery of myth was similar to the imagery of dreams, and, in both cases, Freud thought that this imagery was primarily sexual in nature. *Oedipus* is a story about, at least in part, a sexual relationship. Freud saw sexual imagery in other myths as well.

The second psychological theorist of this century to grapple with myth was Carl Jung. Jung saw myths as reflections of the collective unconscious. In particular, Jung thought that myth draws on archetypes, which are contained in the collective unconscious. By "archetypes," he meant, more or less, recurrent images that exist cross-culturally and throughout time—images such as the image of the wise old man, the earth-mother, the maiden, that sort of thing. Jung thought that myth utilizes these images, these archetypes, and we find myth compelling because we too partake of the archetypes as we partake of the collective unconscious. Because myth, according to Jung, reflected the myths of the collective unconscious, he thought that myths were crucially important, both for the individual and for society. He probably accorded more importance to myth than Freud did.

The psychological approach is only one "universalist"—or to use my terminology "why"—approach to myth. The other main school of thought that has developed around myth in this century is what is called "structuralism."

Structuralism is very difficult to define briefly and simply. The best definition I have found is given by the scholar Walter Burkert, who says that "Structuralism is a system of definable relations between the part or elements of a whole, which admit predictable transformations." The "predictable transformations" part of that definition is what is critically important in it. According to structuralism, the component elements—the system of definable relations between the parts or elements of a whole—will interact with each other in predictable ways. Whether the whole we are talking about is society in general, language, myth, or some other system, structuralism says that its parts interact with one another in a predictable manner.

There are two primary varieties of structuralist theory that I want to look at here. The first is often called the Formalist School, though some people separate it from structuralism entirely and call it "Formalism" instead. It was developed by a Russian folklorist named Vladimir Propp, who analyzed traditional tales based on their surface elements—based on the actual narrative elements that appear in these tales.

Looking at Russian folktales, Propp found one basic pattern of tales which could be called the "Quest Pattern," which he further analyzed into 31 separate elements—or as he called them, 31 separate "functions." An important thing to understand about Propp's kind of analysis, about formalist analysis, is he was not saying that every single tale would have all 31 of these functions. One story might have functions two, three, five, seven, eight, nine, 13, 15, and so forth. Another might have functions one, two, seven, eight, 10, 11, 12, 15, 17, and so forth. But, when you study the entire body of tales, you find the same functions and they appear in the same order. Thus, it is the sequence of functions which creates or defines the tale for a formalist analysis, not the characters who happen to appear in the tale. The characters are not the tales' defining characteristic.

Let me give an example to try to clarify this. We could say that a tale in a formalist analysis may include the elements of a young man being driven out of his home by a wicked elder male relative, going on a journey in which he encounters several monsters, killing at least one of those monsters, and as a reward for those efforts, being given the hand of a princess in marriage. Whether we call that hero Jason or Perseus or Prince Charming or Luke Skywalker makes very little difference. The tale, the story, is the same. That is the basic understanding of formalism.

The second main category of structuralism, and in fact, what most people are talking about when they talk about a structuralist approach to myth, looks at the underlying structure of the myth, rather than at the surface narrative of a myth. This approach was developed by Claude Lévi-Strauss. The main point of Lévi-Strauss's theory is his claim that myth exists to mediate contradictions; that human society and human thought in general operate through a series of binary oppositions, and that myth and other structures in society exist to mediate these contradictions or oppositions—oppositions such as those between nature and culture, which Lévi-Strauss says appears, among other ways, in the opposition between raw food and cooked food— raw food standing for nature and cooked food standing for culture. Another opposition that myth could mediate would be between gods and humans, between death and life.

Lévi-Strauss claims that not just human culture, but human thought itself operates through these binary oppositions, and that many of our cultural structures and artifacts exist to mediate these oppositions. This form of structuralism developed as a subcategory of linguistics. It was applied first to language and then expanded to include other systems such as myth. Under Lévi-Strauss's structuralism, myth is seen as analogous to language, just as the individual components of language (the phonemes) have no inherent meaning in themselves. The sound K *(kuh)* has no meaning in itself, the sound T *(tuh)* has no meaning in itself. Put a vowel in between them to get "cat" or "cut" or "cot" and you start to have meaning. The individual sounds mean nothing. It is their relationship to one another that conveys meaning.

Lévi-Strauss would say that the components of myth—which are sometimes called "mythemes" to press the analogy with phonemes—the components of myth have no independent meaning by themselves. Oedipus by himself means nothing. It is only putting the components into relationship with one another that gives them meaning. One of Lévi-Strauss's most controversial claims is that a myth is made up of all its variants. And by all its variants, he means *all* its variants—not just within the culture that developed it, but also within any culture that refers to it or uses it. Lévi-Strauss says that Freud's interpretation of the Oedipus myth—Freud's theory of the Oedipus Complex—is now part of the Oedipus myth, and if we are going to analyze the Oedipus myth, we have to take Freud into account no less than we have to take Sophocles into account. So, he gives a very broad, elongated-through-time definition of what a myth is.

A more recent development in structuralism is the work of Walter Burkert—the same man whose definition of structuralism I quoted a few minutes ago—who has developed a structuralist approach that differs from both Propp's and Lévi-Strauss's in assigning the basic impetus for certain myths to what he calls "biological programs of action." Burkert's theory resembles Propp's in that he isolates narrative elements that recur in different myths and different tales, and from them identifies certain types of tales. One example is what Burkert calls "the girl's tragedy." In the girl's tragedy, as analyzed by Burkert, there is a sudden break in a young girl's life, which causes her to leave home. She then undergoes a period of seclusion, which comes to an end in a violent encounter with a male—often a god, sometimes a human, sometimes even an animal. This violent encounter results in her pregnancy. She then undergoes a period of tribulation, suffering and punishment, but at the end of the story she is rescued and reintegrated into society—often given a new and higher status in society—often often through the birth of a child, of a son.

Burkert's contribution—so far, so much like Propp—is to say that these kinds of stories reflect underlying biological realities. The girl's tragedy he connects to the stages of a young girl's puberty and maturation, so that the sudden break in her life would be menarche—her first menstruation—followed often in many cultures by actual seclusion in a kind of initiation ceremony. The catastrophe, the violent encounter with the male, would be defloration—her first sexual encounter. The period of tribulation and suffering would be her pregnancy, and the happy ending would be the birth of her child and the emergence of her as an adult woman.

His thesis that these narrative elements are rooted in actual biological realities—biological realities that can be traced beyond early human, all the way back to pre-human culture—is controversial to say the least. By no means does every scholar accept this thesis, but that is Burkert's main contribution. He also assigns great importance to ritual, particularly to initiation rituals, so he is sometimes referred to as a neo-ritualist as well as being a structuralist.

The best-known theorist of myth, at least in America, the best known to appear in recent decades, is Joseph Campbell. Though Campbell is often called a Jungian, and shows many resemblances to Jung's theory of the archetypes in his work, a better term to describe his approach to myth might actually be "metaphysical." Campbell assumes that all myth is the same cross-culturally—that myth functions in the same way in every society, that myth reflects a reality of the human mind that is recognizable and is the same throughout cultures and across time. Like Frazer's, his method depends largely on gathering examples of narrative similarities from different cultures. As anyone who has seen his lectures or read his books will remember, that is one of the main things he does—cite examples of what he sees as the same narrative elements from many different cultures.

He assumes that myth is true in a metaphysical or spiritual sense. By that, I mean that he imputes a spiritual meaning to myth; that he thinks it's constant across societies and across time, but is also crucial for individual psychological and spiritual health. In other words, Campbell sees the main function of myth as an expression of a particular spiritual reality in the human mind. That is what he thinks—claims—myth is. Interestingly, Campbell separates this spiritual element of myth from the specific religious doctrines held by the societies that formed the myths. So rather than thinking that "this is understandable only within a particular culture," Campbell tends to say that myth is most understandable *outside* of culture, because the religious doctrines imposed by culture he sees as distortions of the original spiritual meaning of myth.

Joseph Campbell is an extraordinarily engaging lecturer and author, and he is very popular. But despite his popularity, most scholars (and I include myself here) do not have a very high opinion of Campbell's work. First of all, he never attempts any rigorous demonstration of the validity of his interpretations of myth. Instead, he simply asserts his interpretations as givens. He assumes that all myth reflects one spiritual truth; or rather, he assumes that there is one spiritual cast to the human mind, that that is part of the essence of being human and that myth reflects it.

Both of those assumptions are questionable. Even if we agree, which many people would not, that there is one spiritual cast to the human mind, the assertion that myth reflects that spiritual cast of the human mind needs to be argued and not asserted. As I say to my students when I assign them termpapers, "assertion is not evidence." To simply say that something is so is not to give evidence that it is so. Campbell doesn't ever give evidence; he simply states his belief that myth reflects one spiritual reality and takes that as a given throughout his work. If you agree with him that it does—if you agree with his interpretation—his work can be very compelling. But, if you don't agree, he never gives any reason why you should.

Secondly, he claims to be discussing narratives that occur worldwide—narratives he calls "monomyths." He claims that the same mythic narrative occurs worldwide throughout cultures and throughout time. But, he constructs these narratives by taking one narrative element from a story in one culture, another from a story in another culture, and yet a third from a story in yet another culture. He puts them all together and says, "Here is the monomyth, here is the narrative"—when, in fact, that underlying narrative doesn't exist in any culture.

Now, you may be thinking, "Wait a minute, isn't that what Propp and Burkert do?" There is a difference. Propp works within Russian folktale, within one culture, and finds the elements that make up his tale within one culture. So does Burkert; when he is talking about the maid's tragedy—the girl's tragedy—for instance, he is looking at Greek culture. Campbell ranges across time and across culture. He takes an element from Polynesia, another from native American myth, another from ancient Greek myth, puts them all together and says that they all refer to a monomyth—to a narrative structure that does not exist in any one of these cultures. That is questionable. That is an assumption that many of us find ourselves unable to make.

He also tends to assume that mere multiplication of examples amounts to proof of his interpretation. So, if he can find ten of his examples of a hero going out and slaying a dragon, he assumes that this amounts to proof of his interpretation of what that narrative element means. But, in fact, multiplication of examples and interpretation of what those examples mean are two very different things. A mere listing of examples tells us nothing about the validity or lack of validity of any given interpretation of those examples. Finally, Campbell assumes that similar narrative elements must have precisely the same meanings in different cultures. That is a very, very questionable assumption, to say the least.

To take an example, classical Greek myth—classical Athenian myth—and modern American culture have stories about Amazons; warrior women who fight against male warriors, who live without males, who have sexual relationships without marriage, who do not depend on males to protect or save them in any situation of violence. In Greek myth, they appear all over the place. In fact, I will deal with them in a lecture late in the course. In modern American culture, they appear in such popular guises as the television program, "Xena, Warrior Princess," and the comic book "Wonder Woman" of many years ago.

Despite the fact that these figures are very similar, independent strong women who use violence as much as men use violence, it would be a grievous mistake to think that they have the same implication in Greek society and in modern American society. For the Athenians, the Amazons were examples of exactly what women must *not* be. They were frightening, horrifying, repulsive, and they are constantly overcome by heroes who re-sexualize them and put them back in their places. In modern American culture, at least the fans of "Xena, Warrior Princess" see her as an *affirmation*—an example of a strong independent woman, of what women can do on their own to protect themselves, without men. I have friends who encourage their young daughters to watch "Xena," because they think she is such a wonderful role model. Same idea, same image—and two entirely different meanings in two different cultures.

Clearly, it could be objected that "Xena" is not a myth in the sense I have defined myth. This television program is intentionally written by modern American writers with an agenda, with an ax to grind. Fair enough. But what about a more basic narrative, a more basic element that shows up worldwide? What about snakes?

In Judeo-Christian culture, snakes are symbols of evil. The snake tempted Eve in the garden. The snake led us all astray. The snake is always a symbol of evil. But in Greek culture, snakes *can* be evil--huge, monstrous, dragon-like snakes usually are--but they can also be beneficent. In fact, a dead hero very frequently appears at his shrine to his worshippers as a snake. Snakes can be and often are "good" images in Greek culture. The same image, but we cannot assume that it has the same meaning. The assumption that symbols must mean exactly the same thing wherever they appear—cross-culturally and across time—is a very dangerous assumption to make.

I don't mean to pick too much on Joseph Campbell here. I focus so much time on him because he is so popular, and because many of my students are often very disappointed when they discover that I don't like his work. But, in fact, many of the objections I have just raised to Campbell's approach can also be raised to universalist "why" theories, in general. These theories tend to rest on unproven and improvable assumptions. For instance, let's look at the psychological theories of Freud and Jung again. Both Freud and Jung espouse the idea that myths are in some sense the dreams of the people—that myth is to society as dream is to an individual. But what do they mean by that? This implies—this depends on the idea that a people or a society has the collective mind capable of dreaming, which strikes me at least as a rather odd and very problematic assertion.

I have said in my working definition that myths are stories a society tells itself. But, that similarity of phrase does not indicate a similarity of meaning here. When I say that "myths are stories a society tells itself," that is shorthand for saying that "myths are stories that a great many individuals within a society tell." When we say that a society believes in something—American society believes in freedom of speech—what we mean by that is that most individuals within society believe in freedom of speech. When Freud says, "Myths are the dreams of a society," I don't think he does simply mean that individuals within that society have dreams. I think he is saying something else. I think he is positing that a society can somehow dream, just as an individual can. I don't see how that is possible. I don't see how a society can dream, any more than how a society can feel hunger or thirst or fall asleep.

So, Freud posits that myths are dreams of a society, or function to a society as dreams do to a human. He doesn't ever demonstrate it. He also assumes that the symbols in dreams and in myths have the same significance cross-culturally. One of his main points in his first articulation of the Oedipus complex—one of the points that made Freud think he was on the right track—is a line in that play where Jocasta says to Oedipus, "Many a man before you has dreamed of sleeping with his mother." Freud saw that as proof that throughout time, across cultures, male human beings desire, as small children, to have sexual access to their mothers, feel terrible guilt over this desire, repress it, and it then comes up through their subconscious and manifests itself in their dreams.

If we look at handbooks of dream interpretation that were current in Classical Greece and Hellenistic Greece, we find that a dream of sex with one's mother was often seen as a *good* dream—a good omen. It could indicate that a man was about to return to his native land, for instance—that he was about to get some possessions that he wanted. It does not seem to reflect the guilt and repression that Freud assumes must be operating there. So, even if Freud is right that this guilt and repression operate in twentieth-century male children, that doesn't necessarily prove that they operated in fifth-century-B.C. male children.

Jung posits the collective unconscious and the archetypes, never demonstrating that they exist. Lévi-Strauss assumes that the mediation of oppositions is the driving force of all cultures and, in fact, underlies human thought itself, never demonstrating that this is so. So, the objections I have to Campbell's theory apply really to most of these "why" theories, including Burkert. Burkert assumes that myth is rooted in pre-cultural biological necessity. I find that a fascinating suggestion. I admire Burkert's work greatly, but again, it cannot possibly be demonstrated. It can only be asserted.

So, where does this leave us? The best approach may be to recognize that myth is a varied category, a recognizable category (we all know it when we see it), but it is hard to pin it down to any one theory. To put that a little less discouragingly, the best approach may be to recognize that myth can include all of these theories and more. No one theory that we have looked at of either the "what" or the "why" category seems to be sufficient to explain myth overall as a category.

That doesn't mean that these theories can't be useful for elucidating individual myths. They can, and they certainly are. I would suggest that the best way to proceed is to use these theories in conjunction with one another to see what they can tell us about different myths, but not try to force myth to fit the pattern of any one of them. And, it is fair to say that while these theories can't be proved, they can't be disproved either. There is no way to show that they are incorrect, and therefore, they should and can be employed as tools when and where they are useful.

Now, my own working definition of myth—and I define myths as traditional stories that society tells itself, that encode or represent the world view beliefs, principles and fears of that society—that definition obviously combines elements from several other theories that we have discussed. I think that myths give us a great deal of insight on what a specific culture thinks about the nature of the world in general, and about key elements within the world, and about key questions such as: What is the nature and function of the gods? *Are* there gods? What are they like? What do they do? The relationship that humans ought to have with the gods, what it means to be human, what marks us out from other creatures? Again, as I mentioned in the first lecture, why are there only two sexes? Why can't they get along better with one another? What is all that about? In other words, I tend to see the most interesting approach to myth as one that looks at myths within their originating culture and looks at what the myths can tell us about that culture, rather than looking at them in a more global view.

Obviously, I find the universalizing "why" theories of myth—psychological, structuralist, what have you—less useful than an approach that examines myth within the culture that developed it. That is my own personal bias, or the way my personal intellect works. However, throughout the course, I will, as appropriate, point out particular uses of the "why" theories, particular myths to which those theories have been applied or to which I think they could usefully be applied, and will discuss how they work at key points throughout the lectures.

Now, we have at this point finished our introductory material, our survey of what myth is and how it works. In the next lecture, we will turn to looking at actual classical mythology itself, when we begin looking at the myth of the creation of the gods and the creation of the universe, as told in Hesiod's *Theogony*.

"First Was Chaos"
Lecture 4

These gods don't create the universe; they are part of it. This implies, among other things, that these gods are not omnipotent within the universe. They are extremely powerful, but none of them—not even Zeus, the head god—is altogether omnipotent.

The most complete surviving Greek account of the creation of the universe is Hesiod's *Theogony*. Hesiod probably composed the poem sometime in the 8th century B.C., around the same time as the composition of the *Iliad*. Like the *Iliad* and the *Odyssey*, *Theogony* is a transcription of orally transmitted material; Hesiod did not make *Theogony* up. However, Hesiod does shape his traditional material; other *Theogonies* differed in detail from his. Hesiod's *Theogony* was never an orthodoxy; it was not a "sacred text" in the way that the Bible and the Koran are.

Theogony is both a description of how the material universe came into being and a description of the birth of the gods. In this view, the gods are not separate from the universe itself. This is an excellent example of the multivalent explanatory nature of myth. *Theogony* uses the narrative of the gods' birth to describe events that we would approach through science, philosophy, and psychology. This aspect of *Theogony* means that a character can be both a natural force or element and an anthropomorphic entity with volition, emotion, and bodily functions. This creation story reveals much about the nature of the gods. The gods do not create the universe; they are part of it. This implies, among other things, that the gods are not omnipotent within the universe. No external creator exists outside and beyond the universe itself. These gods are not transcendent. The gods are immortal for at least so long as the universe lasts. The gods are highly anthropomorphic: they eat, drink, sleep, mate, and feel emotions.

> *Theogony* **is both a description of how the material universe came into being and a description of the birth of the gods.**

Theogony posits several primordial entities: Chaos, Gaia, Tartaros, and Eros. "Chaos" in ancient Greek meant a gap or yawning, *not* a state of disorder. Hesiod says that Chaos came first, then Gaia; it is unclear whether Gaia and the other original entities were born from Chaos or simply appeared after Chaos. Gaia (or Ge) is the earth. Because Hesiod's universe was geocentric, she is pictured as the first natural entity to exist. Tartaros is the Underworld, the land that will eventually be inhabited by the souls of dead humans. Eros means "sexual desire." In later versions of myth, he is the son of Aphrodite; but in this account, almost all creation takes place through sexual reproduction. For Hesiod, Eros must be a primary deity.

After the appearance of the primordial deities, birth and sexual reproduction become the standard means of reproduction. Chaos gives birth to Night and Erebos (the gloomy darkness of Tartaros). The latter mate and produce Ether and Day. Gaia gives birth to Ouranos (Sky), Pontos (Sea), and Mountains. In other words, the earth is taking recognizable shape, creating the Mediterranean Sea and the important mountains known to Hesiod.

Gaia mates with Ouranos and produces twelve children, who are called the Titans. These include important natural elements, such as the Sun, the Moon, and the River Oceanos, which flows around the edges of Gaia. Ouranos does not allow the children to be born, but pushes them back into Gaia's womb. With the help of her youngest son, Cronos, Gaia disables Ouranos. Cronos hides inside his mother's body and castrates his father. Cronos throws the severed genitals into Pontos; Aphrodite (goddess of sexual passion) is born from the foam that springs up around them. Ouranos retreats from Gaia and becomes the dome of the sky, leaving room for his children to be born and for other entities to develop. This story shows how myth can work on several levels at once. Gaia is the Earth and Ouranos is the Sky; at the same time, Gaia is a female entity with a womb, who can feel both pain and anger when her husband pushes her babies back into her. We also see the Sky pressing down on Earth so that there is no space for anything to develop between them. With the freeing of Gaia's children, the world enters a new stage of development, represented in the text by a whole flurry of reproduction. This story also lends itself to allegorical interpretation, because Cronos's name resembles the Greek word for "time," *chronos*. According to this interpretation, when Cronos was freed from Gaia's womb, Time came into being. The two words *Cronos* and *chronos* are not actually related, but this does not necessarily invalidate the allegorical interpretation, if Hesiod or his contemporaries *thought* that they were related.

The same basic pattern is repeated in the next generation, when Cronos in his turn tries to prevent the birth of his children. Cronos marries his sister Rheia, and they produce six children: Hestia, Demeter, Hera, Hades, Poseidon, and Zeus. Unlike his father, Cronos does not leave his children in his mother's body and, thus, to some extent under her control. He swallows each child as it is born. Rheia tricks him by giving him a stone wrapped in swaddling clothes in place of the youngest child, Zeus. Zeus is sent to the island of Crete to be reared in secret. Zeus reaches maturity and overthrows his father. Cronos spits out

Zeus, ruler of the Olympian gods.

the children in reverse order. Thus, Zeus is, in a sense, both the youngest and the oldest of his siblings. Zeus and his five siblings, together with several of Zeus's children, come to be called the Olympians. A ten-year war ensues between the Titans (Cronos) and the Olympians (Zeus). Finally, Zeus and his siblings triumph. At this point, the struggle for power ends and the order of rule in the universe is set; Zeus will remain the head god forever. As such, he is often called simply "The Olympian."

One immediately noticeable and intriguing point about this narrative is that it portrays the struggle for power as one involving older female deities opposed by younger male deities. Many scholars argue that this reflects the psychological anxieties of males about their parents' sexuality, about displacing their fathers, and about having to hand power over to their sons in turn. Others see the increased anthropomorphism of each generation and the decreased identification of gods and natural forces as representing the development of civilization. Others point to the apparent anxiety in Greek culture about the power of women, the fear that women would exert control if they could. Other explanations exist. Any effort to find just one "decoding" of the Ouranos-Cronos-Zeus story is probably doomed to failure.

Theogony presents sophisticated and difficult concepts in the guise of genealogies. Compare the creation story as retold by the Roman poet Ovid some 700 years later, in a culture in which literacy was established. Ovid's creation story differs from Hesiod's, both in tone and emphasis. Rather than describing the creation of the universe through the creation of the gods, Ovid assumes the gods and offers alternatives for how the physical universe may have come to be. He runs through scientific theories of his day, suggesting that the universe was composed of discordant atoms, or perhaps of the four elements. He also glances at different theologies, suggesting that a creator god existed or that Nature simply took it upon herself to order the discordant elements of Chaos. Ovid is working in a literate tradition and showing his erudition by glancing at various theories of creation while endorsing none of them. These differences illustrate the problems in discussing "classical" mythology; the same myths are presented in different ways with different emphases. In Hesiod, we can feel fairly confident that we are dealing with a recounting of the myths that remains close to their oral form. In Ovid, we are dealing with a self-consciously literary reworking of the myths, in ways that sometimes may work against their traditional import. Ironically, Ovid is our main source for several very famous myths. ■

Essential Reading

Apollodorus, *Library*, pp. 27–31 (up to "Artemis and Apollo").

Hesiod, *Theogony*.

Ovid, *Metamorphoses*, pp. 3–5 (up to "The Four Ages").

Supplementary Reading

Burkert, *Structure and History*, Ch. 1, Section 5.

Caldwell, *Origin of the Gods*.

Kirk, *Meaning and Function*, Ch. 5, Section 4, pp. 213–220 (on Kumarbi and Cronos).

Questions to Consider

1. What are the implications for a culture of believing in gods who are neither transcendent nor omnipotent?

2. I suggested several possible interpretations for the pattern of "younger male overcomes older female" that we see in *Theogony*. Which interpretation makes the most sense to you? Can you think of any others?

"First Was Chaos"

Lecture 4—Transcript

In our previous lecture, we finished up the introductory material by looking at some of the more important twentieth-century theories of what myth is and how it works. In this lecture, we are going to turn to discussing classical myth itself. We will begin by looking at the creation story as accounted in the book *Theogony,* by the poet Hesiod.

This is the most complete surviving Greek account of the creation of the universe. Hesiod probably lived and composed *Theogony* sometime in the eighth century B.C. We don't know his exact dates, but most scholars think that he wrote around the same time as the *Iliad* and the *Odyssey* were written down—composed. He uses the meter of the *Iliad* and *Odyssey*, and a good deal of the same meter and dialect, same language, as those two poems. Like the *Iliad* and the *Odyssey*, the Homeric epics, *Theogony* is a transcription of orally- transmitted material. Hesiod did not make up the stories he tells in *Theogony*. However, he did organize his material, shape it, decide which particular details to include in *Theogony* and which to leave out. He certainly had an influence on the material. However, *Theogony* is as close as we can get to the actual orally-transmitted myths about creation that were told in Greece before the invention of literacy.

There were other theogonies, other accounts of the creation of the universe and the gods, in ancient Greece. They have not survived. Hesiod's version of the way the world came into being is the most complete Greek creation story that we have. However, it is important to realize that this was never an orthodoxy. Hesiod's work is not something that someone had to believe in order to be a member of a Greek religion that worshipped Zeus and the other gods. Greek religion did not work that way. There was no sacred text. *Theogony* is not analogous to Genesis in the Judeo-Christian Bible, or to the Koran, or to any other set body of doctrine. It is Hesiod's version of the traditional myths about how the world came into being, widely accepted as we can tell in antiquity, very influential on Greek culture, but not in any sense an orthodoxy.

The word *Theogony* actually means "how the gods came into existence." That is what the Greek word means. However, the material that Hesiod presents in *Theogony* is as much a description of how the whole material universe came into existence as it is a description of how the gods came into existence. The reason for this is that in Hesiod's worldview—and the worldview reflected by *Theogony*—the gods are not separate from the universe; they are part and parcel of the universe. We will discuss this throughout this lecture.

This is an example of the multivalent nature of myth—how myth can explain many different things at the same time and through one and only one narrative. *Theogony* uses the narrative of the gods' birth, of the coming into existence of the gods, to describe events that we would approach through science, psychology, philosophy and other such disciplines. Since in Hesiod's worldview the gods comprised the universe, the gods are not separate from the universe but elements within it. When he tells how they came into existence, he is also telling how the world itself came into existence. This means that a character can be, and usually is, at one and the same time, both a natural force or element—the sun, the moon, the sea, that kind of thing—and an anthropomorphic entity with volition, emotion and bodily functions, as we discussed a little bit in the first lecture when I mentioned Gaia and Ouranos, whom we will now find out much more about.

The creation story that Hesiod presents in *Theogony* actually tells us a great deal about the nature of the gods. That is not what he set out to do; he set out to describe how they came into being. In his culture, of course, their nature was already understood. These were "the gods." People knew what kind of gods they were. But for us, looking at the stories from outside, Hesiod gives us a great deal of information about the type of gods that he and his culture worshipped.

These gods don't create the universe; they are part of it. This implies, among other things, that these gods are not omnipotent within the universe. They are extremely powerful, but none of them—not even Zeus, the head god—is altogether omnipotent. None of them is all-powerful, and they are not outside the universe. This further implies that in Hesiod's account of creation, there is no external creator. In fact, "creation" might be a slightly misleading word to use here because there is no creator. As Hesiod tells the story, the universe simply comes into being. The gods, and with them the universe, simply come into existence without any creator setting the process into motion. These gods, in other words, are not transcendent—they are not outside, beyond, separate from the universe. They come into existence as it does.

However, the gods *are* immortal. They cannot die. This has important implications for several points that Hesiod covers in *Theogony*. A god cannot be killed, a god cannot die. So long as the universe lasts, these gods are immortal. If the universe ever ended, the gods would go with it, but as long as the universe it there, these are immortal gods. Furthermore, as we will see in our discussion of *Theogony,* these gods are highly anthropomorphic. They eat, drink, sleep, mate, give birth, have emotions, feel anger, all of that sort of thing.

Theogony begins by positing several primordial entities—gods, deities, entities: Chaos, Gaia, Tartaros and Eros. *Chaos* in ancient Greek does not mean disorder. It simply means a gap, a yawning, an open space. So, basically, Hesiod says first there was an open space, first there was a gap or a yawning. After that, he says, came Gaia. He does not make it clear whether the other original entities were born from Chaos or whether they simply appeared after Chaos. He just says first was Chaos and after her (Chaos is female in Greek) came Gaia.

Gaia, or *Ge*—her name is sometimes spelled G-E—is the Earth. Since Hesiod's view is geocentric—his worldview is a geocentric one; the world is considered the center of the universe—it makes perfect logical sense that the first deity to come into existence would be the Earth herself. *Tartaros*, one of the other four primordial deities, is the underworld—the land that will eventually house the spirits of the dead once there are some dead spirits to go there.

Eros means sexual desire. The god Eros is the personification of sexual desire. This may surprise you, that Eros is one of Hesiod's primordial deities, because in more commonly known versions of Greek myth, Eros is the son of Aphrodite. He is the equivalent of the Latin Cupid—usually shown in Greek art as a youth or a young boy and in Roman art as a baby. He is considered the son of Aphrodite. In Hesiod's work, Eros is one of the primordial deities. This is a good illustration of what I have touched on before about the different versions of myth being used according to what purpose the particular teller of the myth has in mind. Hesiod is going to describe for us how the universe came into existence, and in his account, almost all creation—almost all development within the universe—will take place through the medium of sexual reproduction. That is how he is going to describe how everything comes into existence. If he is going to do that, if he is going to describe how everything comes into existence through the medium of sexual reproduction, sexual desire has got to be there from the very beginning. Eros must be a primordial deity in Hesiod's account, or else none of the development of the rest of the world can happen.

It does not seem to have been a problem for Hesiod or his audience—or later generations of Greeks reading his work—that Eros to Hesiod is a primordial deity and to other authors is the son of Aphrodite. What seems to us to be a contradiction doesn't seem to have troubled them. After the appearance of these primordial deities, Chaos, Gaia, Tartatros and Eros, birth and sexual reproduction become the standard means of development in the world. These first deities simply come into existence, but after that, deities come into existence through birth. Birth is usually, though not always, preceded by sexual conception. Not always, however. Chaos gives birth to Night and Erebos on her own. Night is self-explanatory. Erebos is the gloomy darkness within Tartaros. It is a little bit odd that Tartaros and Erebos should be two separate entities, but according to Hesiod, they are. Night and Erebos mate and produce Ether (that is the bright upper air) and Day. Gaia, on her own without mating with anyone, gives birth to Ouranos (the sky), Pontos (the sea) and mountains. In other words, the earth is taking on the recognizable shape that would have been familiar to the people of Hesiod's day. Pontos, here, means *the* sea, the Mediterranean Sea, the sea in the middle of the known world.

Gaia first exists, it seems, as a flat disc. The Earth is perceived as being disc-shaped. Then, she shapes herself into the familiar earth of the Greeks by making the Mediterranean Sea (Pontos) in the center of the land, and producing the mountain ranges that would have been familiar to Hesiod and his audience. We are picturing a flat disc-shaped earth, and Ouranos, the sky, will come to be a dome over her. Think of a cake dish—a flat round disc with a dome over it—and you will have the picture of Gaia and Ouranos. Tartaros is, Hesiod tells us, as far below Gaia as Ouranos is above her.

Once Gaia has produced Ouranos, she mates with him—her son—and they together beget 12 children. These 12 children, the first generation of gods to be born after Gaia, are called the Titans. The Titans include important natural elements or natural entities, such as the sun, the moon and the river Oceanos—a river which flows around the edges of Gaia. To complete our picture of Hesiod's worldview here, imagine a never-ending river flowing around the edges of that flat disc-shaped Earth. If you were foolish enough to sail out through what we call the Straits of Gibraltar—what the Greeks called the Pillars of Heracles—out of Pontos, the known sea, that is, you would get into this stream of Ocean and you would sail forever without ever reaching land. Ocean flows continually around the edges of Gaia (*Oceanos* is the Greek name).

So, Gaia and Ouranos mate and produce these 12 children. But all is not well, because Ouranos does not allow these children to be born. He pushes each one back into Gaia's womb as each child is born. Ouranos refuses to let his children be born. This causes Gaia great pain as well as causing her great anger. Therefore, she conspires with her youngest son, a Titan named Cronos, to overthrow Cronos's father Ouranos. Gaia produces a sickle—she somehow makes a sickle. Cronos hides inside her body (and I've always thought this was a particularly Freudian-seeming myth) and the next time Ouranos comes to have sex with Gaia, Cronos, from inside Gaia's womb, grasps hold of Ouranos's genitals and cuts them off with a scythe. Ouranos is castrated by his son Cronos, who is hiding inside the body of Cronos's mother, Gaia. Cronos throws the severed genitals into the sea, and out of the foam that springs up around them is born Aphrodite ("Venus" is her Roman name). All these paintings that are so famous in showing Aphrodite being born from the sea seldom tell you where the foam comes from. It comes from Ouranos's severed genitals being thrown into Pontos. For Aphrodite, as the personification of sexual desire, this is a reasonable birth story for her.

At this point, Ouranos retreats from Gaia and becomes the dome of the sky. He never again takes any very active part in anything that happens in *Theogony*. He cannot be killed; as I already said, a god by definition cannot be killed. What Cronos has done is the next best thing. He has disabled his father by castrating him. Obviously, if you can't kill a god, what you are going to do is deprive him of his power to the greatest extent possible, and depriving him of his masculinity is a very clear symbolic way of depriving him of his power. So, Ouranos becomes the dome of the sky that touches Gaia on all sides. He doesn't go away, he is always there—if you go outside and look up, there he is—but he is no longer an active participant in *Theogony*.

This also leaves physical room for the children to be born. The picture that Hesiod is presenting here is, before the castration of Ouranos, Ouranos was not yet the dome of the sky with which we are all familiar. He was pressing down on Gaia; he was flat on Gaia. There was no separation in between them; quite literally, no room for those children to develop. It is only when Ouranos retreats and becomes the sky as we know it that the Titans, the children, can spring forth from Gaia and become powerful entities in their own rights.

As I mentioned briefly in the very first lecture, this story is an excellent example of the way myth can work on several levels at once, because Gaia is the Earth and Ouranos is the sky. At the same time, she is a very anthropomorphic female entity, with a womb, who can feel both pain and anger when her husband pushes her babies back into her, who can conspire with her youngest son, who can create that scythe—or sickle—for Cronos to use in overpowering his father. All of this is going on at one level, while at the same time, we have the picture I just described of sky pressing down on Earth and there being no room for anything to grow between them. You have both a physical picture of the sky and Earth as they "really" are and a story of this proto-war between the sexes, if you like, in which the female conspires with the younger male to over throw the dominant male.

Once Ouranos has backed away, once he has retreated and become the dome of the sky, then there is room for Gaia's children to exist. Not only for them to exist, but to mate and to reproduce in their own rights. This is represented in the text by a whole flurry of reproduction. At this point, Hesiod goes into about three or four pages of text in which he describes all the Titans mating off with one another and producing literally hundreds of children. He lays particular emphasis on all the water, streams, lakes, rivers and so forth that come into existence at this time. So, the physical Earth is completed by the reproduction that can come among the Titans, after Ouranos has let Gaia give birth to her children.

This story of Cronos castrating his father also lends itself remarkably well to allegorical interpretation, due to the resemblance of Cronos's name to the Greek word for time. Cronos is the name of the god; *chronos*, with a slightly rougher "K" sound (represented in our transliteration by an "H"), is the word for "time"—the word we see in words like chronology, chronological. *Chronos*, with the "H" in it, is the word for time. If we go with the allegorical interpretation that the similarity of the name Cronos and the word for time seems to imply, we can say that when Cronos was freed from Gaia's womb, after he castrated his father Ouranos, Time itself came into being. On this interpretation, we are really dealing with a fairly sophisticated concept. Not only is it necessary for there to be space for Gaia's children to develop in, not only does Ouranos back away and leave room for the children to develop, time is also necessary. You have got to have space, and you have also got to have time for development to take place. Only when Cronos, only when Time, has come into true being—according to this allegorical interpretation—can the reproduction that I have just described start taking place, can the world come into full functioning order.

These two words Cronos, the name of the god, and *chronos*, the word for time, are not actually etymologically related to one another. They come from two entirely different roots; they are not two entirely different versions of the same word. I personally don't think that necessarily invalidates allegorical interpretation, if Hesiod and his audience *thought* they came from the same word. Then, that allegory can be working there even though modern linguists know that the resemblance of sound is purely coincidental. This allegorical interpretation was first suggested as early as the sixth century B.C. It is not my own idea. It has a long history behind it, and it makes a lot of sense. I like to point it out because, again, it does show the level of sophistication that can be working under the surface of what, at first sight, is a horrifically gory and outré story—the castration of Ouranos by Cronos.

Once the Titans are freed from Gaia's womb, they become the main actors in the story. As I have already said, they pair off and start mating with one another. The same basic pattern is repeated in the next generation as Cronos, in his turn, tries to prevent the birth, or at least the development, of his children. Cronos marries his sister Rheia, and they produce together six children: three daughters and three sons. The daughters are Hestia, Demeter and Hera. The sons are Hades, Poseidon and Zeus.

You would think that Cronos would have learned from his father's sad fate the futility of trying to prevent these children from developing. He does learn enough from his father that he doesn't leave his children in Rheia's womb, or push them back into Rheia's womb. Instead, he waits until the children are born, and then he swallows them. He swallows each child, in turn, as it is born. So, instead of leaving them in Rheia's body, he takes control of them by placing them in his own body. Rheia, like her mother Gaia before her, is infuriated by this and conspires to overthrow Cronos—to trick Cronos—out of his evil plan. She substitutes for the youngest child Zeus a stone, a rock, wrapped in swaddling clothes, gives that to Cronos, and he swallows it, thinking it is a baby.

A point that I like to make here at this point in the story is that we are not dealing with realism in this kind of story. Very frequently, a hand will go up in my classroom and a plaintive voice in my class will ask, "How can Cronos be so stupid that he didn't know the difference between a stone and a baby?" I think the only answer I can offer to that is that that kind of logic—that kind of realism—is not the way mythic stories operate. I can give you a folktale parallel. When we here the story of Little Red Riding Hood, it doesn't occur to most of us to say, "How could Little Red Riding Hood possibly mistake a wolf for her grandmother, and why is that wolf talking in the first place?" Within the story, we accept the logic of the story. I think we have to do the same thing with this sort of story, as Hesiod recounts it. Within the logic of this story, Cronos does not see the difference in a rock and a baby, despite the unreality of that assumption.

So, Cronos swallows a stone thinking that it is the baby Zeus. Zeus is sent to the island of Crete to be reared in secret. Hesiod doesn't tell us how long it takes Zeus to grow up and reach full maturity, but once he does, Zeus returns home and helps his siblings escape from their father. He also sets into motion the events that will lead to the overthrow of Cronos and Zeus's ascension to power. Hesiod, unfortunately, is very vague about the details of how Cronos is induced to spit out his children. But induced to spit them out he is, and since gods cannot die, Zeus's siblings have remained alive within Cronos's body. They are spat out in reverse order from the order in which they are born. In this sense, Zeus is both the youngest of his siblings and the eldest of his siblings. He is the last born, but the first to reach maturity. The others are spat out in reverse order, so Hestia (the first born) is in some sense also the youngest, the last one to be spat out by their father Cronos.

Zeus and these five siblings, together with several of Zeus's children in the next generation, together come to become the Olympians—the gods who live on Mount Olympus. And a little note about terminology here; when the Greeks talk about "the gods," they very frequently use that to mean Zeus, his five siblings and Zeus's children, also called the Olympians. Yet, all of these entities I have been talking about are gods. The Titans are gods, Gaia is a god or goddess, Ouranos is a god. So, the use of the term "gods" to mean Zeus and his immediate family is a little bit misleading, yet it is very, very common. The ten-year war that ensues at this point between Cronos and his siblings and Zeus and his siblings is very frequently referred to as the war between the gods and the Titans. It would be more appropriate to refer to it as the war between the Olympians and the Titans. Just so you are aware of it, very frequently "the gods" refers to Zeus and his immediate family, despite the fact that all of these entities are actually gods.

The two sides fight for 10 years. Eventually Zeus is triumphant. And at this point, the struggle for power ends, the order of rule in the universe is set, Zeus will remain the head god forever, and as such, is frequently called "The Olympian"—the primary Olympian among all the Olympians.

One immediately noticeable and intriguing point about this narrative is that it portrays the struggle for power among the gods as one involving older female deities opposed by and helped by younger male deities. Gaia is the oldest deity. Ouranos works against her. She enlists the help of a still younger male, Cronos, to overthrow Ouranos. Cronos in turn opposes Rheia, who enlists the help of a still younger male, Zeus, to overthrow Cronos. What is going on with this?

There are many possible answers. Some scholars argue that this reflects the psychological anxieties of males about coming to maturity; having in some sense to replace their fathers as mature men acting in the world, but also worried that their sons will in turn replace them, and worried about the affection that their wives feel for those sons. Other scholars see the increased anthropomorphism of each generation. Gaia is the Earth, Ouranos is the sky, Cronos is sort of time, Rheia is just a goddess who exists to give Cronos children. By the time we get to Zeus's generation, there is no direct connection with natural forces at all; these gods may control natural forces, but they don't personify them. Some scholars see that increased anthropomorphism of each generation as representing the development of civilization; as a society progresses, so does anthropomorphism of the gods.

Others point to the very apparent anxiety throughout Greek culture about the power of women—the fear that women would exert control if they could—and here we see these elder goddesses trying to exert power, though they can only do it through enlisting the aid of younger males. There are many, many possible other explanations, and again, I think it is a mistake to try to find one and only one meaning in this Ouranos, Cronos, Zeus story. The idea of a struggle between older female deities and younger male deities is one that we will come back to a couple of times during the course. It is worth holding in the back of your minds.

Theogony, as we have seen, presents various extremely sophisticated and difficult concepts in the guise of genealogies. Hesiod talks about all kinds of things by narrating the marriage and birth stories of the gods. It is an interesting and useful thing to do to compare Hesiod's version of the creation story with the version told by the Roman poet, Ovid, some 700 later, in a culture in which literacy was fully established. Remember classical mythology covers both Greek and Roman versions of the myths. Here, we have an unusual case of two authors standing at either end of that tradition: Hesiod in the eighth century B.C., Ovid in the first century B.C. and A.D. (he overlaps) telling more or less the same story. That gives us a rare opportunity to see how the story is manipulated by these two different authors in two different cultures.

Ovid's overall creation story is very different than Hesiod's, both in tone and in emphasis. Rather than describing the creation of the universe through the creation of the gods, Ovid simply assumes that there are gods of one type or another. He uses the standard anthropomorphic gods as characters in his work. (I am talking now about his work *Metamorphoses*, which opens with an account of creation.) Rather than describing creation of the universe through creation of the gods, Ovid offers alternatives for how the physical universe may have come to be. He does so by running through all sorts of possibilities.

The opening pages of *Metamorphoses* always seemed to me to be a *tour de force* by Ovid, in which he shows off just how learned, just how erudite he is. He runs through various possible scientific theories of his day. Maybe the universe came into existence when discordant atoms joined together and made the forms that we know. Maybe it happened when the four elements were separated out of chaos, and then came together to make the bodies and the entities that we know. Perhaps—after he has run through possible scientific theories, he touches on possible theologies—perhaps there was a creator god, or maybe Nature took it on herself, there assuming that "Nature" is somehow an entity outside the natural world. Maybe Nature takes it upon herself to shape the world.

He runs through, in a very short space, a great many possible theories—touching on each, showing how familiar he is with each, but not committing to any one of them. Now, Ovid, as I said, is working in a very literate tradition and writing for an extremely literate and erudite audience. He is doing a very different thing than Hesiod is doing, though he is using the same subject matter to do it. This is a good illustration of the problems built into a discussion of classical mythology. In Hesiod, we can feel fairly confident that we are dealing with a recounting of myth that is pretty close to the original oral tradition that the myth draws upon. With Ovid, we are dealing with the self-conscious literary reworking of the myths in ways that may sometimes go directly against the traditional import of those stories. Ironically, Ovid is our main, and sometimes our only, source for some extremely famous classical myths, such as the story of Apollo and Daphne, the story of Narcissus, the story of various others that have come down to us only in Ovid's extremely literary reworking of those myths.

In this lecture, we have begun our discussion of Hesiod's creation story, looked at how the world came into existence, and the three-generation struggle for power that ensued after the world came into existence. In our next lecture, we will focus more on what Zeus does after he comes to power, his consolidation of his power and his matings with various goddesses before he settles down with his permanent wife, Hera.

The Reign of the Olympians
Lecture 5

Hesiod and his contemporaries, and, for that matter, the Greeks who lived some time after Hesiod, did not know that thought takes place in the head. They were not aware of that. As strange as that sounds, we do not feel thought taking place in our head. We don't have any sensory nerve endings in our brains at all. We feel nothing going on in our brains. Hesiod and his contemporaries, and later Greeks as well, believed that thought took place in the midriff—in the torso.

In this lecture, we continue our discussion of *Theogony*. After overthrowing the Titans, Zeus consolidated his power and became the primary ruler of the gods, which he will continue to be for as long as the universe lasts. There will be no further struggles of sons to overthrow their fathers and no further shift of power down the generations. Hesiod does not explicitly state that the universe became fixed with Zeus's ascendancy to power. This omission is justified by reasons that are important to remember throughout the study of myth. Hesiod and his audience assume the reality of Zeus and the other gods. Therefore, "everyone knows" that Zeus will remain in power and that the point of the whole story was Zeus's rise to power. This is an important point to remember in reading any myth. Narrative points that may seem arbitrary from outside the culture that created the myth seem necessary from inside that culture.

Zeus divides power among himself and his brothers, in

After the overthrow of the Titans, Poseidon becomes the ruler of the sea and waters in general.

what is often called the "triple division." Hades becomes the ruler of Tartaros and lord over the souls of the dead. Poseidon becomes the ruler of the sea and waters in general. Zeus becomes ruler of the sky. Theoretically, all three brothers have power over the earth. In practice, the earth too is Zeus's domain, and the division of power is far from equal. Zeus's sisters also have their particular roles. Hera is the patron goddess of marriage. Hestia is the goddess of the hearth. Demeter is the goddess of grain and agriculture.

As ruler, Zeus not only gains physical control over the sky and the earth, but his domain also includes various abstract concepts that concern the orderly functioning of human society. Zeus oversees Justice; in this aspect, he is the patron of oaths and punishes oath-breakers. He also is the god of *xenia*, a very important concept usually translated as the "guest-host relationship." He oversees prophecy, particularly at his shrine at Dodona. Zeus's son Apollo is also a god of prophecy, but it is quite clear that Apollo derives his control of prophecy from Zeus. Zeus's connection with prophecy emphasizes both his wisdom and his power; prophets often say that they foretell "the will of Zeus."

Once he is established as the ruler of the gods, Zeus marries his first wife, the minor goddess Metis. Metis is fated to bear a son who will overthrow his father, thus repeating the pattern seen in the earlier generations. On the advice of Gaia and

Athena, daughter of Zeus. She is the goddess of warfare and is often associated with wisdom and cleverness.

Ouranos, Zeus prevents this by swallowing Metis. Metis is already pregnant with a daughter, Athena, who is eventually born from Zeus's head. The son who was destined to overthrow his father is never conceived and never born. This is one of the very few times that anyone successfully circumvents fate.

Like so much else in *Theogony*, the story of Metis and Athena offers several interesting interpretative points. It highlights the concept of fate, which affects gods as well as humans. Fate, or destiny, plays a crucial role in many classical myths. Fate works independently of Zeus, a reminder that even Zeus is not omnipotent. Fate is sometimes personified as three goddesses, the Fates or *Moirai*. The swallowing of Metis can be seen as the moment at which the male gods assert final power over the goddesses; from now on, the dominance of male over female will be firmly established. This act is also important as the point at which Zeus matures. In this regard, an allegorical interpretation works particularly well. Zeus is a young ruler who has power and dominance; what does he need to rule well? He needs *wisdom*, which is what the Greek word *metis* means. When Zeus swallows Metis, he is literally incorporating wisdom. Hesiod and his contemporaries believed that thought took place in our torsos, not our heads. Despite the very popular modern interpretation, the birth of Athena from Zeus's head is *not* emblematic of wisdom, because the Greeks didn't consider the head to be the seat of thought.

Fate is sometimes personified as three goddesses, the Fates or *Moirai*.

Zeus then mates with various other goddesses and produces several children before marrying his permanent wife, Hera. Hera is the patron of marriage and of married women, yet she and Zeus have difficulties producing acceptable sons. They have two daughters, Hebe ("Bloom of Youth") and Eileithyia, the goddess of childbirth. Despite Zeus's fecundity with other females, he and Hera produce only one son, Ares, the god of war. Hera's other son, Hephaistos, was probably born parthenogenically, because of Hera's jealousy over Athena. Along with these and other goddesses, Zeus also mates with various mortal women, such as Alcmene, the mother of Heracles. Hera is particularly disposed to hate Zeus's sons by mortal women. This hatred is a motivating force behind Heracles's adventures.

Zeus's amatory exploits are not just a matter of a god behaving badly. Many of Zeus's matings are with "conceptual" gods, such as Themis ("right order"), and produce offspring, such as Justice. These unions express his attributes as ruler. His multiple matings also repeat a pattern we saw in the earlier generations. Hesiod is describing the coming-into-existence of everything, including such abstractions as Justice, through the medium of anthropomorphic gods. It is reasonable in this context to describe the process through the sexual matings of different gods. Because Zeus is such an important god, this will necessarily result in his mating with various females. Another explanation for Zeus's frequent matings with minor goddesses and mortal women is that it reflects the synthesis of various local gods and traditions, or syncretism.

By the end of *Theogony*, what sort of picture of the gods do we have? Several important characteristics are worth enumerating. The gods are anthropomorphic, not theriomorphic or a combination of the two, sharing many of humanity's characteristics. They have bodies, though it is taken as a given that in their "natural" state, the bodies of the gods are both much larger and much more beautiful than human bodies. They eat (*ambrosia*) and drink (*nectar*) and have a substance flowing through their veins (*ichor*). They share human emotions and passions, both good and bad. The gods are also very different from humans. They have the ability to move vast distances, more or less at will; they can appear before a human when they want to. Although their normal appearance is anthropomorphic, they can disguise themselves as other creatures or even as non-animate objects (such as a shower of gold). The defining difference between gods and humans is that the gods are immortal. Humans must die, but gods cannot die. One of the most frequent terms used to describe the gods in Greek is *athanatoi*, the deathless ones. Humans, by contrast, are *thnetoi*, those who are liable to death. An oath sworn on the River Styx was, for the gods, the most telling incarnation of their immortality. ■

Supplementary Reading

Graf, *Greek Mythology*, Ch. IV, "The Origin of the World and the Gods," pp. 79–100.

Tyrrell and Brown, *Athenian Myths and Institutions*, Ch. 2.

Questions to Consider

1. I have referred to "allegorical" interpretations of Zeus's swallowing of Metis and marriage to Themis. Is this anachronistic? Put another way,

could Hesiod's original audience have separated out the literal and allegorical senses of these stories?

2. Greek society was strongly patriarchal; marriages were arranged, not based on romantic love. What are the implications of this for our understanding of Hera and her jealousy over Zeus's affairs?

The Reign of the Olympians
Lecture 5—Transcript

In the previous lecture, we talked about Hesiod's delineation in *Theogony* of the three-generational struggle for power, in which power devolved from Ouranos, through Cronos, to Zeus. In this lecture, we are going to continue discussing *Theogony*, looking at how Zeus consolidated his power and divided it with his siblings and the next generation of gods that began to be born through Zeus's various matings with several different goddesses.

After overthrowing the Titans, Zeus consolidates his power and becomes the primary ruler of the gods, which he will continue to be for as long as the universe lasts. There will be no further struggles of sons to overthrow their fathers and no further shift of power down the generations. Zeus is now in control; he is the head god and he will remain so for as long as the universe lasts.

Hesiod never explicitly states any of that, which I have just said. Hesiod never comes out and says, "Zeus is now in power and will remain so. This is the end of the struggle for power that crosses generations. Zeus is going to stay in power forever." He doesn't do so for reasons that are important to remember throughout the study of classical myth—or any mythology for that matter. Hesiod and his audience assume the reality of Zeus and the other gods. For them, these gods are really there. They are *the gods*. They are an accurate picture of how the universe works. Therefore, everyone knows that Zeus will remain in power; there can be no question of Zeus not remaining in power. That is a given of Hesiod's society, and everyone listening to Hesiod's work at the time it was composed would know perfectly well that it was Zeus's rise to power toward which the whole story was tending from the very beginning—that everything was leading up to, was heading toward Zeus's accession to power.

Because this is known by everyone, it is not necessary to state it straightforwardly in Hesiod's narrative. This is an important point to remember any time we look at any myth. Narrative points seen from the outside may seem arbitrary; various different points may seem arbitrary. Why should Zeus become the head god over someone else? Why should

Zeus not be overthrown by a son later on? From within the culture that created these stories, these points are not arbitrary at all. They are necessary because they are reflections of what that culture perceives as reality. Zeus is, and will remain, king of the gods, ruler of the gods. He divides power among himself and his brothers, as one of his first acts, once he is in power. This division is often referred to by Greek authors as the "Triple Division," with no further explanation than that, because everyone knows which Triple Division is being referred to. Zeus has two brothers, Hades and Poseidon, and he allocates power to them as follows.

Hades becomes lord of Tartaros. At this point, Hades goes literally, bodily, into Tartaros and stays there. He becomes king of the dead. He does not ever come back to Mount Olympus where Zeus and his siblings live, and Hades does not take much active part in the doings of myth after this, except as those doings affect or are associated with the land of the dead. His identification with Tartaros becomes so close, in fact, that his name "Hades" comes to be another name for the land of the dead, so that Tartaros can now be referred to as Hades (the god's name becomes the name of the place as well). Poseidon becomes ruler of the seas and of waters, in general. Poseidon doesn't personify the sea; Pontos is still there. Pontos has not gone away, but Poseidon is given power over the seas and over waters, in general. He also is the god who is supposed to send earthquakes. He controls earthquakes as well as water. Zeus becomes ruler of the sky. And, as such, he controls the thunderbolt, which he can hurl as his weapon.

Theoretically, all three brothers share power over the earth. In practice, the earth becomes Zeus's domain. Poseidon very seldom exerts power over the earth; Hades very seldom, if ever, has any direct control over the earth. The earth, in effect, becomes Zeus's domain, as well as does most of the workings of human society. So, while this is called the Triple Division, and supposedly, Zeus divides three shares of power among himself and his brothers, in actuality, it is more as though Zeus divides the world into four parts: earth, sky, sea and underworld, giving one-fourth to each of his brothers and keeping half for himself. Zeus very definitely has the upper hand in this division of power.

Zeus's sisters also have their particular roles. Hera, as we will talk about later in the lecture, is the patron goddess of marriage and married women. She is also Zeus's permanent wife. Hestia is the goddess of the hearth. Hestia's case is a good one for reminding ourselves that myth and religion are not necessarily completely overlapping categories. The reason I say that is that Hestia is goddess of the hearth. Hestia, whose name actually means hearth, must have been one of the most important goddesses in the day-to-day religious lives and religious experiences of most Greek people; the hearth is both the literal and metaphorical center of the household. The hearth—the fireplace—allows for heat, light, heating water to cook, for all the processes that are necessary for life in society. The hearth is absolutely crucial. It can be set as the focal point of the home, and that is actually a pun, because the Latin word *focus* originally meant hearth. That is where we get that word from.

We have almost no myth about Hestia. She does not show up in literature much at all. She is mentioned now and then, but there are almost no stories associated with her. If we judge the importance of a god in religion purely based on that god's appearance in literature, we would have to say that Hestia is negligible. And yet, everything else we know about Greek religion would indicate she is far from negligible. That is just a reminder that the two categories, myth and religion, do not always overlap nearly as neatly as we would like to think they would.

Demeter, Zeus's remaining sister, is the goddess of grain and agriculture. She takes part in some very important myths, most important among them the story of the loss of her daughter Persephone, which I mentioned in an earlier lecture and which we will talk about at length in Lecture Seven.

As ruler, Zeus not only gains physical control over the sky and the earth, he also takes, as part of his domain, control over the governance of various abstract concepts having to do with human society and the orderly working of human society. First and foremost, Zeus oversees justice. Zeus is the god who stands behind justice, who backs up justice. As such, he is the god who punished oath-breakers and who validates the swearing of oaths. He is also the god of *xenia*, the patron god of an extraordinarily important concept in Greek culture. *Xenia* is often translated as the guest-host relationship, or as hospitality. Neither of those captures just how crucially important a concept it was in archaic Greek society. Anyone who has ever read the *Odyssey* will remember how important *xenia* is. Zeus is the god who stands behind that concept as well, and punishes those who violate their duties to guest or host.

He is also the god who overseas prophecy, particularly at his shrine at a place called Dodona. Zeus's son Apollo, whom we will talk about in a later lecture, is also a god of prophecy and is probably the most important god of prophecy in Greek myth. It is Apollo who supervises the Oracle at Delphi, the most important oracular shrine in Greece. But Apollo makes it quite clear several times in literature that his control of prophecy, his prophetic gift, is handed to him by Zeus. It is given to him by Zeus. He even says, at times, that what he is doing when he gives prophecy is prophesying the will of Zeus. Zeus, in other words, is the god who is most directly associated with prophecy. He gives control over prophecy to Apollo as a kind of lending out of his control of prophecy, but Zeus is the main prophetic god.

Zeus's connection with prophecy emphasizes both his wisdom and his power. Prophets like Apollo often say that they are foretelling the will of Zeus. What is going to happen is, at times, described as what Zeus wills to happen. Once he has established himself as ruler of the gods, divided his power with his brothers, overseen the domains of his sisters and set himself up as the god who is patron of these various aspects of human society, Zeus starts to mate with various different goddesses.

His first wife (or his first mate) is the minor goddess Metis. It is not clear if he actually marries her or just mates with her. In any case, she is his first partner, and the important thing about Metis is that she is fated—the Fates have decreed that she would bear a son who would overthrow his father, thus repeating the pattern we saw in the earlier generations. Just as Cronos overthrew Ouranos, and Zeus overthrew Cronos, Metis is supposed to bear a son who will overthrow his father. Hesiod says about Metis:

> It was fated the Metis would bear keen-minded children,
> first, a gray-eyed daughter ... who in strength and wisdom
> would be her father's match, then a male child,
> high-mettled and destined to rule over gods and men.

But Zeus lodged her in his belly before she did all this,
that she might advise him in matters good and bad.

As I said in the last lecture, Cronos takes a hint from the mistakes of Ouranos, and doesn't leave the children inside his wife, but swallows them. Zeus takes a hint from the troubles of Cronos, and doesn't wait until the children are born to swallow them, but swallows the wife before she can conceive the troublesome son. She has already conceived the daughter in question, and the daughter is Athena, who is eventually born from Zeus's head. Just as Zeus's siblings remained alive inside Cronos's body, so Athena remains alive inside Metis's body, inside Zeus's body. Whenever the gestation period is finished with, Athena is born from Zeus's head. There are various works of Greek art showing this moment. Zeus has someone, usually it is the god Hephaistos (the blacksmith god), hit him over the forehead with an ax, his head splits open, and out springs Athena, fully grown and wearing armor. A very interesting subject to be portrayed in art. The son who is destined to overthrow his father is never conceived and never born. Zeus is never overthrown. This is one of the very few times in Greek myth that anyone, even Zeus, successfully circumvents the workings of fate.

Like so much else in *Theogony*, the story of Metis and her daughter Athena offer several interesting interpretive points. First, it is the only time anyone successfully overthrows fate. It highlights and introduces the concept of fate, which affects gods as well as humans. Fate, or destiny, is a huge topic in classical culture and classical mythology. It is very hard to get an exact handle on precisely how it works. It is independent of Zeus. While prophets may say they are foretelling the will of Zeus, side by side with that is the very strong sense that the Fates operate separately from Zeus, and that even Zeus normally speaking cannot counteract the workings of fate.

There is a very famous scene in Homer's *Iliad* in which Zeus thinks about intervening in the battle and saving the life of his human son, Sarpedon, who is about to be killed. Hera reminds him that Sarpedon is fated to die and that Zeus should not interfere with the workings of fate. Zeus agrees and lets Sarpedon die, though he weeps bitterly for him. Thus, the swallowing of Metis and circumvention of the conception of the fated son is a very unusual thing. Normally, fate functions as a reminder that even Zeus is not omnipotent. Fate is sometimes treated as an abstract concept. It is sometimes personified as three goddesses called "The Fates," or *Moirai* in Greek, who are daughters of Zeus and another minor goddess named Themis.

The swallowing of Metis gives us an interesting take on fate. It is the exception that proves a rule, in effect—that fate cannot normally be circumvented. It also can be seen as the moment at which the male power, the power of male gods, is finally irrevocably established over the female goddesses. Up to this point it has been a little bit questionable. These mother goddesses have seemed awfully powerful. They have conspired with younger sons to overthrow fathers, up until this point. When Zeus circumvents any of that by swallowing Metis, one way to read what is going on here is to say this is the moment in which male dominance is firmly established, and remains so in Greek culture and Greek myth.

The act is also important, I think, as the point at which Zeus matures—becomes a mature, fully competent ruler. To explain why I say that, we have to do an allegorical interpretation, which works exceptionally well for this myth. Zeus is a young ruler. He has just come into power. He has power and dominance. What else does a ruler need in order to rule well? To rule well, a ruler needs wisdom. He must be a wise ruler. Guess what the word *Metis* means in Greek? It means wisdom. Metis, like many other minor goddesses ,has a name that is also an abstract concept. She personifies wisdom, just as there are goddesses who personify justice, order, peace. Metis personifies wisdom.

Zeus needs wisdom in order to rule properly, and thus, when he swallows Metis, he is quite literally incorporating wisdom. Hesiod says, "He lodged her in his belly so that she might advise him in matters good and bad." He lodged her in his belly so that she might advise him. In order to explain that, I have to tell you something about ancient Greek views of physiology and the workings of thought.

Hesiod and his contemporaries, and, for that matter, the Greeks who lived some time after Hesiod, did not know that thought takes place in the head. They were not aware of that. As strange as that sounds, we do not feel thought taking place in our head. We don't have any sensory nerve endings in our brains at all. We feel nothing going on in our brains. Hesiod and his contemporaries, and later Greeks as well, believed that thought took place in the midriff—in the torso. That is not quite as bizarre as it sounds if you think about it (with your head). You will realize that we feel emotions, which are pretty closely allied to thoughts anyway, in our torsos. Where do you feel fear, anxiety, happiness, anger? You don't feel them in your brain. You feel them, if anywhere, in your torso. We still have expressions in our language that reflect that. We say that someone loves someone else with all their heart. We say, "I have a gut feeling about this." Those kinds of expressions reflect our realization that we feel our mental states, to a large degree, in our torsos. The Greeks thought that that is also where we thought our mental states—in our torsos.

They weren't stupid. Some of the clearest evidence that thought takes place in the brain that we have is what happens to someone who suffered a severe head injury. We can see—all too horribly—many times, the impact of a head injury on the thought process. In the ancient world, in any time before the invention of modern medicine, an injury severe enough to cause brain damage would almost undoubtedly be severe enough to kill. While the ancient Greeks knew that the stuff in the head (and by the way, that is what "encephalon" means—just "the stuff in the head"), they knew that it was important; you split someone's head open with an ax, and—if the person is not Zeus—he drops dead, but they didn't know exactly what it was important for. One theory was that it was a regulatory system for heat, that it controlled the heat or coolness of the body. Another theory was that it was the source of important bodily fluids such as blood, bone marrow and semen. But it was not the seat of thought.

Again, that means when Zeus puts Metis in his belly, he is putting wisdom right where she needs to be for him to think with her. It also means that the very modern interpretation of the birth of Athena—something that you will see in many modern myth handbooks—that Athena springs forth from Zeus's head because she is a goddess of wisdom and that is the proper place for her to spring from; that won't work. Athena is a goddess associated with wisdom, but that can't be what is associated with her springing out of Zeus's brow. I think that is probably a connection with the belief that the brain is the source of semen, so if a male god was going to give birth, that is a good place for him to give birth from; or it is an association with the head as the top of the body, the highest point, the crowning point. A word that is used for head can also mean the top of a hill or mountain. It gives Athena a kind of majesty that she comes out of Zeus's head.

After the swallowing of wisdom, of Metis, and the birth of Athena, Zeus mates with various other goddesses and produces several children before he marries his permanent and lasting wife, Hera. Hera is the patron goddess of marriage and married women, and yet, her marriage with Zeus is neither happy, nor very productive. She and Zeus have difficulties producing acceptable sons. They have two daughters, Hebe, whose name means youthful beauty or bloom of youth or something like that; the moment at which a young maiden is her most beautiful is her *hebe*. And Zeus and Hera's second daughter is called Eileithyia, the goddess of childbirth. They have one daughter who personifies the exact moment at which a girl ought to be a bride and another who personifies childbirth, both of which fit very well with Hera being goddess of marriage.

However, their son, probably their only son, is Ares, god of war—a god whom Zeus himself says, in the *Iliad,* all the other gods hate. Hera has a second son, Hephaistos, the blacksmith god. But, according to most versions of Hephaistos' birth, he was born parthenogenically. Hera gave birth to him without mating with Zeus because she was angry that Zeus had Athena. While Athena is in many ways the most splendid goddess who exists, Hera's attempt to produce a male child on her own results in Hephaistos, who is lame, ugly and not a very satisfactory god in many ways.

So, Zeus and Hera do not produce flourishing offspring as you might expect they would. Zeus also mates with not only other goddesses, but with various mortal women such as Alcmene, the mother of the hero Heracles. One theme that runs through the Greek hero myth is the idea that Hera hates and makes trouble for Zeus's sons by mortal women. She is not entirely pleased when Zeus has sons by other goddesses either, but she particularly hates the idea that a mortal woman could produce a son with Zeus when she herself has not been particularly successful in that regard. She is particularly disposed to hate Zeus's sons by mortal women.

The hatred of Hera is a motivating force behind most of the adventures of the hero Heracles, whom we will talk about at length in another lecture. But, for right now, just as a comment, this is one reason that I was terribly disappointed in the recent Disney movie about Heracles (or Hercules, the Roman version of his name). In that movie, the story was cleaned up to make Hercules the legitimate son of Zeus and Hera. Well, there are two problems with that. First of all, if both his parents are gods, he ought to be a god, not a hero. It leaves unanswered the question of why he is a human at all. Secondly, and I think more importantly, if you remove Hera's hatred for Heracles, and Heracles is Hera's son, then you remove the entire motivation for almost everything that happened to Heracles throughout his entire life. By getting rid of the illegitimacy, getting rid of the fact that Zeus is an adulterer, they undercut the entire story of Heracles (or Hercules).

Zeus's amatory exploits are not just a matter of a god behaving badly. There are reasons—compelling reasons—within the logic of the mythological narratives for why Zeus mates with so many other females. First of all, many of his matings are with conceptual goddesses. By that, I mean matings with goddesses such as Metis (wisdom) or Themis, whose name means "right order," the right functioning of society and the world in general. These matings produce offspring such as Justice. Zeus mates with Right Order and has a daughter, Justice; that is a fairly transparent way of talking about Zeus's attributes as ruler. Making him the father of Justice underlines the idea that he supervises justice. Justice is part of his domain.

His multiple matings also repeat a pattern that we saw in the earlier generations. Hesiod, as I have said before, is describing the coming into existence of everything, and is using the sexual matings of anthropomorphic gods to describe how everything comes into existence. If you want to have abstractions, such as justice, produced through sexual union, and have Justice herself be an anthropomorphic goddess, then it is reasonable in this context to have Zeus—so important a god as he is—the father of many of the lesser gods. Zeus is almost by necessity paired off with different concepts to produce yet other concepts. That is the means that Hesiod has to talk about how the world came into existence.

Another explanation for Zeus's very frequent mating with minor goddesses, and even mortal women, is that this may well reflect the synthesis of traditions about various local gods. Greek religion, belief in the Olympians and all the stories concerning the Olympians, did not spring full-grown from the earth as Athena sprang full-grown from Zeus's brow. It developed over a period of centuries. It is safe to assume that as it developed, it also spread; some areas of Greece that had not originally believed in Zeus and the Olympians came to believe in them. Most places would have local traditions and stories about their own gods. When they came to believe in Zeus, there would be a strong tendency to say, "The stories we have told about our local god were really about Zeus instead. We called him something else; now we know his name is really Zeus." Along with that, there is probably a reluctance to give up stories about local heroines who had mated with this god, a local queen who had been married by this god, a local goddess who had been married by this god. You simply graft all those stories onto Zeus. That means that Zeus, by necessity, becomes a god who has mated with many, many different females. This process, by the way, is often called "syncretism"—putting together various different traditions, adding other traditions onto the stories about a particular god or goddess.

So, by the end of *Theogony,* what sort of picture of the gods and goddesses do we have? There are several important characteristics that I want to enumerate at this point, just to pull together some of the threads. These gods are anthropomorphic. They share many of humanity's characteristics. We are so accustomed to the classical mythology as our primary example of what mythology is, and how it works, that we know of in this culture of polytheism—belief in many gods—that it may not seem at all surprising that the gods are anthropomorphic. You may be thinking, "Well, of course, they are. How else would a god be portrayed?"

The answer is that a god could be portrayed in many other ways. There are many cultures that have gods who are "theriomorphic," rather than anthropomorphic—that is, gods who resemble beasts, animals, not humans— and there are some cultures that have gods who are a combination of the two. In Egyptian culture, for example, there are gods who have heads of jackals, or a crocodile god. The fact that the Greeks conceived of their gods as anthropomorphic in nature is not a given of a polytheistic system. That is simply how the Greeks happened to do it.

These gods are very anthropomorphic. They have actual bodies. It is taken for granted that in their natural state, as they appear to one another on Mount Olympus, their bodies are larger, more beautiful and more glorious than human bodies—human-like, but better than ours. In fact, they are so glorious in their natural state that if a human being sees a god as the god really is, the human being goes up in smoke. We are incinerated by the sight. We cannot tolerate it.

Though their bodies are larger and more beautiful than ours, they are functioning anthropomorphic bodies. The gods eat; they eat ambrosia; we eat grain or meat. The gods drink; we drink wine; they drink nectar. The gods have a substance flowing through their veins; we have blood; they have ichor. They have fully functional human-like bodies, and they share many human emotions and passions—both good and bad. However, anthropomorphic though they are, they are also very different from human beings. They have the ability to move vast distances, apparently almost instantaneously. When a god wants to appear to a human, he or she can almost just by thinking it— and they very constantly do. They simply appear in front of human beings in many myths. Although their normal appearance, their real appearance, is anthropomorphic, they can and do disguise themselves as other creatures or even as non-animate objects. Zeus is particularly known for this. When he wants to seduce a mortal woman, he may appear to her as a bull, a swan, or, in one memorable case when a girl was locked up in a tower, as a shower of gold that blew through the window and landed in her lap.

The defining difference between gods and humans, the one true dividing line between them and us, is that the gods are immortal. Humans must die, but gods cannot die. One of the most frequent terms used to describe the gods in Greek literature is to call them the *athanatoi*—the deathless ones—whereas humans are called the *thnetoi*—the dying ones or the ones who are bound to death. This helps us understand why the most powerful oath a god can swear is an oath by the River Styx. When a god swears by the River Styx, the god is bound to do as he has sworn. The Styx is a river that flows around Tartaros as Oceanos flows around Gaia. It is therefore the actual dividing line between the land of the dead inside Tartaros and the land of the living. Since the absolute defining characteristic of a god is that he or she cannot die, an oath sworn on the River Styx is, in effect, an oath sworn on the essence of what makes a god a god, their immortality, and is therefore inviolable.

So, in this lecture, we have continued our discussion of Hesiod by looking at Zeus's consolidation of power and his matings with various goddesses. In our next lecture, we will turn to the one missing element we have not talked about yet, human beings, and see how Hesiod treats them, and particularly, what he says about the creation not of the first man, but of the first woman.

Immortals and Mortals

Lecture 6

In actual Greek ritual practice, the human beings ate the meat of the sacrificed animal and the gods were given the bones. Supposedly, the gods enjoyed the smell of the smoke rising up on their altars, but they did not get the meat or the fat, the edible part of the animal.

In this lecture, we turn to Hesiod's depiction of humans. *Theogony* concentrates on the coming-into-being of the gods; it does not contain a creation story for humans at all. The subject of *Theogony* is the gods, and its purpose is to describe how they arranged and developed their society. Humans are largely irrelevant in this context. Humans are mentioned in *Theogony*, but the creation of men (as opposed to women) is not described; they are simply there. Men appear in *Theogony* when Hesiod describes the first sacrifice at a place called Mekone. This leads into the story of Prometheus and of Pandora, the first woman.

Prometheus is a Titan, the son of Iapetos (brother of Cronos). In Hesiod's account, Prometheus tries to trick Zeus into taking the less desirable portion of the first sacrifice so that men will have the better portion. In retaliation, Zeus punishes humans. Zeus's first reaction to Prometheus's deceit is to hide fire from man. Because Zeus is the god of justice, it is striking that he acts here in what seems to be a very unjust way, punishing humans for Prometheus's transgressions. This is our first view of the relationship

According to Hesiod's *Works and Days*, Pandora is sent to Epimetheus with a jar containing all the evils of the world.

between gods and humans in Greek myth. The gods do not love humans or feel compelled to treat them fairly; rather, humans are useful but expendable. In his role as god of justice, Zeus supervises justice between humans; this does not necessarily imply that a comparable form of justice exists between gods and humans. Prometheus steals the fire back for humanity, which brings down further punishment. Prometheus is chained to a pillar to have his liver eaten daily by an eagle, Zeus's sacred bird. The liver regenerates and is eaten again the next day. Men are punished by the creation of the first woman, Pandora. The Prometheus story highlights several of the problems of studying myth through literature that I mentioned in the first lecture. The story includes unexplained elements. Zeus seems to have a particular grudge against Prometheus's entire family, but Hesiod does not say why. Nor does Hesiod say why Prometheus wants to help humans. According to some later authors, Prometheus created humans, but Hesiod does not say so.

Prometheus's story is obviously very important. Notice that fire equals civilization, or "culture." What Prometheus brings men is culture. Later authors specifically make this equation. The impetus for his story—the first sacrifice—is very important in this context. Sacrifice can be seen as representing the transition from pre-civilization to civilization. Burkert believes that sacrifice is a means to displace the guilt felt over hunting and killing animals. The "first sacrifice" would be the moment at which hominids made the transition from guilt-free animals to guilt-feeling humans, the moment at which civilization, or society in general, comes into being. If the myth is read in this way, it is probably no surprise that sex appears at just this point, because one function of society is to regulate the relationship between the sexes. Guilt over killing animals is not the only possible guilt men might feel over sacrifice. When we look at the myth from outside its original culture, we understand why humans eat the sacrificed animal. *Within* the culture that developed this myth, the fact that the gods receive the inferior portion of the sacrifice would be troubling. Thus, the idea that the establishment of sacrifice somehow entailed punishment makes sense.

The story of Pandora also occurs in Hesiod's other great work, *Works and Days*. In *Theogony* the emphasis is on Prometheus's wrongdoing and his punishment, but in *Works and Days* the emphasis is on Pandora herself. In *Works and Days*, the first woman is named; in *Theogony*, she is nameless.

The name Pandora is ambiguous; it may mean "gift of all" or "all-giver." In *Works and Days*, Pandora's creation is described in more detail. She is sent not to men in general but to Prometheus's brother Epimetheus. She has a jar that contains all the evils of the world, as well as Hope. When Pandora opens the jar, the evils fly out, but Hope remains just under the lid of the jar.

Pandora's story is often compared to that of the biblical Eve. The differences seem more striking than the similarities, however, and have several important implications for our understanding of the relationship between the sexes in Greek mythology. Both Pandora and Eve are responsible for the advent of evil into the world. Eve was created in the first place as a helper for Adam. Pandora is evil from her very creation. Eve is created out of Adam's body, but Pandora is a different type of creature. This seems to imply that women are seen as different in kind from men, rather than as simply the female sex of the human species. This is our first example of the deep-seated misogyny that runs through much of classical myth.

Both Pandora and Eve are responsible for the advent of evil into the world.

The presence of Hope in Pandora's jar is both striking and difficult to interpret. The most common modern interpretation is that no matter how bad things get, "we still have hope." This view ignores two points: Hope is still *in* the jar, not out in the world the way the evils are. If Hope is a good thing, why is it in the jar of evils to begin with? Another interpretation is that Hope's retention in the jar is meant to indicate that there is no Hope, that even that small relief of evil is absent for mankind. The key may be that the word translated as Hope, *elpis*, is in fact ambiguous, both good and evil, more like *expectation*. Its being caught under the lip of the jar may indicate the two-edged nature of *elpis*.

The myth of Pandora lends itself especially well to psychological interpretations. The jar can be read as representing Pandora's womb. Pandora—and all women—are responsible for evil in that they are responsible for life itself, by giving birth. At the same time that birth inflicts all the evils of life on the one born, it is also the only hope for continuity available to humans. Thus, the jar/womb contains both evil and hope. On a deeper level, the description of Pandora can be seen as reflecting male anxieties about and resentments of sexual reproduction. In a strongly patriarchal society, it is all-important for men to have sons. The only way to achieve sons is through women. The woman can be seen as controlling the man's ultimate destiny. The jar, which Pandora can choose to open, could represent this fear/resentment of female power. We will see other examples of this anxiety and resentment about women, along with fears of what they would do if they gained power.

At this point, we need to pull together several threads and consider the overall relationship of gods and humans. First, we will recap the essential nature of the gods. The term "god" is regularly used to translate the Greek *theos*, but for modern readers this translation can bring serious misconceptions. Modern Western readers tend to assume that a god must by definition be good, merciful, and just. We tend to assume that a god must by definition be omniscient and omnipotent. We tend to assume that a god must by definition have created the universe and must feel love toward human beings. Despite the anthropomorphic language often used to describe God, we tend to assume that a god does not really have a body or human-like appetites and passions. All these assumptions are false for the gods of classical mythology. They are not consistently good, or merciful, or even (apparently) just. Their anthropomorphism means that they share in humanity's less appealing attributes and emotions; they can be jealous, spiteful, and cruel. Though they know a great deal, they are not omniscient; though very powerful, they are not omnipotent. They are not transcendent. In other words, they did not create the universe but are part of it. According to the earliest traditions, they did not even create human beings. They are not loving, devoted caretakers of humanity. They do not care about us as a species and rarely even as individuals. Although they are more than personifications of natural forces, emotions, or processes, such personification is an important element of their characters. This helps to explain their emotional detachment from humans and their mercilessness. ■

Essential Reading

Hesiod, *Works and Days*, pp. 67–69.

Supplementary Reading

Burkert, *Structure and History*, Ch. 2, Sections 4–6, pp. 52–58.

Kirk, *Myth: Its Meaning and Function*, Ch. 5, section 7, pp. 226–231.

Questions to Consider

1. Why do you think Hope is present in Pandora's jar? Remember that the term *elpis* can mean "false expectation," as well as "hope."

2. I suggested a psychological explanation for identifying Pandora (and women in general) as the source or cause of evil. Can you think of any other explanation?

Immortals and Mortals

Lecture 6—Transcript

In our previous two lectures, we looked at what Hesiod's *Theogony,* which tells us about the gods, their creation, and the creation of the universe through the creation of the gods. In this lecture, we are going to turn to seeing what Hesiod has to tell us about human beings. We will look at the myth of Prometheus and Pandora, as it appears in *Theogony* and in Hesiod's other great work, a poem called *Works and Days.* We will consider the implications of this myth for the Greek view of society and, particularly, of women and gender roles.

Theogony, as I have said several times, concentrates on the coming into existence of the gods. It does not contain a creation story about humans or, at least, about *men* at all. This often surprises modern readers because we, for whatever reason, tend to think that how we came into existence, how human beings came to be, would be one of the primary points of interest in any creation story. What Hesiod is doing in *Theogony* is describing the birth of the gods; humans are largely irrelevant in that context. Therefore, when humans are mentioned in *Theogony,* or when male humans are mentioned in *Theogony,* Hesiod does not describe how they came to be created—they are simply there. They are simply taken as a given.

Hesiod launches into the one place in *Theogony* where he really discusses humans and their relationship with gods by simply saying that when the gods and men met at a place called Mekone, a series of things happened there. He doesn't tell us where the men came from. He doesn't even make it clear immediately that he does mean just men, not men and women, but as the story progresses we find that that is in fact what he means. Though Hesiod doesn't tell us how men came to exist, he does posit an original state in which humans were males only and there were no women.

The men and the gods met at a place called Mekone. Among other things, what they did there was to establish the appropriate ritual for sacrifice, to establish the way in which men would offer sacrifice to the gods. This was the beginning of all of men's troubles. Though they were trying to set up a way to sacrifice to the gods in order to honor the gods, the idea of sacrifice backfired for the following reasons. Prometheus was present when the gods and men met at Mekone to work out the method of sacrifice. Prometheus is a son of Iapetos, one of the original Titans. Prometheus himself is also called a Titan—though actually if you draw a family tree, you will see that he is Zeus's first cousin and that he is in the same generation as Zeus, but he is not one of the Olympians. He is called a Titan as is his father Iapatos, brother of Cronos.

In Hesiod's account, Prometheus tries to trick Zeus into taking the less desirable portion of the first sacrifice so that men will have the better portion. What Prometheus does is he disguises the edible part of the sacrificial animal by putting the meat under the hide, hooves, horns and the parts of the animal that look inedible. The inedible portion he hides under fat so that it looks like it would be the meat, then he tells Zeus to choose whatever portion he desires.

There are a couple of points to notice here. First of all, this reflects an assumption that is very frequent in myth in most cultures, in aetiological myths in particular. The way something is done the very first time is the way that it will be done forever after. If Zeus chooses the worse portion on this occasion, then forever after the gods will get the inedible part of the sacrifice, the humans will get the edible part. Again, there is no logical reason why it should be so. There is no logical reason why the way things are done the first time is the way they are done forever after, but that shows up very frequently in myth. Secondly, though I said at the end of my last lecture that gods eat ambrosia and drink nectar, apparently at this very early stage of society when things were still being settled, the gods could eat meat if they wanted to, because the idea is that Zeus could have chosen the edible part of the sacrifice for the gods and left the inedible portion to the humans.

Zeus is not a fool. Hesiod tells us Zeus knows perfectly well what Prometheus is doing and is angered by it. In retaliation for his anger at Prometheus, Zeus punishes humans. You may remember that in the last lecture I said Zeus is the god who has dominion over justice. This seems like a remarkably unjust way for a god of justice to deal with human beings. Zeus's first reaction to Prometheus's deceit is to punish humans by hiding fire from them. Hesiod says quite distinctly that Zeus is punishing human beings. He says that Zeus plots evil for men in his mind because he is angry at what Prometheus did.

How can we square this with the idea that Zeus is a god of justice when he punishes innocent men for the transgressions of his own cousin Prometheus?

This is the first view we have had of the relationship between gods and humans as it is delineated in Greek mythology, and I think that it is a very important glimpse we are given here of the Greek view of the way humans and gods interact with one another. These gods do not love humans; they do not feel compelled to treat humans fairly. The relationship between humans and gods, as Hesiod relates it, is not a relationship of love, compassion or mercy on the part of the gods. Humans are useful to the gods. We offer them sacrifices. We do nice things for them. They find us useful. They do not find us particularly worthy objects of love, pity or mercy, and they do find us expendable. In his role as god of justice, Zeus supervises justices between humans, justice in human actions toward other humans. He punishes humans who break their oaths toward other humans, or for that matter towards gods. This does not necessarily imply any correlation of a just system between gods and humans. The fact that humans have to treat one another fairly does not imply that gods have to treat humans fairly. They don't have to and they don't, as we will see in a great many of the myths we will study.

So, Zeus decides to punish Prometheus by punishing humans and he steals fire away from human beings. Prometheus then steals the fire back for humanity, which brings further punishment down, both on his own head this time, and on men. Prometheus himself is punished in a way that is extremely famous. He is chained either to a rocky crag, or according to Hesiod, to a pillar, to have his liver eaten out every day by an eagle, Zeus's sacred bird. Every night his liver grows back, so that it can be eaten out by the bird again the next day. (One point I always like to make here is, again, a demonstration of how extraordinarily anthropomorphic these gods are. Not only the external appearance of their bodies is like humans, but even their internal organs are like humans. Prometheus has a liver, and it is his liver that the eagle can eat every day and that will grow back every night.) Zeus apparently intends this punishment to be permanent. Prometheus is supposed to be there forever. In fact, he is freed by Heracles some generations later. Heracles happens to be passing by and unchains Prometheus, and lets him go. So much for Prometheus.

Men are also punished in a way that Hesiod seems to consider no less horrible than what happens to Prometheus. Men get women, and the person of the first woman, Pandora, although she is not named in *Theogony*. The first woman is created and sent to men in general (we are not supposed to think of this too literally, I suppose) as a source of womankind and a punishment and trouble for men. Hesiod delineates very quickly just what a trouble women are. He says they are worthless, they don't contribute anything to their own upkeep, they are a burden and a nag and you don't want to have them around. On the other hand, if you don't have them around, then you can't have any children, and you die old and friendless and strangers get your property. So, he ends on a cheerful note, there is no way to escape the will of Zeus. In other words, men are going to suffer no matter what they do.

The Prometheus story highlights several of the problems of studying myth through literature that I touched on in the first lecture. There are unexplained elements. Zeus appears to have a grudge against Prometheus's whole family, for one thing. Prometheus's brother, Atlas, is the one who is condemned to hold the sky up on his shoulders forever. We are not told why Zeus has a grudge against Prometheus's whole family. That seems to be one of the elements that Hesiod thinks his audience can take for granted. Secondly, and more importantly, Hesiod doesn't tell us why Prometheus wants to help humans. Other gods, as I have said, don't seem particularly interested in helping us or being kind to us. Prometheus goes out of his way and risks dreadful punishment, and suffers dreadful punishment, for helping us. Later authors said that Prometheus was the creator of men, that Prometheus was the one who had created male human beings. That is why he wanted to help them, and that is why Zeus thought he could punish Prometheus by punishing men. That may be. It may be that Hesiod assumes we know this so he doesn't say it, or it may be that later authors made that up to account for Hesiod's portrayal. We just don't know.

Prometheus's story is obviously a very important one. It has many crucial implications for our understanding of the Greek view of the world and of humans' place in it. The first thing to notice is that fire equals civilization. I touched on that when I talked about Hestia and her role as goddess of the hearth. Perhaps it would be better to say that fire equals culture rather than fire equals civilization. Without fire, there can be no human culture as we know it. Therefore, what Prometheus brings men is culture when he brings them fire. When he returns fire to them, he is returning culture to them.

Later authors specifically make this equation. The tragedian Aeschylus in the drama, *Proetheus Bound,* has the character Prometheus say that he brought men all the arts of culture, including even writing, in that account. The impetus for Prometheus's story—the first sacrifice, which leads to the hiding of fire, which leads to the punishment of woman—this is extremely important in this context. Sacrifice here can be seen—Burkert reads it as representing the transition from pre-civilization to civilization or from pre-culture to culture. Burkert, the neo-ritualist I mentioned in my third lecture, thinks that sacrifice is a means to displace the guilt humans felt, in the early stages of culture, over hunting and killing animals. If he is right about this, his argument further continues that the first sacrifice would represent the moment at which guilt-free hominids, animals who are incapable of feeling guilt, made the leap into being humans who can feel guilt. In other words, the first sacrifice—the moment that guilt enters the picture and humans feel the need to expiate that guilt—would also be the moment at which culture or society enters the picture.

If we read the myth in this way, it is probably no surprise that sex appears at this point as well, since one of the main functions of society is to regulate sexual relationships. That connection—sacrifice, sexuality, women, marriage, the problems of marriage—if we follow Burkert's reading, that is not a coincidental throwing together of elements, but a very important connection with the representation of the beginning of human culture.

Guilt over killing animals is not the only possible guilt that humans might feel in connection with sacrifice. I talked a few minutes ago about the choice that Prometheus gives Zeus to choose the better or the worse part of the sacrifice. And, in actual Greek ritual practice, the human beings ate the meat of the sacrificed animal and the gods were given the bones. Supposedly, the gods enjoyed the smell of the smoke rising up on their altars, but they did not get the meat or the fat, the edible part of the animal.

When we look at the myth from outside its original culture, there is no difficulty at all in understanding why that should be so. Ancient Greece was a hard place to live. Culture tended to be subsistence- level only. In such a society, it would make no sense whatsoever to burn, in honor of the gods, precious protein when you have sacrificed an animal. The only reasonable thing to do with it is to have the human sacrificers eat the animal after it has been sacrificed. Protein was hard to come by. That is the only thing that would make any sense at all as a cultural practice. That is looking at it from outside the culture, assuming that these gods don't exist. Looking at it from inside the culture that developed these myths, with the gods who are awe-inspiring dangerous beings, who need to be propitiated to keep them from harming us, it is very problematic, indeed, that we, the humans, get the good part of the sacrifice and throw the bones to the gods, so to speak. And so a kind of sense of guilt over why is that. Why do we eat the animal and only burn the bones for the gods? It is probably very much there in the story. The establishment of sacrifice somehow entails punishment for the establishment, makes sense, that there is something there that needs to be punished. The punishment, as I have already said, is the creation of the first woman.

The story of the first woman occurs not only in *Theogony,* but also in Hesiod's other great work *Works and Days,* which for the most part doesn't deal with myth; it is mainly a farming manual, as it happens. The first few hundred lines of *Works and Days* do deal with myth and, among other things, they retell the story of the first woman. In *Works and Days,* the woman is given the name Pandora. In *Theogony,* the emphasis is on Prometheus's wrong doing and his punishment, and Pandora, the first woman, is mentioned almost as a sideline. In *Works and Days,* the emphasis is on Pandora herself. She is named, while in *Theogony* she is nameless. The name Pandora is ambiguous. It may mean "gift of all" (i.e., gift of all the gods to men) or it may mean "all-giver" (i.e., someone who gives everything herself).

In *Works and Days,* her creation is described in more detail than is the case in *Theogony.* We are told that most of the gods and goddesses unite in giving her something. Aphrodite, Goddess of Passion, makes her irresistibly beautiful. Hermes, the messenger god, whom we will talk about in a later lecture, gives her a thievish nature and the mind of a bitch, as Hesiod puts it. Then she is sent, in *Works and Days*, not to men in general, but to Prometheus's brother, Epimetheus. Perhaps the most important detail in the *Works and Days* story of Pandora is that she has with her a jar—not a box, as later versions of the story tend to say, but a jar. In that jar are contained all the evils that afflict human kind—diseases, old age, care, trouble—all of that kind of thing, as well as Hope. Pandora opens the lid of the jar. The evils fly out, but Hope remains inside just under the lid of the jar.

The story of Pandora is very frequently compared to the story of the Biblical Eve. A lot of mythological handbooks will say it is more or less just the same story—woman brings evil into the world. There are similarities, but I personally think the differences are more significant and more interesting than the similarities. I think the differences are important for our understanding of the relationship between the sexes as it is depicted in Greek mythology. It is true that both Pandora and Eve are responsible for the advent of evil into the world. There is no doubt about that. But Eve was created in the first place as a helper for Adam. God looked at Adam, decided it was not good for him to be by himself, and decided to make a help suitable—"meet"—for him, in the language of the King James Version.

Pandora is evil from her very creation. She is not created to be a help to man; she is created to be a curse to man. She is sometimes referred to as "the beautiful evil." There is a complete difference in motivation in the creation of the first woman. Also, Eve is created out of Adam's own body. She is not the same *kind* of creature he is; she almost *is* the same creature he is. She can be seen as a completion of humanity, made from Adam's own body. Pandora is an entirely different creation. She is made not from the same substance as man, or if she is, we are not told so. She is certainly not made from man's own body. She is created separately—individually—and with malice aforethought.

This seems to me to imply that women are seen in Greek myth and Greek society as different in kind from men; not just as the female of the human species, but as different in kind, different in nature and, in some sense, almost artificial—created as an afterthought. This is our first example of a very deep-seeded misogyny that runs through much of classical myth. We talked in earlier lectures about the anxieties that may be demonstrated by the stories of the mother goddesses competing for power with their male consorts. There is more than just anxiety going on in Greek myth; there seems to be a real distrust and dislike of women that shows up in many of these stories. This is our first example of that.

Let's go back to Pandora's jar and the fact that Hope is in that jar. The presence of Hope in a jar of evils is very striking, but is also extremely difficult to interpret. Many commentaries on Hesiod's *Works and Days*—big learned tones that talk about the meaning of every word of every line—will say things like, "The presence of Hope in the jar seems very surprising," and they leave it at that, which doesn't do us much good. I always like, when I teach myth in the classroom, to send the students away one day to think about what Hope is doing in the jar, then have them come back the next day and tell me what they think about it. The most usual suggestion I get, the most common modern interpretation, is a rather optimistic one: that Hope is there to indicate no matter how bad things get, we still have hope.

That is nice, but I think it ignores two very important points. Hope is still in the jar. She is not out in the world—I say "she" because it is a "she" in Greek—she is not out in the world with the other evils, or with the evils in general. She is still in the jar; she is somehow different, her status is somehow different from the other things that were in the jar. Secondly, if Hope is a good thing, why is she in the jar of evils to begin with? What is she doing there? The other interpretation I get, which is equal but opposite, is extremely pessimistic. Someone will usually say Hope's retention in the jar is meant to say that there is no hope—that even that tiny consolation for humankind is utterly absent, that the Greeks were completely pessimistic. There is no hope, we might as well all lie down and die. I think goes a little bit too far in the opposite direction.

I don't have a good answer for this. I am not sure why Hope is in the jar. What I have worked out over years of thinking about this with my students is that the key may be that the word we translate as Hope, *elpis* in Greek, is not an unambiguously good thing. We, after 2000 years of Judeo-Christian tradition, tend to think that hope is unambiguously good. It is one of the three cardinal virtues: faith, hope, and charity. The Greek word *elpis* might be better translated as "expectation" rather than "hope." It can be good, but it can also be bad. If hope is the only thing that gets you through a dreadful situation and things do come right for you in the end, then hope was a good thing. But what about if you go for years and years with the false expectation that something will happen that never does, and all of your possibilities run out and all of your chances disappear, because of the expectation that was never fulfilled? Then it is a very evil thing. I think the ambiguous nature of Hope may be the key point here—that Hope could be both good and evil. This may explain why it is caught under the lid of the jar. It is not entirely good, so it is in the jar to begin with. It is not entirely evil, so it does not escape into the world. At any rate, that is the best I can do with it.

The whole myth of Pandora lends itself exceptionally well to psychological interpretations. The jar can be read as representing Pandora's womb. I think that is part of why it is important to understand that it is a jar and not a box. It is a womb-shaped object. If we take it that way, we can follow the idea a little bit further and say that Pandora and all women are responsible for evil in that they are responsible for life itself. They give birth. They put new humans into the world to experience life, which—as anyone who has read the *Iliad* will remember from Achilles' words in Book 24—means experiencing a lot of evil. At the same time that birth inflicts all of the evils of life on the individual person who is born, birth also provides the only hope for continuity available to the human race, by providing a new generation. Birth, like Hope in the jar, is ambiguous. It imposes evil on the individual, but it gives hope to the race. In this interpretation, the jar, Pandora, women as source of evil, all work together to make a statement about birth and about life.

On a wider level, the whole description of Pandora can be read as reflecting once again male anxieties about and resentments of sexual reproduction. This is a theme that is surprisingly common in Greek literature. Over and over again, a male character will say something about how he wishes it were possible to get sons, without having to resort to women to get them. In one of Euripides's plays, a character says something about how the gods should have arranged it so that a man could go to a temple at night, leave a certain amount of money, come back in the morning and get a baby boy—none of this dealing with women whatsoever. There is a very strong current in Greek myth of anxiety about and resentment of sexual reproduction on the part of men.

In a strongly patriarchal society, and the society reflected by Hesiod's works is definitely strongly patriarchal, it is all-important for men to have sons.

They have got to have sons to carry on the family, to leave their property to, and so forth. The only way to achieve sons is through women. A woman, or women, can thus be seen as controlling man's ultimate destiny. If the woman remains barren, the man remains barren. The man has children only if the woman provides them. Thus, again, the jar—which Pandora can choose to open but could have chosen to leave closed—could represent this fear of women's power over reproduction.

I want to end this lecture as I did the previous ones by recapping some points about the essential nature of the gods as we saw them in *Theogony,* and picking up some points that I have touched on before. First of all, the term "god" is regularly used to translate the Greek word *theos.* It is a rather surprisingly misleading translation in some ways, because of the assumptions we tend to make about what gods are. I have even toyed with the idea of teaching a course on Greek mythology without ever using the word "god" at all, by keeping the Greek word *theos* in place. The only problem with that is, I would either have to send my students to their books with bottles of whiteout, to whiteout "god" every time it occurred and put in *theos,* or I would have to do all the translations myself. The reason I have even toyed with that idea is that the word "god" brings with it so many unquestioned, unconscious assumptions in our society. Whether we are believers ourselves or not, we come from a society that makes assumptions about what the word "god" means. When we disbelieve in God in this society, we disbelieve in a particular kind of god. We tend to assume that, by definition, a god must be good, merciful and just; that by definition, a god must be omniscient and omnipotent; by definition, a god must have created the universe, including human beings, and must feel affection and concern toward human beings. We tend to assume that a god does not have a body or human-like passions and appetites.

All of these assumptions, as we have seen several times now, are false with reference to the gods of classical mythology. They are not consistently good. They are not consistently merciful. They are not, apparently, even consistently just toward human beings or toward one another. Their anthropomorphism means that they share in humanity's less appealing emotions, as well as in our more appealing ones. They can be cruel. They can be spiteful. They can be jealous, and they frequently are. They know a great deal, but they are not omniscient. They are very powerful, but they are not omnipotent. Those assumptions as well are false with regard to these gods. As I have said before, but it is worth underlining because it seems so strange to our assumptions, they are not transcendent. They are not outside or beyond the universe, they are part of the universe. According to the earliest traditions we have been working with, they did not create human beings. It is almost as though they are a parallel kind of creature. There are three kinds of beings living in the world: gods, humans, and animals. None of them created the others; they are all just there.

They are not loving caretakers of humanity. They do not care about us as a species and they very rarely care about us as individuals. There are examples of gods who feel affection for particular individuals. Athena, in the *Odyssey*, seems to feel affection for Odysseus, for example. There are other stories that work in similar ways. But by and large, the gods do not seem to feel affection for individual human beings, and they certainly do not feel affection for us as a species. We will see this again and again in some of the myths about individual gods that we will see in the next few lectures.

I think part of the reason for this rather unappealing nature of the gods has to do with their role as personifications of natural forces, emotions or processes. They are not *just* personifications; in particular, the Olympians are not just personifications. They are much more than that. Zeus is not just the personification of any one thing. In a system in which the oldest gods—and perhaps, ultimately, in their earliest incarnations, all of the gods—are to some extent personifications of natural forces, it perhaps makes sense to conceive of such entities as being merciless, capricious and not caring about humans. If you are out on the sea on an open boat and a storm comes up, it does no good to ask the sea not to drown you. If you are on land when an earthquake happens, it is useless to cry out to the earthquake, "Why are you being so cruel? I never did anything wrong. Why are you killing me?" If Poseidon is seen on some level as the personification of the sea and earthquakes, it makes no more sense to call out to Poseidon for mercy. Poseidon is acting as natural forces act; mercy doesn't enter the picture. That is not all that is going on with these gods, but I think that explains why they were conceived in the first place as being so detached from emotionally from human beings in so many ways.

We have talked now about the creation of the gods, about their essential attributes and about the creation of female human beings. In our next lecture, we will move on to looking at a specific myth about a specific goddess—the myth of Demeter and her daughter Persephone—and the next several lectures will cover the most important stories about particular individual gods and goddesses.

Demeter, Persephone, and the Conquest of Death
Lecture 7

Athenian women, at least Athenian women of the middle and upper classes, were not supposed to leave their homes. They stayed inside; they were sequestered. They went out of their homes normally only for family funerals and for a few religious festivals per year. This means, if you think about it, that if a daughter moved more than a very short distance away from her family home upon her marriage, she and her mother would quite likely never see one another again.

The myth of Demeter, Persephone, and Hades is recounted in one of the richest works of classical antiquity, the *Homeric Hymn to Demeter*. The *Homeric Hymns* is a series of poems, ranging from only a few lines to several hundred lines, in honor of various gods. The poems are called "Homeric" because they are written in the same dialect of Greek and using the same meter (dactylic hexameter) as the *Iliad* and the *Odyssey*. They were composed at different times; the *Hymn to Demeter* is one of the oldest, dating from sometime between 650 and 550 B.C. This myth lends itself to a variety of interpretations and viewpoints, because it deals with questions of gender roles, sexuality, marriage customs, the relative power of different deities, and human mortality. This myth is one of the few that has a clear connection with a specific ritual, the Eleusinian Mysteries, held at Eleusis, near Athens. It is also one of the most transparently aetiological of surviving myths, because it provides an explanation for the existence of the seasons.

This myth is one of the few that has a clear connection with a specific ritual, the Eleusinian Mysteries.

The basic story of the abduction of Persephone by Hades is fairly simple. Demeter, goddess of grain and agriculture, had a daughter, Persephone. Persephone's father was Zeus. With Zeus's permission, Hades seized Persephone one day as she was gathering flowers and took her to the Underworld to be his wife. Demeter wandered the world looking for her daughter. During her wanderings, she visited the town of Eleusis, near Athens. Eventually, Demeter caused a famine by refusing to let grain grow. Zeus ordered Hades to return Persephone so that humankind would not starve to death. Persephone had eaten a pomegranate seed while she was in Tartaros, which meant that she could not leave Hades permanently. This apparently reflects the idea that eating in the Underworld meant one had to stay there. Under Zeus's mediation, Demeter agreed to a compromise whereby Persephone spends one-third of the year in Hades and two-thirds with her mother on Olympus.

There is more to this story than meets the eye. As told in the *Homeric Hymns*, Demeter's search for her missing daughter and its aftermath give us a window onto many aspects of ancient Greek (or at least Athenian)

Dover Publications.

Persephone, wife of Hades and queen of the Underworld.

life. First, the story reflects marriage practices. A marriage was a contract between the husband and the bride's father. Zeus gives Hades permission to take Persephone. Marriage of an only daughter with no brothers to her uncle was perfectly acceptable. Such a girl was called an *epikleros*. Human marriages were patrilocal. Human mothers and daughters would have greatly restricted contact after marriage. Thus, sorrow was a natural reaction to such an arrangement. The story reflects the human experience of death and separation. Olympians can't or don't go to Tartaros. Hades and Hermes are exceptions to this rule. Demeter's anguish is very close to what a human feels at a loved one's death. This is the only time a god or goddess feels this sort of mourning for another deity. A symbolic connection between death and marriage is common in Greek literature, in part a reflection of high rates of maternal mortality. The story paints a picture of the gods' attitude toward and relationship with humans. Humans are useful to the gods but are not objects of affection. Zeus does not persuade Demeter to lift the famine because he loves humans, or because humans are innocent, or for any other such compassionate reason. He wants the famine lifted because without humans, there will be no one to give the gods sacrifices.

Along with the account of Persephone's abduction, the *Homeric Hymn to Demeter* also contains the story of Demeter's visit to Metaneira, the queen of Eleusis. Demeter wandered to Eleusis, where she met the daughters of Queen Metaneira. Demeter was disguised as an old woman and was pitied. She offered her services to the queen's daughters as a nanny for their baby brother, Demophoön. Demophoön is described as a late-born and much desired son; in a male-centered culture, such a baby would be doubly precious. Infant mortality was high; an old woman who had many years of experience in caring for infants and children would be a logical choice as a nanny. Demeter sets out to make Demophoön immortal by anointing him with ambrosia and laying him in the fire each night. When Metaneira observes what Demeter is doing, she is horrified and cries out in anguish. Demeter becomes angry and throws the child to the ground, declaring that she will no longer make him immortal. The *Hymn* does not recount Demophoön's fate, but Apollodorus and other authors say that he died.

Like the story of Persephone, the Demophoön story offers a window into the nature of the gods it describes and the society that created them. Demeter seems to be using Demophoön as a Persephone-substitute. It is noteworthy that she picks a male child. Demeter is following the same pattern as Gaia and Rheia before her, trying to enlist the help of an infant male son against an oppressive adult father. A male child will not be taken away from her through marriage. Demeter's attempt does not work. This is consistent with the picture given by Hesiod that the order of the universe under Zeus is fixed. Where Gaia and Rheia could succeed, Demeter fails. By trying to immortalize a human child, Demeter is not only providing a substitute child for herself; she is also redressing the balance against Hades. Finally, we again see the gods' unconcern with human emotion and their tendency to see humans as useful, rather than as objects of affection. Demeter does not seem to realize that if she succeeds, she will inflict the same anguish on

Metaneira as Zeus inflicted on her. After Metaneira's interference, Demeter has no further interest in Demophoön. Demeter apparently cannot simply start again; once the immortalization process has been interrupted, it is over.

The *Homeric Hymn to Demeter* is an almost perfect example of the complex and multivalent nature of myth. As such, it can be analyzed according to various theories. Those who espouse Jungian psychology can see the archetypes of Mother, Maiden, and Crone very clearly in the *Hymn*. The *Hymn* can be read, in a more Freudian way, as a wish-fulfillment fantasy for women or for humans in general. Women must often have wished to regain their married daughters, and daughters, to return to their mothers. Human mothers couldn't "unmarry" daughters, but Demeter (almost) can. All human beings wish that death could be reversed. In this case, it is; Persephone returns. Structuralists can find many contradictions to be mediated: acceptance of death, desire to retain childhood, and so on. Adherents of the ritual theory can point to the Eleusinian Mysteries (for which the *Hymn* provides both an aetiology and a charter). Even Frazer's dying god is not too far a stretch, because Persephone can easily be read as representing the grain. None of these theories—or others—seems to account for the entire appeal of the *Hymn*. Each can be used to elucidate a portion of the myth but not its entirety. ■

Essential Reading

Apollodorus, *Library*, pp. 33–34.

Homeric Hymn to Demeter.

Supplementary Reading

Arthur, "Politics and Pomegranates."

Foley, *Homeric Hymn to Demeter*, "The Mother/Daughter Romance," pp. 119–137.

1. Does the idea of the Demeter/Persephone myth as a kind of "wish fulfillment" make sense to you? Can you think of similar "wish fulfillment" stories in modern American society?

2. If the gods have no experience of grieving over death, what are the implications for the human/god relationship?

Demeter, Persephone, and the Conquest of Death
Lecture 7—Transcript

In our previous lecture, we discussed the story of Prometheus and Pandora and looked at some of its implications for the Greek view of gender relationships and the Greek view of gods and humans. In the next several lectures, starting with this one, we will be examining individual Olympian gods, looking at their characters and why they are important. We begin in this lecture by examining the goddess Demeter. We look at Demeter through one of the richest works of literature to survive from the ancient world, the *Homeric Hymn to Demeter*, which describes the story of Demeter's search for her missing daughter Persephone.

Before I talk about the myth itself, I need to explain what the Homeric Hymns are. These are a series of poems in honor of various different gods and goddesses. They range in length from a few lines to several hundred lines—the *Homeric Hymn to Demeter* is several hundred lines long, in fact. They are called "Homeric" because they are written in the same dialect of Greek, using the same poetic meter (dactylic hexameter) and many of the same turns of phrase and vocabulary as we see in the Homeric epics the *Iliad* and the *Odyssey*. The Classical Greeks themselves assumed that the Homeric Hymns had, in fact, been written by Homer, the person they believed to have written the *Iliad* and the *Odyssey*. Modern scholarship finds it problematic to posit even that one man named Homer wrote the *Iliad* and the *Odyssey*. Modern scholars are quite certain that the Homeric Hymns were not composed even at the same time as the *Iliad* or the *Odyssey*, let alone written by the same author. The Hymns in fact were composed over a period of several centuries. The earliest one may well be the *Homeric Hymn to Demeter*. It's certainly one of the earliest. It was probably written down between 650 and 550 B.C.

They are called "Homeric" because they were written in the style of Homer. They are called "Hymns," which in Greek just meant songs. They happen to be songs in honor of various gods and goddesses. The longer Homeric Hymns, in particular, are very useful in understanding the nature of the deities to which they are dedicated, because they tend to tell a story that is in some way key to understanding the nature of the god whom they honor.

The *Homeric Hymn to Demeter* tells the story of Demeter's search for her missing daughter Persephone.

The work is important, not just because it is a beautiful poem from a relatively early era of Greek literature; it is also important because the myth it recounts, the story of Persephone's abduction by Hades, god of the Underworld, and Demeter's search for her is open to a great variety of interpretations. It is a very fruitful myth to look at from all sorts of angles, mainly because it deals with those important questions again; questions of gender roles, of sexuality, of marriage customs, the relative power of different deities, what Demeter can and cannot accomplish to rescue her daughter, and, last but not least, the *Hymn* touches on the whole issue of human mortality, human death, and how we approach death. In addition, the myth of Persephone's abduction and Demeter's search for her is one of the very few myths preserved in ancient literature that has a clear and direct connection with a specific ritual, where we know what the ritual was—at least more or less—and we can see how the myth interacts with it. The ritual, in this case, is a ceremony held in honor of Demeter at Eleusis, a town near Athens. The ceremony was called the "Eleusinian Mysteries;" it was one of the most important festivals of ancient Greece and we will talk about it in detail in the next lecture.

Finally, the *Homeric Hymn to Demeter* preserves one of the most clearly and transparently aetiological of all surviving myths. As I mentioned in a previous lecture, Persephone's disappearance into the underworld and reappearance for two-thirds of each year during which time grain grows—while the grain is gone, she is in the underworld—that very clearly serves as an explanation of an aetiology for the seasons, for why grain does not grow during a portion of the year. This one myth encapsulates all sorts of angles on myth, aspects of myth, as well as being in itself a compelling story.

The basic story of Persephone's abduction by Hades is fairly simple. Demeter, the goddess of grain and agriculture, had a single daughter, Persephone. Persephone's father was Zeus; Zeus and Demeter mated once and produced a daughter, Persephone. With Zeus's permission, Hades goes out of the Underworld, comes out of Hades, out of Tartaros, one day, seizes Persephone as she is picking flowers in a field and takes her down to Tartaros with him to be his bride. This is one of the very few times in myth when

Hades leaves Tartaros and comes back to the world of the living. He does so to get Persephone. Demeter does not know what happened to her daughter. She wanders the world looking for Persephone. During her wanderings, she visits the town of Eleusis, near Athens. Eventually, Demeter forces Zeus's hand to try to get Persephone back by causing a famine, refusing to let any grain grow. If the famine continues, all humankind will die out. Therefore, Zeus strikes a bargain between Hades and Demeter so that humanity will not starve to death. Zeus begins by ordering Hades to return Persephone permanently. However, while Persephone was in Tartaros, she ate a seed of a pomegranate and this means she can't leave Tartaros permanently. The idea, apparently, is that if you eat a substance while you are in the underworld, you have to stay in the underworld. The compromise that is reached under Zeus's mediation is that Persephone will spend one-third of the year in Hades, in Tartaros, with her husband Hades, and two-thirds of the year on Olympus with her mother, Demeter. That is the basic story line.

There is much more going on in this basic story than is immediately obvious. As told in the *Homeric Hymn to Demeter*, Demeter's search for Persephone tells us a great deal about, reflects in great detail, various aspects of ancient Greek life—ancient Athenian life. That is something I haven't really mentioned in detail yet, but when we talk about ancient Greek culture, that is really a rather inaccurate expression. We would probably normally be better off saying ancient Athenian culture, because of all the ancient city-states in Greece, Athens is the one about which we know the most, and the bulk of ancient Greek literature that has survived to today comes from Athens, as does the *Homeric Hymn to Demeter*. It is probably safer to say that the *Homeric Hymn to Demeter* gives us insight on to several important aspects of Athenian life, rather than to say Greek life in general.

First, it reflects quite clearly actual Greek marriage practices. A marriage in Athens was a contract between the groom and the bride's father. It was a business transaction, almost, undertaken by two males, in which the girl was the object that was exchanged between the two males. The girl did not have to consent to the marriage. There was no legal or social requirement that she even had to be told ahead of time that she was going to be married. We can hope that most human fathers did at least tell their wives, and tell their daughters, that they were arranging a marriage for the daughter in question.

Zeus's giving Persephone to Hades without telling Demeter that this is going to happen is a bit extreme, but it is an extreme of normal practice. The idea is that the marriage is arranged between Zeus and Hades, rather than Hades asking Persephone, "Would you like to marry me?" That is completely normal.

Secondly, Persephone marries her own uncle. Now, we have seen a lot of incest already among the gods already. Zeus marries his sister, Demeter is his sister and so forth. But this, the marriage of a girl to her uncle, to her father's brother, would not be considered incest in ancient Athens. In fact, when a man had only daughters—when he had no male heirs—it was not only appropriate, it was considered necessary that his eldest daughter marry his closest male relative, which normally meant her father's brother, her own uncle. Such a girl was called an *epikleros*, a particular term for her. An *epikleros* was a daughter who was her father's heir. Legally speaking, women could not inherit property in ancient Athens. Now, a man wanted his property to remain within his family. Normally, he would hand it down to his sons. A woman cannot hold property in her own right. If she marries outside her family, then the family's property goes to another family. That is considered unacceptable. So, what do you do in this case? You marry the girl to the father's nearest male relative, normally her uncle, and therefore the property stays within her direct male family. Persephone is acting as the *epikleros* when she is married off to her own uncle. She is the only child of the union between Demeter and Zeus, though she is not Zeus's only child in general.

Another point worth making in this context is that human marriages in Athens, and Greece as well, were "patrilocal." That means that the bride moved in with her husband's family. I am always interested in students' reactions, because so often I get the reaction, "Well, of course," or "That's only natural." It is not natural. Nothing about marriage customs is natural. They are all constructed by cultures. The reason we tend to find the idea that the bride goes to join her husband's family, rather than vice-versa, "natural" is because that is the same system that we still have in our culture. We see marriage as a woman joining her husband's family. That is why most American brides take their husband's names. Not all do, but most do, because we see marriage as a woman joining the husband's family, not vice-versa. There have been cultures in which marriage means that a man joins his wife's family.

In ancient Athens, marriage was definitely patrilocal. Persephone's being taken to the Underworld is a rather severe example of that, but, again, part of normal practice. The reason that I stress that, the reason this important, is because in Athenian society, the patrilocal nature of marriage meant that human mothers and daughters would have greatly restricted contact after the daughter was married. Athenian women, at least Athenian women of the middle and upper classes, were not supposed to leave their homes. They stayed inside; they were sequestered. They went out of their homes normally only for family funerals and for a few religious festivals per year. This means, if you think about it, that if a daughter moved more than a very short distance away from her family home upon her marriage, she and her mother would quite likely never see one another again. If the daughter moved next door, undoubtedly Athenian women would talk to the next-door neighbor from time to time. I don't think they were locked up in their houses and unable to go out at all, but they were not able to move through the city freely. Transportation pretty much meant your own feet, or perhaps an animal or a cart that you could be carried in. If a daughter on her marriage moved more than the very shortest distance away, she and her mother would almost never, or ever, see one another again. The fact of marriage for girls and their mothers probably did invoke a great deal of sorrow of the kind that Demeter shows in the *Homeric Hymn*—of mothers longing to get their daughters back and of daughters not being altogether willing to be married. The age of a bride at marriage would have been about 13 or 14. We are talking about very young girls here.

The *Homeric Hymn to Demeter* reflects not only the human experience of marriage, it also reflects the human experience of death and separation, and this is one of the unusual things about this myth. In it, we see Demeter grieving for her daughter who is, in effect, dead. That needs a little bit of explanation. Why doesn't Demeter go to Tartaros and see Persephone? The answer to that is that Olympians can't or at least don't go to Tartaros. Hades is an exception because, in the Triple Division, he was given Tartaros as his domain. He stays there and rules over Tartaros. Hermes is the only real exception to this rule. Hermes is a god we will talk about in a later lecture. He is the messenger of the gods, among other things; but he is also the god who conducts the souls of dead humans to their new abode in Tartaros. Hermes can cross over into Tartaros and come back out again. Aside from that, Olympians normally cannot go to Tartaros. Persephone is there only because Hades has bodily taken her there as his bride. The assumption that Demeter makes when she hears where Persephone is—Helios, the God of the Sun tells Demeter where Persephone is, because from his vantage point in the sky, he has seen her abduction—Demeter's assumption is that Persephone is gone. And Demeter's reaction is very much like a human being's reaction at the death of a loved one. She even goes through some gestures—tearing her robe and so forth—that would normally be gestures a human being would do while grieving for the death of a loved one.

In Demeter's reaction to Persephone's disappearance, we have the only time that we see a god or goddess in effect mourning the death of another god or goddess. Demeter has lost her daughter to marriage, and she has lost her daughter at least to the land of death, if not death itself. This underlines a symbolic connection that we see in a great deal of Greek literature between marriage and death. In part, that is probably because those are two very great transition periods in life. Also, more grimly, it is probably a quite factual connection. A great many women died because they married—they died in childbirth. Infant mortality was high. Maternal mortality was high, as far as we know. It is hard to tell. There are no records, but it seems that maternal mortality would have been very high. A girl who was married at 14 and had a baby a year would quite likely die in one of those childbirths fairly early on in her life. One way we know this is we do have records of men marrying two or three or even more wives as they lived a more normal lifespan—normal by our terms, that is.

The *Homeric Hymn* not only reflects marriage practices and reminds us of the reality of death for humans, it also gives us a picture of the gods' attitude toward and relationship with humans. As we have talked about a little bit before, humans are useful to the gods but we are not objects of affection. We see this in the *Hymn to Demeter* when Zeus strikes the compromise, so Demeter can have Persephone back for part of the year, to keep Demeter from starving the humans to death. That sounds like Zeus is concerned for humans, is worried about us, feels pity for us. Not at all. The *Hymn* says very clearly that Demeter would have killed off the race of human beings and deprived the Olympians of the honor of sacrifices if Zeus had not interfered. What Zeus is concerned with is that he and the other gods will no longer receive honor through sacrifice if the humans die. He doesn't care about the humans in and of themselves. He cares about his own honor through sacrifices humans make to him.

The *Homeric Hymn to Demeter* really consists of two interlocked or intertwined stories—the story of Persephone's abduction and return to her mother (or at least partial return to her mother) is the main story, the framing story. Inside that story, as I have already mentioned, there is an account of Demeter visiting the town of Eleusis, a town near Athens, and the story of what she does while she is there. This second story is no less important in the *Homeric Hymn*, though it is sandwiched in the middle. Between the disappearance of Persephone and the return of Persephone, we have this other story, the story of Demeter's visit to Eleusis. In this second narrative framework of the *Homeric Hymn*, Demeter goes to Eleusis and visits the queen there, Metaneira, queen of Eleusis. There is also a king of Eleusis, but he figures very little in the story. Demeter's interaction is with the queen, the queen's daughters and the queen's baby son.

When Demeter wanders to Eleusis, she is disguised as an old woman, a human being. While she is sitting by a well, she meets the four daughters of Metaneira. These daughters are teenagers. They are presented as being young women, about old enough to get married, so that means they are teenagers. They tell Demeter that they have a baby brother, and Demeter volunteers to be the nanny for the baby brother. Demophoön, that is the baby's name, is described as a "late-born and much desired" son. The implication is that his mother had had these four daughters who are now teenagers, had probably almost given up on ever having another child, and then, finally, has the baby boy, who in the patriarchal society is so crucially important. In other words, this would be a more than normally cherished son. Metaneira is probably near the end of her childbearing years at this point. If Demophoön dies, there is not likely to be a baby brother to replace him.

In a culture where infant mortality is very high, an old woman who has experience caring for babies would be an invaluable addition to a family circle, because she knows what to do—she has experience, she has seen babies through childhood illnesses, she can take care of him. And Metaneira says to Demeter when she hires her as a nanny, "If you nourish him and raise him up to adulthood I will give you great gifts and great honor." We tend to take it for granted that a baby, once born, is going to grow up to adulthood. We see it as an inversion of the natural order if the baby does not reach adulthood. In this culture, it is a very tenuous thing. Having a baby is just the beginning of it. You cannot assume that he will live to maturity.

Demeter is hired to take care of this remarkably precious, late-born, and much-desired child. She, however, has another agenda. She sets out to make baby Demophoön immortal. She does this by anointing him with ambrosia and by putting him in the fireplace, in the fire, every night. The ambrosia apparently keeps him from burning. Metaneira comes in one night and observes what Demeter is doing, and reacts in an understandable way as a human mother. She is absolutely horrified, because what she sees is a crazed old woman burning her baby in the fireplace. Demeter's reaction to Metaneira's horror is to grow angry. Demeter becomes very angry, scolds Metaneira and says that now Demophoön will not become immortal. It is after that that Demeter causes the famine and Zeus strikes the bargain by which she gets Persephone back.

The *Homeric Hymn* does not recount Demophoön's fate after this encounter, but other authors, including Apollodorus, tell us that he died. When Demeter lost interest in him and stopped trying to make him immortal, the upshot was he died. Through this encounter with Demeter, Demophoön probably dies. The *Homeric Hymn* hints at that. It says that when Metaneira interferes, Demeter tosses the baby down on the ground. His sisters run over to try to comfort him, but he won't be comforted because he is used now to an immortal nurse, and the mortal ones do him no good. The *Hymn* seems to hint at a short life for Demophoön.

Like the surrounding story of Persephone, the Demophoön episode offers a window into the nature of the gods it describes and the society that created them. First of all, Demeter seems to be using Demophoön as a Persephone-substitute. She seems to be trying to provide a substitute child for herself. This is a pause in her search for Persephone; she is going to try to get herself another child instead. In this context, I think it is noteworthy and important that she picks a male child. First of all, we can see this as Demeter trying to repeat the pattern that we saw with Gaia and Rheia before her, gaining an immortal son that she is going to bring up to be her helper. Perhaps she is thinking of when he grows up, she will take her vengeance then on Zeus for depriving her of Persephone. Of course, it doesn't work, but that may be the motivation for trying to raise an immortal son. Secondly, and this is the point my students frequently see as the crucial point here, a male child won't be taken away from her through marriage. Why does she pick a male substitute for Persephone rather than getting a baby girl? The male child stays with his mother.

Demeter's attempt to immortalize Demophoön does not work, and that is consistent with the picture we talked about in *Theogony*. Once Zeus is in power, the order of the universe is fixed and it is not going to be possible now for a goddess, no matter how powerful, to bring up a male child that will help her overthrow—her brother, in this case—the child's father, usually. By trying to immortalize a human child, Demeter may also be trying to redress the balance between herself and Hades. What I mean by that is that Hades has taken an entity, a being, that should not belong to him. He has taken Persephone, who ought to be immortal. Perhaps Demeter is in effect saying, "All right, you took one of mine, I will take one of yours." Hades is ruler over all the human souls who have ever died, which means, in effect, all the human souls who ever have or ever will live. One of Hades's titles is the "Lord of All" or the "Receiver of All." He is also described as a very rich god. So when Demeter tries to immortalize Demophoön, she is in effect taking away from Hades a being that ought, in the normal run of things, to belong to Hades.

Again, the next point I want to make about the Demophoön episode is that it shows the gods' unconcern with human emotion, and their tendency to see humans as useful, rather than as proper objects for affection. Demeter does not seem to love Demophoön. As I already said, when she replies to Metaneira's interference, when she grows angry with Metaneira, she throws Demophoön to the ground—she loses all interest in him. She doesn't even look at him after that, as far as we can tell from the text. More importantly, it doesn't seem to even cross Demeter's mind that if she succeeds at immortalizing Demophoön, she will be inflicting precisely the same kind of anguish on Metaneira as Hades and Zeus inflicted on her. She is stealing someone else's baby; she is taking him permanently away from his mother. It does not even seem to cross her mind that she ought to have empathy for Metaneira, that she ought to understand Metaneira's grief if Metaneira loses her child. That doesn't even enter into the picture.

Another point that I want to make here is that Demeter says to Metaneira that this is all her own fault. Demeter says to Metaneira when Metaneira interferes:

> Men are too foolish to know ahead of time
> the measure of good and evil which is yet to come.
> You too were greatly blinded by your foolishness.
> The relentless water of the Styx by which gods swear
> be my witness: immortal and ageless forever
> would I have made your dear son...
> but now it is not possible for him to escape the fate of death.

So, it is Metaneira's fault, and Demeter doesn't even entertain the idea that a human mother might prefer to keep her child with her, rather than have him become a god. Also, those lines reflect something that we have seen before and will see again, the idea that once a process has been initiated that is how it will have to be done forever after. Think of the sacrifice in the case of Prometheus. The flip side of that is, when a process is interfered with, it is over. Demeter can't simply say, "Never mind, Metaneira. I am not burning him; I'm making him immortal. Why don't you go pay attention to your daughters, and I'll start this process over." It doesn't work that way. Once Metaneira has interrupted Demeter, apparently the attempt to confer immortality on Demophoön cannot then continue.

The *Homeric Hymn to Demeter*, along with all its other aspects, is an almost perfect example of the complex, multivalent nature of myth. It works on many levels at once. There are many different approaches to the *Homeric Hymn to Demeter*, many different ways to bring out different aspects of it. It can be analyzed according to every theory of myth that has ever been invented. Those who espouse Jungian psychology love this poem for the appearance in it of the archetypes of the Mother, the Maiden, the Crone—

when Demeter is disguised as an old woman. Demeter is persuaded to agree to the compromise suggested by Zeus by her mother, so Rheia appears as the wise old woman as well. So, the archetypes seem to be very fruitful in this myth.

It can also, obviously, be read in a more Freudian way, as a wish-fulfillment fantasy for women or for humans in general. Human mothers in Athens must at times have wished very strongly that they could "unmarry" their daughters, so to speak, that they could get their daughters back. Human mothers can't. Once a daughter is married off, she is gone. But Demeter almost can. She gets Persephone back, at least for two-thirds of the year, which is pretty good. She undoes the marriage of her daughter, at least to a large extent. Similarly, all human beings, I think it is safe to say, at least at times, wish that death could be reversed. We want to get back those we love who have died. We can't do that, but in this case, death, in effect, is reversed. Persephone comes back from the land of the dead. Both as a wish-fulfillment fantasy for women in regard to marriage and for humans in general in regards to death, the *Homeric Hymn* works very well.

Stucturalists can find all kinds of contradictions to be mediated in this myth. The acceptance of death, as opposed to the desire for life; the desire to remain a child, as opposed to the necessity for marriage; those sorts of things are very present in this myth. Adherents to the ritual theory can point to the Eleusinian Mysteries, which we will talk about in the next lecture, and say, "Look how this myth grew directly out of ritual." Even Frazer's dying god, who you remember was represented by the King of the Wood, was killed each year and annually replaced—even the dying god is not too far a stretch since you can, if you like, see Persephone as personifying the grain that is cut down and buried each year, and returns as new grain in the Spring. That would be a dying goddess, rather than a dying god, but close enough.

None of these theories, or others that I have not run through quickly, accounts for the entire appeal of the *Hymn*. It is a perfect example of what I said at the end of my lecture about theories—that each of them can be useful to elucidate parts of myths, but none of them elucidate myth in general. All of these approaches to the *Homeric Hymn* are valid, but none of them is sufficient.

In this lecture, we have looked at the story of Demeter and Persephone, and we have mentioned how it interacts with the Eleusinian Mysteries. In the next lecture, we will look in detail at the Eleusinian Mysteries themselves, and then move on to look at other views of the afterlife and what happens to the human soul after death.

The Eleusinian Mysteries and the Afterlife
Lecture 8

The Eleusinian Mysteries apparently held out the promise of a happy afterlife for their initiates, and that was a large part of their appeal, because elsewhere in surviving Greek literature, we find views of the afterlife that are considerably less pleasant.

This lecture considers the religious ritual held in honor of Demeter and Persephone, the Eleusinian Mysteries. Demeter's visit to Eleusis is a crucial narrative element in the *Homeric Hymn*; it also has important connections to ritual outside the storyline. Eleusis is a town near Athens, where the great "Mysteries" in honor of Demeter and Persephone were celebrated for over 1000 and perhaps nearly 2000 years. They fell into disuse about 400 AD. "Mysteries" in this context means "secrets"; the ceremonies were open only to initiates. The initiates were forbidden to tell non-initiates about the rites. Initiation was available to men and women, to free people and to slaves; the only requirements were that one must not be a murderer and that one must speak Greek. One had to make the journey to Eleusis—and make a sacrifice—to be initiated.

The requirement of secrecy means that our knowledge of the Mysteries is both limited and quite possibly biased. Although certainly some initiates must have told the secret, the

The requirement of secrecy means that our knowledge of the Mysteries is both limited and quite possibly biased.

surviving written references observe the prohibition. They allude to details of the Mysteries but do not describe them. The only writers who do describe the Mysteries are early Christian authors. Because they wrote with the desire to prove the Mysteries false, their testimony may not be accurate. The sources seem to agree that the high point of the Mysteries was the showing or revealing of something to the initiates. Some sources imply that whatever was revealed was obscene. Other sources say that the revelation consisted of an ear of wheat being cut in silence. Although the details of the Mysteries will probably remain unknown, we know enough to recognize many details in the *Homeric Hymn* as aetiologies for parts of the ritual of the Mysteries. Demeter's visit to Eleusis explains why the Mysteries are celebrated there. On a conceptual level, the connection with death and the afterlife is aetiological, because initiation promised a happy afterlife. If we had more information, we might recognize other details as aetiological.

The Eleusinian Mysteries apparently promised a happy afterlife; elsewhere in surviving literature, we find less pleasant views of the afterlife. The standard view seems to be that the Underworld is a place of dim, shadowy existence, much less desirable than life in this world. The ghost is sometimes called an *eidolon*, or "image"; it is less real than the living person. The word for soul, *psyche*, originally seems to have meant "breath"—that which visibly leaves the body at the time of death. In the *Odyssey*, the spirits in Tartaros are described as being witless, not even knowing themselves. Some exceptionally noteworthy souls are picked out for reward or punishment, but overall there seems to be little sense that one's state in the afterlife was determined by one's actions in this life. The conception of the Elysian Fields, reserved for a very few especially good souls, is alluded to in the *Odyssey* and elsewhere. The idea of punishment for the wicked is more clearly developed, but even it does not apply to the majority of humanity; punishment is restricted to a few famous wrongdoers, such as the "cardinal sinners" Tantalos, Tityos, and Sisyphus.

Dover Pictura Electronic Design Series.

When his wife was killed, Orpheus's music was so moving that Hades and Persephone agreed to return Eurydice to him.

We also have some evidence of a belief in reincarnation. Pythagoras (in the 6th century B.C.) apparently taught a doctrine that included reincarnation (along with vegetarianism). Plato discusses reincarnation in the so-called "Myth of Er" (in *The Republic*). One difficulty in using this as evidence for 4th-century belief is that Plato may have invented this "myth" for use in *The Republic*. Elsewhere, for instance in the *Apology of Socrates*, Plato describes a view of the afterlife that is much closer to the traditional one. Virgil, writing in the 1st century B.C., combined the ideas of reward and punishment and the idea of reincarnation in Book VI of *The Aeneid*. Again, as with Plato, it is difficult to determine to what extent Virgil used the idea of reincarnation purely as a literary device and to what extent it mirrors actual belief.

One of the most important myths concerning the afterlife is the myth of Orpheus and Eurydice. Orpheus, a son of Apollo and one of the Muses, was the greatest poet who ever lived. Orpheus, a human, supposedly had the power to charm animals and even stones and trees with his music. When his wife, Eurydice, died, Orpheus made his way to the Underworld to plead for her release. His music was so moving that Hades and Persephone agreed to release Eurydice if Orpheus not look back at her. Orpheus did look back, and Eurydice returned to Tartaros. This purely mythical Orpheus was associated with a body of writings and a set of religious beliefs called "Orphism." Orphism began to be taught in the 6th century B.C. The Orphic writings (few of which survive) supposedly contain knowledge that Orpheus gained while in the Underworld. Reincarnation is central to the doctrine; only by following the teachings of Orpheus to lead an ascetic life can the soul eventually be freed from rebirth. As in Buddhism, incarnation is a bad thing from which one seeks release. Some Orphic writings contained precise instructions about what one should say and do in the Underworld to avoid reincarnation. Thus Orphism, like the Eleusinian Mysteries, held out the promise of a happy, or at least happier, afterlife.

As in so many other areas of Greek religion, no orthodoxy about the afterlife exists. It seems safe to say that it was generally considered both less important and less pleasant than this life. Greek mythology contains no aetiology for death through, for example, human sin or mistake. ■

Ovid, *Metamorphoses*, pp. 234–237 (on Orpheus).

Supplementary Reading

Bremmer, *Early Greek Concept of the Soul*, Ch. 3.

Burkert, *Ancient Mystery Cults*.

Vermeule, *Aspects of Death*.

Questions to Consider

1. Modern students often find it strange that Greek religion and mythology had no set doctrine about the afterlife and that the different descriptions diverged from one another so greatly. To what extent do you think this lack of unified doctrine can be attributed to the lack of a "sacred book"?

2. The Greeks' relative lack of agreement about the afterlife is often cited as proof that their interest was mainly focused on this world and this life. Do you think this conclusion is valid?

Lecture 8: The Eleusinian Mysteries and the Afterlife

The Eleusinian Mysteries and the Afterlife
Lecture 8—Transcript

In the previous lecture, we talked about Demeter and her search for her daughter Persephone, and noticed how Demeter, during that search, spent some time in the town of Eleusis, where she attempted to immortalize the human baby, Demophoön. In this lecture, we are going to look at the ritual connection of the *Homeric Hymn to Demeter* with the Eleusinian Mysteries. We are going to talk about those mysteries in some detail, and then move in to look at other ancient Greek views of the afterlife.

As I said in the previous lecture, the *Homeric Hymn to Demeter* is one of the very few myths in which we see a direct connection with ritual, or religious, ceremonies that are attested elsewhere than in the myth itself. Here, we are not extrapolating from the myth itself to guess that there was a ritual behind it. We know that there was a ritual, a very important ritual or set of ceremonies performed at Eleusis, the town near Athens which Demeter visited on her travels—and performed in honor of Demeter and also of Persephone.

The great Eleusinian Mysteries that were held annually in honor of Demeter and Persephone were celebrated for well over 1000, and perhaps even as long as 2000 years. We don't know exactly when the worship of Demeter at Eleusis began. Some scholars think it may date as far back as to around 1500 B.C. If that is correct, then the Mysteries were in fact celebrated for around 2000 years, because we know that they fell into disuse near the end of the fourth century A.D. We don't have any account of them ever being celebrated after 395 A.D. This is a religious celebration that had a very long run for its money and was extremely important in Greek culture; Athenian culture, in particular, but also Greek culture in general.

In this context, "mysteries" means secrets. The term "mystery" in Greek originally simply meant something that was kept secret. The reason the ceremonies at Eleusis were called secret is because they were secret to non-initiates. To take part in this ceremony in honor of Demeter, one had to go through an initiation process; and only initiates were allowed, not only to take part in the ceremonies, but to know what happened in those ceremonies.

Non-initiates could not be told about what happened in the Mysteries. So, we don't know precisely what went on in this celebration in honor of Demeter, which is very frustrating. We would love to know precisely what happened detail by detail. We don't. We have only a broad outline, only as vague a description as was considered appropriate for non-initiates to be told.

A great many people were initiated into those ceremonies. Unusually, for Greek religion, initiation was open to both men and women. Normally, Greek religious ceremonies were single sex. Men had certain festivals that they attended; women had certain festivals that they attended. The Eleusinian Mysteries were open to both sexes; males and females could be initiated. Slaves could be initiated as well as free people. The only restrictions imposed were that someone guilty of murder could not be initiated into the Eleusinian Mysteries, and only those who spoke Greek could be initiated into the Mysteries. I am always amused that not speaking Greek is morally equivalent to being a murderer. I don't think it is, but those were the two requirements.

Now, in practice, initiation would have been limited by economic factors. By that, I mean simply that people who could not afford to travel to Eleusis could not be initiated. This was a location-specific religion. That is a rather unusual concept for us, but it was very much present in many ancient religious ceremonies. Here, in order to be initiated into the Eleusinian Mysteries, you had to go to Eleusis. You could not go to them elsewhere. For people who lived in Athens, that was not a problem. For people who lived much further away than Athens—for people who lived in other parts of Greece—you would have the be pretty wealthy to make the journey to Eleusis to be initiated into the Mysteries. Also, initiates had to sacrifice a pig to Demeter. Very poor people or slaves who could not afford a pig to sacrifice would not be able to be initiated for that reason. So, theoretically, it is open; in practice, it is limited mainly to those who live nearby and to those who have enough wealth to offer a sacrificial pig.

The requirement of secrecy means that our knowledge of the Mysteries is both limited and quite possibly biased. It is limited because, while some initiates must have told the secrets to non-initiates—in a religion that lasted for 2000 years with hundreds if not thousands of people being initiated every year, it is beyond reason to think that no one every told a non-initiate what happened in the Mysteries—as far as the written records that we have go, we don't have any accounts by initiates about what happened in the Mysteries. What we do have as far as the written record goes are accounts by early Christian authors of what goes on in the Mysteries. Now, some of those early Christian authors may themselves have been initiated, but then rejected the Mysteries in favor of Christianity. We really don't know. What we do know is that the early Christian authors who wrote about the Eleusinian Mysteries wrote in order to demonstrate their belief that the Eleusinian Mysteries were a false religion, and that Christianity was the true religion. That is why I say that their accounts may be biased. Whether or not they intended to give accurate, unbiased accounts, they were convinced in their own minds that the religion they were describing was a false religion. Even so, we have much less testimony about what happened in the Mysteries than we would like.

The sources seem to agree that the Mysteries consisted of three main parts: things that were done, things that were said, and things that were shown. The things that were done and said may refer to some sort of religious drama or ceremony acted out in front of the initiates. We really don't know. The things that were shown, most sources agree, were the high points of the ceremony. As initiates went through the initiation ceremony, they went further into the great temple complex at Eleusis, which is still there, by the way. You can go and visit it today. Eleusis is now a suburb of Athens and the archaeological site is surrounded by chemical and power plants, which is rather disappointing. It is still a marvelous archaeological site and the remains of the temple are vast. As initiates went through the process of initiation over several days, they went further into the temple complex, and we think the final ceremonies were held underground, so that they were in an underground chamber. The high point was the showing, the revelation of some sacred object to the initiates. What this sacred object was is very questionable. Some of the early Christian authors I mentioned say it was something obscene—obscene figurines, obscene symbols, perhaps even an actual act of sex between a priest and a priestess.

Other ancient authors and many modern authorities think that the high point of the ceremony—the great revelation, the meeting of life and death—was an ear of wheat being cut in silence in front of the initiates. Now, my students very frequently look awfully disappointed when I tell them that. As secrets of life and death go, that seems rather tame. I think it is worth remembering that the power of a religious symbol seen from within a religion does not depend on what that symbol is or how it actually looks from the outside. I can think of no better example to show what I mean than the Christian communion service. Looked at from outside the Christian religion, or let's say the Catholic Communion Mass—looked at from outside of Catholicism, what happens? What happens when a child takes First Communion, for instance? The child eats a rather tasteless little cracker and drinks a small sip of very bad wine. That is, looked at from outside the ceremony. How could that possibly have the emotional and spiritual impact that it has?

The answer is that the objects used as symbols in the ceremony are very close to irrelevant in and of themselves. It is what they symbolize that matters. After days of initiation in a religion that we know had to do with life and death, with issues of mortality and immortality, with Persephone's descent and return from the underworld, cutting an ear of living grain to symbolize the death and rebirth of all life may have been extraordinarily powerful and emotionally moving. We don't know if that is what the high point actually was, but it seems to me that it, at least, could have been nothing more than that.

The details of the Mysteries will probably remain unknown. Unless we discover some heretofore unknown document that lays them out in detail, which is highly unlikely, we will never know the details of the ceremonies that happened at the Mysteries. But we know enough to recognize many details in the *Homeric Hymn to Demeter* as referring to bits of the ceremony that happened early on in the initiation process and were not necessarily secret. For instance, when Demeter arrives at Eleusis, she drinks a particular drink made out of barley meal and mint and pennyroyal. We know that initiates at Eleusis drank a similar drink. That detail is there in the *Hymn* to provide an aetiology for what the initiates do.

On a more conceptual level, rather than the narrative detail level, the connection of the *Hymn* with death and life and the return of Persephone from the dead is also aetiological, because what initiation promised its initiates was a more happy status in the afterlife than they would otherwise have. The *Hymn* says this explicitly. Near the end of the *Hymn*, talking about the Mysteries, the writer of the *Hymn* says, "Whoever on this earth has seen these [Mysteries] is blessed, / but he who has no part in the holy rites has / another lot as he wastes away in dank darkness." The reason people became initiates in the Eleusinian Mysteries was to ensure themselves a happier life, a blessed lot, in the afterlife. The whole connection that we talked about last time of the hymn with death and life can be seen as an aetiology for the Eleusinian Mysteries, for their connection with a better afterlife for humans. If we had more information about what happened at the Mysteries, we might recognize other details in the *Homeric Hymn* as clearly aetiological as well. Some people think that the placing of Demophoön in the fire must have had some connection with something done in the ritual, but we don't know what that might have been.

The Eleusinian Mysteries apparently held out the promise of a happy afterlife for their initiates, and that was a large part of their appeal, because elsewhere in surviving Greek literature, we find views of the afterlife that are considerably less pleasant. The standard view of the afterlife as it appears in Homer's *Odyssey* and elsewhere in Greek literature is really pretty grim. The underworld, Tartaros, as it is described in the *Odyssey*, is described as a place of dim, shadowy existence, much less desirable than life in this world. The ghost, the spirit of the person who exists in Tartaros, is sometimes called an *eidolon,* which is a word meaning image—not a person, but an image of a person. That to me seems to stress the idea that what survives after death is much less real, much less important, than the living person on this earth. Sort of the opposite, I suppose, of the Christian or Islamic view of the afterlife, where in some sense what happens in eternity is real life, the most important thing, and this world is just a preparation. This is the opposite view, that this world is real life, and what survives after death is merely a shadowy image and a rather frail and witless one at that.

The word for soul in Greek, *psyche,* originally seems to have simply meant the breath, the thing that visibly leaves the body at death, the thing that makes the difference between a living body and a dead body. The breath seems to have been the original meaning of the word *psyche.* That too, I think, stresses that whatever survives after death is rather shadowy and unsubstantial. In the *Odyssey*, and in other authors as well, the spirits in Tartaros are described as being witless, as not even knowing or recognizing themselves, not knowing who they are or were, until Odysseus gives them a drink of sacrificial blood which returns their wits to them and allows them to remember who they were when they lived.

Even in Homer's account and in other accounts, some exceptionally noteworthy souls are picked out in Tartaros, either for reward or for punishment. But, overall, the Greek view of the afterlife reflects very little sense that one's state in the afterlife is determined by one's actions in this life. Most souls simply exist as dim, shadowy remnants of their actual human selves in Tartaros, where nothing much ever seems to happen. It is only a very few, very noteworthy souls who are either punished or rewarded in the standard view of the afterlife. The concept of the Elysian Fields—a place in the afterlife or a state in the afterlife that is reserved for a very few especially good souls—is alluded to very elliptically in the *Odyssey*, and a few other really early works, but seems to have been a later development in Classical antiquity than the time of Homer or the *Homeric Hymns*. The idea of punishment for the wicked is more clearly developed, but even it doesn't apply to the majority of humanity. There is no sense that if you were an evil person in this life, you are going to be punished in Tartaros. Those who are punished are sometimes called the "cardinal sinners" of Greek mythology and they are a few really, really noteworthy wrongdoers. Often, the first person to commit a particular evil is one of the wrongdoers who is punished in Tartaros.

For instance, we have the story of Tantalos, who is an exceptional wrongdoer in that he tried to trick the gods into eating human flesh. As we talked about when we were discussing sacrifice, there seems to be an idea that very early on, before things were truly set, the gods could eat meat if they wanted to. Tantalos's story parallels that idea because he invited the gods to a feast, and then, he killed his own son, Pelops, cut him up, cooked him, and served Pelops to the gods as dinner, apparently to try to prove that the gods weren't as smart as they thought they were or some such motivation. It is an odd thing to do, undoubtedly, but that is what he did. The gods recognized that they were being served human flesh and refrained from eating Pelops, with the exception of Demeter who was grieving for Persephone (this was during the time of the year when Persephone was in the underworld). Demeter absentmindedly ate Pelops's shoulder before she noticed what she was doing. When the gods resurrected Pelops, which is what they did, they had to make him a shoulder out of ivory to replace the one that Demeter had eaten when her mind was on Persephone.

Tantalos's punishment in the underworld is to stand up to his neck in a river of water with fruit trees growing on the bank, their branches hanging just over his head so that the fruit is just within reach for him to pick. He is eternally hungry and eternally thirsty. Whenever he reaches up to pick a piece of fruit, a wind comes to blow the branches out of his reach. Whenever he bends down to drink, the water flows away and leaves a sandy riverbed. Eternally hungry, eternally thirsty—within the sight and smell of food and drink. Eternally unable to eat or drink.

Greek myth is very good at coming up with really terrible punishments like that. Prometheus with his liver being eaten out by an eagle, Tantalos tormented by eternal hunger and thirst. (And a side note—that is where we get the word tantalize. To *tantalize* someone is to torment them by showing them something they cannot have, and that is what Tantalos suffers for eternity.) There are other cardinal sinners, such as Titaios, who tried to rape Leto and whose punishment is to have his liver eaten by a vulture, like Prometheus's punishment; Sisyphus, who supposedly was the first murderer—his punishment is to roll a boulder continually up hill, but right when he gets to the top of the hill, the boulder rolls back down again. Then he has to start all over. There are a handful of other cardinal sinners. For most people, for the normal run of humanity, reward and punishment does not enter into the standard picture of the afterlife.

Side by side with belief in the underworld, and the gloomy existence of souls there, there is some evidence that there was some belief in reincarnation at least among some people in the Greek, and later in the Roman, world. The evidence for the belief in reincarnation is tantalizingly vague. We don't know as much about this as we would like to. Apparently, Pythagora—who lived probably in the sixth century B.C.—taught a doctrine that included reincarnation along with a belief in vegetarianism. Pythagoras seems to have taught that souls could be reincarnated not only as other humans, but as animals, and therefore he counseled vegetarianism, since the soul of the animal may at one point have been a human soul, or may be going to be a human soul. This is the same Pythagoras who also developed theories of music and worked in geometry, the same man after whom the Pythagorean theorem is named. But unfortunately, not only do we have none of his own writings, there are no records referring to him or telling us what he taught until the late fifth century B.C., well over a hundred years after the time when he actually lived and taught. It is hard to say what precisely Pythagoras actually taught, but reincarnation seems to have been part of it.

Other references to reincarnation in Greek and Roman literature are much later, and are hard to evaluate as evidence for actual belief because of the type of works in which they actually occur. Plato, for instance, discusses reincarnation in the so-called "Myth of Er," which occurs in Plato's great work, *The Republic*. One difficulty in using this as evidence of actual fourth-century belief (Plato wrote in the fourth century B.C.) is that Plato may have invented this so-called myth, which is not attested elsewhere before him. He may have invented it to make a point he wanted to make in *The Republic*. He tells the story of Er, a warrior who is thought to be killed in battle and remains dead for a period of some days. When he wakes up—when he comes out of what we would call his coma—he recounts what he saw while he was "dead." Among other things, he sees souls being reincarnated, and they are reincarnated according to the kinds of lives they have lived previously. Odysseus, who is famous for his trickiness, his deceitfulness and all that, is reincarnated as a monkey, according to Er.

As I said, Plato may have made this story up to make points about proper human behavior. It is not safe to say that because Plato records the Myth of Er, people in the fourth century B.C. actually believed in reincarnation. Maybe they did, maybe they didn't. We don't know. Elsewhere in his works, for instance near the end of *The Apology of Socrates*, Plato seems to believe in the much more traditional Underworld, where souls remain rather than being reincarnated.

Later, in the Roman world, Virgil, writing in the first century B.C., combines the idea of reward and punishment in the Underworld, in the afterlife, and the idea of reincarnation. In Book 6 of his great epic, *The Aeneid*, he has Aeneas's father, Anchises, who is dead and in the Underworld and whom Aeneas has gone to visit in the Underworld, tell Aeneas what happens to souls after death. Some of them go to the land of the blessed. That is where

Anchises himself is. Some of them, really bad ones, go to Tartaros, parallel to the punishment of cardinal sinners as we saw it in Homer. Most souls go through a period that is very similar to the Catholic idea of purgatory, and after 1000 years of this, drink from the river Lethe—which is the river of forgetfulness—and are reincarnated, not remembering anything about their previous lives.

As with Plato's myth of Er, it is very difficult to determine to what extent Virgil here is reflecting actual beliefs, either his own or anyone else's, and to what extent he is using this purely as a literary device. Among other things, what Aeneas's visit to the underworld accomplishes in *The Aeneid* is it allows Virgil to give an overview of the future, because Anchises shows his son Aeneas a whole long parade of souls who are about to be reincarnated as great Romans of the future. Virgil may be using reincarnation simply as a way of letting Aeneas view the souls of his yet-to-be-born descendants. This is the same problem I have talked about before, of how difficult it is to use literature, literary accounts of myth, as actual evidence of people's genuine beliefs in those myths. The more developed the literary tradition becomes, the more difficult it is to determine exactly what the correspondence between the literary device and actual belief may have been.

One of the most important myths concerning the afterlife is the myth of Orpheus and Eurydice. Orpheus was the greatest poet who ever lived. He was also a son of Apollo, though, and one of the Muses, the nine goddesses of creative ability, so Orpheus ought to have been a god. The fact that he is human is odd and is anomalous. With both his parents gods, he should have been a god. But, for whatever reason, he wasn't. He was a human and the greatest poet who ever lived. Supposedly, his poetry, singing, was so beautiful that he had the power to charm animals and even stones and trees with his music. When his wife Eurydice died—bitten in the heel by a snake on her wedding day—Orpheus journeyed to the Underworld to try to get her back, and played his lyre and sang his poetry so beautifully that Hades and Persephone agreed to let him have his wife back. They agreed to let Eurydice go, with one stipulation of course, the very famous part of the story. Orpheus must not look back at Eurydice as she followed him back out of the Underworld until they had reached the land of the living again. And, of course, as they were walking out of the Underworld, Orpheus did look back, Eurydice faded back into Tartaros, and that time was really dead. He could not go back and try to get her again.

Now, this purely mythical Orpheus—whose story is attested by Roman writers, by the way in detail, not by Greek writers—this purely mythical Orpheus was associated with a body of writings and a set of religious beliefs that are called "Orphism." As far as we know, there never was any real Orpheus. I think we can safely say that he certainly did not go the Underworld to try to get Eurydice back. But there was a set of religious doctrines and beliefs that began to be taught in the sixth century B.C. that we call Orphism, and the adherents of those beliefs thought that they were founded by Orpheus. The idea was that while he was in the Underworld, Orpheus learned all sorts of things about the afterlife, and when he came back, he told those to disciples and wrote them down and gave them to later humans.

Orphism, as I said, began to be taught in the sixth century B.C., the same time that Pythagoras was developing his idea of reincarnation. The Orphic writings unfortunately survive only in fragmentary form. As I have to say so often in this course, we don't have much testimony about this religious belief system. We know much less about it than we would like to know. We know that it was very involved and complex—it contained its own creation story, its own Theogony, for instance. What I want to focus on for here is that these writings, supposedly preserving knowledge that Orpheus gained while he was in the underworld, include a belief in reincarnation. In fact, reincarnation is central to the doctrine of Orphism. Only by following the teachings of Orpheus and leading an ascetic life can the soul eventually be freed from the cycle of birth and re-death.

Orpheus's teaching about reincarnation is in many ways opposite to the standard Greek view that I talked about a few minutes ago, in which life in this world is what counts and is desirable, and life as a disincarnated spirit is seen as only a very poor substitute for life in this world. Orpheus's view of reincarnation was much more like the view that we have in Buddhism, for instance, in which incarnation is a bad thing and the goal of the individual soul is to break the cycle of rebirth and free itself from incarnation. Supposedly, followers of Orphism did this by leading an ascetic life in this incarnation, and also Orphic writings contain precise instructions about what one should say and do in the underworld to avoid reincarnation. So, if you were a follower or Orphism in this life, you would learn what, in effect, were magic spells. You would learn certain things to say and certain actions you should take. Supposedly, when you died, you would find yourself in the Underworld. If you said these words to the right god of the Underworld (there were several minor gods under Hades) and did the right things, then you would not be reincarnated again. You had to be an ascetic in this life, but you also needed to know the proper things to say and do in the next life.

Orphism, like the Eleusinian Mysteries, held out the promise of a happy, or at least happier, afterlife than the standard view of the Underworld as we see it in Greek religion. Clearly, like in other aspects of Greek religion, in the view of the Underworld and the afterlife we don't have anything approaching an orthodoxy. All of these belief systems seem to have existed more or less side by side, and it is even hard to say how many people ever espoused the idea of reincarnation as opposed to the idea of the Homeric gloomy life in Tartaros, as opposed to the idea of some kind of reward and punishment. There wasn't any orthodoxy about the afterlife. But, it does seem safe to say that in most of these systems—Orphism might be the exception here—the afterlife was seen as less important, less real, less worthy of attention than life in this world. Greek thought, in general, tended to focus on what happens in this life as real, and what happens in the afterlife as only a shadowy reflection of reality.

In that context, it is interesting to consider that unlike so many mythologies, Greek mythology does not contain any aetiology for death. There doesn't seem to be any story that implies that humans originally did not have to die, that death was some kind of afterthought, that death was added on either through a mistake that humans made or through a sin that humans committed or anything like that. This is very unusual. Most mythological systems do seem to contain some such story, some sense that we ought to live forever, and that somehow we did something wrong or somebody made a mistake at some point, and death was introduced into the picture but ought not to have been there. That idea seems to be entirely absent in classical mythology. Again, in a system in which the defining characteristic of humans is that we are the *thnetoi*, the dying ones, and the defining characteristic of gods is that they are the undying ones, perhaps death is simply there as a given from the very beginning. Greek and classical mythology, in general, don't seem to suggest that there was ever a time that humans did not die. But, side by side with that, they seem to see this life as the only life worth having, so it is a rather—I don't want to say pessimistic, but perhaps melancholy picture. This life is the only life worth having, but it is short, and what comes after it is less valuable than this life itself.

Apollo and Artemis
Lecture 9

Certainly, at the time of Homer and even in the high point of classical culture in the fifth century B.C., Apollo was not associated with the sun; that association came later. Artemis is associated with the moon, but even there, that is only one aspect of this goddess. Both Apollo and Artemis are far more complex than the identification of them with the sun and the moon would tend to indicate.

Two of the most important younger Olympians are Artemis and Apollo, twin children of Zeus and the goddess Leto. These deities play essential roles both in reference to the other gods and for the Greek construction of human experience. Many dictionaries of classical mythology will say that Apollo is the sun god and his sister Artemis is the moon. Although both did come to have these associations eventually, they are much more complex than these identifications would indicate.

Son of Zeus and Leto, Apollo is the god of youth, medicine, healing, music, and prophecy.

Apollo is a god of youth, medicine, healing, music, prophecy, and, in general, moderation and rationality; however, he is also associated with sudden death for men and with plague. Most of the younger generation of Olympians are depicted in art as young adults in their twenties, but Apollo is represented as the youth par excellence, the ideal of manly beauty. Each generation of Olympians matures to its proper age and remains at that age. He is associated both with medicine and healing and with sudden death and death through disease. The double association of healer and plague-bringer gives a complete and rounded image of Apollo; he is not entirely beneficent towards humans, despite his positive qualities. He is described as wearing a quiver and carrying a bow; when he shoots men with these arrows, they die suddenly. His sister Artemis performs the same function for women. As the patron of music and the arts, Apollo presides over the Muses.

Perhaps his most important role is as the main god of prophecy. He passes on prophecy from Zeus to selected humans. Zeus, too, controls prophecy, but the most famous and important oracle of ancient Greece was in Delphi, sacred to Apollo. Questioners could ask the god anything they wanted and would receive answers through the Pythia, his priestess at Delphi, inspired by Apollo himself. Many of the oracles that we know of are so ambiguous as to be impossible to refute; however, the oracle of Delphi was taken extremely seriously by the Greeks and their neighbors. A priestess could be corrupted, but faith in Apollo was profound. Apollo's role as patron of prophecy at Delphi reflects his overall association with reason and moderation. Greek religion had no prescriptive commandments, but two sayings carved on the temple at Delphi are crucial for understanding the underlying presumptions of the religion. These sayings are *gnothi sauton* and *meden agan*: "Know yourself" and "Nothing in excess." "Know yourself" means know what kind of creature you are, remember your limitations, remember that you are not a god.

These two maxims encapsulate a theme that runs throughout Greek myth: that humans are liable to transgress the boundaries that separate them from the gods, which inevitably brings suffering. Humans must remember their status and not seek to exceed it. In particular, humans should avoid *hubris*, a word that is often translated as "excessive pride" but basically means insolence or wantonness; *hubris* is the kind of excessiveness that leads one to claim more than is one's due. The story of Niobe is a particularly good example of the importance of Apollo's maxims and of the dangers of *hubris*. Niobe, queen of Thebes and sister of Tantalos, boasted that she was more worthy of worship than Leto, mother of Artemis and Apollo, because Leto had only two children but she, Niobe, had fourteen. Apollo and Artemis kill all Niobe's children. When only one remains, Niobe begs for mercy, but even the last is killed. Niobe has failed to remember both maxims; she has not known herself—the vulnerability of her humanity—and she has been misled by the excess of her good fortune.

Like her brother Apollo, Artemis brings sudden death, but in other ways, she is her twin's polar opposite.

Like her brother Apollo, Artemis brings sudden death, but in other ways, she is her twin's polar opposite. She is associated with wildness and wild things, where he is associated with reason and civilization. She is a huntress, the patron of wild beasts, and the protector of the young of all species. Artemis's association with wild animals in various aspects dates back to very early times. Homer calls Artemis *potnia theron*, or "Mistress of Wild Beasts"; many artistic representations recall this title. One of her most important sites of worship was at Ephesus, in modern Turkey, where her role as *potnia theron* seems to have predominated. As a huntress, she carries a bow and wears a quiver; she is often shown in a short robe that would allow for running. Artemis is also associated with women in several ways. She is the protector of women in childbirth. She is a virgin and is particularly associated with young girls before and up to the time of their marriages. She brings sudden death to women. Artemis's status as a virgin and her role as protector of women in childbirth may at first sight seem contradictory; however, both aspects of the goddess tie in to her essential wildness. Women in childbirth are most vulnerable to and most caught up in their animal natures; only in the instant of death are humans so clearly allied to the rest of the animal kingdom. Ancient Greek society associates women with nature and men with culture. Artemis's virginity is not a rejection of sexuality per se; rather, it is a rejection of male domination in sexual intercourse.

Artemis's rejection of sexuality is the impetus for the story of Actaeon, which illustrates the danger of crossing a god. Even unintentional violations of the boundaries between gods and humans can lead to disaster. Actaeon inadvertently saw Artemis nude while he was out hunting. Artemis turned him into a stag, but left his mind cognizant of what had happened to him. Actaeon was torn to shreds by his own hunting hounds. In the worldview represented by classical mythology, intentions are often irrelevant; what matters are actions. Our culture tends to make a strong distinction between actions according to their intent, but the ancient Greeks considered motives much less important. ■

Essential Reading

Apollodorus, *Library*, pp. 104–105 ("Amphion, Niobe, and Their Children").

Homeric Hymn to Apollo.

Ovid, *Metamorphoses*, pp. 61–64 (Actaeon); 133–139 (Niobe).

Supplementary Reading

Burkert, *Greek Religion*, pp. 142–152.

Fontenrose, *Delphic Oracle.*

Questions to Consider

1. The concept that intentions are unimportant and actions are all that matter strikes many modern readers as disturbing. Is there anything in the nature of the classical gods that makes such a worldview comprehensible? What does Actaeon's story tell us about Artemis?

2. I argue that Artemis's virginity is a rejection of male domination, not of sexuality per se. Does this interpretation make sense for Athena as well?

Apollo and Artemis
Lecture 9—Transcript

In the previous lecture, we talked about the Eleusinian Mysteries and other views of the afterlife, and what happens to the soul after death. In this lecture, we are going to resume an examination of individual Olympian gods and goddesses by looking at two of Zeus's children, the twins Apollo and Artemis. These two are among the most important of the Olympians. They are the offspring of Zeus and a minor goddess named Leto. She really has no function in myth except to be the mother of Apollo and Artemis. These two deities play crucial roles, both in reference to the other gods and throughout Greek mythology, for our understanding of the Greek construction of human experience. They are two extremely important deities.

In many modern dictionaries of classical mythology, if you look up Apollo, for instance, will say that he is the god of the sun and that his sister Artemis is the goddess of the moon. They did come to have these associations eventually, although the association of Apollo with the sun is fairly late in classical culture. Certainly, at the time of Homer and even in the high point of classical culture in the fifth century B.C., Apollo was not associated with the sun; that association came later. Artemis is associated with the moon, but even there, that is only one aspect of this goddess. Both Apollo and Artemis are far more complex than the identification of them with the sun and the moon would tend to indicate.

If Apollo is not simply a sun god, what is he? He is a god of youth, medicine, healing, music, prophecy, and, in general, moderation and rationality; however, he is also associated with sudden death for men—when a man drops dead, he is said to have been shot by the arrows of Apollo. And he is the god who brings plague and sickness in general. He is not entirely a positive and beneficent god. He does have a negative side from the human point of view as well. Most of the younger generation of Olympians, not just Apollo and Artemis, but the other younger gods as well, tend to be depicted in art as young adults in their 20s. The older generation of gods, Zeus and his siblings, are depicted as mature adults in or around their 40s. For instance, this illustration on this wall is of Zeus—or Poseidon. We don't know which, some scholars think one, some the other. You can see that is a mature man, probably in his 40s. Apollo is represented as a younger man, as are his siblings, the younger Olympians. Apollo is represented as the ideal of youthful beauty, the young man *par excellence*, the ideal of manly beauty.

One point to bring out here is that the different gods have their appropriate ages, and they seem to age from birth until they reach the age that is considered appropriate or fitting to their role—to their area of power—and then they stop. Zeus is born as a baby, reaches the age of full maturity, and stops there and never ages any further. Persephone we have to perceive as being the right age for a bride, so she is about like a girl of 14 when Hades abducts her. She is not going to age any further either. Apollo and his siblings in his generation are fixed as youths, are fixed as young gods and goddesses.

Apollo, as I said, is associated both with medicine and healing, and with sudden death in general, plague, and death through disease. The double association healer and plague bringer—anyone who has read the *Iliad* will remember how at the beginning of the *Iliad* Apollo brings the plague that devastates the Greek army—this double association, healer and plague bringer, is very good to bear in mind for the complete and rounded picture of Apollo it offers us. He is not entirely beneficent toward humans, despite his many positive qualities. He is often shown in art wearing a quiver and carrying a bow. When he shoots men with the arrows from his quiver, the men fall dead. Deaths that we would explain as being the result of strokes or aneurism, that sort of thing, would, according to the Greek view, mean the man had been shot by the invisible arrow of Apollo. When a woman dies suddenly the same way, she is said to have been shot by the arrows of Artemis.

Apollo is patron of music and of the arts, in general. As such, he presides over nine goddesses called the Muses. I mentioned the Muses in the last lecture when I said that Orpheus is the son of one of them. The Muses, in the earliest stages of Greek culture, were simply the personifications or the representatives of the creative arts in general. They did not yet, in the early stages of culture, have their own proper areas of expertise. Later on, the nine Muses come to be associated with an individual kind of creative endeavor, each one with one individual area. For instance, Clio is the Muse of history; Melpomene is the Muse of tragedy—that sort of thing. In their earliest representations, they are simply together, as a group, the goddesses of creative endeavor. Apollo presides over the Muses; this means that he presides over art, poetry, music, creative ability in general.

Another aspect of Apollo, which is his most important aspect, is that he is the main god of prophecy. Now, I mentioned earlier on in the course that Zeus stands behind prophecy, Zeus gives prophecy to Apollo, which Apollo then passes on to humans. This is true. Zeus is perhaps the primary god of prophecy, and Apollo is in effect his lieutenant in this area. But, the most important prophetic shrine, the most important oracular shrine in Greece, was at Delphi, and was sacred to Apollo, not Zeus. Apollo's role as a god who provides prophecy for humans is central to our understanding of him, and that role is most important in his shrine at Delphi.

People could travel to Delphi to ask the priestess there (in this particular shrine, the oracles were given out by a woman, by a priestess), who was called the Pythia, questions about anything they wanted to know. The idea was that they would give their questions to the Pythia, she would give an oracular answer and that answer would have been given to her by Apollo. She was inspired by Apollo. People would say that they are going to Delphi to ask Apollo for an answer to a question. Oedipus says this, for instance, in Sophocles's play, *Oedipus the King*. Oedipus says he went to Delphi to ask Apollo for an answer. What that means, of course, is asking the priestess, the Pythia, and she tells you what Apollo tells her.

We have preserved for us in literature several examples of the kinds of answers, prophecies, oracles that the Pythia gave to questioners. Many of them are very, very ambiguous. The most famous in that category is the oracle given to the King of Lydia, Croesus, who came to ask Apollo if he, Croesus, should declare war on Persia, whose emperor was Cyrus. Croesus wanted to know, "Should I attack Cyrus's kingdom?" The answer that the Pythia gave him was, "If you cross the river Halys (which was the boundary between their two empires), you will destroy a great empire." Croesus took this as a positive answer, went to war with Cyrus and, of course, destroyed his own empire. That is one kind of oracle that we see frequently represented, a completely ambiguous oracle that can be read either way. Others were given in such symbolic and recherché language that is difficult to tell what exactly they meant.

Looking at the culture from the outside as we do, it is easy to be cynical about this—to say the priestess, the Pythia, very carefully gave responses that were either so ambiguous or so wrapped up in vagueness that they could mean anything, and therefore, she can never be proven wrong. From inside the culture, for whatever reason, the Oracle of Delphi was taken extremely seriously by the Greeks and their neighbors. Cities sent representatives to the oracle to ask for advice before any important undertaking. Athens, for example, when it was being besieged by the Persians in the Great Persian Wars of 490 and 480 B.C., asked Apollo's oracle at Delphi, "What should we do? Should we evacuate our city or should we stand and fight?" This was taken extremely seriously.

There are some authors who recognize that a particular Pythia could be corrupted, that Pythias could sometimes be bribed to give false answers. That does not imply any disbelief in Apollo's prophetic ability and in the possibility of getting prophecies from Apollo. The idea of prophecy, and Apollo as patron of prophecy, is a central factor in Greek culture and Greek myth. Apollo's role as the patron of prophecy reflects his overall association with reason and with moderation, with the idea that there is an order in the world, and that Apollo somehow knows and foreknows this order so that he can tell you what will happen in the future.

Greek religion, as I have said several times before, had no orthodoxy. Along with that, it did not have any prescriptive commandments, no "thou shalts" and "thou shalt nots" that had to be believed in and obeyed in order to be a member of this religion. However, carved on Apollo's temple at Delphi there were two sayings that come as close as Greek religion ever came to commandments, and that are absolutely crucial to our understanding of the presumptions of Greek religion and Greek culture. These two sayings, carved on the temple, two words each, were: *gnothi sauton* and *meden agan*. *Gnothi sauton* means "know yourself." *Meden agan* means "nothing in excess." "Know yourself" in this context is not some sort of pop-psychology, touchy-feely advice to get in touch with your own feelings or your inner child. It means remember what kind of a creature you are.

Remember your limitations; remember above all else that you are not a god. These two sayings together encapsulate or lead us toward a theme that runs throughout Greek myth—the idea that humans are liable to transgress the boundaries that separate them from the gods, and that to do so inevitably brings suffering. If you forget what kind of a creature you are or if you have an excess of anything—particularly an excess of good things—you are in danger of transgressing the boundaries of offending the gods, and you will suffer the consequences of doing so. Humans must remember their own status and must not seek to exceed it.

In particular, humans must avoid *hubris*. *Hubris* is a word that has actually come into the English language directly from Greek. It is often translated as excessive pride, and it can mean that. More basically, it means insolence or wantonness—the kind of excessiveness in behavior that leads a person to claim more than is his or her due. To illustrate the dangers of *hubris*, the importance of Apollo's maxims "know yourself" and "nothing in excess," and the necessity of obeying them, the story of Niobe is a perfect one to turn to at this point.

Niobe was a queen of Thebes. It is interesting how often Thebes pops up in Greek myth as a place where bad things happen to main characters in myths. Niobe was queen of Thebes—sister of Tantalos (so it has its problems already)—and she boasted that she was more worthy of worship than Leto, the mother of Apollo and Artemis, because, Niobe said, "Leto has only a paltry two children," whereas she, Niobe, had 14 children. Niobe claimed that the people of Thebes ought to build a temple to and worship her rather than Leto, because Niobe had seven times as many children as Leto had. Clearly, Niobe has failed to abide by the maxim "know yourself" here. She has forgotten the crucial difference: her children are human; Leto's children are Apollo and Artemis. The result is that Apollo and Artemis get to work with their bows and arrows.

First, Apollo shoots Niobe's seven sons. Her seven sons (described by the Roman poet Ovid as young men out exercising, taking part in exercises in hunting, boxing, wrestling, etc.) all fall dead at Niobe's feet. Does she learn her lesson? No. She says she is still better off than Leto; she still has her seven daughters. Whereupon Artemis starts putting arrows to the bow and starts to shoot Niobe's seven daughters. When only the youngest is left, Niobe begs for mercy, asks Artemis to spare her youngest child, but it is too late—the arrow has already left the bow and even the youngest, normally pictured as a little girl of about two or so, dies at her mother's feet. There Niobe is—surrounded by the 14 corpses of her 14 children who have died because of her own *hubris*. Supposedly, she transforms into a cliff face with water running down it, forever to symbolize her eternal tears for her children.

Now, there are all sorts of points that could be brought out in this story. First of all, it underlines a theme that is quite frequent in classical mythology, and in the mythologies of other cultures as well, that (to use a Biblical phrase) the sins of the fathers will be visited upon the children. Niobe transgresses; her children die as a result of her transgression. But most importantly for the point I am making here, it shows us how those two maxims should be interpreted, and what happens when you fail to abide by them, and how the two maxims work together, almost as two sides of the same coin. Niobe has failed to know herself. She has failed to remember what it means to be human. She has failed to remember that humans are by definition vulnerable to death, and the fact that she has 14 children today does not mean that she will have 14 children tomorrow. She may lose some of them; she may lose all of them. They are human; therefore, they can die at any moment. Human good fortune is an unstable thing. That is stressed over and over again in Greek literature. It is changeable, it is unstable, it can disappear in the blink of an eye.

Why has she failed to know herself? Why has she fallen into the error of *hubris* and so far forgotten the vulnerability that is part of being human, the vulnerability to death? Because of excess. She has so many children, all of them alive, that she thinks she is safe. If two or three die, she would still have 11 or 12. Even if half of them die, she would still have seven. She thinks because of this excess she is safe, she is not liable to normal human experience, and that is her great error. Apollo, as a god of reason and moderation—that is often seen as a very good aspect of Apollo, and in many ways it is, but there is also a kind of warning implicit there, as well as a good thing. We should have nothing in excess, because that is so dangerous. We should practice moderation or else. Even in these two maxims, "know yourself" and "nothing in excess," we see the somewhat dangerous side of Apollo represented, as well as his appealing and good side.

Artemis, as I already said, is Apollo's twin sister. Like her brother Apollo, Artemis brings sudden death, as we saw in the Niobe story; it is Artemis who shoots Niobe's daughters. In other ways, Artemis is almost her twin's opposite. Where he is associated with reason, moderation, rationality, the arts of culture, music, healing, all of those things, Artemis is mainly associated with wildness, untamedness, the wild animal side of nature. She is primarily associated with wild beasts. She is a huntress, the patron of wild beasts and a protector of the young of all species. I used to think that Artemis's roles as huntress was in some way contradictory to her role as protector of the young of all species, until I had hunters in my mythology classes on several different occasions. They saw no contradiction there whatsoever. Hunters are concerned with protecting the young of all species, so that the species will continue to be there in order to be hunted later. I think that is actually a very valid insight that my students gave me in that regard, that Artemis as the huntress, Artemis as the protector of the young, are really two complimentary aspects, not contradictory aspects at all.

Her association with wild animals in various aspects seems to date back to very, very early times. This may in fact be the original characteristic of Artemis. She may have begun as a goddess of wild beasts before she was identified as Apollo's sister, before she gathered any of the other associations that she has. Homer calls Artemis the *potnia theron,* a Greek phrase that means the "mistress of wild beasts" or the "lady of wild beasts." There are several very archaic artistic representations that seem to show her in that role as the lady or mistress of wild beasts. If Apollo's most important shrine was at Delphi, one of Artemis's most important shrines was not in Greece at all, but in modern day Turkey at Ephesus. The western coast of Turkey was Greek-speaking and culturally Greek in the ancient world. Ephesus was Artemis's most important shrine in Asia Minor, and really in all of the Greek-speaking world. It was at Ephesus that Saint Paul preached against Artemis, or Diana, as her Roman name would have it. And, there at Ephesus, her role as *potnia theron,* as the lady or mistress of wild beasts, seems to have been her most important aspect.

Her very famous cult statue there shows her with wild beasts on her headdress, and on her garment, and her torso is covered with objects that may be breasts. She is sometimes called the "many-breasted Artemis" at Ephesus, which seems to show her as the nurturer of the young of all species. Other scholars think that the objects that appear on her cult statue at Ephesus are not breasts at all, but something else. It is questionable what exactly those objects are. In any case, Artemis at Ephesus seems to have been mainly understood as a goddess of wild beasts and wild animals.

As a huntress, she carries a bow and wears a quiver, just like her brother Apollo does. Another way to recognize her hunter aspect in art is that she wears a dress which is belted up to her knees to allow her to run. So, if you see an image in Greek art, statue or painting, of a goddess with a short tunic that would let her run, that is almost definitely Artemis.

Now, along with this association with beasts and with the young of all species, Artemis is also associated with women in several important ways. First of all, she is the protector of women in childbirth. Hera, as we talked about a few lectures back, is the patron goddess of marriage. And, Hera's daughter, Eileithyia, is the daughter who embodies childbirth, who comes to a woman and allows the child to be born. Artemis is the goddess to whom women would pray for protection in childbirth, to whom they would pray not to die in the process of labor. Artemis is also a virgin. There are three goddesses who remain forever virgins: Artemis, Athena and Hestia. Artemis is a virgin and is particularly associated with young girls before and up to the time of their marriage. There were ceremonies that young, unmarried girls performed in honor of Artemis, and she is seen as somehow their patron in the way that Hera is the patron of married women. And, she is the bringer of sudden death to women, so she is associated with crises of women's lives, with virginity up to the point of marriage, with childbirth after marriage, and with death of women.

Her status as a virgin and her role as the protector of women in childbirth at first glance seem contradictory. Why would a goddess who is a virgin herself, who will never undergo childbirth herself, why would she be given the role in a culture of protecting women in childbirth? I think that this particular apparent contradiction really is not a contradiction at all, if we see both of these aspects of Artemis as tying in to her essential wildness, to the side of her nature that makes her the patron of wild animals. In human existence, I think, there are two main times when it is almost impossible to deny our connection to the animal kingdom, to see us as in some way separate from or different from other animals. Those two instances are birth and death. In those two times, in those two crises of our lives, culture falls to one side, does us no good, doesn't separate us from the animal kingdom in any significant way. Another way of saying this would be to say that when women are giving birth, that is when they are closest to wild nature, closest to animal nature, closest to other animals.

Artemis's role as the protector of the young of all species comes in here as well, because she is the protector of human babies as well as the babies of other species. I think the crucial aspect here is that women, when they are giving birth, are women or humans at their wildest, at their least impacted by culture. Greek thought in general makes a strong distinction between nature and culture, and tends to identify women with nature, men with culture. Artemis as a god of wildness, Artemis as a god of nature as opposed to culture—which her brother Apollo represents—is a fitting goddess to be associated with women in childbirth, with women in their role as representatives of nature, rather than of culture.

Similarly, I think Artemis's virginity is understandable through and because of her association with wildness. To understand why I think that, we have to talk a little bit about the Greek view of sexuality, of what sex implies and of the roles of the two sexes. We talked in the lecture about the *Homeric Hymn to Demeter*, about Greek, or at least Athenian, marriage practices, and I pointed out then that marriage was a contract between the groom and the bride's father. This implies—though I don't think I specifically said so in that lecture—an underlying assumption about the relative roles, importance, and authority of both sexes. In ancient Greek culture in general, and ancient Athenian culture in particular, there is no doubt that men were seen as being in authority and women were seen as being submissive. Males were dominant in every respect; males had authority. Women were seen as quite definitely secondary—second- class citizens, if you want to put it that way.

This carried over into the view of sexuality and how sexuality worked. The act of sexual intercourse was seen as domination of the female by the male. I think it is this that Artemis rejects when she remains a virgin. I don't think she is rejecting sexuality per se; I don't think she is rejecting sexual pleasure as somehow inappropriate to her. I think she is rejecting domination by a male because of her essential wildness—domination by anyone, but specifically domination by a male.

One interesting little tidbit of the Greek language that I think backs me up in this interpretation is that a word for wife in Greek (not the only word, but one word) is *damar,* which literally means tamed. A wife was a tamed woman. What a man did when he married (and it was pictured as catching a wild creature) a young, unmarried woman was taming her, domesticating her, and then she was a wife. I think what Artemis rejects is precisely that; being tamed, being controlled. So I don't see her virginity as contradictory to her role as protector of the young and a goddess of childbirth, but rather as complementary.

Her rejection of sexuality in any form is the impetus for another myth that illustrates the danger of crossing a god or transgressing the boundaries between humans and gods, as the myth of Niobe did. In this story, the story of Actaeon, we see how even unintentional violations of the boundaries between gods and humans can lead to disaster for the human. Actaeon was a great hunter. He was out in the woods one day—he was also from the town of Thebes, by the way—hunting with his friends, and was separated from his companions. As he was wandering through the woods, he came to a grove of trees. He pushed his way through the trees and discovered that they surrounded a lake. In the lake, Artemis and her attendant nymphs were bathing naked.

Actaeon did not intend to see Artemis naked. He did not decide he was going to go spy on Artemis. He saw her unintentionally, by mistake, he did not mean to. This matters not at all. Artemis punishes him for seeing her naked by turning him into a stag, a deer, but leaving his mind perfectly aware of what has happened to him. He has an animal body, but a human mind. That might seem to be torment enough, but just wait. As Actaeon, now a stag, runs through the woods, his own hounds pick up his scent. With his friends encouraging them, the hounds tear Actaeon to shreds and kill him, while his friends stand around wondering where Actaeon is, Actaeon is missing the sport, Actaeon would enjoy this so much. One of the most dreadful stories that I know of in Greek mythology.

The point I want to close with here is that this tells us something very important about the worldview represented in classical mythology. In this worldview, intentions are quite frequently irrelevant. Actions are what matter. Our culture tends to make a very strong distinction, in most cases, between intentions and actions. If I kill someone and don't intend to do it, we call that involuntary manslaughter. If I stalk my victim and plot ahead of time how to kill him or her, we call that first-degree murder. We consider those two actions very different in kind, and we punish them very differently, despite the fact that the result is the same—the person I kill is dead. In the worldview represented by the myth of Actaeon, that would be nonsensical. What matters is not what Actaeon intended. What matters is what Actaeon did. He saw Artemis naked. He suffers the consequences. This idea that intentions are less important than actions comes up in a great many Greek myths, though the story of Actaeon is probably the most obvious example of it.

In this lecture, we have looked at Apollo and Artemis. We have seen how, in many ways, they are polar opposites of one another: he representing culture and moderation, she representing nature and wildness. In the next lecture, we will move on to talk about two other very important children of Zeus, the gods Hermes and Dionysos.

Hermes and Dionysos
Lecture 10

Dionysos's connection with frenzy is represented in myth by the idea that he literally possesses his followers. He enters into them, possesses them and drives them mad, makes them do things that in their right minds they would never either consider doing or be able to do.

*Z*eus's two youngest sons are Hermes and Dionysos. Hermes is the son of a minor goddess, Maia, and Dionysos is the son of a human woman, Semele. Hermes is often identified simply as the "messenger of the gods," a description that does not do him justice. Like his siblings Apollo and Artemis, Hermes presides over a group of characteristics that at first glance seem unconnected. He is the patron god of messengers, heralds, merchants, thieves, beggars, travelers, and roads; cattle and cattle-herders; liars and tricksters. In addition, he is the god who conducts the souls of the dead to Tartaros. Hermes is often described as a god of boundaries and transitions. Another way of looking at him is to see him as the god of exchange and commerce.

The souls of the dead belong to Hades and are often described as his wealth.

The *Homeric Hymn to Hermes*, which narrates his birth story, supports the idea that Hermes is a god of exchange. The first thing the newborn god does is create a lyre out of a tortoise shell. This he later barters to Apollo in exchange for Apollo's cattle. If we view Hermes as primarily a god of exchange, then the association with both merchants and thieves makes sense. His association with cattle also makes sense, because cattle are a primary means of determining wealth. His association with messengers and heralds can be explained in two ways. Messengers and heralds preside over the exchange of information, which is a logical development from the exchange of goods. Messengers and heralds often perform other tasks having to do with the exchange of goods. Even his role as *Psychopompos*, or Guide of Souls, makes sense under the rubric of exchange. The souls of the dead belong to Hades and are often described as his wealth; thus, Hermes presides over another sort of exchange, from the realm of Zeus to that of Hades. In the *Hymn*, Hermes is clearly a trickster figure, who is clever, manipulative, and very good at speech. These traits, too, fit well with his role as god of exchange.

Hermes was also associated with *herms*, pillars that stood in the marketplace, in front of private houses, and at crossroads. This reflects his aspect as a god of boundaries. Hermes's association with the herm is probably the oldest element of this god's essential character. "Herm" originally meant simply "pile of stones"; the pillar gave its name to the god, not the other way around. Hermes very likely began as a personification of these marker-stones. Herms were pillars topped with a head and featuring an erect phallus. This is unique among Greek statues of their gods, which were usually fully anthropomorphic. The erect phallus is something of a puzzle. Its most obvious function would be to symbolize fertility, but this is not an aspect of Hermes. The

Often identified as the "messenger of the gods," Hermes' role is actually far more complex. He is a god of boundaries and transitions and of exchange and commerce.

© iStockphoto/Thinkstock.

pillars are often described as *apotropaic*, or frightening away evil spirits, but this leaves unanswered the question of why the phallus should serve that function. Burkert suggests that this representation of Hermes has its origin in primate behavior; in certain monkey species, males who guard the group sit facing outward, with erect phalluses. Whatever the origin of the herms, they were important elements of public (and private) religion; defacing a herm was a serious offense in Athens.

Zeus had one more important son, Dionysos. He is a complex god whose domains include fertility of plants, wine, frenzy, irrationality, and drama. As a god of plant fertility, Dionysos complements Demeter. Demeter's domain is grain, specifically the controlled growth of grain in agriculture. Dionysos's domain is the growth of fruitful, moist plants, such as grapes and figs, and of rapidly growing, luxuriant plants, such as ivy. Dionysos is associated with madness, frenzy, and irrationality. In this aspect, he is directly opposed to Apollo. This opposition is shown in myth by the fact that Apollo leaves Delphi during the winter months each year and Dionysos takes up residence there. In *The Birth of Tragedy,* Friedrich Nietzsche identified the "Dionysian" and the "Apollonian" as the two main strands of Greek thought, constantly in tension with one another. Dionysos's connection with frenzy is represented in myth as his possession of his followers; under his influence, they do things completely at odds with their usual personalities. In myth, Dionysos's male followers are Satyrs, creatures who blend human and animal characteristics. His mythic female followers are the Maenads, women constantly under his influence and gifted with exceptional abilities, who rip animals apart and eat their flesh raw. Actual worship of Dionysos, so far as we know, did not include such behavior. The most common definition of Dionysos is "god of wine." His association with wine unites his associations with growing plants and with irrationality and frenzy. Dionysos is also the patron god of theatre, though the exact reason for his connection with drama is still a matter of scholarly debate. Tragedy and comedy were both performed at festivals in honor of Dionysos. One theory is that tragedy and comedy both developed out of rituals in honor of Dionysos. However, the surviving plays contain little evidence of such ritual origin. We can say that a god whose domains include possession and behavior inconsistent with one's normal character is appropriate for a theatrical tradition in which actors were masked.

Many aspects of Dionysos are unusual or even unique among the Olympian gods. The first such aspect is his birth from a human mother. Dionysos's mother was Semele, princess of Thebes, who had an affair with Zeus. Hera was jealous and decided to destroy Semele. Hera visits Semele disguised as her old nanny. Hera suggests that Semele's lover is simply a man claiming to be Zeus. She suggests that Semele should induce him to promise to do whatever she asks, then ask to see him as he appears to Hera. Semele follows Hera's advice, Zeus reveals his true form to her, and Semele is incinerated. Zeus snatches the infant Dionysos from Semele's womb and implants him in his own thigh. Dionysos is later born from Zeus's thigh, thus receiving his epithet "twice-born." Dionysos apparently gains his immortal status from his incubation in Zeus's body.

Dionysos and his worship seem somehow less "given" in Greek myth than those of any other god; there are several stories of people resisting his worship and denying his divinity. The most important of these concerns his cousin Pentheus, king of Thebes. Semele's sisters did not believe that their sister could have been the mother of a god. In Euripides's *Bacchae*, Dionysos returned to Thebes as an adult, disguised as a human priest. He had two purposes to accomplish there. He wanted to punish his disbelieving relatives. He wanted to establish his religion in Greece. His first step is to drive the Theban women mad. Pentheus, king of Thebes and Dionysos's first cousin, refuses to accept this new god. His punishment is to be torn to pieces by his own mother and aunts, who think that he is a mountain lion. Dionysos thus proves both his power and his divinity.

Scholars used to believe that all these aspects of Dionysos's myth—his unusual ancestry, the resistance to his worship, his general unruliness—were evidence that he was, in fact, a late importation into Greece from Asia Minor. Evidence now shows that Dionysos was worshipped in Greece as early as most of the other Olympic gods; he is not a late arrival. The questions of why Dionysos is so different and why he is represented in myth as a latecomer to the pantheon are left open. Some scholars think that the representation of Dionysos as a latecomer reflects the Greeks' own discomfort with and distrust of irrationality and frenzy. Another possibility is that Dionysos's association with young, verdant, growing things carries over into his myths as the idea that he himself is young, i.e., recent. No definitive answer exists. ∎

Essential Reading

Apollodorus, pp. 101–103 ("Semele and Dionysos").

Homeric Hymn to Hermes.

Ovid, pp. 64–66 ("The Story of Semele"); 73–80 ("The Story of Pentheus and Bacchus").

Oxford Classical Dictionary, "Dionysos."

Supplementary Reading

Burkert, *Greek Religion,* pp. 222–225 ("Dionysos").

————, *Structure and History,* pp. 39–41, on herms.

Euripides, *Bacchae.*

Sale, "The Psychoanalysis of Pentheus."

Questions to Consider

1. Does Burkert's suggestion that primate behavior may help us understand herms strike you as plausible? Could it ever be *dis*proven?

2. Can you think of any explanation (other than the ones I suggested) for Dionysos's "difference" from the other Greek gods? Why is this god a latecomer whose worship is often resisted?

Hermes and Dionysos
Lecture 10—Transcript

In the previous lecture, we discussed Apollo and Artemis, two of Zeus's most important children, and talked about some of their attributes, their characteristics, their domains and so forth. In this lecture, we are going to continue our examination of individual Olympian gods by looking at two more of Zeus's children, his two youngest sons, Hermes and Dionysos.

Hermes is the son of a minor goddess, Maia. As I said Leto really exists to be a mother for Apollo and Artemis, so Maia has no distinguishing characteristics of her own except that she is the mother of Hermes. There are no independent stories about her. Dionysos, interestingly, is the son of a human mother, a woman named Semele. We will talk about the oddity of a god having a human mother later in the lecture when we deal with Dionysos.

Just as Apollo and Artemis are often identified simply as the god of the sun and the goddess of the moon, so Hermes tends to be identified overly simplistically as the messenger of the gods. That is one of his roles; he takes messages for Zeus to other gods, in particular, but he is a much more complex god than merely describing him as a messenger would tend to indicate. That description does not begin to do him justice. Like his siblings, Apollo and Artemis, Hermes presides over a group of characteristics that, at first glance, seem almost bizarrely unconnected with one another. He is, among other things, the patron god of messengers, heralds, merchants, thieves, beggars, travelers, roads and crossroads; cattle and cattle-herders; liars and tricksters. In addition, he is the god who guides the souls of the dead to the Underworld. In that regard, he is given the title *Psychopompos* in Greek, which means guide of souls, the soul-guide.

Is there any way to unify all these different attributes of Hermes, as I attempted to do with unifying Artemis's different attributes under her central characteristic of wildness? I think that there is, with Hermes. Many scholars say that his primary characteristic is to be a god of boundaries and transitions; boundaries and the crossing of boundaries. Property crosses boundaries in commerce or in thievery or in other such activities over which Hermes presides. Taking the souls of the dead to the Underworld is very clearly crossing a boundary. That is one way of giving him a unifying characteristic. Another way, which I tend to use to look at Hermes, is to see him as a god whose primary characteristic is an association with exchange and commerce—exchange of all kinds, exchange of goods, but also exchange of other things.

The *Homeric Hymn to Hermes,* which is a very important document for understanding this god, describes his birth-story, and in its description of Hermes's birth and his first day on earth, the *Homeric Hymn to Hermes* supports the idea that he is, first and foremost, a god of exchange. The very first thing he does as a newborn is to go outside the cave in which his mother Maia gives birth to him, find a tortoise, kill it, strip it out of its shell and then use the shell to invent the lyre—the musical stringed instrument that was essential in Greek music and poetry. In other words, the very first thing he does after his birth is provide himself with an item that he can later exchange. And exchange it he does. Later on in the *Homeric Hymn to Hermes*, he steals Apollo's cattle. When Apollo catches him and wants the cattle back, Hermes proposes a trade, a barter. He trades the lyre that he has invented to Apollo in exchange for authority over Apollo's cattle. Right there, in this little story about Hermes, we see him providing for exchange with the lyre which he exchanges for the cattle; presiding over stealing because he steals them in the first place; presiding over barter because he strikes a bargain with Apollo. I think it is significant that his very first action after birth is to start giving himself the means of exchange, something that he can later trade for something else.

If we view him primarily as a god of exchange, then Hermes's association with both merchants and thieves becomes understandable. In our normal way of looking at things, it would seem odd to have one god the patron of merchants *and* the patron of thieves, because you would expect the merchants to want this god to protect them against the thieves, and vice-versa. But if we zero in on the idea of exchange, then these two seemingly opposite areas work together and make sense, because in both the legitimate selling of property and the stealing of property, in thievery, property exchanges hands. I think Hermes is less concerned with the means by which it exchanges hands, whether a merchant is paid for the goods or whether a thief takes them, than he is concerned with the actuality of the exchange of goods itself.

His association with cattle also becomes intelligible if we look at him as mainly a god of exchange, because in the earliest strata of Greek culture, as well as in so many cultures, cattle were a primary means of reckoning wealth. A man's wealth was reckoned early on in many cultures in terms of the number of cattle that he owned. An interesting linguistic fact about the Latin language, not the Greek language in this case, is that the word for money, *pecunia,* is derived from, related to, the word for a herd of cattle, *pecus.* In other words, the Latin word for money preserves the idea that cattle were the original means of describing or amassing wealth. The association with cattle and cattle herding also ties into Hermes's role as a god of exchange.

What about his association with messengers and heralds? If we look at him as primarily an exchange god, I think there are two ways to explain that. First of all, we can expand the idea of exchange past the exchange of material goods and say that messengers and heralds preside over the exchange of information, which they do, so that Hermes could be here concerned with information traveling from one person to another, rather than with the exchange of goods. Another way of viewing his association with messengers and heralds is that in an ancient society in which travel is difficult, when a messenger is sent from one city to another to take a message from one ruler to another or when a herald gives a proclamation, very frequently, such a person would be entrusted with other tasks to accomplish as well. You are not going to go to all the trouble of sending a messenger from Thebes to Athens and not see to it that if there are any goods to be delivered—any messages other than his primary one that needs to be delivered, letters and so forth—you are going to see to it that he takes those things along as well. Messengers and travelers, in general, are associated with the exchange of goods in a culture in which travel is difficult and only undertaken by a few people.

Even Hermes's role as *Psychopompos*, as the guide of souls, fits into this overall view of him as a god of exchange. The souls of the dead, as I have mentioned before when discussing Demeter's attempt to immortalize Demophoön, the souls of the dead belong to Hades. They are his property. While humans are living, they are mainly under the control of Zeus, but once they die, they become the property of Hades. When Hermes escorts the soul of a newly dead person from the land of the living to the land of the dead, he is presiding over a kind of exchange of goods—the exchange of a soul from being under Zeus's dominion to being under Hades's dominion.

Last, Hermes in the *Hymn to Hermes* is clearly a trickster figure. He is clever, manipulative, very good at speech. He is very good at getting his own way by dazzling other people, or other gods, with the power of his rhetoric. This, too, would be a characteristic that would certainly be useful in a person associated with a god of exchange, particularly in a culture where barter is still very much a part of the exchange process. The ability to talk someone else into your view of things, to drive a good, clever bargain, very much works to underline Hermes's role as a god of exchange.

Along with these characteristics that I have been talking about—which are all, to some extent, highlighted in the *Homeric Hymn to Hermes*—Hermes was also associated with a very unusual kind of statue, very common in Ancient Greece, but very unlike other statues that came out of Ancient Greek culture. Hermes is associated with what are called *herms*. Those are pillars that stood in the marketplace, in front of private houses and often at crossroads. This association with this particular kind of pillar statue, called a *herm*, pretty clearly reflects Hermes's aspect as a god of boundaries. The *herm* was a marking pillar. It was a way to indicate: "This is where the marketplace begins and other parts of the city end," "This is where my property begins and my neighbor's ends," that sort of thing.

Hermes's association with these marking pillars, with *herms*, is probably the very oldest element of this god's essential character. The word *herm* originally just meant pile of stones in Greek. This means that the pillar, the pile of stones that was later schematized into a pillar, gave its name to the god, rather than the other way around. Hermes, in other words, at first, was probably simply a personification of a boundary marker, a personification of a boundary stone, or pile of stones, or a pillar.

Herms are, as I have been saying, pillars. They are very unusual pillars. They are topped with a very realistically carved head, anthropomorphic head, usually showing Hermes fully bearded. Despite the fact that he is a young god, he has a full beard. Other than that, the pillars are featureless— no hands, arms or legs—except that they also contain or feature an erect phallus about midway up the pillar. They are extremely unusual statues, both because other Greek statues of their gods were fully anthropomorphic, were carved to show their other gods' bodies presented as a beautiful human body, and very naturalistically done. In the case of *herm*s, we have a pillar with a head and a phallus and nothing else. The presence of the erect phallus on a *herm* is something of a puzzle to scholars. We don't really know why that aspect of the statue should have developed or should have been maintained. Its most obvious function, what you would think was going on with that, is that it was a symbol of fertility. That is a pretty easy guess to make; yet, Hermes is not, anywhere that we know of, associated with fertility. Whatever it is, it is probably not a symbol of fertility. That is not one of his areas of control or an important part of him.

Many scholars say that the presence of the phallus on the *herm* is supposed to be *apotropaic*. That is a word that simply means "turning away;" an *apotropaic* symbol is one that is supposed to turn evil away. Gargoyles on Gothic cathedrals are considered *apotropaic*; they are supposed to frighten away evil spirits. Maybe that is what the phallus on the *herm* was there for, but that leaves the question of why a phallus should be considered *apotropaic*. Why would it scare away evil spirits?

Burkert, the scholar I mentioned in earlier lectures who traces many elements of myth back to biological patterns of behavior, has made a very intriguing suggestion about this—again, one that cannot be proven but is at least worth considering. He suggests that this representation of Hermes, the pillar with a head and an erect phallus, has its origin in pre-human primate behavior. In certain monkey species, according to Burkert, males who guard their particular tribe, clan, flock or whatever we should call a group of monkeys, sit around the edges of the group facing outwards and their penises are erect as they sit there. Burkert theorizes that the *herm*, this representation of Hermes, is a reflection in human culture of this very archaic biological reality in which that is part of how a male guards his territory. His idea for why that should be so is that it is a symbol to other male monkeys, who may be thinking of invading the group to try to steal the females, that this group already has fertile males, "Back off; keep away; these females are spoken for."

If Burkert is right, then here we have an example of human culture reflecting an extremely ancient, pre-human primate behavior. It is a fascinating suggestion. I don't see any way that it could either be proven or disproved, and it certainly hasn't been accepted by every scholar who studies *herms*. Whatever the origin of the *herm*, they were important elements of public and private religion. Modern people talking about them tend to find them comical. We don't really know how to deal with this kind of statue so we tend to laugh at it. In ancient Athens, where we know most about their use and their function, they were anything but comical. Defacing a *herm* was considered a very serious offense, indeed. We know of at least one time this happened, when a group of rowdy young men, near the end of the fifth century B.C., got drunk one night, went around Athens and knocked all the phalluses off all the *herm*s. This was not considered amusing. This was not considered merely a matter of adolescent high spirits. It was taken very seriously as an act of sacrilege. The fact that we find these *herm*s amusing because of our own views of sexuality and nudity and so forth—they were not considered amusing in their own culture.

So much for Hermes, a god of exchange, of boundaries who is represented by this strange kind of statue. What about his brother Dionysos? When we turn to Dionysos, we are looking at perhaps the most complex and unusual god in the Olympian pantheon. He has power over, or his domains include, the fertility of plants; wine; frenzy; irrationality; and drama or theatre. It is hard to make a unified statement about Dionysos. He has so many different aspects. Perhaps the irrationality and frenzy is as close as we can get to isolating one characteristic essence of Dionysos.

As a god of plant fertility, the first element in his character that I mentioned, Dionysos complements Demeter. Demeter, as you remember, is the goddess of grain and the harvest. She is usually described as a goddess of controlled growth, the controlled growth of dry, self-contained plants. Dionysos is the god of wild, uncontrolled growth, of wet, moist, fruit-bearing plants like the grape, like the fig, and also of extremely rapid-growing, luxuriant plants such as ivy. He is often shown in art crowned with a wreath of ivy. If Demeter supervises controlled, dry plants, Dionysos supervises wild, uncontrolled, wet plants.

He is also associated with madness, frenzy and irrationality. In this aspect, he is directly opposed to his elder half-brother Apollo. This opposition is represented in myth by the idea that Apollo leaves Delphi each year during the winter months, and Dionysos takes up residence there instead. The idea that Apollo and Dionysos are somehow complementary to one another, mirror images of one another, is reflected in the idea that Dionysos, for part of the year, lives in the shrine that is normally associated with Apollo. Of course, very famously, Friedrich Nietzsche identified the Dionysian and the Apollonian as the two main strands of Greek thought that were constantly in tension with one another. In *The Birth of Tragedy,* Nietzsche saw these two elements as productive in many ways of Greek culture. The tension between the reason of Apollo and the irrationality of Dionysos, he thought, was one of the motivating forces of Greek culture.

Dionysos's connection with frenzy is represented in myth by the idea that he literally possesses his followers. He enters into them, possesses them and drives them mad, makes them do things that in their right minds they would never either consider doing or be able to do. In myth, Dionysos has two main groups of followers, a male group and a female group. His male followers are called "Satyrs," and they are creatures who are at least partly animal, mainly human but with some animal characteristics. In classical Greek art, they are normally shown as men with animal-like ears (that look like goat's or horse's ears) and a horse's tail. In later art, particularly Roman art, they are shown as human from the waist up, goat from the waist down. They are always male, and their main characteristics are drunkenness and extreme sexual aggressiveness.

Dionysos's female followers—in myth, not speaking in reality—are called Maenads. Those are human women who are under the influence of Dionysos, are driven entirely mad and are given unusual strength and unusual abilities. The Maenads are said to be able to tear animals apart with their bare hands and eat the flesh raw. They can handle snakes without suffering any harm. There is one very famous Greek painting of a Maenad who has a living snake wound around her head as a wreath or garland and is holding a leopard by the hind foot at the same time. They are also able to do things like making milk, honey and wine flow out of the ground when they hit it with a stick. They have both magical powers and extreme strength that allows them to tear an animal apart with their bare hands.

It is worth pointing out that, as far as we know, actual worship of Dionysos—worship of Dionysos done by actual, normal, every day humans—did not include ripping animals apart with one's bare hands or even eating raw meat, as far as we know. These frenzied celebrations in honor of Dionysos, these completely wild patterns of behavior in which the eating of raw animal flesh figures as a larger part, seem to have happened only in mythic stories about Dionysos, rather than in actual practice in his worship.

The most common definition of Dionysos, the thing that you will find if you go to that handbook of mythology I keep mentioning as a possibility, and look him up, the same place where you will find Apollo as the sun, you will find Dionysos as the god of wine. He is certainly associated with wine; that is an association that unites his rule over growing plants with his attribute of frenzy and irrationality, because obviously wine, taken in large amounts, drives one into irrational and mad or even manic behavior. Dionysos is said to have invented wine. In that regard, he is a beneficent god to human beings. Wine is considered a very great good; it was the main drink of classical culture. He is also a very dangerous god, because he can inflict irrationality upon his followers.

Finally, Dionysos is also the patron god of theatre, though the exact reason for his connection with drama is still a matter of scholarly debate. We know that both tragedy and comedy were performed in Athens at festivals in honor of Dionysos, and tragedy and comedy were both originally purely Athenian phenomena. They were invented in Athens; they were performed in Athens. We know that they were performed at festivals in honor of Dionysos specifically, and only at festivals in honor of Dionysos. There was no way in which theatre was performed year-round in a secular context. Theatre was part of a celebration in honor of Dionysos. But why were tragedy and comedy performed at festivals in honor of Dionysos? Here is where the scholarly consensus is not so easy to come to.

One theory is that tragedy and comedy both developed out of rituals in honor of Dionysos. There were originally rituals performed for the god and those took on a dramatic character as time progressed. Drama then detached itself from its purely ritual function and became a matter of playwrights writing plays that were performed in honor of Dionysos, because they had originated in rituals in honor of Dionysos. This could be so. The problem is there is very little evidence of such ritual origins in the surviving plays themselves. Most of the tragedies written by the three great Greek tragedians, Aeschylus, Sophocles and Euripides, have nothing whatsoever to do with Dionysos. Most of the plots do not involve Dionysos, and in some of the plays, he is not even mentioned. The one exception, Euripides's play *Bacchae*, is about Dionysos. He is the main character in it, but it is the only one that is about him.

The mere fact that the plays were performed at festivals in honor of Dionysos does not prove that they must have originated in rituals in his honor. The Homeric epics the *Iliad* and the *Odyssey* were recited at festivals in honor of Athena, for instance, but no one has ever suggested that those epics developed out of rituals held to worship Athena. At the very least, we can say that a god whose domain contains possession—behavior inconsistent with one's normal character, acting out of things that one would not normally do—is an appropriate god to be associated with a theatrical tradition in which the actors wore masks, in which an actor actually put on the face of another character before taking part in a drama. It may simply be that Dionysos is seen as the appropriate god to supervise an art form in which people are acting as something that they are not. Other than that, I don't think the exact origin of drama has yet been fully explained.

Along with his unusual association with irrationality and frenzy, many aspects of Dionysos's story are unusual or even unique among the Olympian gods. The first such aspect is his birth from a human mother. Normally, the offspring of a god and a human is a human, and so Dionysos should have been. He was the offspring of a sexual union between Zeus and a human named Semele. And yet, Dionysos is a god. The reason for this originates in Hera's jealousy over Semele's affair with Zeus. Hera disguised herself as Semele's old nanny, went to visit the girl and persuaded her that she needed proof from her lover that he was, indeed, Zeus. Hera suggested to Semele that her lover might be a human being who was simply saying he was Zeus in order to seduce her, and suggested that Semele should inveigle Zeus into swearing on the River Styx that he would do whatever she asks. Then, once he has promised, she should ask him to show himself to her in his full glory as he appears to Hera on Mount Olympus.

Semele followed the advice of, as she thought, her nanny (in actuality, Hera); got Zeus to promise on the Styx that he would do whatever she liked; asked him to show himself to her in his full glory; when he regretfully did so, because he could not break his promise, Semele was incinerated. Remember, human flesh cannot withstand the sight of the gods in their full glory. Semele went up in a puff of smoke, but she was already pregnant with Dionysos. Zeus snatched the embryo from Semele's womb as Semele was being incinerated, implanted the embryo of Dionysos in his own thigh, and within a few months Dionysos was born out of the thigh of Zeus. This gives Dionysos his epithet "twice-born." He is often called the "twice-born god." And, apparently, it accounts for Dionysos's immortal status. I think the idea behind it is that it would be inappropriate for Zeus, the greatest of the gods, to produce a child out of his own body who was human rather than god. It is because of his gestation within the body of Zeus that Dionysos turns out as a god.

Throughout Greek myth, Dionysos and his worship seem to be somehow less "given" than those of any other god. There are several stories about people resisting the worship of this god. There are several stories about people not thinking that he really is a god. There are several stories that indicate that he somehow is a late arrival and is different from the other gods. One of the most famous of such stories involves Dionysos's cousin Pentheus, King of Thebes. (Did I mention that Semele was from Thebes? We have Thebes in this story again.) Semele's sisters did not believe, after her death, that she had ever had an affair with Zeus at all. They thought she had an affair with a human and had been punished by Zeus for claiming it was Zeus. Therefore, they and Dionysos's extended family did not think that Dionysos was a god at all.

In the play *Bacchae,* by Euripides, Dionysos comes to Thebes to prove his divinity—and to avenge the slight on his mother's honor. He does this by driving all the Theban women mad; and in their madness, they rip apart Pentheus, Dionysos's cousin who refuses to believe in him. Pentheus is ripped apart by his own mother and aunts, who think that he is a mountain lion. They are under an illusion that they are tearing apart a lion, when they are actually tearing apart Pentheus. By the end of the play *Bacchae*, Dionysos has proven his power, his divinity, and avenged the slight against his mother by those who say she was not the mother of a god, she did not have an affair with a god.

All of these aspects of Dionysos—the idea that his worship was somehow something that people resisted, that he was different, that he was born of a human mother, that he was a late addition to the pantheon of the gods, born after the other gods were already there—all of those aspects, scholars used to think, could be accounted for by the hypothesis that Dionysos really *was* a latecomer. There used to be a theory that seemed to make a great deal of sense, that Dionysos was actually a Near Eastern god, a god from Asia Minor, who had been brought into Greece, whose worship had been introduced into Greece, relatively late, and therefore he was seen as being different in kind. His worship was somehow different. He was seen as being a latecomer. He was seen as somehow being an invention—reflected in myth in the idea that he had a human mother.

This seemed to make perfectly logical sense; it was a very compelling theory. Unfortunately, recent archaeological evidence in the form of very early inscriptions has indicated that Dionysos was worshipped in Greece as early as the rest of the Olympians. Whatever he is, he does not seem to be a late arrival on the scene of the Olympian pantheon. The questions of why Dionysos is so different from the other gods and why he is represented as a latecomer to Greek myth are thus left open. Some scholars think that the representation of Dionysos as a latecomer reflects the Greeks' own discomfort with and distrust of irrationality and frenzy. They say this god is late, an addition, somehow not part of the original group of gods, as a way of distancing themselves from his irrationality and from the less attractive aspects of his worship. Another possibility is that Dionysos's association with young, verdant, rapidly growing things carries over into his myths and the idea that he himself is young, that is, a recent arrival in the pantheon. I don't think there is any definitive answer to account for the difference in character of Dionysos from the other gods. It is simply a given that we have to bear in mind when we look at him and his myths.

In this lecture, we have looked at Zeus's two youngest sons, Hermes and Dionysos, and described some of their essential attributes. In the next lecture, we will talk about the one remaining crucially important Olympian deity, Aphrodite, the goddess of sexual passion.

Laughter-Loving Aphrodite
Lecture 11

What about a goddess bearing a human child? What about the idea that Aphrodite will now be pregnant with a human baby, will give birth to a mortal child, will bear a son who will live for 60 or 70 years at most and then die? This is seen as degrading, as beneath a goddess's dignity.

Our last key deity is Aphrodite, the goddess of sexual passion and desire. According to *Theogony*, Aphrodite was born from the foam that appeared around the severed genitals of Ouranos when Cronos tossed them into the sea. In the *Iliad*, she is the daughter of Zeus and a goddess named Dione. In either case, she is usually depicted as among the younger Olympians, in the same generation as Athena and Artemis, rather than Hestia, Hera, and Demeter. As the goddess of sexual desire, she is extremely powerful. She can and does subdue even Zeus to her will. The only beings she cannot touch are the three virgin goddesses, Hestia, Artemis, and Athena. She is the goddess of sexual passion, not love or companionship.

Aphrodite appears in many works of literature. However, for understanding of her essential nature, once again a *Homeric Hymn* is our starting point. The *Homeric Hymn to Aphrodite* tells the story of her sexual encounter with the human Anchises. This affair is attested elsewhere in literature, because it resulted in a son, Aeneas, the title character of Virgil's epic *The Aeneid*. Aphrodite's maternal relation to Aeneas also appears in the *Iliad*. The *Homeric Hymn*, however, concentrates on the relationship between Aphrodite and Anchises; the birth of Aeneas is predicted but is not the focus of the work.

The *Homeric Hymn* begins by stating that Zeus was angry at Aphrodite for causing him and other gods to become sexually involved with humans.

The *Homeric Hymn* begins by stating that Zeus was angry at Aphrodite for causing him and other gods to become sexually involved with humans;

Botticelli's *Nascita di Venere* depicts the birth of Aphrodite (called Venus by the Romans), the goddess of sexual passion and desire.

therefore, he decided to give her a taste of her own medicine. Zeus's reaction implies that sexual involvement with humans is beneath the gods' dignity, something that they regret afterward. Another implication involves the separate spheres of influence of the gods and Zeus's relationship to them. Usually, one god either cannot or does not trespass on another god's sphere of influence. Aphrodite does not cause earthquakes, Poseidon does not inspire people with sexual passion, and so on. This respect for the boundaries of one another's spheres probably stems from the fact that these gods *embody* the emotions and activities they govern. Aphrodite, in a sense, *is* sexual passion. However, Zeus is able to inflict Aphrodite with her own essence.

Zeus inspires Aphrodite with passion for the young Trojan prince Anchises, whom she seduces. Aphrodite appears before Anchises in disguise as a young girl and tells him that she is destined to be his bride. Anchises recognizes that she is a goddess and asks her for appropriate and proper blessings, but he believes her when she says she is human and agrees to go to bed with her immediately. Anchises's words embody the maxims of Delphi; he remembers his own status and is careful not to ask for excessive blessings. His adherence to these maxims does not protect him; Aphrodite lies to him to get her way. After the two have sex, Aphrodite reveals herself to Anchises and admits that she is a goddess. Anchises is terrified and begs for mercy.

Anchises's statement that men who have sex with goddesses are never left unharmed has several implications for our understanding of the narrative and of Greek society. Gods and mortals can interbreed; their offspring are human but usually exceptional. Although mating with a god often has disastrous consequences for a woman, these consequences are not inevitable, and some women who mate with gods live normal lives afterward. Anchises articulates the idea that men who mate with goddesses have committed a great transgression.

The reason for this imbalance has to do with views of sexuality and gender roles and with the nature of the relationship between gods and humans. Sex is seen in Greek culture as a process of domination. The male penetrator dominates his partner. Because Greek culture was strongly patriarchal and women were supposed to be subservient, this paradigm of sexuality was considered appropriate for male-female relationships. During sex, the man was dominant and the woman submissive, which was "how it should be." When sex occurs between a god and a human, the gender of each partner becomes very important. If a male god has sex with a mortal woman, there is no imbalance; a more powerful being (god, male) is dominating a less powerful one (human, female). When the male is human and the female is a goddess, the relationship is contradictory, because a less powerful human is dominating a more powerful goddess. Furthermore, when a god and human mate, a child always results. Again, if the female is the human, this causes no discomfort to the gods. Her child is still human but greater, more beautiful, more excellent than would otherwise have been the case. For a goddess to bear a human child to a mortal father is disgraceful, even (one senses from Aphrodite's words) disgusting.

Aphrodite's attempt to reassure Anchises falls flat, because she tells him about Tithonos. Tithonos was the lover of the dawn goddess Eos, who wanted to keep him forever. Eos gave Tithonos eternal life but forgot eternal youth. Thus, Tithonos grows older forever, until finally Eos shuts him away into a room and only his voice is left. This story is a chilling example of a recurring theme in Greek myth—humans may desire immortality, but it is not appropriate for us. The *Hymn* does not tell us whether Anchises was harmed. Other sources tell us that Anchises revealed who his son's mother was and was lamed as a result. Aphrodite's other human lover, the beautiful youth Adonis, died as a result of their affair.

We can isolate the following characteristics of sexual passion as delineated in the *Homeric Hymn to Aphrodite*: Sexual passion is seen as an external force, imposed on humans (or gods, or animals). Passion is, by its nature, transitory. You may feel passion for one person today, but another person next year or next week or even tomorrow. Sexual passion is not, in itself, emotionally significant; this is far different from our own conception. Sappho's one extant complete poem asks for help from Aphrodite, a compelling image of sexuality as an outside force. Later authors give an emotional significance to sexual passion that is absent in the earlier works. Ovid's story of Pyramus and Thisbe, a pair of suicidal lovers, is a good example. Aphrodite remains a capricious goddess of passion rather than one of devoted, long-lasting love.

Aphrodite is an excellent goddess through whom to contemplate some of the implications of gods who are personifications of natural forces. With this type of god, "belief" is not a matter of debate the way it is in a monotheistic religion. To ask, "Do you believe in Aphrodite?" is, on one level, as absurd as asking, "Do you believe that sexual attraction exists?" The question of whether personification is an appropriate way to represent these forces remains, and some classical authors would answer that it is not. Aphrodite also illustrates the irrelevance of expecting compassion, mercy, or pity from personified natural forces. Inappropriate sexual desire can devastate and destroy innocent lives, just as Aphrodite does. We can see a similar phenomenon in Dionysos; misuse of wine can destroy, and it is useless to ask the wine to feel pity. The personification of these natural forces carries with it a certain contradiction; as sentient beings, the gods should be able to act compassionately, but as natural forces, they cannot. ■

Essential Reading

Homeric Hymn to Aphrodite.

Ovid, *Metamorphoses*, pp. 83–86 ("Pyramus and Thisbe").

Sappho, *Hymn to Aphrodite.*

Questions to Consider

1. We have seen that it is considered acceptable for a god to mate with a human woman and for her to bear his children, but it is inappropriate for a goddess to mate with a human man. Can you think of any analogs to this system, in which gender relationships are factored into a wider pattern of supposed superiority and inferiority?

2. In their aspect as personified natural forces, the Greek gods do not feel pity or show mercy. What are the implications of this for their "personalities"? Do they end up being *less* admirable than human beings, in some sense?

Laughter-Loving Aphrodite
Lecture 11—Transcript

In the previous lecture, we looked at Hermes and Dionysos, Zeus's two youngest sons among the Olympians. In this lecture, we are going to conclude our discussion of individual gods and goddesses and their individual functions by looking at Aphrodite, the goddess of sexual passion and desire.

According to *Theogony,* as you will remember, Aphrodite was born in the foam that appeared around Ouranos's severed genitals when Cronos tossed them into the sea. That is one version of her birth story. According to another, which appears in the *Iliad*, she is the daughter of Zeus and a goddess named Dione. Like many other gods, Aphrodite has at least two versions of how she came into existence. Whichever version is followed, she is normally portrayed as a young woman at the high point of sexual attractiveness. If Hesiod's version of her birth is followed, then actually she is one of the very oldest of goddesses, but she is not portrayed as a mature woman, unlike Hera, Demeter or Hestia. She is portrayed as a young woman, which makes sense for a goddess who personifies sexual desire.

As the goddess of sexual desire, Aphrodite is extremely powerful. She can and does subdue even Zeus to her will. She can inflict sexual desire on Zeus, make him have affairs with mortal women, with other goddesses, with whomever she wants him to have an affair with. The only beings she cannot touch are the three virgin goddesses: Hestia, Artemis and Athena. They are sacred, immune to Aphrodite, but every other living being—god, human and animal—is vulnerable to Aphrodite's power. By the way, I call her the goddess of sexual desire or passion, rather than the goddess of love, as she is so often described, because I don't think she *is* a goddess of love. She is not a goddess of affection or devotion or lifelong companionship or soulmates. She is a goddess of sexual passion, which, as we will see later in the lecture, can be a remarkably transitory thing in Greek myth.

Aphrodite appears in many, many works of literature. It might almost be safe to say in most works of ancient literature there is at least some reference to her. However, for understanding her essential nature, once again, we are going to turn to a Homeric Hymn as our starting point. The *Homeric Hymn to Aphrodite* recounts the story of Aphrodite's affair, or sexual encounter, with a human man named Anchises. This affair is well-attested elsewhere in ancient literature because the son that resulted from it was Aeneas, the hero of Virgil's epic *The Aeneid,* and supposedly the ancestor of the Roman race. Elsewhere in literature, we hear mentioned the idea that Aphrodite had an affair with Anchises and by it conceived a son, Aeneas. This is mentioned not just in *The Aeneid,* but also in Homer's *Iliad.* However, in the *Homeric Hymn,* the author concentrates not on Aeneas, the offspring of the union, though he is mentioned near the end of the poem. Rather, the *Homeric Hymn* concentrates on the affair itself, on Aphrodite's encounter with Anchises.

The *Hymn* begins by stating that Zeus was angry at Aphrodite for causing him and other gods to become sexually involved with humans. Zeus resented this, was angry about it, and therefore decided to give Aphrodite a taste of her own medicine, so to speak. One implication of this is that Zeus and the other gods see sexual relations with humans as somehow beneath their dignity, somehow degrading. Zeus is angry at Aphrodite because she makes him take part in these encounters, which he regrets later as being beneath his dignity. Another implication of the idea that Zeus punishes Aphrodite by infecting her with desire for Anchises has to do with the idea of gods having separate spheres of influence. Normally, in Greek myth, the gods do not trespass on one another's domains. Aphrodite does not cause earthquakes. Poseidon does not imbue people with sexual passion. Hermes does not shoot arrows that kill men suddenly. The gods tend, by and large, to respect one another's separate spheres of influence.

This respecting the boundaries of influence probably has to do with the fact that these gods embody, or personify, the emotions and activities they govern. In other words, there is a sense in which Aphrodite *is* sexual passion. She is sexual passion itself given a visible, tangible body. Zeus, as the ruler of the gods, has the ability, though the *Hymn* doesn't explain how, to inflict sexual passion itself—or herself—with sexual passion. He turns Aphrodite's powers against her; he makes her feel irresistible desire for Anchises as she, Aphrodite, has so often made Zeus feel irresistible desire for many different human women.

Zeus inspires Aphrodite with passion for the young Trojan prince, Anchises, whom she will seduce. This happens, by the way, in the generation before the Trojan War. Anchises is a young man at this point; he is an old man during the time the Trojan War takes place. Aphrodite appears before Anchises in disguise as a young girl and tells him that she is destined to be his bride. Remember, gods and goddesses can appear in any form they choose. Demeter, for instance, appears in the *Homeric Hymn* before Metaneira as an old woman. Here Aphrodite disguises herself as a young girl, just at the right age for marriage—just about 13 or 14 years old. She tells Anchises that Hermes had picked her up in her own native land and literally carried her to where Anchises is, and put her down in front of him, and she tells him that he is supposed to marry her. Anchises recognizes from Aphrodite's extraordinary beauty that she must be a goddess, and the first thing he says to her is to ask her for appropriate blessings. However, once she tells him she is a human being, he allows himself to be persuaded, because she is so beautiful and so desirable that he would like to think she is a human being.

The first thing he says to Aphrodite, when he sees her, embodies the maxims of Delphi in a very interesting way. Anchises both remembers his own status as a human and is careful not to ask for excessive blessings from this goddess—and and he is sure she is a goddess who has appeared before him. He looks at her and he says, "Lady, welcome to this house, whoever of the blessed ones you are: / whether you are Artemis, or Leto, or golden Aphrodite, / or well-born Themis, or gray-eyed Athena"—and then he goes on and names several other goddesses just to make sure not to insult anyone by leaving her out. Then, he says:

> Upon a lofty peak, which can be seen from all around,
> I shall make you an altar and offer you fair sacrifices
> in all seasons. And with kindly heart grant me
> to be an eminent man among the Trojans,
> to leave flourishing offspring behind me,
> and to live long and behold the light of the sun,
> prospering among the people and so reach ... old age.

I have always found that particular prayer, as I said, to be a perfect embodiment of what it is appropriate for a human to ask for. He doesn't ask for 14 or

20 or 25 children. He just asks for flourishing offspring, offspring who will survive. He doesn't ask for a lifespan of 200 years, he just asks to reach old age. He doesn't ask for exceptional riches, he just asks to be prosperous. He is doing exactly what he ought to do, honoring the goddess and asking her for blessings that are appropriate to his status as a human being.

Anchises's adherence to the Delphic maxims, his ability to know himself and to avoid excess, does not protect him. Aphrodite lies to him in order to get her own way despite the fact that she knows it will have bad consequences for him, as we will see in a few minutes. Aphrodite persuades Anchises that she is indeed a human being and, as I said, tells him that he is supposed to marry her. I always feel sorry for Anchises at this point of the *Homeric Hymn*; the poor man hasn't got a chance. Sexual passion itself is standing there in front of him bent on seducing him. There is no way he could avoid going to bed with Aphrodite, and, in fact, he doesn't avoid it. After she has persuaded him that she really is a human, he says in effect, "Great, I'll marry you, but let's go to bed *right now*," which, of course, is what she too has in mind. After the two have sex, after Aphrodite and Anchises go to bed together, Anchises falls asleep. Aphrodite wakes him by revealing herself to him as a goddess. She doesn't reveal herself to him in her full true form, of course, or he would be incinerated. But, she does show enough of her glory that it is quite clear she's not a human. For instance, her head brushes the roof beam of the building they are in, and she asks him, "Do I look the same way as I looked before?"

Anchises is terrified when he realizes that he has, in fact, slept with a goddess, and he asks her for mercy in very interesting words. He says,

> Goddess, as soon as I saw you …
> I knew you were divine, but you did not tell the truth.
> Yet by … Zeus I beseech you
> not to let me live impotent among men,
> but have mercy on me; for the man who lies
> with immortal goddesses is not left unharmed.

"The man who lies with immortal goddesses is not left unharmed." That is a very interesting statement, and I think it has important implications for our understanding of the *Hymn,* and again, for our wider understanding of the culture that developed these myths.

Gods and mortals can interbreed. Their offspring are human, but they are usually exceptional humans, more beautiful, more noble, braver, something like that, than everyday humans. While mating with a god often has disastrous consequences for a human woman, it does not inevitably lead to disaster. There are stories of human women who have sex with a god, bear his child, and continue to live perfectly normal, uneventful and even happy lives. Alcmene, the mother of Heracles, would be one of the examples of such a woman. When Anchises says the man who lies with immortal goddesses is not left unharmed, he is not stating a principle that holds for humans, in general, when they lie with divinities. He is talking specifically about male humans who have sex with female divinities. There must be something about that particular combination, male human with female goddess, that comprises a very great transgression.

To understand why that is a transgression, the imbalance and the consequences for female and male humans of sex with a divinity, we have to look again at Greek views of sexuality and gender roles, and at the nature of the relationship between gods and humans. In Greek culture, as I mentioned briefly when we were discussing Artemis, sex—sexual intercourse itself—is seen as an act of domination. The active partner dominates the passive partner. I put it that way, rather than saying the male dominates the female, because many parts of Greek culture, including Athenian society in the fifth century B.C., accepted certain forms of homosexual behavior. Homosexual behavior was acceptable, so long as the active partner, the penetrating partner, was a mature man and the passive partner, the penetrated partner, was an adolescent boy. In other words, what was seen as crucial was who was penetrating whom, who was dominating whom. Domination, penetration, are appropriate activities for an adult male. The partner who takes the passive role and is penetrated is seen as being in some sense feminized by that act.

This was appropriate for an adolescent boy, a boy whose beard had not yet grown, because he was not yet considered a fully adult male. Greek culture did despise and look down on adult males who took the passive role in a homosexual relationship, who allowed themselves to be penetrated. Rather than the gender of the partners involved being the crucial element of sexuality as the Greeks understood it, the crucial element is who is dominant and who is submissive—who is penetrating and who is being penetrated.

In a heterosexual relationship, in a male-female relationship, there is no problem at all, because men are seen as dominant by nature, women are seen as submissive by nature. Therefore, in the sexual act, when a man penetrates a woman, the already dominant partner is dominating the already submissive partner. No problem; that is how, according to Greek culture, it ought to be. That is the "natural" order of things. When sex occurs between a god and a human, then the gender of each partner suddenly becomes very important. If a male god, say Zeus, has sex with a female human, say Alcmene or Semele, there is no problem. The superior partner is dominating the inferior partner. The god is dominating the human, the male is dominating the female, no problem. The female may suffer disastrous consequences like Semele does, but it is not inevitable because she has not committed any transgression of the proper boundaries of behavior between gods and humans. What happens when the male is human and the divinity is the female? Then we have a real contradiction in terms in the relationship as it is seen in Greek culture. We have a male dominating a female, so far so good. But we have a human dominating a goddess. So far, so very not good, indeed. That is the problem. By having sex with Aphrodite, Anchises has dominated, asserted authority over, put himself in the superior role with regard to, a goddess, and that is why he is terrified. That is without question a transgression.

Furthermore, when a god and human mate, a child always results. There was even a proverb about that, which is usually translated something along the lines of: "The unions of the gods are always fruitful." When a god and human mate there is always a child conceived, without exception, as far as I know. Again, the gender of the two partners, which one is the human, becomes very important here as well. If the human is female, then there is no inherent problem in her conceiving a child to a god. Her child will be greater than he would otherwise have been. (I say "he" because it almost always is a "he." Sometimes it is a "she" as in Helen of Troy, but usually the child of a god and a human is male.) For a human mother to bear Heracles, for instance, is better than for her to bear a normal human child. She gets a child who is more glorious and is better in most regards than the child she otherwise would have borne. So, no problem.

What about a goddess bearing a human child? What about the idea that Aphrodite will now be pregnant with a human baby, will give birth to a mortal child, will bear a son who will live for 60 or 70 years at most and then die? This is seen as degrading, as beneath a goddess's dignity. In fact, in the *Hymn*, Aphrodite talks to Anchises about this. She tries to reassure him. She says he won't be harmed as long as he doesn't tell anyone who the mother of his son is. She says once the child is born, she will bring him to Anchises, leave him with Anchises and Anchises must not tell that Aphrodite is his mother. Aphrodite puts this in very strong terms. She says that she will name the child Aeneas, which is related to the term for grief, because great grief has seized her over the fact that she shared a bed with a human. And, she puts it in terms that seem to indicate that she is disgusted with the idea already, very quickly; a morning-after reaction that she is already disgusted with the fact that she slept with Anchises and conceived a son with him.

Aphrodite's attempt to reassure Anchises in the *Homeric Hymn* falls very flat, indeed, because she tells him as the main thread of her attempt to reassure him the story of his kinsman Tithonos. She says, "Your family has always been particularly appealing to the gods, we really like you, the Trojan royal family. Remember Tithonos, a kinsman of yours, and the dawn goddess Eos?" To try to reassure Anchises that he need not worry about being harmed, she recounts the story. It is a horrifying story indeed.

Eos, the dawn goddess, had an affair with the human Tithonos. She wanted to keep him around, she enjoyed him so much that she wanted to make him immortal, and she did make him immortal, but she forgot to make him ageless. Tithonos lives forever. Tithonos cannot die. Tithonos has mortality taken away from him but he continues to age, he grows older and older and older until, eventually, there is nothing left of him but a voice—a complaining voice which Eos shuts away in a back chamber of her palace so she won't have to pay any more attention to him.

As reassuring stories go, this one is remarkably unreassuring. It also is a very good example of a theme that occurs over and over in Greek myth, the idea that humans may desire immortality, we may think that we want immortality, but it doesn't work for us, we are not that kind of creature. There are various stories about humans who attempt to gain immortality, and it almost always results in total disaster. Tithonos is one of the worst examples, because he gets older and older forever. He is still there, he can't die—he will never die—but he continues to age. There are similar stories. There is one about a female lover of Apollo, the Sybil, who, when she was in Apollo's good graces asked for as many years of life as there were grains of sand on the shore of the sea. This was granted her but eternal youth was again left out, and when the Sybil angered Apollo he intentionally kept eternal youth back from her. She too grows older and older. She will eventually die. The grains of sand are finite, but it is going to take a very long time. There are stories about her in which she has withered away into a little thing that sits in a cage. Boys go by and torment her by asking her, "Sybil, what do you want?" and her one and only answer is, "I want to die."

Very grim stories about the attempt to get immortality. Aphrodite, as I have said before, tells Anchises he won't be harmed if he keeps the secret of who Aeneas's mother actually is. Apparently, he did not keep the secret. For one thing, we know who Aeneas's mother was. The *Hymn* seems to imply that Anchises did indeed tell someone. Also, other sources tell us that Anchises did reveal that Aphrodite was his son's mother—it would be awfully hard not to brag about having had an affair with Aphrodite herself—and that he was in fact harmed, he was lamed, crippled, after his encounter with Aphrodite.

Aphrodite has other human lovers—most notably the human Adonis, who is killed because of his affair with Aphrodite. The idea that human men are harmed by sexual relationships with goddesses is reiterated over and over again in almost every circumstance in which such a relationship occurs.

Looking at Aphrodite as she is presented in the *Homeric Hymn*, we can isolate the following characteristics of sexual passion as she represents it. Sexual passion is seen as an external force, something that comes swooping in from the outside, grabs you, makes you crazy, and makes you do things you normally would not do. It is also seen as being by nature transitory. This is not a lasting, emotionally significant relationship that Aphrodite inflicts on gods and humans. It is a transitory madness. I am using "madness" because it is often described that way in Greek literature, as madness or sickness. The transitoriness of it is one of its main identifying characteristics. You may feel it one day for one person, next year, next week or even tomorrow for someone entirely different. The idea that we have in our culture, that sexual attraction is a lasting emotional state on which a marriage can and should be based, would have struck the ancient Greeks as the rankest insanity. That—the idea that it could be stable and lasting enough to base a marriage on it—simply is not there.

One of the clearest articulations I know of, of the Greek view of sexual passion, happens to be the one complete poem that has remained by the ancient Greek poet, Sappho, one of the few female writers we know of from antiquity, who lived in the early sixth century B.C. and wrote poems about and to other women, as far as we can tell. Her one complete poem that has survived is often called the *Hymn to Aphrodite,* and in it, Sappho asks Aphrodite for help in seducing the current object of her passion. This is a translation of the poem that I did a couple of years back that I would like to read to you, because I think it points out some very important aspects of Aphrodite and of sexual passion.

So, Sappho says:

> Iridescent-throned Aphrodite, deathless
> Child of Zeus, wile-weaver, I now implore you,
> Don't—I beg you, Lady—with pains and torments
> Crush down my spirit,
>
> But before if ever you've heard my pleadings,
> Then return, as once when you left your father's
> Golden house; you yoked to your shining car your
> Wing-whirring sparrows;
>
> Skimming down the paths of the sky's bright ether,
> On they brought you over the earth's black bosom,
> Swiftly—then you stood with a sudden brilliance,
> Goddess, before me;

Deathless face alight with your smile, you asked me

What I suffered, who was my cause of anguish,

What would ease the pain of my frantic mind, and

Why had I called you
To my side. "And whom should Persuasion summon
Here to soothe the sting of your passion this time?
Who is now abusing you, Sappho? Who is
Treating you cruelly?

Now she runs away, but she'll soon pursue you;
Gifts she now rejects—soon enough she'll give them;
Now she doesn't love you, but soon her heart will
Burn, though unwilling."

Come to me once more, and abate my torment;
Take the bitter care from my mind, and give me
All I long for; Lady, in all my battles
Fight as my comrade.

Notice what Sappho does not say. She does not say, "I am so emotionally bound to this person I cannot live without her." She does not say, "This is my one and only true love." She says, "Come to me again, help me this time, be my comrade in all my battles." The image of Aphrodite swooping down from Mount Olympus to help her devotee, to cause the object of Sappho's desire to return the desire, I think is a very compelling image of sexuality as an outside force imposed on us that comes for a while, then goes away and leaves us alone until the next time it comes and infects us.

Later authors do give an emotional significance to sexual passion that is absent in the *Homeric Hymn to Aphrodite*, in Sappho and in earlier and classical Greek works. By the time we get to Roman authors, such as Ovid, whose *Metamorphoses* I have mentioned before in this course, we find an idea that sexual passion can be emotionally significant; or, rather, that a significant emotional state can include sexual passion as one of its components. Ovid tells the story, for instance, of Pyramus and Thisbe, a young couple who are forbidden to marry by their parents, who run away together and who end up committing suicide: Pyramus when he thinks Thisbe is dead, Thisbe when she discovers Pyramus's body. Yes, very much like Romeo and Juliet. Even in Ovid's account where emotional, romantic love seems to be taken as a significant relationship which could be a basis for marriage, sexual passion itself, and Aphrodite as the embodiment of it, remain capricious, rather than Aphrodite being a goddess of devoted, long-lasting love.

The last thing I want to look at in this lecture on Aphrodite is the way she works as an example through which we can explore the question—which I am very frequently asked by students—of whether the ancient Greeks actually believed in these gods or not. That strikes many modern people as a very crucial question about a religious system. I'd like to use Aphrodite as a means to discuss it, because I think she gives us a very good insight into the way in which that question is almost unaskable with this kind of god.

With gods who are personifications of natural forces, the question of belief is not really a matter of debate, is not something that comes up as it does in a monotheistic religion. Aphrodite personifies sexual passion, controls sexual passion. If we could summon up a fifth-, sixth- or seventh-century B.C. Greek person, and ask him or her, "Do you believe in Aphrodite," there is a sense in which that would be as foolish a question as if I looked at you and asked, "Tell me, is there such a thing as sexual passion? Do you think it exists?" The question is ludicrous; of course, there is such a thing as sexual passion. Of course, it exists. In a system in which gods and goddesses like Aphrodite are personifications of that kind of natural force, to ask, "Do you believe in Aphrodite, do you think such a thing as Aphrodite exists?" is as meaningless or silly as asking, "Do you think such a thing as sexual passion exists?" Of course, they exist. All human experience tells us they exist.

The question of whether personification is an appropriate way to represent these forces of nature, that is a question that can indeed be asked. As philosophy developed in Athens in the fifth and fourth centuries B.C., thinkers did begin to question, "Is personification an appropriate way to represent these forces of nature?" The question of belief that is so crucial in monotheistic religions, that, in fact, is the defining point of monotheistic religions—if you do not believe in Christ, you are not a Christian; if you do not believe in Allah, you are not a Muslim—that kind of question simply doesn't apply in a polytheistic system such as we have with the Olympian gods.

Aphrodite is also an excellent illustration of the irrelevance—not just the futility, but the irrelevance—of expecting compassion, mercy or pity from this kind of personified natural force. It is a reality of human experience, regret it though we may, that inappropriate sexual desire can devastate and destroy innocent lives. We see that all the time. I am sure everyone has some experience of that through friends, at least, if not in their own lives. Similarly, if we look at Dionysos, it is a sad fact of human experience that inappropriate use of alcohol, wine, can devastate, destroy innocent human lives. It is meaningless to ask Aphrodite to feel pity or mercy, or to ask Dionysos to feel pity or mercy when we think of them of personifications of sexual passion, of wine. They can destroy us, they do destroy us, they feel no mercy for us—that is what they are, that is what they do. That is the kind of entity they are.

That means that the personification of these natural forces carries with it a kind of contradiction, built into the system as it were. As sentient beings, Aphrodite, Dionysos and the rest ought to be able to feel pity. The fact that they cannot makes them in some sense less than, not greater than, humans. It is this kind of contradiction—this sense that sentient beings should be able to feel pity, and yet these personified natural forces can't and don't—that contradiction starts to be explored in some of the great literature of the fifth century B.C. and in philosophy as well.

In this lecture, we have finished our survey of individual Olympian deities. In the next lecture, we are going to take a slightly different tack and step back a bit from Greek culture, and look at the cultural and historical background that is at play in some of the myths that we have studied so far.

Culture, Prehistory, and the "Great Goddess"
Lecture 12

In the previous lecture, we finished our discussion of individual gods and goddesses with an examination of Aphrodite and her role as the embodiment of sexual passion. In this lecture, we are going to look at the possible cultural and historical background material that may have helped to shape the myths we have been discussing so far. We will consider the similarities between Mesopotamian myths and the myths we have seen so far, in *Theogony* in particular.

At this point, we can consider the backgrounds of the Greek gods and goddesses. No culture exists in a vacuum; Greek religion and mythology must have been influenced by other cultures with which the Greeks came in contact. In polytheism, new gods and myths are easily accommodated. A culture's mythology does not simply appear all at once; the myths must have been influenced by events in Greece's prehistory. Determining the exact nature of such influences, across cultures or through time, is extremely difficult. We will take the question of a prehistoric "great goddess" as a test case.

The Greek creation myths recounted by Hesiod share many points in common with Mesopotamian creation myths. To take just one example, the Hesiodic story of Cronos shows strong parallels with the Mesopotamian story of Kumarbi. Cronos and Kumarbi are both sons of a god whose name means "sky" (Ouranos, Anush). Each gains power by castrating his father. Each is in turn overthrown by a younger god who is associated with storms (Zeus, Teshub). This parallel demonstrates a relationship between the myths of these two cultures, through direct influence or through derivation from a common source. However, the details differ from culture to culture. Kumarbi castrates Anush by biting off his genitals; Cronos castrates Ouranos with a sickle provided by Gaia. Kumarbi swallows Anush's genitals and becomes pregnant; he bears Teshub through his penis. Kronos swallows his children (who have been conceived and born normally), then spits them out.

The other important formative influences behind Greek myth were the prehistoric cultures of Greece itself, the Minoan and Mycenaean cultures. Minoan culture was located on Crete and the nearby island of Santorini. One of the great archaeological discoveries of the late 19th and early 20th centuries was the uncovering of Minoan civilization, which reached its high point from about 2000 to about 1470 B.C. Sir Arthur Evans set out to demonstrate that the myths that recalled a great thalossocracy ("sea-based kingdom") on Crete had some basis in fact. At Knossos, Evans found extensive ruins of a huge palace, which he associated with King Minos of myth. From this, the culture he uncovered came to be called "Minoan." Evans had found evidence that there had indeed been a great seafaring culture based on Crete, just as the myths said.

Minoan culture is still a puzzle in many ways, mainly because the Minoans left little behind them in the way of written records.

Minoan culture is still a puzzle in many ways, mainly because the Minoans left little behind them in the way of written records. They did have two writing systems, Linear A and Linear B. Linear A has never been deciphered. Linear B was deciphered in the 1950s and turns out to be an ancient form of Greek. The records in this writing are inventories of palace supplies, which tell us little about the culture of the Minoan people. Furthermore, Linear B only came into use after the Minoans had come under the domination of the Greek-speaking Mycenaeans. Historians have to try to interpret the architecture, artifacts, and especially the art of Minoan Crete without the context that written works usually provide. Minoan culture is not known to be related to any other culture; thus, we cannot turn to the written records of other cultures to try to reconstruct Minoan myth. Minoan art shows many scenes that may be religious, but it is difficult to interpret these without any context to guide us.

The other great pre-classical civilization of Greece was the Mycenaean civilization, the direct ancestor of later Greek culture. Mycenaean civilization, which flourished from about 1600 to about 1050 B.C., was discovered by Heinrich Schliemann, who also excavated the site of Troy. He excavated Mycenae, Agamemnon's city, which had never been completely lost. He found other cities that clearly belonged to the same culture. These cities correspond astonishingly well geographically to the cities mentioned by Homer. The Mycenaeans were descendants of Indo-European migrants who came into Greece probably around 2200–2000 B.C. Their language was an early form of Greek. They gained dominance over Minoan culture by the 15th century B.C. The Minoan use of Linear B is one piece of evidence of this dominance. Like the Minoans, the Mycenaeans used Linear B mainly to make lists of supplies. After the fall of Mycenaean civilization during the 11th century, Greece entered its Dark Ages. Writing was not reintroduced until the 8th century. The fact that myths written down in the 8th century and later refer to Mycenaean cities must indicate cultural continuity through oral tradition. Therefore, it seems likely that some of the myths associated with those cities have their origins in Mycenaean culture. The Trojan War is the most obvious example.

How much can we plausibly deduce about prehistoric Greek religion and myth from our knowledge of these cultures? As a demonstration of the difficulties, let us look at the theory of the great mother goddess. There is a widespread modern belief that classical myth (and ancient European and Near Eastern myth in general) contains traces of a prehistoric, pre-Indo-European worship of the great mother goddess. Although this belief has become almost an article of faith for many modern people, the evidence for it is not straightforward. The primary problem is that of interpreting archaeological evidence without any written context to explain its use. The literary evidence often brought to bolster the claim of a proto-goddess is ambiguous at best. Many of the same objections can be made to the goddess theory as can be made to psychological explanations of myth. Female figurines are widespread throughout ancient European and Near Eastern cultures, but their interpretation is not straightforward. We have no compelling reason to assume that the figurines must represent goddesses. Even if they are goddesses, we have no reason to assume that they must represent the same or a single goddess.

Some of the widest-reaching claims about a great goddess are made for Minoan civilization, based largely on its art. Minoan art features powerful female figures. The most famous of these is the so-called Snake-Goddess. This arresting figure must have had some important significance in Minoan culture. But was she a goddess? Other possibilities have been dismissed with little consideration. Without knowing more about Minoan religion beyond the images preserved by art, we cannot know what the Snake-Goddess figurines represent. We cannot assume that every figurine must have been used for ritual or religious purposes; they may be decorative instead. We cannot deduce religious practice, let alone religious belief, from an image. Reasoning that tries to do so is often circular: "Because the Minoans worshipped a goddess, this must be her image. Because this is the image of a goddess, then Minoans must have worshipped her."

Some scholars read Hesiod's *Theogony* as providing evidence for a clash between Minoan religion, focused on a mother-goddess, and Indo-European religion, focused on a father-god, that was brought to Greece by the Mycenaeans. The three-generation struggle for power can be seen as reflecting the slow process of the newer culture (represented by the younger male gods) gaining power over the older (represented by the female mother goddesses). This reading of Hesiod is fascinating and can be very persuasive. It overlooks the fact that similar stories exist in Mesopotamian cultures in which no similar Indo-European invasion took place. One could just as persuasively explain the repeated pattern of a younger male gaining power from an older female in psychological terms, as reflecting the maturation of men and their rejection of their mothers' control. In short, if we assume that the Minoans worshipped a great mother goddess, *Theogony* can be seen as reflecting the ongoing process of her overthrow and assimilation. If we do not start from this assumption, *Theogony* will not lead us to it.

In sum, we have little good evidentiary reason to believe in an original great mother goddess for ancient Europe and the ancient Near East. The goddess hypothesis perhaps shows a monotheistic bias. Many modern Westerners find polytheism uncongenial and assume that it must be a later development out of a proto-monotheism. This assumption is ahistorical. We have no compelling reason to assume that all representations of a female divinity must be representations of the *same* female divinity, unless one starts from that assumption. In fact, the goddess may well be a modern myth, not an ancient one. She provides a "charter" for those women who find themselves dissatisfied with the patriarchal cast of much traditional religion. She reflects the common mythic sense of a Golden Age, a time in the remote past when things were much better. Thus, her adherents assume that goddess worship implies high status for women in society (despite much evidence to the contrary). The story of her defeat by the Indo-European sky-father-god provides an explanation, or aetiology, for how society came to be as it is. The great goddess is just one example of the pitfalls involved in trying to reconstruct the origins and development of classical myth. ■

Essential Reading

Oxford Classical Dictionary, entries on "Minoan civilization," "Mycenaean civilization," and "Religion, Minoan and Mycenaean."

Supplementary Reading

Fitton, *Discovery of the Greek Bronze Age.*

Gimbutas, *Living Goddesses*, Ch. 7 and 8. A succinct statement of the standard goddess-based interpretation.

Goodison and Morris, "Beyond the Great Mother."

Kirk, *Myth: Its Meaning and Function*, Ch. 5, sections 4–5, pp. 213–226.

Penglase, *Greek Myths and Mesopotamia.*

Pomeroy, *Goddesses, Whores, Wives, and Slaves*, pp. 13–15.

Tringham and Conkey, "Rethinking Figurines."

Wood, *In Search of the Trojan War.*

Questions to Consider

1. Can you think of any sort of evidence *other than* written material that could prove that the Minoans worshipped a great mother goddess?

2. I suggested that the modern belief that there was once a prehistoric great goddess functions in many of the ways that theorists have delineated for

myth. Can you think of any other modern beliefs about ancient history or prehistory that work in the same way?

Culture, Prehistory, and the "Great Goddess"
Lecture 12—Transcript

In the previous lecture, we finished our discussion of individual gods and goddesses with an examination of Aphrodite and her role as the embodiment of sexual passion. In this lecture, we are going to look at the possible cultural and historical background material that may have helped to shape the myths we have been discussing so far. We will consider the similarities between Mesopotamian myths and the myths we have seen so far, in *Theogony* in particular. We will also look at the possible influence of two great prehistoric cultures in and around Greece, the Minoan and Mycenaean cultures, and what we can and cannot theorize about their influence on Greek myth as it has come down to us.

No culture exists in a vacuum. Greek religion and Greek mythology must have been influenced to some extent by other cultures that were in the general area. Trade took place between ancient Greece and other cultures such as the Mesopotamian culture and Egyptian culture, and so on. When people meet to exchange goods and to take part in trade, they also, of course, talk to one another. They tell one another stories. There are all sorts of possibilities for cultural influence, for stories about gods and goddesses to be passed from one culture to another.

It is an important fact to understand about polytheism, that opposed to a monotheistic system, in which believers in one god have to say "if our god is true then your gods are false," in a polytheistic system, it is almost infinitely expandable. There is room for many more gods and many more myths. If you meet people who talk about a god you have never heard of before, that is not a difficulty in a polytheistic system. You simply say there is another god we have not heard of before. The possibility of cross-cultural borrowing between Greece and Mesopotamia, or Greece and Egypt, is much greater because Greece's religion was polytheistic than it might have been otherwise.

Furthermore, a culture's mythology does not appear complete and finished all at once. The myths as we have them developed over centuries and must, almost inevitably, have been influenced by events in Greece's prehistory. By prehistory, all I mean is the period before we have written records; that is, the period before about the eighth century B.C. The myths that have come down to us after Greece became literate have to have been influenced, to greater or lesser degrees, by the centuries before writing was introduced.

To greater or lesser degrees. However, determining the exact nature and extent of such influences—whether the cross-cultural extent of such influences of myths developed in other societies, or the historical influence through time of Greece's prehistory—to determine the exact extent of either of those kind of influences is extremely difficult, again almost by definition, since we are dealing with events that are not described for us in our written record. To try to examine the difficulties inherent in this kind of effort, I am going to take as a test case, the question, the idea of a prehistoric "great goddess," the idea that there was once a "great mother goddess" worshipped in Greece and in other cultures. At the end of this lecture, we will look at that supposition and see to what extent the evidence we have does or does not support it.

Let's begin by looking at the influence of Mesopotamian myth, in particular, on Greek myth. There is no longer any doubt that the Greek creation myths, as recounted by Hesiod, share a great many points in common with Mesopotamian creation myths. The literature of Mesopotamia is a fairly recent discovery. It has only been translated in the last century or so, and so up until fairly recent times, Hesiod was considered in a vacuum; we were not able to look at cross-cultural influences. Now that Mesopotamian myths have been studied, analyzed and translated, it is possible to do a comparison of Hesiod and Mesopotamian myth. There are so many points in common that there has got to be some sort of cross-cultural influence at work here.

To take just one example, the Hesiodic story of Cronos shows strong parallels with the Mesopotamian story of a god named Kumarbi. Cronos and Kumarbi are both sons of a god whose name means sky, Ouranos in Hesiod, Anush in the Mesopotamian story. Each one gains power by castrating his father, and each is in turn overthrown by a younger god who is associated with storms: Zeus, in the case of Cronos; Teshub, in the case of Anush. This sort of parallel demonstrates a relationship of some kind between the myths of the two cultures. The parallel is too exact for it to be purely coincidental.

Either there was a direct influence, Mesopotamian stories were told to Greek travelers who then took them back to Greece, for instance, or the two stories derive from a common source; we could posit yet another myth further back in time from which both Mesopotamian and Greek stories derived.

There is some kind of connection between the two. However, the details differ from culture to culture. To give just a couple of examples from this same story: Kumarbi castrates his father Anush by biting off his genitals. Cronos, as we saw, castrates Ouranos with a sickle provided by Gaia. Kumarbi swallows Anush's genitals and becomes pregnant. He then gives birth to Teshub through his penis. (You thought that the Hesiodic story was strange. The Mesopotamian one was even stranger.) Cronos swallows his children who were conceived and born normally, and then spits them out. In both cases, you have castration of the father. In both cases, you have swallowing, the male god being in some sense pregnant with his own children, but the details are quite different. Another way of putting that would be that the Greek myths—wherever they came from, whatever the Mesopotamian influences might have been—the Greek myths are characteristically Greek. The plot may have traveled, but the details are worked out within each culture and have implications and resonances within each individual culture.

Cross-cultural influence between Mesopotamia and Greece, for instance, is only one of the kinds of formative influences that I want to talk about here. The other important formative influence behind Greek myth, as we know it, would be the prehistoric cultures that existed in Greece itself. There are two primary cultures that I want to talk about. First, there is a culture that existed on ancient Crete called "Minoan" culture. Secondly, there was a culture that was important in mainland Greece itself, called "Mycenaean" culture. Minoan culture centered on the isle of Crete and the nearby island of Santorini, flourishing between about 2000 and about 1470 B.C. That was its time of greatest development and influence. One of the great archaeological discoveries of the nineteenth and early twentieth centuries was the uncovering of Minoan civilization. This was a civilization that had been entirely lost. No one knew that it had ever existed until in the late nineteenth century. An English scholar named Sir Arthur Evans decided to try to discover if any of the Greek myths about ancient Crete might have some basis in historical fact.

As Heinrich Schliemann decided to see if the Homeric epics had any basis in historical fact by excavating until he found the site of Troy, so Evans did to see if any of the myths about Crete, particularly Theseus and the myths about his visits to Crete, were based in fact.

Evans went to Crete and began to excavate there, and did uncover evidence of a great thalossocracy, a great "sea-based empire" that had existed on Crete. At a site called Knossos, Evans found extensive ruins of a huge palace, which we will talk about more in a lecture on Theseus, and he connected this palace he found at Knossos with the legendary King Minos of myth, and that is why we now call this culture "Minoan." We have no idea what they called themselves; we call them Minoan after the legendary King Minos on Crete. Evans had found evidence of a great sea-faring culture on Crete just as he hoped he would. Minoan culture, although very developed, extremely artistic, is still a great puzzle to scholars in many ways mainly because, as you may have guessed by this time, we don't have written records to explain what was going on in Minoan culture.

The Minoans left very little behind them in the way of written records. They did have two writing systems called Linear A and Linear B (very boring names—they are called that because they are both linear in nature, and A and B are simply ways of distinguishing the two systems from one another). Linear A has never been deciphered. We don't know what language it is, we don't know what system it is, we have not ever been able to decipher it, so the few records that exist in Linear A are still a closed book to scholars. Linear B was deciphered in the 1950s and it turns out to be a very ancient form of Greek. The story of the deciphering of Linear B is one of the great triumphs and one of the great disappointments of twentieth century ancient studies, because it was a marvelous bit of detective work to decipher Linear B at all, to discover that is was in fact a very early form of Greek and to be able to read the clay tablets that are inscribed with Linear B. Once that was done, what did those clay tablets say? Well, they turned out to be mainly inventories of palace supplies. If you can imagine being a scholar who worked for years and years and years to decipher the Minoan's writing system, hoping that you would find some very early versions of myths or maybe one of the earliest versions of an epic or some great poetry or something like that, and you find instead a list that says: "10 jars of olive oil,

19 sheep, 15 robes"—it is incredibly disappointing. It is useful to a social historian, but it doesn't tell us the kind of thing that many of us would like to know about Ancient Minoan culture.

Furthermore, Linear B only came into use in Minoan culture after the Minoans had come under the domination of the other great historic culture I am going to discuss, the Mycenaeans, who were Greek speakers. We assume that in the earliest stages of Minoan culture they did not speak Greek; they spoke some other language, probably the language preserved in the Linear A tablets, which we can't read. Historians have to try to interpret the architecture, artifacts, painting, artwork and so on of the Minoans pretty much in the absence of any written works that might tell us what is going on in these archaeological artifacts. Unfortunately, Minoan culture is not known to be related to any other culture. We can't look at sister cultures of Minoan culture and see what they say about their beliefs or their myth system, because we don't know of any related culture to Minoan culture.

To make things even more obscure, Minoan art shows many scenes that may well be religious, that may have some connection therefore with myth, but it is extremely difficult to interpret these scenes without any context to guide us. Minoan culture is fascinating and frustrating in about equal proportions. It probably, almost undoubtedly, had some kind of influence on later Greek civilization. It was an extremely sophisticated and important culture. When it waned—that doesn't mean that all the Minoans simply packed up and went away. They were still there, they intermarried with Mycenaeans, their descendants would have been among the peoples of later Greece. They almost undoubtedly did have some influence on the development of Greek culture and the development of Greek mythology, but we can't know just exactly what that influence might be or, at least, it is very hard to determine what that influence might be.

The other great pre-classical civilization of Greece was Mycenaean civilization, the direct ancestor of ancient Greek culture. With the Mycenaeans, we are on slightly less shaky ground than we are with the Minoans. Mycenaean culture flourished from about 1600 to about 1100 or 1050 B.C. It was discovered by Heinrich Schliemann, the same man who excavated the site of Homer's Troy. He also excavated Agamemnon's city. He looked for the Trojan site of the

Trojan War myth; he also looked for the Greek site and excavated the city associated in Homer with Agamemnon, a city called Mycenae.

Unlike Minoan culture, which had disappeared entirely—which no one knew existed at all—the site of Mycenae had never been lost. Parts of that citadel, including its great gate which features stone two lions as the crowning part of the gate, had never disappeared under the level of the earth, so everyone knew where Mycenae was. What they did not know was how huge and intricate a site it was until Schliemann investigated it. Schliemann also found many other cities dotted around mainland Greece that clearly belonged to the same culture as the citadel he found at Mycenae. And, most importantly for our purposes, the cities that Schliemann found dating from Mycenaean times, which is the period about 1600 to about 1100 B.C., corresponded remarkably well with the cities mentioned by Homer in the *Iliad*. When Homer said there was a city at a particular place in Greece, Schliemann very frequently found the ruins of a Mycenaean city on that site. When Schliemann found the ruins of a Mycenaean city, Homer almost always mentioned that there had been a city at that spot. There is a correspondence; in other words, the Greek cities that Homer talks about seem to be, to a large extent, the Mycenaean cities of which Schliemann found the ruins. This implies a couple of things for us. It implies that Homer in some sense remembered some of the actualities of Mycenaean culture. I will get back to that point in just a minute.

The Mycenaeans were descendants of Indo-European migrants, that is, people who spoke the parent language which later developed into most of the modern languages of India and Europe. Those are called the Indo-Europeans. They migrated widely throughout Europe and India in prehistoric times. The Mycenaean Greeks were descendants of a band of Indo-European immigrants who came into Greece around 2200 to 2000 B.C. The Mycenaean language is a very early form of Greek. The Mycenaeans interacted with the Minoans, with this other pre-historic culture that I just talked about, and by about the fifteenth century B.C., the Mycenaeans had gained dominance over the Minoans. One of the ways we know that is the Minoan use of Linear B. Again, Linear B is Greek. The fact that the Minoans had begun to speak Greek probably indicates that by this time, they were under control of the Mycenaeans.

The Mycenaeans too, used Linear B, just as the Minoans did, but like the Minoans, the Mycenaeans used Linear B mainly to make lists of supplies. Once again, we don't have any proto-epic or any Mycenaean myth recorded for us. We have lists of supplies. Now, Mycenaean civilization waned during the eleventh century B.C. for reasons we are still not sure about. It lost its ability to make great citadels, its artwork declined sharply, and most importantly, for our purposes, the Mycenaeans lost the art of writing. They forgot how to use Linear B. So, from the eleventh century B.C. until the time when the Greek alphabet that we know was introduced into Greece in the eighth century B.C., Greece went through a period that is often called the "Dark Ages"—a period in which Greece was once again illiterate. There is a gap of three to four hundred years between the waning of Mycenaean civilization and the reintroduction of writing in the eighth century B.C.

Once writing had been reintroduced, the Homeric epics were among the first things to be written down. There is an implication here that is worth contemplating. The Homeric epics were written down in the eighth century B.C. As I just said, they referred to cities that had flourished in and before the eleventh century B.C. That implies that there was a continuous oral tradition, remembering those great Mycenaean cities, that covered that gap when there was no writing, no way those cities could have been memorialized in writing. They were remembered in the oral tradition. That means, or that implies at least, if the Homeric epics remember the location of some of the Mycenaean cities, and there are details about those cities and those details are reflected in the Homeric epics written down centuries later, it is at least possible that many other details in the Homeric epics—including some of the storylines, the myths, and so forth—may also stretch back to Mycenaean times.

Greek myth, as we know it, probably has a fairly strong Mycenaean origin and some fairly strong Mycenaean elements in it. The Trojan War is the most obvious example of this sort of thing. There probably was some sort of war between Mycenaean Greeks and the people who lived in what we call "Troy." The epics that describe that war undoubtedly have been exaggerated, mythologized, made into legend, however you want to put it. But there is some sort of actual trace of Mycenaean culture still present in the myth of the Trojan War.

When we are dealing with this kind of thing, all of it is obviously rather vague and rests on a lot of supposition, and a very obvious question is, how much can we safely deduce about prehistoric religion or prehistoric mythology from either the comparative method—looking at other cultures that flourished around the same time—or from looking at these prehistoric cultures, the Minoans and the Mycenaeans? To demonstrate the difficulties involved in trying to talk about prehistoric religious practices, belief, myth, I want to look at the theory of the "great mother goddess" to demonstrate some of the difficulties inherent in this kind of reconstruction of prehistory.

There is a widespread modern belief that classical myth and ancient European myth and Near Eastern myth, in general, contain traces of a prehistoric, pre-Indo-European worship of something that is often called the "great mother goddess." There are all sorts of books out now about goddess worship; there are all sorts of people who identify themselves with the idea that there was a great mother goddess in prehistory, and that the Indo-Europeans came in and suppressed her religion, but that she was there to begin with.

This belief has become almost an article of faith for many modern people, but the evidence for it is not nearly so straightforward as we might wish for it to be. The primary problem, again, is that of interpreting archaeological evidence without any written context to explain the archaeological evidence. The literary evidence that is often adduced to argue that there was, in fact, a great mother goddess is ambiguous at best, and many of the same objections can be made to the goddess theory that I discussed when I was talking about psychological theories of myth. Its adherents tend to simply assert their ideas about what may be true, and then treat those assertions as established fact. We are on very shaky ground when we do that in any case, and here, when we are dealing mainly with archaeological records, with images that have no text associated with them, it becomes all the more dangerous to say an image that appears in this culture, this culture and another culture must be an image of the same type of goddess, or even of the same goddess.

There is no doubt that very ancient female figurines are widespread throughout ancient European and Near Eastern cultures. They are all over the place; there are lots of them. There are many very famous examples, but the interpretation of these figurines is far from straightforward. Whether they represent goddesses at all is uncertain, and if they do represent goddesses, whether they represent a great mother goddess is yet more uncertain. There is no compelling reason to assume that a figurine, simply because it is a figurine of a female, must represent a goddess. Even if they are goddesses, there is no reason to assume that they are the same goddess. It is worth thinking for a minute about figurines. My famous future archaeologist that I refer to sometimes in this course, who comes back in 2500 years, excavates a McDonalds and thinks that it is a Gothic cathedral, might also find figurines from this culture. If this person assumed that all figurines served the same function, then he or she would assume that statues of the Virgin Mary from the Catholic Church and Barbie dolls from a Toys-R-Us had to be representations of the same goddess. They are both figurines; they are both female figures. We can't assume that they served the same function even within a culture, let alone assume that they served the same function cross-culturally.

Some of the widest reaching claims about a great goddess are made from Minoan civilization, based largely on its art. Minoan art, without question, features powerful female figures. The most famous of these is the so-called "Snake-Goddess." She is a figurine about so big, who holds in either of her outstretched hands a snake; she has two snakes. Powerful staring eyes, wearing a bell-shaped skirt, bare-breasted, and she is holding these snakes. She is without doubt a very beautiful and extraordinarily arresting figurine, and I think it is safe to say that she must have had some important significance in Minoan culture.

What was her significance, was she a goddess? People have tended to assume that she is an image of a goddess without ever really considering other possibilities. She could be an apotropaic image of a demon. She could be a snake-demon rather than a snake-goddess. She could be a priestess performing some sort of ritual ceremony in honor of a goddess. She could be a ghost figure used to frighten children. She could be any one of a number of things. There is no immediate reason that we are seeing that she must be a goddess, and yet, any other possibility tends to be dismissed with little or no consideration.

Without other information about Minoan religion beyond the images preserved by art, we simply can't know what the "Snake-Goddess" figurines represent. I have described the most famous one; there are others as well.

There are several of them. We need not assume that every figurine must have been used for ritual or religious purposes. There could be figurines that were there for merely decorative purposes. I myself have a collection of figurines of pelicans in my house. This does not mean that I worship a great pelican god; it means that I like pelicans and I like the way the figurines look on my shelf. The possibility that figurines are merely decorative, it seems to me, is worth considering. Even if we assume that the figurine of the "Snake-Goddess" was a goddess, we can't deduce religious practice, let alone religious belief, from an image alone. This is perhaps a point that does not seem immediately obvious to some people, but I think it is true.

Again, a future archaeologist excavating Notre Dame de Paris would probably come to the conclusion that that cathedral was built to honor a great mother goddess. After all, her image is all over the place, Mary enthroned, holding the much smaller Christ child on her lap. Yet we know that Roman Catholicism is not a religion that worships a primary mother goddess. It worships a primary father god. Mary is there in that cathedral, but that does not imply that the religion, in general, held her as its highest entity.

Reasoning that tries to deduce religious belief from artistic imagery is very often circular. Many of the arguments about the Minoan Snake-Goddess seem to go something along the lines of: "If the Minoans worshipped a goddess, this must be her image. Therefore, since this is the image of a goddess, the Minoans must have worshipped her." You really can't reason that way. That doesn't work.

What about literature? Some scholars read Hesiod's *Theogony* as providing evidence for a clash between mother-goddess-focused Minoan religion and father- god-focused Indo-European religion that was brought in by the Mycenaeans and overthrew the Minoan religion. The three-generational struggle for power under this reading can be seen as representing or reflecting the slow process whereby, through interaction and intermarriage, the newer culture, represented by Zeus and the younger male gods, gained dominance over the older culture represented by the older female mother goddesses. That is a fascinating reading of Hesiod, and it can be a very persuasive one. When I first started teaching mythology, I really liked it, and I used it in my classes. Unfortunately, it overlooks the fact that similar stories exist in

Mesopotamian myth, as we saw, and Mesopotamia did not undergo any Indo-European invasion.

One could just as persuasively come up with other explanations for the three-generational pattern in Hesiod, as we talked about in the lecture on Hesiod. In fact, one of the most easy and obvious explanations of it is to say that the pattern of a younger male gaining power over an older female simply represents, in psychological terms, the maturation of men and their separation from their mother. We don't have to posit an actual clash of a mother-goddess-worshipping civilization and a father-god-worshipping civilization to account for it. If we assume that Minoan civilization worshipped a great mother goddess, *Theogony* can be used to provide evidence for that. If we don't assume it, *Theogony* alone isn't going to bring us to it.

To sum up, there seems to be little good evidentiary reason, as opposed to desire, to believe in an original great mother goddess in ancient Europe and the ancient Near East, for various reasons. The goddess hypothesis perhaps shows a monotheistic bias. Many modern westerners find polytheism uncongenial, and tend to assume that polytheism must be a later development from, or degradation of some kind, of original proto- monotheism. That is ahistorical. That is not how the history of religion seems to have worked. Polytheism seems to have been the original form; monotheism would have come later. As I have said before, there is no compelling reason to assume that all representatives of a female divinity must be representatives of the *same* female divinity, unless one starts from that assumption. In other words, there is no reason to assume that the Greeks originally worshipped one great mother goddess who later fragmented into Demeter, Aphrodite, Hera and all the others. If we start from the assumption that there must have been one unified goddess, then we can see those later ones as fragmentations of her. If we don't start from that assumption, there seems to be no good reason to come to it.

In fact, it seems to me that the goddess may well be a modern myth, not an ancient one. She functions in many of the ways that we talked about myth functioning. She provides a charter for modern women who find themselves dissatisfied with the patriarchal past of much traditional religion. She reflects the very common mythic sense of a Golden Age, a time in the past when things were better. Thus, her adherents tend to assume that goddess worship must imply a society in which women have a very high status, despite all sorts of evidence to the contrary; cultures that worship goddesses do not, by and large, accord high status to their women. Classical Greek culture is a perfect example of that. The Athenians worshipped Athena with great devotion and reverence. They also kept their women sequestered and accorded them almost no civil rights whatsoever. So, worshipping a goddess does not equate to high status for women, and yet, modern adherents of the great goddess theory assume that it did. The story of her defeat by the Indo-European sky-father-god provides an explanation or an aetiology for how society came to be as it is. So, I think she is a myth, but I think she is a modern myth rather than an ancient one.

The great goddess is just one example of the pitfalls involved in trying to reconstruct the origins and development of classical myth in prehistory. I picked her because I think she is a fascinating example, but there are many others. This is a problem that confronts us at almost every turn in studying classical myth. In the next lecture, we will turn back to looking at classical myth itself and will examine humans, and particularly heroes, as Hesiod and other authors describe them to us.

Humans, Heroes, and Half-Gods
Lecture 13

I think it is fair to say that Hesiod's account of the five races gives a very pessimistic view of human existence in general.

We have seen that Hesiod's *Theogony* does not recount the origins of humans. *Works and Days*, however, does contain an account of the creation of humans. This account is often referred to as the "Myth of the Five Ages" or "Myth of the Five Races." Hesiod describes five successive races of humans, starting with the Golden Race and ending with our own race. The overall pattern is one of degeneration and increased hardship.

The first race, the Golden Race, was created by the immortals who dwelt on Olympus during Cronos's reign. They had no cares or troubles, and old age did not exist; they did not have to work for food; and they died out but became benign spirits. The Silver Race, also made by the Olympians, was greatly inferior to the Golden. They lived as children, nourished by their mothers, for one hundred years. On reaching adulthood, they lived a short while but were violent and irreverent. Zeus destroyed them. The Bronze Race was made by Zeus from ash trees. They were warlike and violent and used bronze for everything, including their homes. They too died out. The fourth race was the Race of Heroes, which was better and more just than the Bronze Race. Zeus created the heroes. Hesiod calls them "demigods" and says that they were the men who fought around Thebes and Troy. The fifth and worst race, Hesiod's own and, by implication, ours as well, is the Race of Iron. No creator is mentioned. Hesiod describes the Iron Race's lot as one of increasing hardship and toil. The only end in sight is that conditions will get worse and worse, until finally Shame and Retribution flee the earth, and society breaks down entirely.

This account apparently contradicts the "Pandora" story, told only a few lines before it in *Works and Days*, in several ways. This is a reminder that Hesiod was not attempting to provide an orthodoxy. The question of where humans came from is not the most pressing issue in Greek mythology. These myths are, by and large, more concerned with how humans should act and how society should function than with our origins.

Hesiod's story of the Five Races paints a very pessimistic view of the human condition. Ovid, writing in Rome in the 1st century B.C., used the same basic myth but gave it a very different emphasis. In discussing the creation of humans, Ovid recaps Hesiod's Myth of the Ages but with significant differences. Ovid's account has no Race of Heroes between the Bronze and Iron Races. We are not the Iron Race; rather, the Iron Race was destroyed by a great flood. We are the offspring of Deucalion and Pyrrha, who survived the flood and threw stones over their shoulders to repeople the earth. Thus, Ovid says, we are a hardy race, showing our ancestry. As we saw in Ovid's account of the creation of the world, we see here myth used as a self-conscious literary device, rather than recorded as a still-dynamic living force. Because we are separated from the earlier races, we can be more optimistic about our future than Hesiod was.

> **Just as "god" is a misleading translation of the term *theos*, so too "hero" is a misleading translation of *heros*.**

Who are these "heroes" whom Hesiod places right before our own day and Ovid leaves out of his picture of the races? Just as "god" is a misleading translation of the term *theos*, so too "hero" is a misleading translation of *heros*. The heroes of classical myth are not necessarily noble, good, or morally exemplary; sometimes they are quite the opposite. This is one reason that many scholars find fault with Campbell's discussion of heroes. He takes it as a given that "the hero" is motivated by a desire to provide a "boon" for his fellows, but this is not the case in many, if not most, Greek hero-tales. The word *heros* had three basic meanings in ancient Greek: *Hero* could refer to a dead person who was revered and to whom sacrifices were offered and who was considered protective of a particular site or city (often because he had founded it). This status by no means implied that he had been a good man, simply an extraordinary one. *Hero* could refer to someone who lived in the past, particularly up to the time of the Trojan War. Again, moral qualities were not decisive. *Hero* could refer to a human with one divine parent. Achilles, Heracles, and Perseus are all heroes in this sense. A fourth sense, *hero* as the main character of a tragedy, is post-classical and need not concern us here. The three main senses of the term have a great deal of overlap. Hesiod refers to his Race of Heroes as both demigods and men who fought around Thebes and Troy. These same legendary heroes were often claimed as ancestors and as the founders or protectors of cities. Remember, however, that some of the most famous heroes of Greek mythology, such as Oedipus and Agamemnon, do not have divine parents.

The stories of heroes involve the sense, often found in myth, that things were different in the past. This "difference" often implies that, at one time, humans had more power or greater powers than they now have. The difference also involves the idea that gods and humans once interacted much more freely than they do now.

Classical mythology's emphasis on heroes is unusual. Most cultures do not have nearly as many heroes in their mythology as Greece does, nor are those that they do have nearly so important. Mesopotamian myth, for instance, includes almost no heroes at all (with the notable exception of Gilgamesh). It is possible that because Greek culture placed so much emphasis on the opposition of mortal and immortal, the heroes were a means of mediating that opposition. The idea that gods and humans could interact was limited to the remote past. Another possibility is that a kernel of historical truth may lie in the Greek stories of greater ancestors and a lost Golden Age. Mycenaean civilization waned after c. 1100 B.C.; it did not suddenly disappear entirely. Mycenaean cities, including some quite impressive architecture, would have remained more or less intact for some time. Mycenaean artifacts, such as pottery and jewelry, would have continued to be used. The skills needed to construct such buildings or to create such artwork, however, would have been lost within one or two generations. Memories of Mycenaean culture could be preserved in oral poetry, which is what seems to have happened to some extent with the Trojan War. Thus, the Greeks of Hesiod's time might well have the sense that their own culture had been preceded by a greater, more accomplished one, whose people were in some sense their ancestors. ■

Apollodorus, *Library*, pp. 36–37.

Hesiod, *Works and Days*, pp. 70–72, line 201.

Ovid, *Metamorphoses*, pp. 5–16 (up to "Apollo and Daphne").

Supplementary Reading

Kirk, *Myth: Its Meaning and Function*, Ch. 5, section 7, pp. 232–238.

————, *Nature of Greek Myths*, Ch. 7 and 9.

Questions to Consider

1. Do you think the Greek view of the human condition is overly pessimistic? Does Ovid's treatment of the Ages strike you as less pessimistic than Hesiod's?

2. The myth of a lost Golden Age is common in many cultures. Why do you think this is? What desire or experience may that myth reflect?

Humans, Heroes, and Half-Gods
Lecture 13—Transcript

In the previous lecture, we concluded our examination of the gods of Greek mythology by discussing the possible cultural and prehistorical background for the myths we looked at. In the second half of the course, we are going to move on to concentrating on the heroes of Greek myth, and we are going to begin our examination of the heroes by setting them in context by looking at the story of how humans were created, as Hesiod tells it in *Works and Days*.

As you will remember, we saw that Hesiod's *Theogony*—his main account, in general, of the creation of the Universe, in general, and the gods, in particular—does not contain a creation story for men, though it does mention the creation of the first woman. However, in *Works and Days,* Hesiod's other great poem, he does include an account of how humans, in general, came into being. This story that he tells in *Works and Days* is often referred to as the "Myth of the Five Ages" or "Myth of the Five Races," because in it, Hesiod describes five successive races of human beings starting with the Golden Race, or Golden Age, and ending with his own kind, his own group of humans whom he describes as being a "race of iron." The overall pattern in Hesiod's account of the five different races of human beings is one of degeneration and increased hardship.

He begins by describing the first race of humans, the Golden Race. He says that the Golden Race was created by the immortals who dwell on Mount Olympus and that the Golden Race was created during the reign of Cronos. Far back in time, before Zeus overthrew his father Cronos, before the universe was set into the form that it would hold thereafter, according to the "Myth of the Five Ages," there was a Golden Race. Their existence was characterized first and foremost by the lack of any kind of care or trouble. They had no difficulties, and specifically, old age did not exist. According to Hesiod, people in the Golden Age did not have to work for food; the earth simply produced food for them. There was no necessity for work, for toil, no cares, no hardship and no old age. They did, however, die out, and Hesiod says they became benevolent spirits who still are around watching out for later human beings. Even in the Golden Age, Hesiod does not suggest that there was ever a time when humans did not have to die. As we talked about before, mortality is there for human beings, as a defining characteristic of human beings, from the very beginning.

After the Golden Race came the Silver Race, and there you see the the beginning of the pattern of degeneration. Silver is less than gold, and so the second race of humans is less than the first race. They too, Hesiod says, were created by the Olympians. They are a rather odd race in that their main characteristic is they lived for 100 years as children, nourished by their mothers, Hesiod says. They had a 100-year-long childhood. Then, when these people reached maturity, they lived a short while because they were violent and irreverent. In particular, they refused to pay proper sacrifice to the gods. So, Zeus wiped them out. Zeus destroyed the Silver Race of human beings.

Then, Hesiod says Zeus himself created the third race of humans, the Bronze Race. They, according to Hesiod, were made from ash trees. That seems like an odd source for a race of human beings. Probably the implication there has to do with the fact that the word that means ash tree in Greek is also used by Homer, in particular, to mean a spear, because the handle of the spear was made from the wood of the ash tree, and so the word itself came to mean spear. Probably what Hesiod is implying here is that the Bronze Race was extremely violent and warlike, and that they owed their origin to the same material from which spears are made. He said that they used bronze for everything, including their homes, and that they were extraordinarily warlike. They too died out. Hesiod seems to imply that they killed each other off.

Following the pattern of degeneration as symbolized by metals of lesser value, you would expect the next race after Bronze to be the Iron Race. In fact, Hesiod inserts here the "Race of Heroes" to whom he does not assign a metal and who, he says, were actually better than superior to, the preceding Bronze Race. So there is a little bit of a break in the pattern, which allows Hesiod to account for the Race of Heroes who are so important in the myths that he and his culture know. The Race of Heroes, Hesiod said, was also created by Zeus as the Bronze Race before them had been. Hesiod calls them "demigods;" by that he is probably referring to the idea that many heroes had one parent, usually the father, sometimes the mother, who was a god.

He calls them "demigods," and he says that they were the men who fought around Thebes and Troy; i.e., these heroes, this fourth race of human beings, whom Hesiod calls the heroes, are the people who figure in the stories of Greek myth, the stories of the Theban cycles such as Oedipus the King and his family, and the stories of the Trojan War. They too died, according to Hesiod. Most of them died and went to the Underworld, where humans normally go. Some, he says, Zeus settled in the Islands of the Blessed, referring to that idea we discussed before that a very few, very extraordinary humans get some sort of happy afterlife. But, most of the Race of Heroes simply died off.

This brings us to the fifth and worst race, the race of Hesiod's own day, which he calls the Race of Iron. For the fifth race, no creator is mentioned. Hesiod describes the fifth race, the Iron Race's lot, as one of increasing hardship and unhappiness. He says, describing it:

> I wish I were not counted among the fifth race of men,
> but rather had died before, or been born after it.
> This is the race of iron. Neither day nor night
> will give them rest as they waste away with toil
> and pain. Growing cares will be given them by the gods,
> and their lot will be a blend of good and bad.

He goes on to say that Zeus will eventually destroy this race of mortals as well when children are born already gray-haired. That is a vivid and, I think, very chilling description of the increasingly bad lot of the Iron Race. One of the main characteristics of the Iron Race's trouble is old age, disease and care. Children being born gray at the temples seems to imply that there will come a time when human beings are old from the moment of birth, when—just as the Golden Age never suffered old age—there will come a time when the Iron Race will know nothing but old age, and at that point, Zeus will destroy us as well.

The only end in sight for the Iron Race as Hesiod describes it is for things to get worse, and worse, and worse. He goes through a list of how bad things will get. He says that as the Iron Race continues to deteriorate, sons will not reverence their fathers, friends will not be trustworthy with one another, brothers will fight brothers, and eventually, he says, Shame and Retribution, *aidos* and *nemesis* in Greek, will veil their faces and flee the earth. Then, in effect, society will break down entirely. Without Shame and Retribution, there will be no controls on human activity whatsoever. The Iron Race, Hesiod's own race, is painted in very, very pessimistic tones indeed. The only slight element of hopefulness in this picture is that Hesiod states he wishes he had been born before or *after* the Iron Race, which seems to imply that there will be an after, that there may be another race of humans, eventually, created.

One thing to notice about this Myth of the Five Ages or Five Races is that it seems to contradict the Pandora story, which Hesiod has recounted just a few lines before the Myth of the Five Ages in *Works and Days*. If it doesn't flat-out contradict the Pandora story, at the very least, the Myth of the Five Ages does not dovetail neatly with the Pandora story, because, for instance, there are mothers in the Silver Age. The Silver Race lives for 100 years as babies, "nourished by their mothers," Hesiod says. Where do those mothers come from? If there are no cares or evils in the Silver Age, and there aren't, then how can there be mothers when Pandora, just a few lines before, is said to be the source of all females and to bring cares and troubles with her? This should remind us that Hesiod is not attempting here to come up with the one and only orthodox account of the creation of human beings. Just as we talked about before with *Theogony*, so here too, he is not attempting orthodoxy. Rather, he is using the traditional myths that he knows to look at the realities of human society from one angle, then from another angle. The fact that the myths sometimes don't fit quite perfectly with one another is only a problem if you are trying to construct an overall coherent, logical narrative, and that is not what he is trying to do here. Rather, he focuses first on the Pandora story, and secondly on the Myth of the Five Ages.

Another implication here is that the question of where humans came from is not the most pressing issue by any means in Greek mythology. That often surprises modern readers. We tend to think that our origin—how we got here, what we are doing in the world—has got to be the focal point of any religious or mythological system. For Greek myth, it isn't. Humans, particularly male humans, are more or less just a given, and the myths that we have looked at so far and will continue to look at are far more concerned with how humans should act, given that we are here, and how society should function than with the origins of human beings.

I think it is fair to say that Hesiod's account of the five races gives a very pessimistic view of human existence, in general, and of the Iron Race, in particular. With the exception of the Race of Heroes, we have an overall deterioration from good to not so good, from bad to really bad. And, Hesiod doesn't offer any hope for people of his own race that things will ever get better. Once again, I want to compare Hesiod's account with the account given by the Roman author Ovid in his work, *Metamorphoses,* some 700 years later. You will remember Ovid was writing in the first century B.C. and first century A.D.; he was right on that dividing line in Rome. In *Metamorphoses,* which he begins by giving his version of the creation of the universe, Ovid also recaps and modifies Hesiod's story of the different ages or races of humans. I think it is interesting to see the different emphasis that Ovid puts on the story, and how he makes it a far more optimistic account than it is in Hesiod's presentation.

Ovid recaps the Myth of the Ages, but there are significant differences in his telling of this myth. Most importantly, there is no intervening Race of Heroes. Ovid simply takes the underlying pattern—Gold, Silver, Bronze, Iron—and leaves the heroes out entirely. He agrees with Hesiod that the Iron Race was absolutely terrible and that it would eventually be destroyed by Zeus (or Jupiter, to give him his Roman name since Ovid is a Roman author). In Ovid's presentation, all of that is in the past. The Iron Race is in the past, as much as any of the other races are, and he tells us that, in fact, Zeus did destroy the Iron Race. He wiped them out by a great flood. So, who, then, are we?

Well, we are descendants, through a very odd process, of the two survivors of that flood. Just one quick side note here. Obviously, the flood story is a very clear example of cross-cultural parallels in different mythic traditions, perhaps of cross-cultural influence. There is the flood story as recounted for us by Ovid in classical mythology. There is a flood story in Mesopotamian myth, and of course, the most familiar flood story occurs in Genesis with the story of Noah. Here again, we may have cross-cultural influence between these mythologies coming up with a very similar story. According to Ovid, the only two people to survive the great flood, the only two members of the Iron Race to survive, were Deucalion and Pyrrha. Deucalion is the man; Pyrrha is the woman. Their little boat ran aground on Mount Parnassus, which is where Delphi is, and they went to ask the oracle of Delphi. (Now, how there can be an oracle speaking in Apollo's temple, if everyone including the Pythia is dead, Ovid doesn't bother to tell us.) They go and ask the oracle what it is that they should do. They are the only two surviving humans in the world. What should they do? The oracle tells them: "Throw the bones of your mothers over your shoulders." They react, at first, with horror at the idea of desecrating their mothers' graves, until they realize that what the oracle means is to throw the stones of the earth over their shoulders. The earth is the great mother of all living things; rocks, stones, are to her as bones are to the human body. Therefore, they are not sure it will work, but as Ovid says, "How can it hurt to try?" They pick up rocks, throw them over their shoulders as they walk. The rocks that Deucalion throws become men, and the rocks that Pyrrha throws become women.

Let's think for a moment about the implications of that. In Ovid's presentation, not only are we not the Iron Race, we are not even related to the Iron Race. We are a whole different, separate creation. We grow out of the rocks of the earth that Deucalion and Pyrrha throw over their shoulders. And Ovid says, "We show our origin in the fact that we are a hardy race able to endure a great deal of toil and trouble. We show where we came from by our hardiness." Once again, as I talked about very briefly when we discussed Ovid's creation story, we can see here how Ovid is using the traditional Myth of the Five Races, as Hesiod preserves it, as a literary device, rather than as a still-functioning living tradition. He puts in a lot of authorial comment, like "How can it hurt to try" throwing the stones over their shoulders. He also writes in a tone that is much less serious than Hesiod's tone. There is a lot of humor in Ovid.

More particularly, I think we see in Ovid a kind of self-conscious pointing out of the aetiological nature of the story as he tells it, where Hesiod, or myths that are closer to oral tradition (to the original status of myth), don't say, "Now look, we come from stones, that is why we are hardy." That may be implicit in the traditional myth, but it is not spelled out. Ovid spells it out for us. Ovid is almost doing a commentary on the myths that he recounts. Also, another aspect of Ovid's telling of the story is that since we are separated from the earlier races, since we have no real connection with the Iron Race that was destroyed by the flood, it is easy for Ovid to be more optimistic about the future of whatever he would call us. I guess we would have to call ourselves the Stone Age, misleading though that might be. It is easier to be more optimistic about our future than Hesiod allows for, because all of the trials and tribulations Hesiod describes, Ovid puts firmly in the past.

As I said, Ovid simply omits the Race of Heroes. What I want to do now is turn to discussing who these heroes are, whom Hesiod places right before our own day and who seem to be so important in Hesiod's account of the different generations of humans, that he has to put them in even though they break the pattern of metals, and they break the pattern of degeneration. Who are they? Why are they so important to Hesiod? What is implied by Ovid leaving them out?

Just as "god" is a misleading translation of the word *theos,* as I discussed before, so too "hero" is a misleading translation of the Greek word *heros*—or at least, the modern understanding of what is implied by the term "hero" in modern American culture is misleading when we look at the heroes of Greek mythology. The heroes of classical myth are not necessarily noble, good or morally exemplary. Sometimes they are quite the opposite. Sometimes they are extraordinarily bad people, rather than extraordinarily good people. By the way, this is one reason many scholars find fault with Joseph Campbell's treatment of heroes, particularly in his discussion in his book, *The Hero with a Thousand Faces.* Campbell takes it as a given that cross-culturally and across time, the hero is motivated by a desire to provide a "boon," as Campbell calls it, for his fellow humans; that is, what motivates the hero's adventures is the desire to bring a boon back to humanity. In the case of many, if not most, Greek hero tales, this is emphatically not the case. Many Greek heroes undergo adventures, and sometimes their actions in those adventures may have beneficent consequences for humans, but the heroes' motivation is not normally to help other humans, and at times, in fact, his actions have bad repercussions for other human beings.

What does the word *heros* in Greek mean if it doesn't mean an exceptionally good, morally exemplary person out to help his fellow human beings? Well, it has three basic meanings in Ancient Greek. *Hero* could refer to a dead person who was revered and to whom sacrifices were offered. This is the meaning of "hero" when you hear about hero sacrifice, hero worship and so forth. These dead people, who were seen as somehow still being spirits to whom sacrifice could and should be offered, were very frequently associated with one particular city. Often a hero would be considered protective of a particular city, because he had founded it or ruled over it, though that is not always the case. In this meaning, the term *hero* really can refer to a person who has died at just about any period. They don't necessarily have to be in the remote past. In other words, these heroes are not necessarily connected with myths at all.

There is one example, for instance, of a hero named Cleomedes who died in 492 B.C. The historian Pausanias tells us he was a boxer who, in anger over a judge's judgment that had gone against him, that he lost a contest, Cleomedes went on a rampage, pulled down a school building, destroyed a school building. There happened to be 60 children in the school at the time, who were all killed. Cleomedes's fellow citizens obviously were unhappy about this, they pursued him, and he miraculously disappeared. His fellow citizens were told by an oracle that he had become a hero and they should offer sacrifices and worship to him. Clearly, that indicates that a hero does not have to be a good man. He has to be extraordinary in some sense; there has to be some aspect of his story that is unusual, but he can be unusual for performing an extraordinarily bad deed as well as for performing an extraordinarily good one.

The second main meaning of *hero*, apart from someone who is offered sacrifices after death, is someone who lived in the remote past, particularly someone who lived up to and into the time of the Trojan War. This is the sense that is most important for us, because the heroes of myth are almost, without exception, the people who took part in the stories gathering around the Trojan War, and the generations before the Trojan War. When a Greek author referred to a hero, he could mean someone who lived up to that past time, in the time of the Trojan War. A third meaning: *hero* could be used to refer to a human who had one divine parent, as we have seen in several stories already. Achilles, Heracles, Perseus are all heroes in that sense. A fourth sense, *hero* meaning the main character of a tragedy or other literary work, is post-classical, and we don't really have to worry about it here. Classical writers did not refer to the main character of a tragedy or another literary work as its "hero."

We have got the three basic senses: someone who is worshipped after death, someone who lived in the past up to the time of the Trojan War, someone with one divine parent. There is a great deal of overlap between those senses. Hesiod, you will remember, refers to the Race of Heroes as both demigods (i.e. people with one divine parent) and men who fought around Thebes and Troy. He is combining those two senses in saying that the people who fought the Trojan War and who fought in the great expedition of the seven against Thebes were also men with one divine parent. These same legendary heroes, these same heroes who fought at Thebes and Troy, were very frequently claimed as ancestors by families who lived in the classical period of Greek culture. They were very frequently claimed as ancestors and very frequently were revered as founders of cities, so there you see a combination with the idea of hero as a dead person who receives sacrifice after death. It could very well be that you could offer sacrifices to someone who had died back at the time of the Trojan War, and who was a hero in that sense as well.

It is worth remembering, however, that the three senses are not always present in the same hero. In particular, many of the most famous heroes in Greek mythology, such as Oedipus and Agamemnon, or for that matter, Odysseus, do not have one divine parent, but have only two human parents. So, *hero* is a rather malleable term. We will mainly use it in the rest of this course to refer to the men and women who took part in the stories of Greek mythology, i.e., *hero* in the second sense I outlined—people who lived up to the time of the Trojan War.

The stories of those heroes, the stories of the heroes of the remote past, often involve the sense that we have talked about before, that myth so frequently reflects, that things were different before, that there was a time when the world operated in a different way than it now operates. We are so accustomed to classical mythology that we may not see how unusual it is to have so strong an emphasis on heroes as classical myth has. Actually, that is an unusual aspect of classical myth. We see that both in the free interaction of humans and gods—that is the way in which classical myth reflects the idea of how things were different in the past—and we also see the unusual emphasis on heroes when we compare classical mythology with the mythology of other cultures. Many, many other cultures do not have nearly so many heroes in their mythology as classical myth does. For instance, Mesopotamian myth, which we have used before as a comparison to classical myth, contains almost no stories of heroes. Mesopotamian myth, by and large, is about the gods. Gilgamesh is a notable exception to that; there is a very famous Mesopotamian myth about the hero Gilgamesh. For the most part, Mesopotamian myth does not focus on humans; rather it focuses on gods. The heroes of classical mythology, however, play an absolutely crucial role in classical mythology. Most, I think it is safe to say, of the stories of classical myth are stories that involve heroes in one way or another.

Why is this? Why does classical mythology lay such an emphasis on heroes when that is not necessarily an element of mythology at all? There are several possible ways to answer that question, as is so often the case. It is possible that because Greek culture, as we have seen, laid so much emphasis on the dichotomy mortal-immortal, saw that as the primary defining characteristic of humans, that we must die. It is possible that the heroes were a means of mediating that opposition, a means of bridging that gap. Men who had one divine parent could be seen, in some sense, as partaking of the state of being that the gods enjoy. Also, the interaction between gods and humans at the time of the heroes could be seen, in some sense, as mediating that difference, making a transition between gods and humans. By the way, it is worth noting that the way gods and humans could interact with one another and could interbreed with one another is very much restricted to the remote past. I don't think any young Athenian girl, say in 430 B.C., who found herself pregnant out of wedlock would have gotten very far if she tried to tell her father that Zeus had fathered her child. Everyone knew that Zeus did that kind of thing in the remote past. Everyone also knew that he didn't do it anymore.

Another possibility, that I find absolutely fascinating, to account for the heroes of Greek mythology is that they preserve a kernel of historical memory in their stories. Remember in the last lecture, I talked about those two great prehistoric cultures that flourished in Greece, before the development of what we call "classical civilization," the Minoans and the Mycenaeans. Let's think for a moment about Mycenaean culture and how it might be reflected in the stories of the heroes and the idea of a lost Golden Age. As I mentioned in the previous lecture, Mycenaean culture waned after about 1100 B.C. When we say a culture waned, we don't mean that it just suddenly disappeared. The Mycenaeans did not just all pack up and leave Greece and go somewhere else. We mean that for reasons that historians still are unsure about, in the case of Mycenaean culture, the culture went into a period of decline in which many of their skills were lost very, very rapidly. They lost the ability to build their magnificent buildings (which were excavated in the nineteenth and twentieth centuries); they lost the ability to make their extraordinarily beautiful and intricate jewelry; and so forth.

Their descendants would have continued to live, probably, in and around the same sites that had been occupied by Mycenaean culture at its high point. These descendants would have been, therefore, living within view of the architectural ruins from the earlier state of the culture. They probably would even have been using, for at least a couple of generations, the implements the Mycenaeans had made at their high point; jewelry, pottery, other artifacts would be handed down and continue to be used. The Mycenaeans' descendants would have been confronted on a daily basis with the fact that they were living in and around cities, and using artifacts, that they could no longer themselves create, that showed a level of skill, a level of cultural development far beyond what they themselves had. Also, all tradition would have—and we know from the Homeric poems that all tradition *did*—preserved memories of Mycenaean culture, some traces of Mycenaean culture. The Homeric epics have several references in them that refer directly to Mycenaean culture, not just the names of cities, but also of artifacts; for instance, a particular kind of helmet described in Homer, a boarstooth helmet—a helmet that is covered with the teeth of boars—that corresponds perfectly to actual helmets that excavations have found in Mycenaean cities.

Oral tradition preserves the memory of the people who built these cities. Their descendants lived, therefore, surrounded by artifacts that they can no longer create, and with an oral tradition telling them who created these artifacts and telling them that those people were their ancestors. By the time you get to the eighth century B.C., when Hesiod writes down *Theogony* [sic *Works and Days*], with the myth of the heroes in it, I think it is quite possible that what we have there is folk memory of a greater culture that actually, in fact, did precede classical Greek culture and that was the ancestor of classical Greek culture.

In this lecture, we have begun our examination of heroes and their role in Greek myth by looking at Hesiod and Ovid's stories of how human beings came into existence and by suggesting some possible interpretations. In the next lecture, we will focus on one particular hero, Theseus, the legendary hero of Athens.

Theseus and the "Test-and-Quest" Myth
Lecture 14

Theseus is probably less well known to modern non-specialists than heroes such as Heracles or Jason, who have tended to be focused on much more in modern culture. But he is a particularly good example of how hero-myth works, largely because of the role he played in Athens.

The stories of several heroes fit what has been called the "quest" pattern. Among these, Theseus's story is particularly rich for investigating mythic themes and presenting possibilities for interpretation. As the legendary *synoikistes* ("unifier") of Attica, he was an important figure in Athenian myth. In Theseus's case, myth became a charter for Athenian hegemonic control of Attica. Perhaps because of his important role in Athens, various stories accrued around Theseus, and it is difficult to work out a consistent chronology for his adventures.

His birth, childhood, and young adulthood show typical "hero" elements, reminiscent of folktale. Oddities and ambiguities surround his conception, not the least of which is an apparent double-fatherhood. His human father was Aigeus, king of Athens. His mother, Aithra, was raped by Poseidon on the same night that she slept with Aigeus; thus, Theseus's parentage was uncertain. This explains how he was a top-notch hero who, at the same time, inherited his father's throne. Aigeus left sandals and a sword under a boulder, with instructions that his son should come to him in Athens when he was strong enough to lift the boulder and retrieve the tokens. Theseus does so and sets off for Athens. Theseus's journey to Athens to claim his patrimony involves a series of encounters with monsters. The most famous of these was Procrustes, who had a bed that he forced all visitors to fit. This is the origin of the term *procrustean.* Others included the giant Sinis the "pinebender" and a monstrous boar. Theseus "unifies" the countryside by eliminating these dangers. When Theseus reached Athens, he was received as a guest by Aigeus and Aigeus's current wife, Medea. Medea, better known for her previous involvement with Jason, was a sorceress. She was pregnant and feared that Theseus (whom she recognized as Aigeus's son) would displace her own child. She persuaded Aigeus that the young guest planned to kill him, and Aigeus agreed to poison the youth. At the dinner table, Theseus drew his sword to cut his meat. Aigeus recognized the sword and stopped Theseus from drinking his poisoned wine, just in time.

After his recognition by his father, Theseus embarked on a dangerous journey to Crete to try to free Athens from its tribute to the Minotaur. The Minotaur was a man-eating half-man and half-bull that belonged to Minos, king of Crete. Athens was obligated by a treaty to send seven young men and seven young women to Crete every year to be eaten by the Minotaur. Athens and Crete had gone to war after Minos's son Androgeos was killed in Attica, either by a great bull whom Aigeus sent him to fight or by other young men who were jealous of his athletic prowess. Minos declared war on Athens, and the war ceased only when Athens agreed to let Minos name whatever recompense he wanted. Minos instated the annual tribute to the Minotaur. Theseus volunteered to be a member of this delegation.

Theseus's adventures in Crete are the most famous part of his story. He was helped by Ariadne, the daughter of Minos. As in other "test-and-quest" stories, the young man is helped by a young woman. Ariadne gave Theseus a ball of thread so that he could find his way out of the Minotaur's labyrinth. In return, he agreed to take her with him when he left Crete. Theseus killed the Minotaur in the labyrinth, then found his way out with the aid of Ariadne's thread. He and Ariadne fled Crete. They stopped for the night on the island of Naxos. When Theseus set sail in the morning, he left Ariadne behind, apparently forgetting her. Dionysos rescued her and married her, and she became a goddess. Before leaving Athens, Theseus had promised Aigeus that if he succeeded in killing the Minotaur, he would change the black sails of his ship for white. He forgot to do so. Aigeus watched daily for the returning ship; when he saw the black sails, he leapt to his death. Theseus thus became king of Athens.

After the loss of Ariadne, Theseus married at least two more times. Theseus and his friend Pirithous agreed that they should both marry daughters of Zeus. For Theseus, they kidnapped Helen (later of Troy) who was too young for marriage but already extraordinarily beautiful. The plan was to keep her until she was old enough to marry. For Pirithous, the two men journeyed to the Underworld to kidnap Persephone. At the invitation of Hades, they sat down on stone chairs and became stuck there. Theseus remained stuck in the Underworld for some years until Heracles rescued him. Pirithous remained there forever. Theseus also married an Amazon named Antiope or Hippolyta. He traveled to the Amazons' land and abducted their queen. The Amazons responded by besieging Athens, but they were defeated. The son of this marriage was Hippolytos. Finally, Theseus married Phaedra, daughter of Minos and Pasiphaë of Crete. This marriage produced two sons but ended unhappily. Phaedra was smitten by Aphrodite with passion for her stepson, Hippolytos. When he rebuffed her, she committed suicide and left a note saying that Hippolytos had raped her. Theseus cursed his son, who was dragged to death by his own horses. Only too late did Theseus discover that Hippolytos had been innocent.

These later adventures of Theseus demonstrate a common problem in studying classical myth, that is, chronological inconsistencies.

These later adventures of Theseus demonstrate a common problem in studying classical myth, that is, chronological inconsistencies. According to most accounts, Minos lived generations before Heracles, and Heracles lived at least one generation before the Trojan War. But Theseus is involved with two daughters of Minos, kidnaps Helen, and is rescued by Heracles. The Trojan War was fought because a Trojan prince abducted Helen when she was already the wife of the Greek Menelaos. How, then, can Heracles have rescued Theseus after Theseus kidnapped the child Helen? How can Theseus live at the same time as Minos and Helen? This sort of inconsistency is probably the result of attempts to gather diverse strands of myth from different times and places into one coherent narrative. Theseus's story is worth going through in detail because, as we shall see in the next lecture, it offers scope for many different interpretations. ■

Apollodorus, *Library*, 138–143.

Graf, *Greek Mythology*, pp. 50–53.

Walker, *Theseus and Athens*, pp. 15–21.

Questions to Consider

1. Theseus's "forgetfulness" is rather surprising, even in the logic of myth. Can you think of any explanation for why he forgets Ariadne *and* forgets to change the sails?

2. Modern readers are often troubled by chronological inconsistencies, such as the ones I have outlined here. Is this an anachronistic concern? In other words, are we expecting a kind of logical and chronological consistency in these myths that would not have occurred to their original audience?

Theseus and the "Test-and-Quest" Myth
Lecture 14—Transcript

In our previous lecture, we began looking at heroes and discussed the three basic meanings of the term "hero" in Greek mythology: a person who is worshipped after death, someone who lived in what is often called the "Heroic Age" (i.e., the time period that ended with The Trojan War), and an ancestor of people who live in the present age. In this lecture, we are going to move on to discussing one particular hero, Theseus, and see how important a role he plays both in terms of Athens's local mythology and for Greek myth in general.

There are a good many heroes in Greek myth whose stories fit what is sometimes called the "test-and-quest" pattern, the pattern of an adventure story where a young man goes out and performs various deeds of valor. Among these, Theseus's myth is a particularly valuable one for investigating some of the mythic themes that appear in this type of story and for possibilities of interpretation. Now, Theseus is probably less well known to modern non-specialists than heroes such as Heracles or Jason, who have tended to be focused on much more in modern culture. But he is a particularly good example of how hero-myth works, largely because of the role he played in Athens.

As I have mentioned before, Athenian literature makes up the bulk of the surviving literature that we have from classical Greece. A hero who is especially associated with Athens is a hero who shows up in a great deal of literature, indeed. Theseus's connection with Athens is that he is seen as being the legendary *synoikistes*, as the Greeks would call it, of Attica. *Synoikistes* means more or less "unifier." What this refers to is the idea that Theseus persuaded all the various small and independent towns of Attica— the peninsula on which Athens is located—to unify, to come together under one centralized control, and the centralized control was, of course, focused in Athens. Theseus is seen as the hero who unified Attica under Athenian control. This element of his myth, this role of being the *synoikistes* of Attica, really, as far as we can tell, developed for Theseus fairly late, in the sixth century B.C., and it seems to parallel, pretty neatly, political developments that were actually going on in Athens in the sixth century B.C. In other words, as Athens actually was gaining control over Attica, over the surrounding towns and villages in the area, it simultaneously developed myths saying that Theseus had done this in the far past. There we can see where myth serves as a validation or "charter," in Malinowski's term, for political realities. The Athenians apparently felt a need to have a mythic predecessor, a mythic justification for their own political developments in the sixth century B.C., and Theseus provided that justification.

It is perhaps because of the important role Theseus plays in Athens that a great many stories accrued around him, a great many adventures were attached to his name, which makes it very difficult to work out a consistent chronology for him, as we will see later on in the lecture. However, the earliest part of his life—conception, birth and early adulthood—is fairly easy to describe and fairly well set. We don't get into chronological difficulties until we get to later parts of his story.

In his birth and childhood stories, Theseus demonstrates typical "hero" elements (i.e., typical elements of narrative which appear in stories about many heroes). These are what Vladimir Propp, whom we discussed in earlier lectures, would call the "functions" of Theseus's story, by which he means, more or less, individual narrative elements—such as an idea that there is a difficulty surrounding the hero's birth—that appear over and over again in different stories about different characters. In Theseus's story, we very clearly see the idea that there is some sort of oddity or ambiguity surrounding his conception and birth. For Theseus, the strangest thing about his conception is an apparent double fatherhood. He is said to be the son both of the human Aigeus and of the god Poseidon (or, in some versions, he is said to be son of one; in other versions, he is said to be son of the other).

The reason there is confusion about his fatherhood is as follows: Theseus's human father, the man who is credited with begetting him, was Aigeus, King of Athens. Aigeus had gone to consult the oracle at Delphi to find out what he needed to do to have a son, because he was, at this point in his life, childless. The oracle told him in a typical oracular fashion that, to be sure of begetting a son, he should not "loosen the dangling foot of the wine skin" until he returned home to Athens. Aigeus had no idea what this meant. On his way back to Athens from Delphi, he stopped overnight at a place called Troizen, which is close to Attica but not actually in Attica, and asked the king there what this oracle could possibly mean. The king recognized that what it meant was Aigeus should not have sexual intercourse until he returned home to Athens, the implication being that the next time Aigeus did have sex with anyone, he would beget a son.

The king, therefore, wanting to connect his family with the royal house of Athens, offered his own daughter to Aigeus as a sexual partner for that night. This woman was Aithra, Theseus's mother. Aigeus and Aithra go to bed together on the advice and consent of her father and have sex with one another. Later that night, Aithra is told in a dream that she should go to a particular temple. She gets out of bed, dresses, and when she goes to this temple, she is raped by the god Poseidon. This means that on the same night, Aithra has had sexual intercourse with both Aigeus and Poseidon. Therefore, no one will ever know who Theseus's real father is.

I think here we can see a very clear logic at work behind this story. Theseus is the great hero of Athens. As such, Athenian myth wants him to be a top-notch hero, and top-notch heroes have a god that is their father. So, Theseus must have a god as his father; there is a story about Poseidon. Theseus is also the most important legendary king of Athens. How do you become king? You inherit the kingship from your father. So, Theseus must have a father who is king of Athens, and therefore, there is a story about Aigeus's parentage. Since Theseus has to fill both of these roles—really top-notch true hero who needs a god as a father, absolutely legitimate king of Athens who needs a king of Athens as a father—he is given two fathers, and the two are left side-by-side without any decision ever being made in the myths of Theseus about which one is really his father.

Aigeus, when he left Aithra and continued on his way to Athens, performed another element that comes up very frequently in folktale and in hero myth: he left tokens for his son to discover at a later time in his life. Specifically, Aigeus put a pair of sandals and a sword under a boulder. He told Aithra that if she bore a son, when that son was old enough to lift the boulder and retrieve the sandals and the sword, he should make his way to Athens, show these tokens to Aigeus, and Aigeus would recognize that this was indeed his son. If Aithra bore a daughter, Aigeus apparently doesn't want to know about it; that is not what he is interested in. Notice also that Aigeus is perfectly happy to have Aithra have all the trouble, expense and worry of bringing the baby up. Aigeus only wants him once he is grown, once he is big enough to lift that boulder and make his way to Athens. So, Theseus grows up, lifts the boulder, retrieves the tokens and sets off on a journey to Athens to claim his patrimony.

His journey to Athens, which he makes by foot, is a series of encounters with monsters and brigands—that is, wild outlaws who are terrorizing the people of Attica. The most famous outlaw whom Theseus encounters as he walks from Troizen to Athens is named Procrustes. Procrustes is famous for his bed. He had a bed in which he compelled all travelers who passed by his house to sleep. Procrustes insisted that the traveler had to fit the bed precisely. So, if the traveler was too tall for the bed, Procrustes lopped his legs off to make him fit. If the traveler was too short for the bed, Procrustes put him on a rack and stretched him out to make him fit the bed. This is where we get the term "procrustean." If someone says that a particular solution is a procrustean solution to a problem, by that they mean that the problem is made to fit the solution rather than the other way around.

Procrustes is the most famous outlaw Theseus encountered and killed on his way to Athens. Another was Sinis, surnamed the "Pinebender." He was a giant who had a habit of bending two pine trees down, tying a hapless traveler between them and then letting the pine trees go, which of course rips the traveler into two pieces. Theseus killed him as well. Theseus also killed a monstrous boar who was ravaging the countryside.

These adventures, again, seem to work allegorically, or symbolically, or however you want to put it, to underline the idea of Theseus as the *synoikistes*, the unifier of Attica under Athenian rule. What is he doing? He is ridding Attica of danger, of things that make Attica unsafe for people to travel in, make it unsafe to go from one town to another town. These mythic monsters and outlaws whom he overcomes seem pretty clearly to represent the idea of lawlessness, of lack of unification, of lack of safety on the roads. So, Theseus, as the person who wipes out these monsters, parallels the idea of Theseus as the person who unifies Attica under Athenian control.

When Theseus reached Athens, he was received as a guest. He did not declare who he was; he was in disguise. According to some versions, he was dressed as a girl. He presented himself to his father Aigeus. Now, Aigeus, at this point, was married to a woman named Medea. Medea is, of course, much more famous for her previous marriage to the Greek hero Jason, the man who sailed the Argo to get the Golden Fleece. Medea is a sorceress, a witch, one of very many powerful women who use magic and who show up throughout Greek myth. In this particular element of her story, Medea was pregnant with Aigeus's child, and she feared that Theseus, whom her magic allowed her to recognize as Aigeus's son, would supplant her own as yet unborn child in Aigeus's estimation. Therefore, Medea acted as Medea always does. She was not a lady who was at all averse to killing her enemies to get them out of her way. She persuaded Aigeus that this young stranger-guest was planning to kill him, Aigeus. And, she persuaded Aigeus that to protect himself, Aigeus should poison the guest before he had a chance to kill him. Aigeus went along with this idea, terrible violation of the guest-host relationship though it might be, and at dinner presented Theseus with a cup of poisoned wine.

Here we get yet another element that is very common in folktale, in myth, in traditional tales in general—the idea that a disaster is averted just in time, that a stranger is recognized as being a relative just in time. Theseus was sitting at the dinner table; the poisoned goblet of wine in front of him. Before he drank it, however, he drew his sword to carve his meat (that tells you something about ancient table manners). He drew his sword to carve his meat, Aigeus recognizes the sword, realizes that this is his son, tells him not to drink the wine. Medea beats a hasty retreat. One very noteworthy element of Medea's story is that she always manages to escape before she pays the consequences of her crimes. So she does in this circumstance.

Aigeus and Theseus recognize each other as father and son. They have a joyous reunion and the next element in Theseus's story gets into what, as I have already said, is called the "test-and-quest" kind of a hero's story. He sets out on a dangerous journey to the island of Crete, and he goes specifically to try to free Athens from the dreadful tribute that it has to pay every year to the Minotaur. The Minotaur is a monster who lives in Crete. Its body is that of a man; its head is that of a bull. It is a human-eating monster, a monster who devours human beings. Athens has the obligation of sending every year seven youths and seven maidens, seven young men and seven young women, to Crete to be eaten by the Minotaur.

The reason Athens has to do this is because of a war that had been fought between Crete and Athens and the treaty that ended that war. Minos, king of Crete, had a son Androgeos who had been visiting Aigeus in Attica. Androgeos had died while he was in Attica. Either he was killed by a great bull whom Aigeus sent him out to fight, or Androgeos was killed by young Athenian men who were jealous of his athletic prowess. Either version, the result is the same. Androgeos is killed, and Minos declares war on Athens to avenge his son's death. The war ceased only when Athens agreed to let King Minos name whatever recompense he wanted, whatever terms of a treaty he wanted. What he wanted was fodder for his monster, the Minotaur. Minos imposed this tribute on Athens of seven youths and seven maidens every year, who will be fed to the Minotaur in Crete.

When Theseus learns of this dreadful tribute from his father Aigeus, he volunteers to be a member of the delegation that year, to be one of the seven youths that will go to face the Minotaur in Crete. Of course, Theseus is intending to kill the monster if he possibly can, and therefore lift this tribute from Athens. Theseus's adventures in Crete are the most famous part of his story. His encounter with the Minotaur and the help that he gets from the Cretan princess Ariadne, daughter of Minos, are the most famous elements of any story about Theseus.

Again, we are dealing with an element that comes up in many stories of this "test-and-quest" pattern. Ariadne, the princess, helps Theseus. This is a very common element, that the young man attempting to perform an all-but-impossible feat is helped by a young woman who has fallen in love with him, usually a princess. Ariadne has in fact fallen in love with Theseus at first sight, and so she decides to help him to overcome the Minotaur. Ariadne does this by giving Theseus a ball of thread so that he can find his way back out of the Labyrinth in which the Minotaur is imprisoned. The Labyrinth is a maze so intricate that once you had gone into it, you could never find your way back out again. The Minotaur supposedly lives in the Labyrinth. The seven youths and seven maidens will be driven into the Labyrinth; they could not find their way out again. The Minotaur would hunt them down and eat them. Ariadne gives Theseus a ball of thread so that he can tie one end of it to the doorpost and then retrace his steps, find his way out again.

This is often called the "clue" of Ariadne, and "clue" in English originally simply meant a ball of yarn. Our use of the word "clue" to mean the one element that leads you out of your perplexity to an understanding comes from the story of Ariadne. It is originally a metaphorical use of that term. In return—Ariadne has to get something out of this as well—in return, Theseus agrees that he will take Ariadne with him when he leaves Crete, as well he might. Minos is not going to be particularly pleased that his daughter has helped this Athenian to kill the Minotaur and end Athens's tribute to Crete. So, Theseus agrees he will take Ariadne with him.

With the help of Ariadne's thread, Theseus succeeds—after he kills the Minotaur in the Labyrinth—in finding his way back out again. He and Ariadne do then indeed leave Crete. They stop to spend the night on the nearby island of Naxos, supposedly sleep together, spend the night together. And the next morning, when Theseus wakes up, he sets sail and leaves Ariadne behind, alone on the island of Naxos. Now there are various different versions for why he did this, but the most common one that most authors seem to espouse is that he simply flat-out forgot her. He got up in the morning, forgot about Ariadne entirely and set sail without her. When Ariadne wakes up, she is abandoned, all alone on an island, all by herself.

Unusually for myth, she has a happy ending to her story. The god Dionysos supposedly comes, finds Ariadne, rescues her, marries her and turns her into a goddess. The outcome for Ariadne is very good. That is so unusual an ending—both in the idea that a woman would become a goddess and in the fact that this kind of story doesn't normally have a happy ending—that many scholars think what is going on here is that Ariadne originally was a goddess, perhaps even a Minoan goddess. Her name seems to imply that. The name Ariadne means "very holy." Her name may indicate that she was originally a goddess. If she was, if the story originally was that a Cretan goddess helped Theseus, then it would make more sense that after she helped him, Dionysos married her. It would be a god marrying a goddess rather than a god turning a human woman into a goddess. But as the story developed, for whatever the reason, Ariadne was downgraded to being a human being and we get the story of Theseus leaving her behind on Naxos and Dionysos rescuing her.

This was not the only devastating episode of forgetfulness on Theseus's part. Before he left Athens, he had promised his father, Aigeus, that if he succeeded in killing the Minotaur, Theseus said, he would change the sails on his ship from black to white. When the ship set sail every year for Crete with the seven doomed boys and the seven doomed girls aboard, it had black sails. When it came back, having left its human cargo in Crete, it still had black sails. Theseus promised Aigeus that if he was successful, if he was actually coming home in triumph on the ship, he would change the sails to white. He forgot to do so, and Aigeus, who had been standing either on the Acropolis of Athens or on Cape Sounion—the southernmost tip of Attica— keeping watch every day for the returning ship, saw the ship coming back, saw that the sails were still black, thought that his son Theseus was dead, and leapt to his death, committed suicide, because he thought Theseus was dead. Theseus then became King of Athens. Aigeus is dead; Theseus enters into kingship in his father's place.

It is at this point, after the loss of Ariadne and after Theseus becomes king, that his story gains all sorts of different elements that become difficult to work out in exact chronological order, exactly how they relate to one another and how each element happened. We know that after the loss of Ariadne, Theseus married at least two more times, and before he married two more times, he attempted a marriage that did not work. Theseus had a dear friend, Pirithous, and they agreed that the two of them should each marry daughters of Zeus. A rather hubristic idea, but that is what they wanted to do. Theseus decided that he wanted to marry Helen, she who would later be known as Helen of Troy. Now, at this point, Helen was only a child. Some sources say about seven years old, some say a little bit older. She was already extraordinarily beautiful, and she grows up to be the most beautiful woman who has ever lived. Theseus went to Sparta where Helen lived, kidnapped her and brought her back to Athens with the intention of keeping her until she grew up—or at least, grew up to the age of 14 or so and was old enough to marry.

Pirithous set his sights even higher, or it might be better to say set his sights even lower, because Pirithous decided that he wanted to marry none other than Persephone, wife of Hades and, therefore, Queen of the Underworld. Theseus and Pirithous journeyed to the Underworld to try to kidnap Persephone. They should have known it wouldn't work, and in fact, it did not work. When they got to the Underworld, Hades invited them to sit down and rest on two stone chairs. When they sat down, they were caught, could not get up again. The chairs were magic, and they were frozen in their place, stuck to the chairs in the Underworld. They remained there for several years until Heracles, who was in the Underworld for reasons of his own—which we will discuss in a couple of lectures when we talk about Heracles—rescued Theseus. However, Heracles left Pirithous there. Pirithous never comes out of the Underworld again. He is stuck in his stone chair forever.

When Theseus returned to Athens, after however many years he spent stuck in the Underworld, he discovered that Helen's brothers had come and rescued her and taken her back to Sparta. So, Helen is not there waiting for him to marry. At some point, either directly after this or a little bit later, Theseus also marries an Amazon, one of that race of legendary warrior women whom, as we will see later on in the course, heroes tend to encounter as a test of their true "hero-hood." An encounter with an Amazon is an essential part of several famous heroes stories. Theseus goes to the land of the Amazons, and either seduces or flat-out abducts their queen, whose name is given variously as either Antiope or Hippolyta. He brings her back to Athens with him as his wife, with the results that the Amazons stage a rescue operation. The Amazons supposedly invade Attica and besiege Athens to try to get their queen back. Theseus and the Athenian men defeat the Amazons, but somewhere in this whole set of circumstances, in the battle or perhaps in childbirth, the Amazon queen Hippolyta dies. Theseus is left a widower. So, he marries an Amazon, he defeats the Amazons who try to get their queen back, but the Amazon queen does, in fact, die and so Theseus is still left without a wife.

The marriage with Hippolyta does produce a son, named Hippolytos. The story of Hippolytos is a side story to Theseus's own narrative, but a very important one for our understanding, both of Theseus and of other elements of his story. Hippolytos is a difficulty for Theseus in Theseus's final marriage. Theseus marries last of all, Phaidra, daughter of King Minos and Queen Pasiphaë of Crete, and yes, the sister of Ariadne. Now it has always struck me as extraordinary that Minos would let his daughter Phaidra marry Theseus after Theseus had, first, killed the Minotaur, and second, abandoned Ariadne, but there it is. For whatever reason, Minos lets Theseus marry Phaidra. This marriage produces two sons, but ends unhappily. Phaidra is undoubtedly a great deal younger than Theseus. By this time, Theseus must be fairly old. Phaidra is a young woman, and Aphrodite infects her with passion for her stepson Hippolytos, Theseus's son by the Amazon queen Hippolyta. When Hippolytos rebuffs Phaidra, when he refuses to be seduced by her (according to the playwright Euripides), this is not just because Hippolytos is disgusted by the idea of having sex with his father's wife, but also because Hippolytos has sworn to be sexually chaste, has sworn never to follow the ways of Aphrodite. When Hippolytos rebuffs Phaidra, Phaidra commits suicide and leaves a note saying that Hippolytos had raped her. Theseus believes this note, curses his son, and as a result, Hippolytos is dragged to death behind his own horses. Theseus only learns the truth, that Phaidra tried to seduce Hippolytos, not vice-versa, after his son is dead. This again is a very common narrative element; it shows up in the biblical story of Joseph and Potiphar's wife, it shows up elsewhere in Greek myth—the idea of an older woman trying to seduce a sexually chaste young man, and the disastrous consequences that accrue to the young man himself.

As I have said already, these later adventures of Theseus and many others that I haven't had time to discuss—his different marriages, his age at the time of his different marriages, how long he spent in the underworld—all of those are very difficult to reconcile with one another chronologically. In fact, Theseus's whole life is difficult to reconcile with the rest of Greek myth, chronologically. This is a problem that is fairly common in studying classical myth. When various different strands of narrative are brought together in one more-or-less coherent myth, there are frequently times when the chronologies just don't quite line up. We will see another example when we talk about the Trojan War in a few more lectures.

What is the problem with Theseus? According to most accounts, Minos lived some generations before Heracles, probably three generations before Heracles. Heracles lived at least one generation before the Trojan War. Yet

Theseus is involved with two daughters of Minos and is rescued by Heracles after he has kidnapped Helen. Theseus's story pictures Minos and his family and Heracles as all alive at the same time. Furthermore, Theseus is rescued by Heracles after he kidnaps Helen. Bu, it was the abduction of Helen after she was grown up and married by Menelaos, it was her abduction by the Trojan prince, Paris, that sparked the Trojan War. So, if Helen is the cause of the Trojan War, and Heracles lives at least one generation before the Trojan War, and Minos lives a few generations before Heracles, how can Theseus be involved with all of these people? The chronology is impossible; it simply won't work. How can Heracles have rescued Theseus after Theseus kidnapped Helen? How can Theseus live at the same time as both Minos and Helen, who are separated by a fairly long stretch of time according to the normal mythic chronology, as it is worked out for all Greek mythology? The obvious answer is that it simply doesn't work, that the chronology is, as scholars say, hopelessly confused. (That is kind of a set phrase for this kind of thing—"hopelessly confused.") We can't make sense out of it.

The question I want to look at to end the lecture though is, why is the chronology hopelessly confused? What is it about Theseus that accounts for this connection with Minos, Heracles, and Helen, when the people who recounted these stories must have realized as we do that there was a chronological problem? The simple answer is that, as we have seen before and we will see again, any time you attempt to gather disparate threads of narrative—stories that have grown up about Theseus in one place, stories that have grown up in another—any time you try to gather those and make them into one story, there are going to be some problems.

Perhaps more interestingly, I think this has to do, again, with Theseus's important role as a founder-figure for the Athenians, as the Athenians' main and primary hero. He is important enough that his myth in Athens wants for him to be connected with just about every other important episode of myth. You want Theseus to interact with Heracles. Heracles is a kind of justifier or validator for other heroes. People who have read the *Odyssey* will remember Heracles's encounter with Odysseus in the Underworld, where he greets Odysseus as, in some sense, a fellow—an equivalent of Heracles. The myth wants Theseus to interact directly with Heracles. It also wants Theseus to be connected with the most important episode of myth, the Trojan War.

And the connection with Minos and Crete is even more important than that, and that is what we will talk about in the next lecture. Theseus's story has been worth going through in detail, I think, because it offers scope for many different interpretations and many different readings, and those, as well as the connection with Minos in Crete, we will cover in the next lecture.

From Myth to History and Back Again
Lecture 15

In the previous lecture, we looked at Theseus's story and ended by discussing why the myth of Theseus connects him with Heracles and with the Trojan War through Helen, despite the chronological impossibilities there. In this lecture, we are going to concentrate on his connection with the Minotaur and King Minos, and through that story with Crete in general.

This lecture continues our examination of the myths of Theseus by looking at some of the theoretical and interpretative issues raised by his encounter with the Minotaur. At first sight, the myth of the Minotaur in the Cretan labyrinth seems to be one of the most purely imaginary among Greek myths and one of the least likely to have any historical connection. The Minotaur is a monster that is half-man and half-beast. He is conceived in a particularly improbable way. Pasiphae, queen of Crete, develops a passion for a bull. At her request, Daidalos, the great artisan, builds a wooden cow. Pasiphae hides in the cow and mates with the bull. When the Minotaur is born, at Minos's command, Daidalos builds the labyrinth to contain him. The Minotaur is not only a monster but also a man-eating monster. The fact that the story shows many folktale elements, such as Theseus's reliance on Ariadne's help, makes it seem unlikely that it could have any kernel of history in it.

Theseus's encounter with the Minotaur offers a great deal of scope for differing interpretations of myth in general and of his story in particular.

Theseus's encounter with the Minotaur offers a great deal of scope for differing interpretations of myth in general and of his story in particular. Neo-ritualist theorists see it as a paradigm for male initiation rituals. Theseus arrives in Athens wearing women's clothing, according to one tradition; initiates arrive at their initiation as less-than-males. Theseus journeys to Crete; male initiates are removed from their villages. Theseus is doomed to be killed by the Minotaur but kills it instead;

the initiates are in some sense "dead" while away from their homes and often encounter demons during their sequestration. Theseus meets Ariadne and "marries" her; the initiates are prepared for sexuality by their initiation. Theseus returns home and (when his father dies) becomes the king; initiates are fully adult males upon their return from initiation.

This story lends itself so well to psychological interpretations that it seems almost a test case for the theory that myth arises from the human psyche. The Minotaur imprisoned in the heart of the labyrinth has been interpreted as representing the hidden, inadmissible desires of the human subconscious. This monster was born from sexual transgression. The labyrinth was fashioned by the greatest artisan of all time; culture imprisons our more bestial desires. The labyrinth itself is susceptible to interpretation; Campbell sees it as the tortuous path to enlightenment. Theseus's encounter with the Minotaur leads to the death of his father. This can be seen as a variation of the Oedipal desire. Theseus's later destruction of his son Hippolytos repeats the Oedipal pattern but reverses it.

Given the fecundity of this myth for interpretations, it comes as something of a surprise that archaeology gives us reason to suppose that some remembered history is hidden beneath its fantastic elements. Sir Arthur Evans's discovery of the palace at Knossos was the first indication that the society of King Minos might have existed. Among the frescoes Evans found at Knossos was one that has become world-famous, often called the "bull-leaping" fresco. This painting shows three young humans and a bull. The bull is shown with all four legs extended in what appears to represent charging or running. One human, painted with white skin, seems to be dangling from the bull's horns, holding the horns with her arms. A red-skinned youth is somersaulting over the bull's back. The third figure, white-skinned, is standing behind the bull, arms extended, apparently having just landed on the tips of her toes. The most common interpretation of this scene is that it shows an athletic event, in which athletes of both sexes seized the bull by the horns, somersaulted over its back, and landed gracefully behind it. Without any written context for the scene, however, it is impossible to know just what is being portrayed here. If it is a sport, it is an extraordinarily dangerous one. It might also be a form of punishment, even execution; the figure who is dangling from the bull's horns appears to have been gored by one of those horns. It could be a representation of some religious ritual. It could be purely symbolic. The mere fact that an activity is shown in a work of art doesn't mean it necessarily happened. Whatever the exact reference of the scene, bulls and young men and women leaping (or being tossed by) bulls appear over and over in Minoan art, in statuary as well as frescoes. Even the Minotaur shows up on some Minoan seals.

What is the connection with the myth of the Minotaur? The myth recounts a dangerous encounter between youths and maidens, in a labyrinth, with a bull-like creature that kills the young people. Archaeologists found a labyrinthine palace that contained a representation of youths and maidens encountering a bull in a manner that would undoubtedly have led to the deaths of some of them. The story may have been transformed through repeated telling. Thus, one of the strangest of all Greek myths appears to have a kernel of remembered history at its core. Even the tribute paid by Athens to Crete could have some basis in fact. After all, Minoan civilization was predominant during the early development of Mycenean culture.

To say that the myth of the Minotaur may reflect dimly remembered history is not, of course, to invalidate other interpretations. The myth may well have developed as it did because of the connection with male initiation, or because of psychological imperatives, or for other reasons. The ruins of Knossos serve as a warning against assuming that even the most "obvious" symbols in myths are only symbols. ■

Supplementary Reading

Fitton, *Discovery of the Greek Bronze Age*, Ch. 5.

Walker, *Theseus and Athens*, Ch. 1–5.

Questions to Consider

1. Is tracing the myth of the Minotaur back to the bull-leaping at Knossos merely an updated form of Euhemerism? Put differently, while the ruins of Knossos are fascinating historically, can they and their frescoes tell us anything useful about the *myth* of the Minotaur?

2. I sketched out one possible psychological interpretation of the Minotaur and the labyrinth. Can you think of others or of other theoretical approaches to this myth?

From Myth to History and Back Again
Lecture 15—Transcript

In the previous lecture, we looked at Theseus's story and ended by discussing why the myth of Theseus connects him with Heracles and with the Trojan War through Helen, despite the chronological impossibilities there. In this lecture, we are going to concentrate on his connection with the Minotaur and King Minos, and through that story with Crete in general.

At first sight, the myth of the Minotaur in the Cretan Labyrinth seems to be one of the most purely imaginary and fantastic among Greek myths. It seems impossible that such a story could have any connection with historical fact whatsoever. The Minotaur, to start with, is a monster, half-human, half-animal; something that cannot actually exist in nature. This monster is conceived in a particularly improbable way, just to add to the fantastic-ness of his story.

The Minotaur is the child of Pasiphaë, Queen of Crete and wife of King Minos. Minos had once promised the god Poseidon that he would sacrifice to Poseidon a particularly beautiful bull that he had among his flocks. Minos then went back on his word, decided to keep this particularly beautiful bull for himself, and sacrifice a lesser animal for Poseidon. This, of course, angered Poseidon, who enlisted Aphrodite's help and punished Minos by infecting Queen Pasiphaë with an irresistible passion for the bull. So, Pasiphaë desires the bull that should have been sacrificed to Poseidon. She enlists the help of an artist named Daidalos, supposedly the greatest artisan who ever lived. Daidalos builds for Pasiphaë a hollow wooden cow in which she can hide. Pasiphaë hides inside the cow, the bull is then brought to the cow, the bull mates with what he thinks is a cow, and thus, Pasiphaë conceives the Minotaur. A completely bizarre story, and of course, one that is completely impossible as well.

Just to add to the oddity of the story of the Minotaur, he is not only a monster, he is a man-eating monster. This is, on the face of it, unlikely; even if we accept that there can be a creature that is half-man and half-bull, why should it be carnivorous? Bulls, cattle, are not carnivorous animals. But the Minotaur is, and once he has been born, it is because of his carnivorous and fearsome nature that Minos instructs Daidalos, the same artisan who built the wooden cow, to build the Labyrinth to contain the Minotaur. Of course, as we talked about last time, the monster has to be fed, and so, we have the tribute from Athens of seven youths and seven maidens annually to feed the Minotaur.

Along with the monstrous nature of the Minotaur, the very fact that his story, the story of Theseus's encounter with the Minotaur, contains so many elements that are reminiscent of folktale, such as Theseus's reliance on Ariadne's help—that also makes it seem unlikely that this story could be anything other than a traditional tale, a purely imaginary traditional tale. The monstrous nature of the Minotaur, the very obvious folktale elements in the story, all of those make it seem unlikely that we could have any historical background here at work at all, any historical kernel in the story.

Furthermore, the story of Theseus and the Minotaur offers a great deal of scope for differing interpretations of myth, in general, and of the story of Theseus and the Minotaur, in particular. It seems to work almost as a perfect example of how myth ought to function, because it can be interpreted by so many different theoretical schools that we have studied. To take one example, neo-ritualist theorists like to see this story as a paradigm for male initiation ritual. In many cultures, boys go through an initiation ritual to mark their transition from childhood to adulthood, as do girls go through a separate initiation ritual to mark their entrance into adult womanhood. Neo-ritualists identify various elements in the story of Theseus that seem to parallel with remarkable precision stages of a boy's initiation, as we know them from societies in which initiation rituals are still used.

First of all, Theseus arrives in Athens—as I mentioned in the last lecture— wearing women's clothing, at least according to one version of his story. Initiates arrive at their initiation as less than males. Whether they are dressed as females or not, part of the point of the initiation is that when the boy arrives at initiation, he is not yet fully male. He has to become male through the initiation ritual. Theseus journeys to Crete, where he will encounter the Minotaur. Male initiates are normally removed from their villages and towns, put in a different place, isolated from their society by traveling to another area. Theseus is doomed to be killed by the Minotaur, though he manages to kill it instead. Initiates are often conceived of by their society as being in some sense "dead," while they are in their isolation, while they are going through their initiation ceremony, to be reborn as adults after the ceremony. Also, very frequently in many cultures, initiates have to counter and overcome demons, or are believed to be encountering and overcoming demons during the initiation ritual, as Theseus encounters and overcomes the Minotaur. Theseus, of course, meets Ariadne and, at least in some sense, marries her—at least, spends a single night with her. One of the main points of initiation is to prepare boys for adult sexuality and, by implication, for marriage. Finally, Theseus returns home and becomes king after the death of his father. When the initiates return from their initiation ceremony, they are then fully adult males who can take their own role in society as fully adult males, just as Theseus assumes the kingship of Athens when he returns from his encounter with the Minotaur.

Now, these parallels are indeed very striking, and it is certainly worth considering the possibility that the Theseus myth does reflect initiation ritual. Unfortunately, we do not have any records of this kind of initiation ritual in Athens itself. We know of it in other cultures, including some that still exist today, but we don't have any evidence that this kind of initiation was ever done in Greek culture itself, unless of course, we take the myth of Theseus as evidence for such a ritual, as I have talked about in one of the opening lectures. If we assume that all myth must reflect ritual, then we can say Theseus's myth clearly reflects initiation ritual. If we don't start with that assumption, then we might decide that the Theseus myth itself is not enough to prove initiation ritual in ancient Greece. Certainly, the parallels are striking.

Another way of interpreting the myth of Theseus and his encounter with the Minotaur is to look at psychological interpretations of it. In fact, this myth is so fruitful for psychological interpretations that it can almost been seen as a test-case for the idea that myth rises from the human psyche. Or, a better way to put it might be that myth reflects realities of the individual human psyche that each individual must deal with in his or her lifetime. The Minotaur imprisoned in the heart of the Labyrinth has been interpreted by many theorists as representing the hidden, inadmissible desires of the human subconscious. Those things that all of us on some level desire or would like to do that we must keep imprisoned, that we must hide away from ourselves, can be seen as represented by this savage monster imprisoned in the Labyrinth. If we take this interpretation of the story, then it is probably significant that this monster was born from a particularly hideous kind of sexual transgression; that it was Pasiphaë's desire for a relationship with a bull, that it was bestiality, that gave birth to this monster who can be read as representing all the suppressed and repressed desires of the human psyche.

The Labyrinth that keeps the Minotaur imprisoned was, as I already mentioned, constructed by the greatest artisan who ever lived, and that can be interpreted as representing the way culture constructs a means by which we can control our more animalistic desires. If we see Daidalos as a representative of culture, and the Labyrinth as a representative of what culture does for humans, then we can make that comparison, that culture does allow us to control our more distressing, hidden, animalistic desires as the Labyrinth controls the Minotaur. The Labyrinth itself is susceptible to all kinds of interpretation. Followers of Campbell tend to see it as the tortuous path to enlightenment, the path that each human soul has to tread, whereby we go to the heart of our own Labyrinth, slay our own monsters, and then find our way back out again. The whole idea of the Minotaur in the Labyrinth lends itself to various different psychological interpretations. I am just scratching the surface here.

Another way to look at it is to remember that the encounter with the Minotaur leads to the death of Theseus's father Aigeus, and Theseus's ability to assume the throne of Athens. This can be seen as a variation on the Oedipal desire, the desire of the young male to supplant his father, to get rid of his father, to take his father's place. Later in Theseus's story, his destruction of his son Hippolytus can be seen as an inversion of the standard Oedipal story; a story in which the mother, or at least, stepmother, desires the son, not vice-versa, and in which the father, Theseus, kills the son, not vice-versa. So, the story of Hippolytus can be seen as an inverted version of Oedipus myth.

Given the fecundity of this myth for interpretation, given the fact that the story of Theseus and the Minotaur lends itself very well and very fruitfully to all sorts of interpretations, it comes as something of a surprise to realize—as I have been hinting at so far in this lecture—that archaeology does, in fact, give us good reason to suppose that there is actually some remembered history hidden beneath the fantastic elements of this story. As unlikely as that seems at first sight, this is one place in which what archaeology has discovered and the story that is narrated by a myth most obviously coincide with one another, and come together in some very surprising ways. And, it is all the more surprising, since this myth—as I said at the beginning of the lecture—is one that no one would ever have suspected as having a kernel of historical truth behind it.

You remember, from the lecture in which I discussed Minoan and Mycenaean culture, that the prehistoric culture of Minoan Crete was discovered by Sir Arthur Evans, who excavated a site called Knossos on Crete and discovered a huge, extraordinarily complex palace there at Knossos. When Sir Arthur Evans discovered the palace of Knossos, this was the first evidence that anyone ever had that the society of King Minos, the society recounted in the myth of the Minotaur and elsewhere, might actually have some basis in fact, that there had indeed been a large, complex and highly sophisticated society operating on Crete in the prehistory of Greece.

When Evans discovered the palace at Knossos, among the most remarkable discoveries he made there were many extraordinarily elaborate and very beautiful frescos. The walls of the palace had been adorned with fresco paintings. These, of course, had crumbled by the time Evans excavated them, but they have been meticulously restored, put back together, rather like working a jigsaw puzzle. Some of them are so damaged that it is hard to tell what they represented, but among one of the best preserved and one of the most famous is a fresco that is often called the "bull-leaping" fresco from the palace of Knossos. It is now in the archaeological museum at Heraklion, the capital of Crete.

This painting, the so-called "bull-leaping" fresco, features three apparently young human beings and a bull. The three humans are painted with different skin tones; two of them are white-skinned, one of them is red-skinned. In Minoan art, as in Egyptian art, as in the art of later Classical Greece, generally speaking, light-skinned figures are normally female, dark-skinned figures are normally male. We can assume that in the painting, the "bull-leaping" fresco from Knossos, the two light-skinned characters are meant to be female and the dark-skinned one is meant to be male.

What are these three humans and this one bull doing in the fresco? Well, the bull is depicted with all four legs extended and what pretty clearly is meant to mean either charging or running, galloping. The three humans are all depicted as interacting with the bull in one way or another. The first one, to the left of the painting, a white-skinned young woman, is shown dangling from the bull's horns. She is holding the horns, propping herself up on the horns, her feet are not touching the ground, so she is in some sense dangling from or suspended from the bull's horns. The red-skinned youth, whom we can assume to be male, is somersaulting over the bull's back. He is painted with his head and arms down toward the bull's back and his feet extended upward so he seems to be performing a somersault over the back of the bull. The third figure, also white-skinned, therefore, also female, is standing behind the bull with her arms upraised and balanced on the tip of her toes as though she has just landed behind the bull coming out of a somersault.

What is going on here? The most common interpretation of this scene is that it shows an athletic event. Most books of art criticism or most books about Minoan Crete that you will read will tell you that this was an athletic contest (called the "bull-leaping contest"), and we are told that it is a demonstration of athletic prowess. Supposedly, what happened was that each athlete would literally grab the bull by the horns, vault over its back, perform a neat somersault, and land behind the bull with arms extended and balanced on the tip of the toes. Supposedly, the painting shows three different athletes in the act of performing this particular athletic event; the first one suspended from the bull's horns, the second in full somersault over the bull's back, and the third one landing.

Maybe this is what is going on in the fresco. Maybe it is, in fact, an athletic event, but it has always seemed to me that, if it is an athletic event, that it is, at the very least, an extraordinarily dangerous one. The humans are painted as being really almost nude. They are wearing loincloths, but not much more than loincloths, so they have no protection at all. They are small in relationship to the bull, and the idea of seizing the horns of a charging bull, performing a perfect somersault over its back, and landing nicely *en pointe* on the other side of the bull has always struck me as a little unlikely. Perhaps some athletes could do it but, at the very least, this would be an extremely dangerous form of athletic competition.

As I have mentioned several times before, we have the same problem here as we have in looking at the Minoan snake-goddess or in trying to interpret archaeological evidence, in general. We have no written context to tell us what this fresco refers to. We assume it is an athletic contest, but it might be something else. It has occurred to me it could be a form of punishment. Perhaps people were pitted against this bull to punish them for misdeeds, with the idea that they would probably be killed by the encounter. Or perhaps it is indicative of some kind of religious ritual. In other words, perhaps it is purely symbolic, and does not represent any action that any genuine human beings ever really performed in connection with bulls on Minoan Crete.

The suggestion that it is purely symbolic may seem a little bit odd at first sight. We tend to assume, when looking at archaeological remnants of ancient cultures, that anything that is depicted in the culture's art must somehow have really happened. We tend to make that assumption, but I think it is a false one. The mere fact that an activity is shown in artwork does not necessarily mean that it ever actually happened in the culture. There is another very famous Minoan fresco that shows a monkey picking crocuses to harvest saffron. I find it highly unlikely that the Minoans actually trained monkeys to pick crocus to harvest saffron. I think that has to be a purely imaginary scene.

Let's take an example from our own culture. At this time of year—I am recording these lectures in early December—our culture is permeated with pictures of Santa Claus being pulled in a sleigh by his reindeer. That picture of a human being with a group of reindeer, being pulled in a sleigh, is all over the place this time of year. We see it everywhere, and we all have a sense of what it means. That does not imply that in our culture, in actuality, there is really a human being being pulled in a sleigh by reindeer. Even though we have this story, we almost never act it out. We never harness actual reindeer to a sleigh and have them pull Santa Claus around. We recognize the referent of the image, but that does not mean that the image has any direct corresponding real action. So, I think it is at least worth considering the possibility that the "bull-leaping" fresco at Knossos could be purely symbolic, could refer to some meaningful narrative element in Minoan culture that Minoans would recognize when they saw the symbol, without our necessarily having to assume that anyone ever really did perform this leap over the bull's back.

Whatever the reference of the scene—and I don't think we are ever going to know exactly what it refers to—bulls, and young men and women leaping over their backs or being tossed by their horns, depending on how you interpret it, is an image that shows up over and over again in Minoan art, not just in frescos, but also in statuary. Clearly, it must have had some important meaning for Minoan culture. Furthermore, the Minotaur himself, the half-bull, half-human image shows up on a couple of Minoan seals (little objects that were used to make an impression in wax). So, we know that Minoan culture did at least sometimes represent a man and a bull combined into one form.

What is the connection, if any, of the "bull-leaping" fresco with the Minotaur? What is the connection of the palace of Knossos with the myth of the Minotaur? This is where the possibility of actual historical memory is absolutely fascinating to consider. What does the myth of the Minotaur tell us? It recounts a dangerous encounter between young men and young women, the seven youths and the seven maidens, in a Labyrinth—that is, in a very elaborate maze-like structure—with a bull-like creature at the center of the Labyrinth that kills the young people. When Sir Arthur Evans set out to excavate on Crete, he cannot really have expected to find the Minotaur or any trace of the Minotaur. What did he find?

He found a palace that is so elaborate that calling it a "Labyrinth" is perhaps not an exaggeration. I myself became lost in the ruins of Knossos the first time I visited it and wandered around in it. The palace consists of various different passages filled with right angle turns, so it is very easy to lose your sense of direction, all sorts of small rooms coming off of these passages ,and in its original form, apparently it stood at least three stories high. It was absolutely enormous, very complicated, very difficult for someone from a less sophisticated culture to find their way around in. Evans found a palace that it is hardly a stretch of the imagination to call a "Labyrinth." And within that palace, he found a representation, a painting, of youths and maidens encountering a bull in a manner that very likely would have been fatal for at least some of them. Not encountering the Minotaur, true, but encountering a bull in a manner that would have lead to the deaths of at least some of those youths and maidens.

In the intervening centuries between the waning of Minoan culture, which went into its decline sometime in the fifteenth century B.C., and the writing down of the myths about Theseus, I think it is not at all beyond the realm of possibility that, as these stories were told over and over again, the bull-leaping games, ceremonies, or punishment, or whatever they were, of Minoan Crete transmogrified into the idea of a monster at the heart of the labyrinth that ate youths and maidens. That is the kind of change that a story can go through over generations where it is recounted, where the kernel of truth—something happened in the middle of that palace in Crete that was dangerous to young people—remains but is changed into a mythic form, changed into a monster that eats the young people. This very strange myth, that is one of the oddest of all Greek myths, seems to have, perhaps, a kernel of remembered history at its core.

Even the idea that Athens paid tribute to Crete could have some basis in fact, could also reflect remembered history. Again, to recap just a little bit from an earlier lecture, Minoan culture was the first great prehistoric culture to exist in the area we would call Greece. Mycenaean culture was the second great culture. The two overlapped. Mycenaean culture began to develop while Minoan culture was at its high point. If Mycenaean culture began about 2000 B.C., and waned in 1100, Minoan culture waned in the fifteenth century B.C. There is several hundred years of overlap there. At some point, the Mycenaeans gained the ascendancy. At some point, Mycenaean culture took over Minoan, and probably even began to govern the Minoans. We know this in part because we know that the Minoans, at first, did not speak Mycenaean Greek, and later began to speak Mycenaean Greek. We know that from their use of Linear B, from the tablets which have been deciphered both in the Minoan palaces on Crete and in Mycenaean palaces on the mainland.

One culture almost never adopts another culture's language unless there has been some kind of conquest. The peoples of South America only began

247

speaking Spanish after the Spanish conquest, for instance. The fact that the Minoans began to use Mycenaean Greek at a particular point in their history indicates a conquest by the Mycenaeans. However, before that conquest, there must have been a time when Minoan culture was still predominant and Mycenaean culture was still beginning to develop. At that time, it is quite likely, at least, that the Minoan overlords, the Minoans who controlled trade throughout their end of the Mediterranean, may have imposed some sort of tribute on the developing Mycenaean cities of Greece. So, you see where I am going with this? The idea that, at some point, Athens had to pay a tribute to Crete, at some point, Athens had to send precious cargo to Crete each year because Crete had dominance over Athens, may very well reflect an actual folk memory of the situation when Minoan culture was dominant and Mycenaean culture was not yet the main leader of the area.

I think it is highly unlikely that the Mycenaeans actually had to send youths and maidens to take part in the bull-leaping, but that is how myth works. You would remember sending a tribute of whatever it was—grain, olive oil, whatever—and that would change into a more memorable and a more horrible tribute through the passage of time. All of these elements— the tribute, the dangerousness, the strangeness of the culture in Crete, the monstrous nature of the Minotaur—all of those can be seen as reflecting a dim memory of the interactions between Minoan and Mycenaean culture.

Now, to say that the myth of the Minotaur may reflect dimly remembered history is not, by any means, to invalidate other interpretations of that myth. I am not trying to be Euhemeros here. I am not trying to say that the myth of the Minotaur is "only" misremembered history about Minoan Crete and its interaction with Mycenaean Greeks. The myth developed over the centuries, between the time of those two cultures and the time when it was written down in the form that we now have it. The myth developed and changed, and took on characteristics that it now has. It may well have developed as it did, in part, because of the connection with male initiation rights, or because of the psychological imperatives that work in the human psyche, or for many other reasons. Merely to say that there is some remembered history in this myth does not, in and of itself, invalidate any other way of interpreting the myth. The various different interpretations should always work together and be considered together. I have always found it fascinating, from the first time

I visited Knossos in my early twenties, to consider that that extraordinarily bizarre story of monsters, and princesses, and magic and all the rest of it may reflect actual prehistorical fact. It strikes me as fascinating and well worth bearing in mind.

Also, the ruins of Knossos and their possible connection with the myth of the Minotaur, I think, can serve to remind us that other very strange Greek myths—the story of Perseus and the monster Medusa, who had snakes for hair and whose gaze turned him into stone, is one, for instance—it is possible that these other very strange myths might also have some concealed kernel of history hidden in them in a way that would be impossible for us to imagine, unless and until archaeology finds it for us. No one before Sir Arthur Evans would ever have imagined that the Minotaur could reflect any historical actuality at all, and yet clearly he does. Other Greek myths, as well, may have some historical connection that we cannot yet see.

In this lecture, we finished our examination of the myth of Theseus by looking at some possible interpretations of his encounter with the Minotaur, and discussing the possible connection with Minoan and Mycenaean culture. In our next lecture, we will turn to an examination of the greatest Greek hero of all, the very famous Heracles.

The Greatest Hero of All
Lecture 16

In this lecture, we are going to turn to looking at the greatest Greek hero of all, Heracles. Now Heracles, who may be more familiar in the Latin form of his name, Hercules, is not just the greatest hero within Greek myth itself, he is also, I think it is fair to say, the most famous hero of classical myth on into the modern day.

The greatest and most famous Greek hero of all is Heracles (Latin Hercules), son of Zeus and the mortal woman Alcmene. Unlike many heroes who are associated with only one city, Heracles was a pan-Hellenic hero, claimed by all of Greece. Heracles is mentioned in epic, tragedy, history, and most other genres of Greek and Roman literature, but none of them tells his complete story. Fortunately for us, Apollodorus gives an account of Heracles's life, as he does for Theseus, which allows us to understand the more illusive references to him in other authors.

Like those of many other heroes, Heracles's conception and babyhood were unusual. Heracles is the son of Zeus and Alcmene, wife of Amphitryon. Zeus tricked Alcmene into sleeping with him by disguising himself as Amphitryon, who was actually away at war. Amphitryon returned the next day, much to Alcmene's surprise. Alcmene conceived Heracles by Zeus and his twin, Iphicles, by Amphitryon. This story clearly recalls Theseus's dual parentage by Aigeus and Poseidon. Hera always hated Zeus's sons by other females, and she particularly detested Heracles. Her hatred reflects the fact that Heracles was destined to be the greatest of all heroes. She sabotaged him from the day of his birth. Zeus declared that a descendant of Perseus who was about to be born would rule over Mycenae; knowing that Zeus meant Heracles, Hera persuaded the goddess of childbirth to extend Alcmene's labor and to hasten the birth of a cousin of Heracles, Eurystheus. Heracles's name apparently means "glorious through Hera." Even as a baby, Heracles showed strength and courage. When Hera sent snakes to kill him in his cradle, the baby Heracles strangled them.

When Heracles reached maturity, he was characterized not only by extreme strength and courage, but also by other extremes: of sexual appetite, of hunger and thirst, and of rage. Among the first of Heracles's adventures was his encounter with the fifty daughters of Thespios, when he was only eighteen. He slept with all fifty of them. His appetite for food and drink was no less voracious. He was given to excessive rage, even madness (perhaps sent by Hera). In one such episode of madness, he killed his own children by his first wife, Megara. This act led directly to his famous labors. On the advice of the Pythia, he served Eurystheus for twelve years and performed the labors that Eurystheus ordered. The Pythia promised that the reward for accomplishing the labors would be immortality.

Heracles's Twelve Labors are examples of the "test-and-quest" type of hero tale.

Heracles's Twelve Labors are examples of the "test-and-quest" type of hero tale. The labors involve an ascending degree of difficulty and of distance that Heracles must travel, and each of the labors would have been impossible or fatal for a lesser man. The first six labors all take place in the Peloponnesus and involve animals. With the exception of the Hydra, these animals are not imaginary monsters, but each of them has some extraordinary attribute that makes it exceptionally dangerous. The Nemean Lion. Heracles killed and skinned it. The Lernaean Hydra. This was a snake with nine heads, one of which was immortal. When a head was cut off, two grew in its place. Heracles finally vanquished it with the help of his nephew Iolaus. The Cerynian Hind. This golden-horned deer was not dangerous in itself but was sacred to Artemis. Heracles captured it. The Erymanthian Boar. Eurystheus demanded that Heracles capture this savage beast and bring it to him alive. The Augean Stables. This labor differs from the rest in that it was difficult but not particularly dangerous. The stables had never been cleaned; Heracles diverted two rivers to flow through them. The Stymphalian Birds. These birds, which lived in a swamp, could shoot their arrow-sharp feathers from their wings. Heracles killed them all. The next three labors take place outside of the Peloponnese, moving steadily further away and becoming steadily stranger. The Cretan Bull. This may be the same bull that sired the Minotaur; Heracles caught it and brought it to Eurystheus. The Mares of Diomedes. Heracles tamed these man-eating mares and fed their master, Diomedes, to them. The Belt of Hippolyta. Hippolyta was an Amazon queen, and Heracles had to take her belt away from her. The final three labors take Heracles to the very edges of the world and pit him against emblems of mortality and immortality. (The order of the last two labors is sometimes reversed.) The Cattle of Geryon. Geryon was a triple-bodied monster who lived in the far west. Heracles drove his cattle back to Eurystheus. The Apples of the Hesperides. These daughters of Night had a tree with golden apples, also in the far west, guarded by a dragon. With Atlas's help, Heracles got the apples. Cerberus. Heracles descended to Tartaros to fetch back this guard dog of the Underworld. Eurystheus didn't know what to do with him, and Cerberus found his way back to Hades.

© Photos.com/Thinkstock.

Heracles, son of Zeus and Alcmene. Unlike many heroes, who were associated with only one city, Heracles was a pan-Hellenic hero, claimed by all of Greece.

Heracles has various other adventures beyond the labors, in what are sometimes called the *parerga*, or "side works." Heracles is unlike most other heroes in that he is neither a king nor primarily a warrior. It is clear from his labors and *parerga* that his primary role is as a fighter of animals, particularly extraordinary or dangerous animals, and monsters. One interpretation of this role is that it represents the spread of Greek culture; Heracles takes Greek civilization with him wherever he goes. He traveled widely in his labors. The killing of monsters can be read as representing the "humanizing" of unknown lands.

Heracles is one of very few humans in Greek myth to become a god. His road to immortality was caused not by exceptional goodness, but by exceptional wrongdoing and suffering. Heracles's second wife was Deianira. His marriage to her was beset with difficulties that included two encounters with semi-animal beings. Before he could marry Deianira, Heracles had to wrestle the river god Achelous, who had the head of a bull. As Heracles was returning home with Deianira, the centaur Nessos tried to rape her. Heracles shot him with an arrow that had been dipped in the Hydra's venom. As Nessos was dying, he told Deianira to gather some of his blood as a love-charm. Years later, when Heracles fell in love with another woman, Deianira gave him a robe dipped in Nessos's blood. The robe burned Heracles's flesh but did not kill him. In agony, he mounted a funeral pyre and burned himself to death. Only his body died, however; he became immortal and took his place on Olympus, where he married Hebe. This reiterates the idea, seen in the stories of Demophoön and Dionysos, that passing through fire is a necessary step for immortality.

So many stories cluster around Heracles that it is very difficult to construct a unified, coherent picture. He can best be analyzed by identifying a series of polar oppositions that seem to underlie his myth. He is both admirable and horrifying, powerful and powerless. The hero who overcomes monsters and marks out the civilized world is also the madman who kills his wife and children. The greatest of Zeus's human sons is twice a slave. He is supremely ill-fated and supremely fortunate. He is persecuted by Hera from before his birth, and he dies shamefully, in agony. This all-too-human hero is also the one human to achieve immortality and become a god; yet he continued to receive sacrifices as both a hero and a god. His persecutor, Hera, allows him to marry her own daughter, Hebe. He both resists Death and intentionally embraces it. His last three labors are all in some sense conquests of Death. In another story, he wrestled with and defeated Death himself. Yet his own death comes through voluntary self-cremation.

Heracles is both a serious, even tragic, figure and a comic figure of excess. He is both masculine and feminine; in one of his *parerga*, the ultra-masculine strongman wears women's clothes and is the slave of a queen. Syncretism may account for some of these differences but seems inadequate to explain them all. Theoretical interpretations may be more satisfactory; for example: Heracles can be read as a kind of "everyman" figure who clearly displays a Jungian "shadow" side. He can also be seen as embodying (and thus mediating between?) both Nature and Culture. ■

Essential Reading

Kirk, *Nature of Greek Myths*, Ch. 8 ("The Mythical Life of Heracles").

Supplementary Reading

Burkert, *Structure and History*, Ch. 4, pp. 78–98.

Galinsky, *The Herakles Theme*.

Questions to Consider

1. Heracles clearly violates at least one of the Delphic maxims, "nothing in excess." What is the implication of this, given that Heracles is the great pan-Hellenic hero?

2. Does the idea of Heracles as a projection of "everyman," with exaggerated virtues and exaggerated faults, make sense to you? How else could we account for the many contradictions in this hero?

The Greatest Hero of All
Lecture 16—Transcript

In the previous two lectures, we looked at Theseus, the primary hero of Athenian myth, and talked about some of the elements of his story and their significance. In this lecture, we are going to turn to looking at the greatest Greek hero of all, Heracles. Now Heracles, who may be more familiar in the Latin form of his name, Hercules, is not just the greatest hero within Greek myth itself, he is also, I think it is fair to say, the most famous hero of classical myth on into the modern day. He still shows up in things such as the recent Disney movie; there is a television series currently about Hercules. He has continued to be a figure in popular imagination up to our own day.

He was the son of Zeus and a mortal woman named Alcmene. Unlike many heroes, such as Theseus, who are associated primarily with one particular city as Theseus is with Athens, Heracles is often called a pan-Hellenic hero, which simply means that he is a hero claimed by all of Greeks. He is not associated primarily with one particular city; rather he is worshipped throughout Greece by most, if not all, Greek people. Heracles is mentioned as the great pan-Hellenic hero all over the place in Greek literature. References to him show up in epic, in tragedy, in history and in most other genres of Greek and Roman literature. None of these references tell his complete story. Often an author will simply allude to him, will use him as a point of comparison for someone or something else. Because Heracles is so well known, he could be referred to in that very allusive sense without any explanation of what it is the author is referring to. Fortunately for us, Apollodorus, in the *Library of Greek Mythology,* gives a fairly full account of Heracles's life, which allows us to understand these allusive references to him in other authors. Apollodorus, by the way, also gives his account of Theseus's life, which is where we get a good deal of our information about Theseus.

Now, like many heroes, Heracles has a conception and a babyhood that are fraught with difficulties or, at least, with unusual elements. As I already said, his father is Zeus and his mother is the human woman, Alcmene. Heracles is conceived when Zeus tricks Alcmene into thinking that he is actually her husband Amphitryon. Amphitryon was away at war, and Zeus appeared to

Alcmene disguised as Amphitryon. Remember, a god can appear in any guise he chooses. Alcmene went to bed with Zeus, thinking that her husband was home unexpectedly from the war. The next day, the real Amphitryon came home, and there was a rather surprising scene in which Amphitryon couldn't understand why Alcmene was not happier and more surprised to see him, and Alcmene couldn't understand why Amphitryon insisted that he hadn't been home for ages. Eventually, they figured out that it must have been a god that had visited Alcmene the day before. Alcmene conceived Heracles by Zeus, thinking that it was her husband Amphitryon, and she conceived Heracles's twin, Iphicles, the next night by Amphitryon. Heracles has a twin brother who is actually only his half-brother. They are conceived on successive nights. Iphicles is a perfectly normal everyday human being. He is not exceptionally brave, strong or in any other way marked out for unusual status as Heracles is.

This story very clearly recalls Theseus's dual parentage by Aigeus and Poseidon. I think it is instructive to look at the difference, as I talked about last time. Theseus has to be both a legitimate king of Athens and the son of a god. Because he needs to fulfill both of those functions, he is given two separate fathers, and the decision is never made which one is really his father. Heracles is not the king of any particular city. He is not directly associated with any particular city, so there is not the same need to have him the son of an actual, legitimate human father. Therefore, the human father's role in his conception is displaced onto Iphicles, and Heracles is, unquestionably and without doubt, the son of Zeus.

As I mentioned early on in the course, Hera always hated Zeus's sons by other females, particularly by human females. She had a particular detestation for Heracles. This hatred for Heracles on the part of Hera reflects the fact that Heracles is destined to be the greatest hero ever. Therefore, he incurs the most hatred and jealousy from Zeus's wife Hera. She sabotages him even from before his birth. She is out to make trouble for him and make life difficult for him from the very beginning, from before the day of his birth. When Heracles was about to be born, Zeus decreed that on this particular day there would be born a descendant of Perseus, the great hero, who Zeus said would rule over the great city Mycenae. Hera knew that Zeus meant Heracles, but Zeus did not actually say Heracles. He simply said "a descendant of Perseus." Hera persuaded the goddess of childbirth, who was after all Hera's daughter, to keep Alcmene in labor longer than she should have been and to hasten the birth of a cousin of Heracles, a man named Eurystheus, also a descendant of Perseus. Thus, Eurystheus is born on the day that Heracles should have been born, and Zeus's decree that on this day shall be born a descendant of Perseus who will rule over Mycenae, gets displaced onto Eurystheus, though he intended it for Heracles.

That is the first time that Hera steps in and sabotages Heracles. Now, interestingly enough, as people often notice when they have read a good deal of Greek literature, Heracles's name seems to have some connection with the name Hera. The first two syllables are exactly the same. The "-cles" element is similar to the word, or the same word actually, as *kleos*, which means glory. Heracles's name seems, in some way, to have something to do with glory and with Hera. Some scholars have tried to say it means "the glory of Hera," but that makes no sense whatsoever, since Hera hates him and persecutes him. I think a better suggestion is to read Heracles's name as meaning "glorious through Hera." Heracles achieves his glory because of all the hardships that Hera forces him into, because of the actions he has to take to overcome those hardships. Therefore, in a sense, he receives glory through Hera, or is glorious through Hera.

Even as a baby, Heracles showed great strength and courage. His first real noteworthy deed was when Hera sent two snakes to kill him in his crib, and the baby Heracles, instead of being frightened, strangled the snakes with his bare hands. Iphicles is often shown in artistic representations of this, cowering off in one side of the crib looking like a normal baby, and little Heracles is sitting bolt upright strangling the snakes. From babyhood on, Heracles was clearly very unusual, and not just unusually courageous, but unusually strong as well.

When he reached maturity, Heracles was characterized not only by exceptional strength and courage, but also by exceptional or excessive appetites and powers in other regards as well. He is characterized by extremes of sexual appetite, of hunger and thirst, and of rage. His first adventure as a young man involved his encounter with 50 daughters of a king named Thespios. Heracles is 18 years old at the time. He spends the night with King

Thespios, and supposedly has sex with all 50 of Thespios's daughters—according to some authors, one daughter per night for 50 continuous nights, according to most authors, all 50 on the same night. Heracles clearly has both exceptional sexual desire and exceptional sexual abilities or prowess. His appetite for food and drink is no less voracious. There are various stories, particularly by comic authors, that refer to Heracles as a kind of prototypical glutton and drunkard—someone who eats and drinks way too much, very, very excessively.

On a less comic level, Heracles is also noted for excessive passion, including the passion of rage. There are various times when he gives way to excessive rage, even to the extent of madness. The madness is usually, most likely, sent by Hera. In the most famous such episode of madness, Heracles kills his own children by his first wife Megara, and perhaps kills the wife as well. Authorities differ on that. Heracles is susceptible to extreme rage, in which he does things that normally he would not do. It is because of the killing of these children that he undertakes his famous Twelve Labors.

After Heracles kills his children, he goes to the oracle at Delphi to ask the Pythia what he should do to cleanse himself of this terrible crime, how he can expiate the guilt that he has incurred for killing his children. The Pythia tells him that he must serve his cousin Eurystheus—that cousin that was born on the day Heracles should have been born—as a slave, in effect, for 12 years, and must perform whatever labors Eurystheus orders him to perform during that time. The Pythia also promised Heracles that if he successfully accomplishes the labors that Eurystheus sets for him, his reward will be immortality; a very, very unusual aspect of Heracles's story that we will come back to in a few minutes.

The 12 Labors Heracles performs are clear examples of the "test-and-quest" type of hero tale, the type we talked about in the first lecture on Theseus. Just as Theseus performed six labors, Heracles performs 12. In many ways, many scholars think that Theseus is almost a kind of echo of, or modeled on, Heracles—that Theseus is to Athens as Heracles is to Greece, in general. If Heracles has 12 Labors, Theseus has got to have at least six. That sort of parallelism seems to be very clearly at work in the Theseus story. Heracles undertakes 12 Labors that are characterized by an increasing level of difficulty as the Labors proceed, and by increasing distances that Heracles must travel to perform them. Each one of the Labors that he undertakes would have been impossible for a lesser man; many of them would have been fatal for a lesser man. Heracles manages to accomplish them all.

The Labors fall into three clearly recognizable groups. The first six take place in Peloponnesus—the main area of Greece, the central area of Greece—and involve animals. The second group, Labors Seven through Nine, take place a little further away, still in the Greek-speaking area of the world, but further away from central Greece than the first six. The final three labors, Labors Ten through Twelve, take place in the Far West and seem to have to do with issues of mortality and immortality.

The first six, the Peloponnesian Labors, involve animals. With the exception of Labor Number Two, the Hydra, these animals are not mythical or imaginary monsters. They are regular, everyday animals, but each of them has some extraordinary attribute or ability that makes them exceptionally difficult to overcome or exceptionally dangerous. To run through them very quickly: the First Labor involves killing the Nemean Lion. This lion is invulnerable to wounds that would pierce it. It cannot be pierced by the arrow, spear, sword or any other sharp object. Heracles clubs it to death, and then uses its own claws to skin it. After he has skinned the Nemean Lion, he takes the lion's skin as his cloak. This becomes his most recognizable attribute in art. Heracles normally carries his club and wears his lion-skin cloak. The cloak is usually shown with Heracles's face looking out from between the lion's jaws, so the lion's head becomes the hood of his cloak.

The Second Labor involves killing the Lernaean Hydra. The Hydra was a snake with nine heads. One head was immortal, which makes it very difficult to kill the Hydra. To make it even more difficult, whenever Heracles cut off one of the Hydra's heads, two more would grow in its place. The more he tried to kill this monster, the more powerful the monster became. Eventually, he enlisted the help of his nephew Iolaus, Iphicles's son. When Heracles cut off one of the Hydra's heads, his nephew would cauterize the neck to keep the heads from growing back. When Heracles cut off the immortal head, what he did was take it and bury it under a boulder. So, he overcame the Hydra.

The Third Labor involved the Cerynian Hind,or deer, a deer with golden antlers sacred to Artemis. The only danger there is that Artemis might be angered by Heracles's injuring her deer. Instead, he captures it and takes it back to his cousin Eurystheus live. He also, in Labor Number Four, captures a very dangerous boar, the Erymanthian Boar, and takes it back to Eurystheus. There are some wonderful examples of artwork in which Eurystheus is hiding inside a huge storage jar to try to avoid the Erymanthian Boar that Heracles is bringing back to him at Eurystheus's command.

Labor Number Five—my own personal favorite because I rode horses a lot as a child and have cleaned many a stable myself—is the Labor of the Augean Stables, stables which had never been cleaned in all the years they existed. In order to clean them, Heracles diverted two rivers, which he made flow through the stables and wash them out. Labor Number Six, the last of the Peloponnesian labors, is the Stymphalian Birds. These birds had feathers which were arrow-sharp and which they could fire from their wings. Heracles killed all of them, either by shooting them with his bow and arrow or by using a slingshot.

The next group of three Labors, as I said, takes place a little further afield and becomes a little bit stranger or more dangerous, progressively, as we go on. The Seventh Labor had to do with catching the Cretan Bull. This may very well be the same bull that fathered the Minotaur. We are not sure about that, but some authors say it is. Heracles caught this same bull and brought it back home to Eurystheus. The Eighth Labor, the second Labor in the second group, involved the Mares of Diomedes. Diomedes was the king of Thrace, an area north of Greece, and had mares who ate human flesh—very dangerous horses. Heracles has to tame these mares and, as a part of doing so, feeds Diomedes, their murderous master, to them to give Diomedes a taste of his own medicine.

The most interesting in many ways of this second group of Labors is a Labor that is usually called the "Girdle of Hippolyta." I tend to call it the "Belt of Hippolyta," because "girdle" has such a different meaning in modern English; we are talking about a belt, not about a girdle in the modern sense. Hippolyta was an Amazon queen, perhaps the very same Hippolyta whom Theseus married, and Heracles had to go and get her belt, her ornate sash, away from her and bring that back to Eurystheus. Obviously, an Amazon queen is not going to hand her belt over to anyone who asks for it, so, the implication is that Heracles had to fight her, overcome her and forcibly take the belt away from her.

Now, his final three Labors, out of the canonical famous Twelve great Labors, all take Heracles to the edges of the world, specifically to the Far West, and pit him against emblems of mortality and immortality. The order of the last two Labors is controversial. The one that I have listed as next to last is sometimes given as the last one, and vice-versa, but I list them in the order that I think is most logical and makes the most sense. The Far West, by the way, is itself an area associated with death and immortality. Going to the Far West in Greek mythology tends to indicate, in some way, approaching the land of the dead or leaving the land of the living. The very location of these last three Labors, in part, indicates that they are concerned with mortality and immortality.

In the first of these three Labors, the connection is perhaps not so obvious. This one, Labor Number Ten, involves the Cattle of Geryon. Geryon is a monster who lives in the Far West, triple- bodied. He is one monster, but he has three bodies. Heracles has to fight him, defeat him, steal his cattle and, of course, drive them back home to Eurystheus.

The Eleventh Labor, called the "Apples of the Hesperides," takes Heracles even further afield. The Hesperides are three goddesses, daughters of Night, who live on an island in the Far West. Their name, Hesperides, simply means "daughters of the West." They have a tree guarded by a dragon. On the tree grow golden apples. Many authors seem to indicate that these golden apples are themselves, in some way, food of immortality—that if you ate these apples, you would gain immortality. Heracles has to not only get past the Hesperides, but past the dragon to retrieve these apples. He does so with the help of Atlas. Atlas, Prometheus's brother, is the Titan who was condemned to hold the sky upon his shoulders. Heracles supposedly made a deal with Atlas that he, Heracles, would hold the sky for a period, while Atlas went to get the apples. Atlas did this, came back to Heracles with the three golden apples, and in effect, said, "Thank you very much, I have no intention of taking the sky back. You can keep it." Whereupon Heracles said, sadly,

"Well, Atlas, you have got the better of me, but please, my shoulders are really sore; would you take the sky back just for a minute while I fold up my lion-skin cape and make a pad for my shoulders?" Atlas did take the sky back. Heracles said, "Well, thank you very much," picked up the apples and went on his merry way. Atlas is still holding the sky.

The final Labor is the labor of Cerberus, the three-headed dog of the Underworld. (His name ought to be pronounced Kerberus, by the way, but it has become so famous in English as Serberus that that is how I pronounce it.) Heracles descended to Tartarus to fetch this three-headed guard dog of the Underworld, and this is the clearest example of Heracles being pitted against the forces of death. To be able to go into the Underworld, steal the guard dog who is there to keep souls from getting out and people from getting in, and bring the dog back with him, is pretty clearly emblematic of a conquest of death. Of course, he takes Cerberus back with him to Eurystheus who has no idea what to do with the dog, lets him go, and Cerberus finds his way back to Tartarus where he belongs. It is during this episode that Heracles frees Theseus from the Underworld.

Along with these 12 "canonical' Labors, so called, Heracles has all sorts of other adventures which are often called the *parerga,* or "side works," in Greek. Many times, when he is on his way to perform a Labor in Greece, he turns aside and has another adventure while he is on his way to the Labor. Throughout all of these, there are some notable characteristics of Heracles that are worth bringing out here. Unlike most other heroes we encounter in Greek myth, Heracles is neither primarily a warrior, nor primarily a king. It is clear, both from his Labors and from his *parerga*, that his primary role, his main reason for existence, is to be a fighter of animals and of mythical monsters. That seems to be what he is there for. Unlike Achilles who was a great warrior, or a king such as Oedipus, Theseus, Agamemnon and others, Heracles exists to fight animals.

One interpretation of this—there are probably many possible ones, but one primary interpretation of this—is that Heracles represents the spread of Greek culture, that as Greek civilization came into contact with other civilizations throughout the Greek world, and as other civilizations spread through colonies that were planted in other places, so Heracles is imagined as traveling in his Labors ever further afield, ever further away from Greece during these travels, killing monsters and overcoming wild animals as he goes.

Again, a comparison with Theseus is helpful. Remember how I talked about Theseus's killing of the monsters and brigands on his way to Athens, as representing freeing Attica of dangers for travelers and so forth? Similarly, Heracles's encounters with animals and monsters can be seen as representing the humanizing of unknown lands. The Greek assumption was that their civilization was superior—that when they took Greek civilization to other lands, they were somehow improving, civilizing, humanizing those other lands—and Heracles may represent that in his role as a pan-Hellenic hero.

Perhaps the most notable aspect of Heracles is that he is one of the very few humans to successfully achieve immortality and become a god. He does become a real, genuine god, not just a minor god. He joins the Olympians on Olympus. He marries Hebe, daughter of Zeus and Hera. How does this come about? His road to immortality is caused not by exceptional goodness, despite what modern reworkers of his story try to imply, but rather by exceptional suffering and exceptional wrongdoing. His death is caused immediately by his wife Deianira. He marries her after the death of his first wife Megara. He marries Deianira, but his marriage to her is beset by difficulties from the very beginning. When Heracles first tries to marry Deianira or wants to marry her, he has to wrestle a river god in order to win her hand, and this river god has the head of a bull. This river god, whom Heracles has to wrestle, is himself a part-animal monster. After Heracles has married Deianira and is taking her home with him, they have to cross another river that is guarded by a centaur—that is, a creature that is a horse in its body and a man from the waist up, where the horse would have its neck and head.

This centaur, Nessos, attempts to rape Deianira, and Heracles in vengeance kills Nessos, shoots him with an arrow. He shoots the centaur with an arrow that was dipped in the Hydra's venom, which makes it irrevocably poisonous. Now, as Nessos is dying, the centaur persuades Deianira that she should catch and save some of his blood. If Heracles ever loses interest in Deianira, Nessos tells her that his blood will act as a love charm. Deianira, for whatever reason, believes this. There is no good reason to think that

Nessos would be friendlily inclined toward Deianira and Heracles, but Deianira does believe him. She keeps his blood, and years later when Heracles does, in fact, lose interest in Deianira and wants to marry another woman, Deianira gives Heracles a robe smeared with Nessos's blood, with the centaur's blood. Heracles puts the robe on, and it begins to burn and eat away his flesh. It does not kill him, but it begins to devour his flesh. The centaur's blood sounds almost like some kind of acid, hideously painful and hideously destructive. In agony, Heracles has a funeral pyre built; he mounts the funeral pyre, and voluntarily immolates himself, burns himself to death, to escape from the agony of the robe that Deianira has given him.

But, and this is the unusual element here, only his body dies. His psyche, his soul, his better part—however you want to put it—becomes a god, goes to Mount Olympus, and marries Hebe. One thing that is going on here, very briefly, is we have got the fullest statement of an idea that has been hinted at before, that passing through fire is somehow a necessary part of becoming immortal for a mortal human being. Remember when Demeter tried to immortalize Demophoön? She put the baby in the fireplace. When Dionysos is born out of Zeus's thigh, he gets into Zeus's thigh in the first place because his mother Semele has been incinerated. In both of those myths, there seems to be an implication that passing through fire is a necessary first step. It may not be sufficient in itself, but it is a necessary first step to achieving immortality. Here, with Heracles, he achieves immortality by burning his mortal body, intentionally.

Many different stories cluster around Heracles—I've really only looked at a very few of them—that it can be extremely difficult to construct a unified, coherent picture of this hero. To come up with a description of the essence of Heracles is not an easy thing to do. I think the best way to analyze him may be to identify a whole series of polar oppositions that seem to underlie the myth of Heracles. There are many different ways in which he is, in himself, a contradictory character, in which he portrays two contradictory characteristics. To begin with, he is both admirable and horrifying, both powerful and powerless. The hero who overcomes monsters, marks out the civilized world, is also the madman who kills his own children. He is both very admirable, and very horrifying. The greatest of Zeus's human sons— nobody disputes that Heracles is the greatest human son that Zeus ever conceived—is also someone who twice serves as a slave, to Eurystheus and to a queen named Omphale. He is both the most powerful of humans and one of the most powerless.

Another contradiction: he is supremely ill-fated, and at the same time, supremely fortunate. He is persecuted by Hera, as we saw, from before his birth and throughout his life. He dies shamefully. Being killed by your wife would be considered a very shameful death for a Greek hero. He died shamefully and in great agony. If you just look at that—persecuted by Hera from before birth and throughout his life, finally killed by his wife and dying in great agony—you could say this is the most ill-fated, unlucky man who ever lived. But this all too human, all too ill-fated hero also is the one human who achieves immortality and becomes a god. There, he is the most fortunate imaginable man.

I think it is interesting that he is offered sacrifice in Greek culture, Heracles is sacrificed to, both as a hero and as a god. The ceremonies of sacrifice were different for heroes and for gods. Heracles continues to receive both kinds of sacrifice, which I think indicates recognition that when he becomes a god, he does not lose his hero status. He is both, both the unfortunate hero and the fortunate god. Of course, these two sides of him are summed up in the fact that Hera allows him to marry her own daughter, Hebe.

Another contradiction: he both resists Death, and intentionally embraces it. The last three Labors are all, as I talked about, in some sense conquests of Death. In another story, he wrestles and defeats Death himself, when Death comes to get a woman who has volunteered to die in place of her husband. Heracles meets Death at her bedroom door, wrestles him and sends him packing. Heracles has these stories in which he overcomes Death, and yet at the end of his life he voluntarily embraces Death. Another contradiction: he is both a serious (even tragic) figure as we have been talking about, but he is also a comic figure of excess—the glutton, the drunkard, the man with the voracious sexual appetite. He is both masculine and feminine. He is the super-macho masculine hero throughout most of his stories, but when he is a slave to queen Omphale, he dresses in women's clothes and does women's work, including spinning and weaving.

Syncretism—again, that means a gathering together of different narrative traditions around one hero—may account for some of these differences, but I don't think it is sufficient to explain all of them. I think theoretical interpretations are more satisfactory here. For example, two very quick suggestions: Heracles can be read as a kind of "everyman" figure who clearly displays a Jungian "shadow" side. We see in him both our best and worst potential. Or, perhaps even more interestingly, he can be seen as embodying, and thus mediating between, nature and culture. His brutish, excessive, violent side can be seen as representing nature. His civilizing side, the side in which he overcomes monsters and eventually overcomes even Death itself, can be seen as representing culture. If we read in that way, then this greatest Greek hero mediates that opposition which lies behind so much Greek thought, between nature and culture.

In this lecture, we have looked, all too briefly, at the greatest Greek hero, Heracles. In the next lecture, we will turn to look at the most famous episode of Greek myth, the Trojan War.

The Trojan War

Lecture 17

[The] fame of the Trojan War results from the fact that it was considered an especially important event by the Greeks and Romans themselves, and therefore played an especially important role in classical literature.

The Trojan War is the most famous episode of classical myth. The Greeks of the classical age saw the Trojan War as the episode that marked the end of the "heroic" age and the beginning of purely human history. Heroic myth ends about a generation after the Trojan War. Some myths exist about the sons of Trojan War heroes but none about their grandchildren or great-grandchildren. The heroes of the Trojan War were seen as the last of the great race of heroes; they were also often claimed as ancestors by families living in the classical age. Thus, the Trojan War is a "liminal" (mediating) episode; it looks back to myth but at the same time looks forward to human history. Probably because of this liminal nature of the Trojan War myth, it became the most fruitful episode of all Greek mythology for literature. The most obvious example of this importance is that the two great Greek epics, *The Iliad* and *The Odyssey*, deal with events during and after the Trojan War. The greatest surviving Latin epic, *The Aeneid*, also takes the aftermath of the Trojan War as its subject. Many of the most famous Greek tragedies also deal with either the Trojan War or its aftermath. The Trojan War is exceptionally well represented in literature, which means that it has continued to be, in some regards, the primary classical myth for later Western culture as well.

The greatest surviving Latin epic, *The Aeneid*, also takes the aftermath of the Trojan War as its subject.

Despite its importance for Greek culture, no major surviving ancient work tells the entire story of the Trojan War. The great epics narrate only episodes from before and after the war. The *Iliad* focuses on events that happened during the last year of the war, and the *Odyssey* deals with Odysseus's further adventures after the war. Other Greek epic poems, now lost, told the rest of the story of the Trojan War. The *Aeneid* recounts the wanderings of the Trojan prince Aeneas after the defeat of Troy and his eventual arrival in Italy, where he became the ancestor of the Romans. It includes the fullest extant description of the sack of Troy. The tragedies tell even fewer details of the war; they focus on specific incidents and the effects of the war on non-combatant groups. As is often the case, Apollodorus gives a good summary of the story.

The story of the Trojan War is basically quite simple; however, many allied stories link into the story of the Trojan War in one way or another and make the overall topic quite complex. The basic story is as follows: The most beautiful woman in the world, Helen, daughter of Zeus and wife of the Greek Menelaos, was abducted by the Trojan prince Paris. Under the command of Menelaos's elder brother Agamemnon, the Greeks mustered an army to go to Troy and fight for Helen's return. The war against Troy lasted for ten years. The fighting was fairly evenly balanced; each side had its foremost warrior (Achilles for the Greeks, Hector for the Trojans). The greatest Trojan warrior, Hector, was killed by the greatest Greek warrior, Achilles, who was himself killed by Paris. Finally, the Greeks resorted to trickery. Using the famous ruse of the Trojan Horse, invented by Odysseus, they infiltrated the walled city of Troy and sacked it by night. The traditional date for the destruction of Troy was 1184 B.C.

This basic story of the Trojan War attracted many related stories over the centuries. One such connected story has to do with the birth of Achilles. The ultimate cause of the war was a prophecy about the hero Achilles, before he was conceived. Achilles's mother was Thetis, a sea-goddess. She was desired by Zeus, but he heard a prophecy that she would bear a son who would be greater than his father. Therefore, Zeus decided to marry Thetis off to a human being. The human picked for the purpose was Peleus. Thetis was less than pleased with this marriage; to placate her, Zeus hosted a magnificent wedding feast, to which all the gods and goddesses were invited except Eris, goddess of Strife. In anger at her exclusion, Eris threw onto the table a golden apple inscribed "for the fairest." Hera, Athena, and Aphrodite each claimed the apple as her own. Zeus appointed the Trojan prince Paris to judge among these three goddesses. This "Judgment of Paris" provided the immediate cause for the war, because each goddess offered him a bribe if he would award the apple to her. Hera offered him sovereignty over many cities. Athena offered him power in battle. Aphrodite offered him the most beautiful woman in the world for his wife. Paris chose Aphrodite, which led to his abduction of Helen and Menelaos's determination to get her back. The "Judgment of Paris" is not directly mentioned in either the *Iliad* or the *Odyssey*; scholars disagree on whether Homer knew of this detail of the story or not. As we know, myth develops over centuries; it is not static. This explanation of the causes of the Trojan War contains an interesting chronological inconsistency. Achilles was the most important Greek warrior in the Trojan War and was old enough to have a son who fought in the war as well. Yet the Apple of Discord, which sparked the war, was thrown down on the table at the marriage feast of Achilles's parents. To harmonize the chronology, we have to account for a missing period of some twenty or twenty-five years. Again, probably the best explanation is that the incongruities are caused by disparate strands of tradition being woven into a whole.

The events leading up to the war are also closely connected with the story of the family of Agamemnon and Menelaos. Their entire past and future are bound up with this war. The most obvious connection, of course, is that Helen was the wife of Menelaos, and her half-sister Clytemnestra was Agamemnon's wife. The abduction of Helen was an offense against the honor of Menelaos's whole family and a profound offense against the Greek notion of *xenia*, or guest friendship. Because Agamemnon was the elder brother, the task of leading the expedition to get her back fell to him. When the fleet gathered to sail, the winds blew against them for a month. The seer Calchas declared that Artemis was angry; Agamemnon must sacrifice his own daughter, Iphigeneia, to get a wind for Troy. Agamemnon kills Iphigeneia, and the winds blow for Troy. Homer does not mention the adverse winds or the sacrifice of Iphigeneia. Thus, the Greeks' expedition to Troy began with a terrible act of impiety, which is mirrored by their misdeeds during the sack of Troy.

The events that occurred during the Trojan War affected the Greeks' attempts to return home. The return to Greece was neither easy nor simple. The Greeks committed many outrages against the Trojans during the sack of Troy, which angered the gods. King Priam was killed at his household altar. Priam's daughter Cassandra was raped in the temple of the virgin goddess Athena. Before leaving Troy, the Greeks sacrifice Priam's daughter Polyxena to the ghost of Achilles; their expedition both begins and ends with the sacrifice of an innocent girl. Because of the gods' anger, the surviving Greeks suffered many hardships on their way home. Agamemnon was killed by his wife and her lover. Odysseus spent ten years wandering on his way from Troy. Menelaos and Helen were blown off course and spent seven years in Egypt. Stories were also told about the surviving Trojans; the most important of these was Aeneas, son of Aphrodite and Anchises and a cousin of Hector. The *Iliad* says that Aeneas was destined to survive and found another city elsewhere. Roman tradition said that he made his way to Italy and became the ancestor of the Romans.

In all these connected stories, we can see how complex the interaction is between the gods' commands and individual responsibility. The war was inevitable. Although it was caused by the actions of several individuals (most notably Paris), all the actions were sanctioned by the gods; thus, the individuals involved could claim necessity. Yet this necessity does not mitigate the horror of the individuals' wrongdoings on both sides. Paris violated the guest-host relationship, or *xenia*, by his abduction of Helen. Agamemnon's sacrifice of his daughter Iphigeneia was a great transgression. In both cases, the actions had the sanction of a goddess, but this does not spare the doers from the consequences. Add to this the concept of Fate, and we have a very complicated system indeed. ∎

Essential Reading

Virgil, *Aeneid*, Book II.

Supplementary Reading

Gantz, *Early Greek Myth,* Vol. 2, Ch. 16. A detailed account, listing all the ancient sources for each detail of the legend.

Woodford, *Trojan War in Art*, Ch. 1–2. A simple, easily readable account of the background events.

1. The Trojan War served as a kind of dividing line between "then and now" for classical culture. Does modern American culture have any similar "dividing line" myths? If so, what are they? If not, can you speculate why not?

2. Does the concept that *having* to commit an action does not excuse one from its consequences strike you as realistic? Is it just?

The Trojan War
Lecture 17—Transcript

In the previous lecture, we looked at Heracles, the most famous hero of Greek myth. In this lecture, we are going to turn to the Trojan War, the most famous episode of Greek myth. The Trojan War is still the episode of classical myth that most people know most about. Even people who know almost nothing about classical myth at all have probably heard of the Trojan War, probably are at least vaguely familiar with the idea of the Trojan Horse, and maybe even know the names of some of the characters of this myth, such as Helen, Achilles, Hector, and maybe others as well. This fame of the Trojan War results from the fact that it was considered an especially important event by the Greeks and Romans themselves, and therefore played an especially important role in classical literature.

The Greeks of the classical age, and following them, the Romans, saw the Trojan War as the episode that marked the end of the "heroic" age and the beginning of purely human history. To recap Hesiod's depiction of things again, the Trojan War is the time at which the Age of Heroes, or the Race of Heroes, ends and the Iron Race begins. Other authors aside from Hesiod, in classical Greek thought in general (as far as we can tell), agreed with this. The Trojan War marks the end of the time in which heroes existed and performed their adventures. Heroic myth actually ends about a generation after the Trojan War. There is a slow petering out of mythic stories. There are some stories, myths about the sons of Trojan War heroes, but none, so far as I know, about their grandchildren or great-grandchildren. After the Trojan War and the generation immediately following, after that, normal, everyday, regular humans appear on the scene, and normal, everyday, regular human history takes over from myth.

Now, the Greeks themselves would not have expressed this as a difference between myth and history, or a dividing line between myth and history. Those are modern concepts that I am using to describe what is going on. The Greeks themselves did identify a change, a difference, and they did see the Trojan War as the point at which the heroes disappear and the kinds of actions—the kinds of interactions with the gods, for instance—that the heroes have end with, or shortly after, the Trojan War. Furthermore, the heroes of the Trojan

War were not only seen as the last of the great race of heroes, they were often claimed as ancestors by families in the classical age. To be able to trace your decadence back to a hero of the Trojan War was rather like an American being able to say that an ancestor came over on the Mayflower. The heroes of the Trojan War were identified as ancestors of people living in modern day (by that I mean fifth century B.C.) Greece. The Trojan War, thus, is what is often called a "liminal episode," a "threshold episode," an episode that looks in two directions at once. It looks back to myth and the great Age of Heroes, but it also looks forward into human society, since those heroes are considered ancestors of great human families.

Just as the heroes perhaps mediate between gods and humans, between the categories of immortal and mortal, as I suggested before, so too perhaps the Trojan War can be seen as mediating between myth and history. To put it in more correct ancient Greek terms, between the Age of Heroes and the Iron Race. It is a liminal, or mediating, episode in many regards. It's probably because of this important liminal nature of the Trojan War that it became the most fruitful episode of all Greek mythology for literature. By that, I mean the episode of Greek mythology which appears in the most literature that we have existing today, and, as far as we can tell from titles of lost works, it was also the most common episode to appear in literature that no longer exists from this time period.

The most obvious example of the Trojan War in literature is, of course, the two Greek epics, the *Iliad* and the *Odyssey*, both of which deal with episodes either after or during the Trojan War. Similarly, the great Roman epic, Virgil's *Aeneid*, deals with events that happened after the Trojan War. It is not just in epic that the Trojan War is crucially important. Many of the most famous Greek tragedies as well, the tragedies that were written in the fifth century B.C. by Aeschylus, Sophocles and Euripides, also deal with either the Trojan War, its immediate aftermath, or the events that are leading up to it. There are 32 surviving Greek tragedies. Of those, nine deal with Trojan War subjects; so that is just over one-quarter, and that is a remarkably high percentage to deal with one main mythic episode when you consider all the things that happened in the totality of classical myth. The Trojan War is exceptionally well represented in literature, which means that it continues to be, in some regards, the primary classical myth for later Western culture as well, because where do we get what we know about classical myth? We get it from literature. If the Trojan War is especially well represented in literature, we are naturally going to know more about it than we know about many other episodes of classical myth.

Despite—or because of—the importance of this myth for Greek culture, there is no major surviving ancient work of literature that tells the entire story of the Trojan War. We don't have a great epic describing what happened in the war from beginning to end. Rather, the Homeric epics deal with only small portions of the overall Trojan War story. The *Iliad* focuses on events that happened in the last year of the war; the *Odyssey* deals with Odysseus's further adventures after the war. There were other Greek epic poems that filled out the rest of the story of the Trojan War, but those no longer exist. The *Aeneid*, the Roman epic, recounts the wanderings of the Trojan prince Aeneas after the defeat of Troy, and describes his eventual arrival in Italy where he became ancestor of the Romans. For trying to reconstruct the Trojan War myth, the *Aeneid* is particularly valuable to us because it includes the fullest description of the Sack of Troy, of what happened on the fateful night when the Greeks came out of the Trojan Horse and destroyed the city of Troy.

The tragedies tell us even less about the war overall, give us even less of an overall picture of the war than do the epics. The tragedies tend to focus on specific incidents, one or two days frequently, or specific individuals, or the effects of the war on noncombatant groups. All of these forms of literature assume in their audience a very full knowledge of the story of the Trojan War, so that they can hone in on fairly small episodes and develop those at great length. Fortunately for us, as is often the case, Apollodorus gives us a good summary of the overall story, which allows us to reconstruct the background against which to read the epics, the tragedies, and other such works. Many of the details that we know about the Trojan War are gleaned not from Apollodorus's summary, but from the other surviving works of literature, which means there must be many more details, many other episodes that, at one point, had been very fully filled out which we no longer have access to.

Now, the basic story of the Trojan War—what happened, when, where and why—is basically very simple. It is the many allied stories, the many other myths that get connected to it, pulled into it, so to speak, that make it quite complex. The basic story of the Trojan War is more or less as follows. The most beautiful woman in the world, Helen, daughter of Zeus and wife of the Greek king Menelaos, was abducted by the Trojan prince Paris. He ran away with Helen and took her back to Troy with him. Under the command of Menelaos's elder brother Agamemnon, the Greeks mustered an army to go to Troy and fight for the return of Helen. This war between the Greeks and the Trojans, which we call the Trojan War, lasted for 10 years. For most of those 10 years, the fighting was fairly evenly balanced, and each side had its foremost great warrior. Achilles was the great warrior of the Greeks; Hector was the great warrior of the Trojans. As the war lasted for 10 years, the fighting was fairly evenly balanced, but eventually the great Trojan warrior Hector was killed by Achilles, and Achilles was killed by Paris, the same Paris who had abducted Helen and started the whole thing going. Finally, after 10 years of fighting that was getting them basically nowhere, the Greeks resorted to trickery to overcome the Trojans. They used the famous ruse of the Trojan Horse, which was invented by the hero Odysseus, who was the cleverest of the Greek heroes. Hiding their warriors in the Trojan Horse, the Greeks gained access to the city, and when night fell, they sacked the city by night.

The traditional date for these events, the traditional date for the destruction of Troy, was 1184 B.C. That was the year that the classical Greeks themselves identified as the year that Troy fell, although they did not call it 1184 B.C.; they used their own chronological system. That is the year that is the traditional date for the fall of Troy, and that it in itself an interesting fact; because remember what we have talked about with Mycenaean culture. If Mycenaean culture is definitely in its waning period, in its declining period by 1100 B.C., a date of the fall of Troy of 1184 fits pretty well. That is the last great adventure of the heroic age. This again gives support to the idea that the heroic age supports in myth the actualities of Mycenaean culture, and the Trojan War is the last great act of Mycenaean culture and the last great episode of the heroic age in myth.

Just as the heroes Heracles, Theseus, and others attracted many elaborate stories to themselves, and thereby became extremely complicated to reconstruct chronologies for or to summarize briefly, so also this basic story of the Trojan War attracted many related stories and elaborations over the centuries. One such connected story has to do with the birth of Achilles and its being, in effect, the cause of the war—the first and foremost cause of the war in the first place. The ultimate cause of the war was a prophecy about Achilles, a prophecy that was given before Achilles was even conceived. Achilles's mother was Thetis, a sea-goddess. Thetis was desired both by Zeus and by other gods until they learned of a prophecy concerning Thetis, a prophecy that said that she would bear a son who would be greater than his father; very similar to the story about Metis that we talked about in *Theogony*, that she would have a son that would overthrow his father. This kind of repeating of the same basic narrative element in different myths is called "doubling," or these repetitions can be called "doublets." In this regard, Thetis is a doublet of Metis. There is a prophecy that Thetis is going to have a son who will be greater than his father. This means that none of the gods want to risk mating with her, desirable though she may be. None of the gods want a son who will overthrow them when he comes to maturity.

Zeus decides that the only safe thing to do, the only way to handle the timebomb that Thetis represents, is to marry her off to a human being, because human beings, oddly enough, like for their sons to be better than they are. A human father is not going to be threatened by the idea that his son will be greater than he. This makes sense from Zeus's point of view, and the human being he picks for the purpose is a man named Peleus. However, Thetis is less than pleased with the idea that she will be married to a human being. Remember from the *Homeric Hymn to Aphrodite,* we talked about how that was seen as degrading to a goddess, bearing a child to a human being, sexual relations with a human being were seen as degrading. To try to placate Thetis, Zeus hosted a great, magnificent wedding feast for her and invited all of the gods and goddesses to come to the wedding of Peleus and Thetis. Only one goddess was left out, that was the goddess Eris, the goddess who personifies strife, discord, quarrelsomeness.

Now, this was an area where allegorical interpretation of the myth almost demands to be given. If you are hosting a marriage feast for someone who does not particularly want to get married, and you are trying to make everyone as happy as possible and trying to make everything go smoothly, the last thing in the world you want at that marriage feast is strife, discord, quarrelsomeness. The exclusion of Eris can be read allegorically as trying to keep discord out of the picture, which, of course, doesn't work. Eris is offended at not being invited and so she makes trouble by tossing down onto the banquet table, when all the goddesses and gods are seated there, a golden apple inscribed in Greek *têi kallistêi,* which in Greek means "for the fairest female." Greek is a language with gender, so the idea that this is for a female is right there in the word itself.

"For the fairest," says the apple. Hera, Athena and Aphrodite each say, "Ah, a gift for me. How nice," and reach out to pick the apple up. Each one of those three goddesses assumes an apple identified "for the most beautiful, for the fairest" must belong to her. Now, Zeus is not going to want to judge between those three particular goddesses. Think about the three they are: Hera is his wife, with whom he has a rather troubled relationship at the best of times; Athena is his favorite daughter, born from his own brow; and Aphrodite is Aphrodite, who is known for making trouble for Zeus whenever she can. Rather than having to decide which one of these three goddesses is the most beautiful, he does what the gods so frequently do in myth; he pushes a difficult task on to a human being, and picks the Trojan prince Paris to judge among the three goddesses.

The "Judgment of Paris" provides the immediate cause for the war, because each goddess offers Paris a bribe if he will pick her. They are not content simply to stand back and let Paris look at them and decide who is most beautiful; they try to bribe him. Hera offers Paris sovereignty over many cities, political power, if he will choose her. Athena offers him great prowess in battle; she will make him the greatest warrior who ever lived, if he chooses her. Aphrodite offers him the most beautiful woman in the world as his wife, if he will choose her. In a stunning reversal of the values that Greek culture would have considered important for a young man, Paris goes for sexual pleasure over political power or power in battle, and awards the apple to Aphrodite as the most beautiful among the goddesses, therefore guaranteeing himself the most beautiful woman in the world as his wife. But the most beautiful woman in the world is Helen, and Helen is already married. This is why Paris goes to Sparta, where Helen and Menelaos live, and either seduces or flat- out kidnaps Helen (different sources disagree on whether she was a willing participant or not), and takes her back to Troy with him as his wife. This, of course, leads to Menelaos's determination to get Helen back and to the Trojan War itself.

Now, this so-called "Judgment of Paris" is not directly mentioned in either the *Iliad* or the *Odyssey,* and scholars disagree on whether Homer was aware of this story or not. I personally think he was. There are several hints in the *Iliad* that I think indicate that Homer did know about the "Judgment of Paris," but it is not absolutely certain. Some scholars think he did not. That is an interesting reminder, I think, that myth develops, myth is not static. As I talked about in the very first lecture, the version that we happen to have of a myth is not necessarily the only version in which that myth ever existed or even the most important version. Myth develops over centuries; it grows over centuries. It is quite possible that, when the *Iliad* and the *Odyssey* were written down, that the "Judgment of Paris" had not yet developed; that later on, as the story of the Trojan War continued to be told, this story was added to it as an explanation of why Paris went to fetch Helen in the first place.

One very notable point about this addition of the "Judgment of Paris" story to the basic Trojan War narrative is that it involves a chronological inconsistency, that, I have to admit, I had been teaching myth for some years before I actually noticed, and I didn't actually notice it. A student raised his hand in class one day and asked me about this chronological inconsistency, and floored me completely because I had no answer. Here it is. Here is what my student thought of, that had never occurred to me. Achilles was the most important Greek warrior in the Trojan War, was old enough not only to fight in the war, but old enough that he had a grown son who fought in the war as well near the end of the war, a young man named Neoptolemos. The Apple of Discord, which sparked the Trojan War, was thrown onto the banquet table at the marriage feast of Achilles's parents. There is a gap of about 20 or 25 years that does not fit. If Achilles fathered his son at the earliest possible age, let's say Achilles was 14 when he fathered Neoptolemos, we still come out to about 20 or 25 years bare minimum missing in the chronology of the story.

Now, once a student had asked me about this, I tried to figure out what was going on, and I found all sorts of ingenious explanations because this has occurred to other people throughout the centuries. Some people have tried to say things like, "Well, the gods live outside human time, so Hera, Athena and Aphrodite smoldered and stewed over which was the most beautiful 20 to 30 years before Zeus got around to having the 'Judgment of Paris.'" I think that is a mistaken approach. I think again, we have to say as we did with

Theseus, that what we have here is a chronological inconsistency that simply isn't going to work. There isn't any way to get rid of this chronological inconsistency. All we can do is note it, look at it, and think about what it tells us about the way myth works. The gathering together of various different stories is sometimes going to entail problems like this, and that is part of what we are dealing with when we are dealing with myth.

The events leading up to the War are also very closely connected with the whole story of the family of Agamemnon and Menelaos. Another area of myth that has been more or less pulled into the Trojan War story, or has been more or less developed with the Trojan War story, is the whole story of Agamemnon's family, which we will talk about in more detail in the next lecture. The entire past and future of Agamemnon and Menelaos's family is bound up with this war. The most obvious connection, of course, is that Helen is Menelaos's wife, and her half-sister Clytemnestra is Agamemnon's wife. The abduction of Helen is an affront against the family of Agamemnon and Menelaos. When Helen is abducted, since Agamemnon is the older brother, responsibility falls on him to lead the expedition to Troy to get Helen back.

This kind of offense against *xenia,* against the guest-host relationship— and what Paris has done is about as bad an offense against the guest-host relationship as you can possibly imagine; one is not supposed to run off with one's host's wife—this offense against *xenia* is seen as an offense, not so much against Menelaos as an individual, so much as against the whole family, and the honor of the whole family of Menelaos and Agamemnon. Agamemnon is the elder, so he is in charge of leading the expedition to Troy to retrieve Helen. When Agamemnon's fleet gathers to sail, they gather at a port called Aulis, on the eastern coast of Greece to get ready to sail over to Troy, which is located in modern day Turkey. When the fleet gathers to sail, the winds blow against them for an entire month, and they cannot leave port. Agamemnon, as the commander-in-chief, asks his seer, his prophet, Calchas, to tell him what is wrong, why the winds won't blow. Calchas tells Agamemnon that Artemis is angry, and that Artemis demands a sacrifice from Agamemnon in order for the winds to blow and the fleet to sail to Troy. The sacrifice that Artemis demands is Agamemnon's eldest daughter Iphigeneia. Agamemnon must sacrifice his own child, as though she were an animal, to the goddess Artemis to get a wind for Troy.

Agamemnon does this. He makes the decision to kill his own child, sacrifices Iphigeneia to Artemis, and the winds blow so that Agamemnon can lead his army to Troy. Now this is yet another detail, the sacrifice of Iphigeneia, that Homer does not mention, and, in this case, it seems pretty clear that at the time the *Iliad* and the *Odyssey* were written down, the story of Iphigeneia's sacrifice had not yet developed. The question of the "Judgment of Paris" is just that, a question; there are some people who think that it is alluded to in Homer. There seems to be no allusion whatsoever to the sacrifice of Iphigeneia in Homer. Here, we pretty definitely have a later strand of narrative, and we will see in the next lecture why that strand of narrative might have developed as it did.

Looking at the overall picture of the Trojan War with the fully developed narrative as we have been doing, the Greeks' expedition to Troy thus begins with a terrible act of impiety, slaughtering a girl as though she were an animal. Human sacrifice is a dreadful and horrifying act, even when it is directly ordered by a goddess, as it is by Artemis. Because the Greeks begin their expedition with this act of impiety, it comes as no surprise that they also act badly during the Sack of Troy at the end of the war. In fact, the events that occur at the end of the Trojan War, what the Greeks do while they are sacking the city of Troy, impede the Greeks' attempts to return home. They commit enough outrages during the Sack of Troy that their own attempts to sail back home again are hampered, as revenge brought by the gods against them. The return to Greece is neither easy nor simple because of this.

The Greeks commit many outrages against the Trojans during the Sack of Troy, and all of these outrages incur the gods' anger. Just to mention the three most important ones; there are many things that the Greeks do, but first of all, King Priam, the king of Troy, an aged and venerable man, is killed at his household altar by Achilles's son Neoptolemos. Priam is holding on to his altar, which ought to make him inviolable, ought to put him under the gods' protection. Neoptolemos kills him there in front of Priam's wife Hecabe. She sees him killed.

Perhaps even more horrifying, Priam's daughter Cassandra goes to a temple of Athena for refuge and is embracing the statue of Athena within the temple. It is important to understand that in Greek culture, when someone is inside the temple of a god and touching the statue, that person is considered directly under the god's protection. That is so strong a belief that there is an account—and this happened in historical time, this is a real account, or at least we think it is—of a group of people who had retreated inside a temple in Athens to protect themselves from their enemies. When they were asked to come out for negotiations, they tied a thread to the statue of the goddess and came out holding onto it, so that they would still in a sense be touching the statue. They thought that would protect them. In fact, it didn't. Their enemies killed them, but their enemies were then under a curse for having killed people who were under the protection of the goddess, because they were holding onto a thread that attached to her statue. When Cassandra is actually in Athena's temple, actually with her arms around Athena's statue, she is directly under protection of Athena. When a Greek warrior, Ajax, comes into the temple, drags Cassandra away from Athena's statue and rapes her in the temple, he has committed about as horrible an outrage in every regard as one can possibly imagine. The fact that it is Athena's temple, and Athena is one of the three virgin goddesses, just makes it worse.

Finally, before they left Troy, the Greeks sacrificed Priam's young daughter Polexena to the ghost of Achilles. Their expedition both begins and ends with the sacrifice of an innocent girl. It is, I think, fascinating that Greek literature gives such a horrifying and, in many ways, realistic picture of warriors sacking a vulnerable enemy city, gives such a horrifying picture of what the Greeks themselves did during the Trojan War. This is not prettied up in any way at all. Because of the gods' anger, the surviving Greeks suffer many hardships on their way home. Agamemnon arrives home to be killed by his wife and her lover. Odysseus spends 10 years wandering, so added to the 10 years of the Trojan War, Odysseus is away from home for a total of 20 years. Menelaos and Helen are blown off course on their way back home to Greece, and spend seven years in Egypt.

There are all sorts of stories about the surviving Trojans. The most important of these is Aeneas, the son of Aphrodite and Anchises, as you will remember, and also a cousin of Hector. The *Iliad* tells us that Aeneas was destined to survive the Trojan War and found another city elsewhere. Roman tradition took that hint in the *Iliad* and developed it into the idea that Aeneas made his way to Italy and became the ancestor of the Romans.

In all of these connected stories, among other things that we can see, one element that comes out quite clearly is how very complex the interaction is between the gods' commands and individual responsibility. Over and over again, in all of these stories I have been sketching out having to do with the Trojan War, we see the idea that a god may command something, but that in no way absolves the individual of the responsibility for any actions that the individual takes under the god's command.

The war was inevitable. While it was caused by several individuals, especially Paris, all of those actions were sanctioned by the gods, and thus, the individuals could claim necessity. Paris did not just go off and abduct Helen because he felt like it. Paris went off and abducted Helen because Aphrodite had told him that Helen was his rightful wife. Paris could say, "But Aphrodite gave her to me." Yet that in no way absolves Paris from the guilt that accrues to him for violating the guest-host relationship, for stealing his host's wife, and that in no way lets his society off the hook. His whole society suffers terrible repercussions because of Paris's misdeed, despite the fact that Aphrodite told Paris to do it. Similarly, Agamemnon sacrifices his daughter Iphigeneia. That is a terrible transgression. It is the worst thing a father could possibly do, but he was directly commanded to do it. Artemis said for the wind to blow, that is what you must do. Again, the fact that this transgression was ordered by a goddess does not absolve Agamemnon from guilt, as we will see in the next lecture.

The goddesses or gods may tell humans they must do something, but if the action they are commanded to do is impious or wrong or a transgression, those humans still suffer the normal consequences for their actions. Add to this the concept of fate—that these individuals may be fated to perform the actions they perform—and we get an extremely complex, many-sided picture, indeed; again, one in which individual motivations are much less important than individual actions, as we talked about before.

In this lecture, we have looked at the Trojan War and how it is linked with various other episodes of myth concerning specific kingdoms and families. In the next lecture, we will look in detail at one such family, the so-called House of Atreus, the family to which Agamemnon and Menelaos belong.

The Terrible House of Atreus
Lecture 18

Of all the unhappy families who dot the annals of classical myth, and there are many of them, the House of Atreus is perhaps the worst. I like to call it the "archetypal dysfunctional family," because in this family we have multi-generational stories of murder, incest, adultery and cannibalism repeated, over and over again. The family labors under a hereditary curse that repeats itself, works itself out again and is reestablished, generation after generation.

The House of Atreus functions under a hereditary curse that repeats itself each generation. The concept of a "hereditary curse" implies that moral guilt is inheritable, just as monetary debts are inheritable. "The sins of the fathers" will be passed on to their children. This curse manifests itself through (and is caused by) inappropriate and excessive intergenerational violence: parents kill children; children kill parents. The curse also exhibits a strong connection with inappropriate eating and inappropriate sexuality.

The founder of the family was Tantalos, and his actions began the curse on his descendants. Tantalos (who was Niobe's brother) tried to trick the gods into eating human flesh, specifically the flesh of his own son Pelops. Another, milder version is that Tantalos tried to steal nectar and ambrosia from the gods (thus to steal immortality). Tantalos's transgression has to do with blurring the lines between mortal and immortal and is expressed through inappropriate eating. Tantalos, one of Greek mythology's "cardinal sinners," is punished in Tartaros by being eternally tormented with hunger and thirst. Tantalos's punishment fits his crime; because he offended the gods through food, he is punished with hunger.

Pelops was resurrected by the gods, though he, too, incurred a curse on himself and his descendants through violence. In his case, however, the violence was not directed at a family member, and Pelops doesn't seem to personally suffer ill effects after being resurrected. Pelops wanted to marry Hippodameia, princess of Pisa, whose father had decreed that before marrying her, a suitor must first defeat him in a chariot race. If the suitor failed, he would be killed. Pelops won the race by bribing the charioteer Myrtilos to remove the linchpins from the king's chariot and replace them with wax. The wax melted, the king was killed, and Pelops fled with Hippodameia and the charioteer Myrtilos. When Myrtilos tried to rape Hippodameia, Pelops threw him to his death from a cliff; Myrtilos screamed out curses against Pelops's family.

Pelops's children labor under the weight of a double curse; they have inherited the guilt of their grandfather, Tantalos, and they are directly cursed by Myrtilos. Pelops has several children, but the most important are Atreus and Thyestes. The story of the interactions between these two brothers is extraordinarily complicated, but the basic outline is as follows: The brothers quarreled over the kingship of Mycenae. At Thyestes's suggestion, they agreed that the kingship would belong to whichever of them had the fleece from a golden lamb. Atreus had such a fleece, but his wife, Aerope, gave it to Thyestes, who was her lover. However, the gods sent an unmistakably clear omen—the sun setting in the east—that Atreus should be king. Atreus thereupon banished Thyestes. Atreus found out that Aerope and Thyestes had been lovers and decided to take a terrible revenge on his brother. He summoned Thyestes and his sons back to Mycenae on the pretense of reconciliation. Atreus killed Thyestes's sons and served their flesh to their father at a banquet. Thyestes eats the flesh of his own children, only to have Atreus show him what he has done. Atreus then banishes Thyestes again. When Thyestes realizes what he has done, he curses Atreus and Atreus's descendants. Atreus's and Thyestes's deeds reiterate the pattern established by Tantalos and add the element of sexual misconduct. Once again, we have a man killing children of his bloodline in order to force an unsuspecting victim to cannibalism. The adultery of Aerope and Thyestes forms a new thread in the pattern, which will be picked up in the next generation. On the advice of an oracle, Thyestes fathered a son by his own daughter, so that he would have an avenger. This son, Aigisthos, would be crucial in the further playing out of the family curse.

Atreus's sons were Agamemnon and Menelaos. By their generation, the curse is tripled: They are affected by the misdeeds of Tantalos, Pelops, and Atreus. Menelaos seems largely to escape the impending doom.

Agamemnon's sacrifice of Iphigeneia can now be seen in its full context; the sacrifice reenacts the pattern of his family curse. This adds yet a greater sense of inevitability to Agamemnon's actions; not only does he have to obey Artemis, but he is also doomed by his family history. At the same time, the curse also makes Agamemnon's action seem even worse; surely he should know just how horrific the slaughter of children is. Fate, then, does not negate individual responsibility. The sacrifice of Iphigeneia reiterates the "father kills child" motif and obliquely raises the related motif of impious feasting. Iphigeneia is sacrificed in place of an animal. A sacrificial animal was almost always eaten by the sacrificers. The very fact of sacrifice hints at a meal to follow. Iphigeneia's sacrifice thus mirrors the slaughter of Pelops; each of these can be seen as a horrific inversion of proper sacrifice and an affront to the gods.

The secondary motif of adultery also occurs in this generation. While Agamemnon is at Troy, Clytemnestra and Aigisthos become lovers. When Agamemnon returns, Clytemnestra and Aigisthos kill him. Several years later, Agamemnon's son Orestes returns from exile and, with the help of his remaining sister, Electra, kills Clytemnestra and Aigisthos.

This multi-generational story of murder, cannibalism, incest, and adultery clearly addresses many anxieties and fears. The fear of intergenerational violence runs throughout Greek myth. Just as in *Theogony*, this myth reflects the anxiety that fathers may become overly powerful and kill or subdue their children. Elsewhere, most notably in the myth of Oedipus, we see the fear of sons becoming overly powerful and killing their fathers. A patriarchal society in which a great deal of power is invested in the father of an extended family must keep these two fears in balance. The myth of the House of Atreus also speaks to the Greek anxiety about women's trustworthiness, loyalty, and sexuality. Aerope and Clytemnestra's infidelities lead to their husbands' ruin. In each case, the woman's lover is a close male relative of her husband. In each case, the motive is assumed to be ungoverned female sexuality, a theme that runs

This multi-generational story of murder, cannibalism, incest, and adultery clearly addresses many anxieties and fears.

throughout Greek myth. In a patriarchal society, a woman's fidelity is the only assurance of continuing the legitimacy of a bloodline. These themes make the House of Atreus myth particularly resonant in Greek culture and particularly suited to the genre of tragedy. All three of the great Greek tragedians wrote plays on aspects of the myth of the House of Atreus. The most important of these was Aeschylus's great trilogy, the *Oresteia*. ∎

Essential Reading

Apollodorus, *Library*, pp. 143–146.

Supplementary Reading

Gantz, *Early Greek Myth*, Vol. 2, pp. 531–556.

Lyons, *Gender and Immortality*, pp. 137–157. Examines variant traditions about Iphigeneia and what happened to her.

Questions to Consider

1. Is the idea of a hereditary curse simply a metaphorical way of saying that families tend to repeat the same pathologies, or does it imply more than that?

2. The myth of the House of Atreus seems to associate sexual transgressions and cannibalism. Can you explain why these two forms of transgression should be grouped together in this way?

The Terrible House of Atreus
Lecture 18—Transcript

In the previous lecture on the Trojan War, we noted how closely interwoven with the Trojan War story are the myths of the House of Atreus, the family of Agamemnon and Menelaos, and it is to that family that we are going to turn in this lecture, to concentrate on the story of the House of Atreus. Now, of all the unhappy families who dot the annals of classical myth, and there are many of them, the House of Atreus is perhaps the worst. I like to call it the "archetypal dysfunctional family," because in this family we have multi-generational stories of murder, incest, adultery and cannibalism repeated, over and over again. The family labors under a hereditary curse that repeats itself, works itself out again and is reestablished, generation after generation.

The concept of a hereditary curse is one that is foreign to our culture. Very basically, the idea is that moral guilt, no less than financial debts, are heritable, can be inherited. Just as we think if someone dies with a great deal of financial debt, that person's heirs are obligated to pay off the financial debt, so the culture reflected in this myth thinks if someone dies with a great deal of moral guilt, his heirs will inherit that guilt, just as they will inherit that monetary debt. The sins of the fathers are passed on to their children, whether they like it or not. In the case of the House of Atreus, the hereditary curse manifests itself through, and is caused by, inappropriate and excessive intergenerational violence. In this family, parents kill children, and eventually, children kill parents. The curse also exhibits a strong connection with inappropriate eating and inappropriate sexuality, and we will look at all of those manifestations of the curse—violence, eating and sexuality—throughout the lecture.

The founder of this family was Tantalos, the same Tantalos that we discussed before who killed his son Pelops, cut him up and fed him to the gods. That is the first example of intergenerational violence, of a father killing his child—also the first example of an attempt at inappropriate eating. It was Tantalos's actions that began the curse on his family, and as I mentioned before, Tantalos was Niobe's brother. There you see from the very beginning this is a family that has difficulty understanding or abiding by its appropriate position with respect to the gods. Tantalos tries to trick the gods into eating

Pelops's flesh. Niobe thinks that she is more worthy of worship than Leto because she has more children. Brother and sister both mistake their own position with respect to the gods.

There is a parallel version of Tantalos's story, which is much less horrific. Rather than killing Pelops and trying to feed him to the gods, this other version says that Tantalos tried to steal nectar and ambrosia from the gods, thus, in effect, to steal immortality; because, supposedly, if one could drink nectar and eat ambrosia, one would become immortal. You remember in *The Homeric Hymn to Demeter*, Demeter anoints the baby Demophoön with ambrosia before she puts him in the fire. In fact, the words "nectar" and "ambrosia" both have roots that seem to have to do with immortality. Nectar seems to be somewhere along the lines of "not-killing," and ambrosia is etymologically related to the word "immortal," though it does not much look like it. Both of those substances carry in their very names the idea that they conceal the essence of immortality.

In either case, whether we go with the more common and more hair-raising story that Tantalos killed Pelops and fed him to the gods, or if we go with the idea that Tantalos tried to steal immortality by stealing nectar and ambrosia, in either case, Tantalos's transgression has to do with inappropriate eating— either trying to get the gods to eat Pelops or himself trying to eat food that belongs to the gods. His punishment in Tartaros, where he is tormented by eternal hunger and thirst, is very appropriate to his transgression.

Pelops, as I mentioned before, was resurrected by the gods, but he, too, incurred a curse upon himself and upon his descendants. Now, Pelops is an anomaly in a couple of ways in this family. First off, his wrong actions, violent actions, are not directed against a member of his own family but rather against his future father-in-law and that father-in-law's charioteer, a slave named Myrtilos. Secondly, Pelops does not himself seem to suffer any of the ill effects of the family curse once he has been resurrected. I suppose being killed by your father could be considered suffering and ill effect, but, once Pelops is resurrected, he does not later on suffer from the family curse, so he is a little anomalous in the overall picture of the family.

He does, as I said, incur a curse on himself, and more importantly, on his descendants through his actions when he wants to marry a women named Hippodameia, a princess of Pisa. Hippodameia's father had decreed that, in order to marry her, a suitor had to defeat him, her father, in a chariot race. If the suitor failed to defeat the father in a chariot race, the suitor would be killed. Again, this is a fairly common folktale element. It shows up in several other Greek myths of a task or a feat that has to be achieved in order to marry a young woman, and failure in the feat equates to death. Pelops wanted to marry Hippodameia, but he did not want to die. He decided to win her hand by trickery, by cheating, rather than taking his chances in the chariot race. He bribed the charioteer, Myrtilos, to remove the lynchpins from the king's chariot (the lynchpins are the ones that hold the wheels on to their axles) and to replace them with wax. This meant, of course, that as soon as the chariot got underway and the wheel heated at all, the wax would melt, the wheel would come off the axle, and, as it did indeed happen, the king would be killed, thrown out of the chariot and killed.

Myrtilos agreed to this on the assumption that Pelops would not only take Myrtilos with him after the king was dead, but also would reward Myrtilos. In fact, when the three—Pelops, Hippodameia and Myrtilos—fled after the death of Hippodameia's father, Myrtilos assumed that his reward was to be Hippodameia herself. When they stopped for the first night, Myrtilos tried to have sex with Hippodameia. Pelops, who had not thought that that would be Myrtilos's reward at all—and you notice that what Hippodameia thought doesn't even seem to come up in this story—but Pelops, who had not thought that Myrtilos should have access to Hippodameia, killed Myrtilos by throwing him over a cliff. That is Pelop's act of violence, those two acts actually; first killing Hippodameia's father, then killing Myrtilos.

As Myrtilos fell to his death, he screamed out a curse against Pelops and all of Pelops's descendants forever. This means that by the time Pelops's children are born, they are already suffering under the weight of a double curse. They have inherited the familial guilt incurred by their grandfather Tantalos, and they are also directly cursed as Pelops's children by Myrtilos. Now, Pelops has several children, but for our purposes, the most important are the two brothers, Atreus and Thyestes. The story of the interactions between these two brothers is extraordinarily complicated, but the basic outline is as follows.

First, the brothers quarreled over kingship of the city of Mycenae. Mycenae was, at this point, without a king, and its people had received an oracle telling them that they should ask a son of Pelops to be their king—that the family of Pelops should become the royal family of Mycenae. Atreus and Thyestes disagree over which of them ought to be the king, which ought to be invited to be king of Mycenae. At Thyestes' suggestion, the two brothers agree that the kingship will belong to whichever one of them has possession of the fleece of a golden lamb. Now this is not the famous Golden Fleece that Jason seeks with the Argo; this is another golden fleece from another lamb.

As it happened, Atreus had such a fleece and therefore agreed to Thyestes's suggestion, but what Thyestes knew, and Atreus did not, was that Thyestes had seduced Atreus's wife Aerope, and Aerope, therefore, gave Thyestes the fleece. Thyestes suggests that this should be the deciding point because he knows he can get his hands on it. Aerope gives him the fleece; Thyestes says, "All right then, I am the king of Mycenae." Atreus asks the gods for an omen to indicate whether or not they approve of Thyestes becoming king. The gods send one of the clearest omens they send anywhere in Greek mythology; they make the sun set in the East, which is a pretty clear sign of displeasure. Therefore, Atreus becomes king and banishes Thyestes.

All might be well at that point, except that Atreus apparently brooded on the question of how Thyestes had gotten his hands on that golden fleece to begin with, and eventually, it dawned on Atreus that Thyestes and Aerope had probably been lovers, as in fact, they had been. Atreus decides to get vengeance on his brother Thyestes for the seduction of his, Atreus's, wife. Atreus summons Thyestes back to Mycenae and tells him to bring his small sons with him—Thyestes has either two or three sons at this point. Atreus does this on the pretense of a reconciliation. He says to Thyestes, "Let's let bygones be bygones. Come back home and bring your sons with you, and we will have a great feast to celebrate out reconciliation." When Thyestes and the boys get to Mycenae, Atreus, unbeknownst the Thyestes, takes Thyestes's children—Atreus's own nephews—kills them, cuts them up, cooks them and serves them to their father Thyestes at the celebratory banquet. Thyestes eats the flesh of his own children without knowing what it is that he is doing. After he has eaten, Atreus has a platter with the boys' hands and feet brought in to him, lifts the lid to the platter and says to Thyestes, "Do you recognize what kind of animal you have eaten?"

Thyestes goes back into banishment and, obviously, curses Atreus and Atreus's descendants. Atreus has incurred a curse on himself through his actions; he is also directly cursed by his brother Thyestes. Atreus's and Thyestes's deeds reiterate the pattern established by Tantalos, and add to it the element of sexual misconduct as well. Once again, we have a man killing male children of his bloodline, though in this case it is Atreus killing his nephews, not his own sons, but we have an elder generation male killing males of the next generation, and doing so in order to force an unwitting victim into cannibalism—the gods, in the case of Tantalos killing Pelops; Thyestes, the boys' own father, in the case of Atreus killing Thyestes's children.

We also have a new thread in the pattern, the adultery of Thyestes and Aerope, which sets up the idea of sexual misconduct in this family as well, which will continue into the next generation, as we will see in a few minutes. Atreus and Thyestes have brought together several lines of hideousness. The cannibalism is not now just cannibalism, but cannibalism of a father against his children. The murder is reiterated, and the idea of adultery, and incestuous adultery, is added to the picture. That is not the only episode of incest in this remarkably unpleasant family. On the advice of an oracle, Thyestes decides to father a son to take vengeance against his brother Atreus for what Atreus did to Thyestes's earlier sons. Thyestes needs a son to be his avenger. On the advice of an oracle, he begets this son with his own daughter, Pelopeia, named after her grandfather Pelops. Versions differ on whether Thyestes intentionally commits incest with Pelopeia or not. Some versions say that the oracle tells him, "Father a son by your own daughter," and he does so. Other versions say that they oracle tells him to go by night to a certain fountain, find a girl who will be there, and rape her, basically. Then he does so, and finds out only later that it was his own daughter, Pelopeia. In either case, he begets a son. This son, whose name will be Aigisthos, is going to be crucial in the further playing out of the family curse.

By the time we get to this generation, the generation of Aigisthos and also of Atreus's sons, Agamemnon and Menelaos, we have all the most hideous elements imaginable at play, murder, rape, incest, adultery and cannibalism, all coming together in this one family. This means that Atreus's sons Agamemnon and Menelaos, and for that matter their cousin Aigisthos, are dealing with a triple-bodied curse—if not by this time, quadruple-bodied—but certainly a triple-generational curse. They are affected and cursed by the misdeeds of their greatgrandfather Tantalos, their grandfather Pelops, and their father Atreus. They are, without question, doomed to reiterate and reenact the same pattern of the curse in their own generation. Interestingly, Menelaos seems largely to escape this fate. Perhaps because he is the younger brother, or because he is married to Helen, a daughter of Zeus, and as such has some exceptional status. That is hinted at in the *Odyssey*, when Menelaos is told by a prophet that he and Helen go to the Islands of the Blessed, rather than going to the Underworld like most people do.

Agamemnon suffers the full brunt of this disastrous curse in his own life. At this point, we can see Agamemnon's sacrifice of Iphigeneia in its full context. I said in the last lecture that the sacrifice of Iphigeneia seems to be unknown to Homer; that does not seem to be part of the story of the Trojan War, as Homer knows it. It is a later development. Now that we have seen the pattern established in the family of Agamemnon, the family of Atreus, Pelops and Tantalos, we can see why such a story almost inevitably had to develop around Agamemnon. Homer may not have known it. The whole story of the House of Atreus, the cursed house of Atreus, may not have developed by the time of Homer. As that story developed it is almost inevitable that Agamemnon, too, is going to have to kill one of his children and do so in a terribly distressing way. So he does.

The sacrifice of Iphigeneia by her father Agamemnon reenacts, restates, and remotivates the family curse. That is one of the aspects of this curse; the reenactment in each generation remotivates the curse, so it becomes stronger and stronger down the generations. Now, this idea that the sacrifice of Iphigeneia is a reenactment of his family curse adds a greater sense of inevitability to the sacrifice. Agamemnon is not only acting under the direct command of Artemis when he chooses to sacrifice his child, but he is also doomed to do so by his own family history. Yet, at the same time, the very fact of this family curse it seems to me makes Agamemnon's actions seem even worse. If ever there was anyone who ought to know what a dreadful thing it is to kill your own child, and if ever there was anyone who ought to be able to see how doing so brings nothing but ill effects for your entire family, that someone ought to be Agamemnon. Of all the men in the world who ought to find some way not to kill his child, you would think that Agamemnon would head the list.

Here again we are dealing with the very complex, interrelated questions of fate and individual responsibility. Agamemnon is a member of a cursed family, and that seems to imply that at least the eldest son in each generation of this family reenacts the curse, whether he wants to or not. Agamemnon is also, as are all characters in Greek mythology, undoubtedly given a fate of his own, and one could say that he is fated to kill his daughter. Yet that does not in any way negate his individual responsibility and the after-effects; the consequences that he suffers for killing Iphigeneia are terrible indeed. We will get back to those consequences in just a moment, but there is a little bit more that I want to say about the sacrifice of Iphigeneia herself.

This story, the sacrifice of Iphigeneia, does more than simply reiterate the "father kills child" motif. That parallelism, with Tantalos killing Pelops and with Atreus killing his nephews, is very clearly there. There is a further parallelism that is not so immediately obvious. The killing of Iphigeneia also obliquely raises the related motif of impious feasting, of inappropriate eating; because Iphigeneia is not just killed, Iphigeneia is sacrificed. She is sacrificed specifically in place of an animal.

There are some versions of her myth which make it a little bit more bearable, which make it—at the very last moment Artemis substitutes a deer for Iphigeneia on the altar, spirits Iphigeneia away to another country where she makes her a priestess of Artemis. In those versions, the actual sacrificial knife falls on the throat of a deer, not on the throat of Iphigeneia. In the version that I tend to follow, the version recounted by the playwright Aeschylus in his great trilogy the *Oresteia*, Iphigeneia herself is killed. She is killed as a sacrifice; i.e., she is killed in place of a sacrificial animal.

Now, remember from the discussion of the Prometheus myth in *Theogony*, way back at the beginning of the course, we talked about how a sacrificial animal is almost always, invariably, eaten. That is the inevitable aftermath of sacrifice. You sacrifice the animal, burn the bones to the gods, to allow them to enjoy the savor of smoke rising up from the burning bones, but the human worshippers eat the sacrificial animal. I am not trying to suggest that in any version of this myth, Agamemnon and his followers sit down and feast on Iphigeneia's dead body. They don't. Nobody ever says that; it is never spelled out. But, I think, implicit right there in the very fact of sacrifice, there is at least the suggestion of a meal to follow because that is the inevitable—not quite inevitable, but normal—consequence of a sacrifice. There was a form of sacrifice done by very wealthy sacrificers in which the entire animal was burned on the altar for the god, but only the very wealthy could afford to do that, and it was normally done only in circumstances of either extreme need or extreme thanksgiving. It was, by the way, called a "holocaust." That word simply means "burning the whole thing." It is only in this dreadful twentieth century of ours that "holocaust" has come to have another, and even more horrible, meaning.

Normally, a sacrificial animal was eaten after the sacrifice; and so the very fact that Iphigeneia is sacrificed sets up almost the expectation, or the remembrance, or the hint of a feast to follow. If Iphigeneia were a member of any other family than the family of which she is a member, I might not try to press that idea. Given the family she belongs to, given the eating of Thyestes's children, given the attempt to serve Pelops to the gods, and the fact that actually Demeter did eat a little bit of Pelops, then, in this family, the sacrifice of a daughter, the offering of a daughter to the gods on an altar, does hint at the impious feasting that could follow. Thus, Iphigeneia's sacrifice mirrors the slaughter of Pelops in two ways. Each of these can be seen as—the first, most obvious way it mirrors it is the father killing the child—but each of these killings can be seen as a particularly horrific version of proper sacrifice and an affront to the gods.

In the case of Pelops, the inversion of the sacrifice is the offering of Pelops, rather than an animal, to the gods for them to eat. In the case of Iphigeneia, it is not quite as dreadful; it is simply the offering of Iphigeneia to the gods in the place of an animal without the direct eating. In both cases, there is the idea of perverted sacrifice and a direct affront to the gods. The fact that the sacrifice of Iphigeneia is directly ordered by one of the gods, again, does not in any way lessen the horror of it.

Another point to make about the Agamemnon-Menelaos generation is that the secondary motif of incestuous adultery that we saw in the affair between Thyestes and Aerope is reiterated in this generation as well. While Agamemnon is off at war, Clytemnestra becomes the lover of Aigisthos, the child born to Thyestes and Thyestes's daughter, Pelopeia, to be an avenger of Thyestes's slaughtered sons. Aigisthos is grown by this time, and he becomes the lover of Clytemnestra, specifically to try to gain control of Mycenae, to try to take back the kingship of Mycenae for Thyestes's line. Remember, Atreus and Thyestes quarreled over who should rule Mycenae. Atreus got the rulership of Mycenae; it has been inherited by Agamemnon, but Aigisthos sees Atreus as a usurper—thinks his father Thyestes should have been ruler all along—and if that were true, then Aigisthos is the rightful ruler of Mycenae.

In Agamemnon's absence, Aigisthos establishes himself in Mycenae through becoming the lover of Clytemnestra, Agamemnon's wife. When Agamemnon returns home from the Trojan War, Clytemnestra and Aigisthos together kill him. Now, the theme of murder in this family has moved into a new resonance or a new manifestation. Now, we have a wife killing her husband, a cousin killing his cousin, rather than a father killing his children. That is not the end of it. Several years later, Agamemnon's son Orestes, who has grown up in exile—Clytemnestra had sent him away to grow up elsewhere—comes back home, and with the help of his remaining sister, Electra, who has been there all the time, Orestes avenges the death of his father, Agamemnon, by killing his mother, Clytemnestra, and her lover, Aigisthos. By the time we get to the generation of Iphigeneia, Electra and Orestes, I have lost count of how many manifestations of murder, slaughter, cannibalism, incest, adultery and so on we have. Orestes, Electra and Iphigeneia are laboring under an absolutely crushing familial burden of inherited guilt and an inherited curse.

Now, this multi-generational story of murder, cannibalism, incest, and adultery pretty clearly addresses many deep-seated anxieties and fears that run throughout Greek literature. First of all, the fear of intergenerational violence comes up frequently in Greek myth. We saw this in *Theogony*, the fear that, the anxiety that, fathers if they become overly powerful will kill or subdue their children. Remember Ouronos not letting his children be born, Cronos swallowing his children. That seems to reflect, on the level of the gods, the same kind of anxiety we see with Tantalos and Atreus and Agamemnon; an overly powerful father may kill or otherwise subdue his children, or at least, not allow them to take their proper place in society. Elsewhere in Greek myth, most notably in the myth of Oedipus, we see a reflection of the fear that sons may become overly powerful and kill their fathers. The fear of intergenerational violence between males, in particular, works in both directions. Why is that?

We are dealing with an extremely patriarchal society in which a great deal of power is extended in the father. The father of an extended family in a patriarchal society is a very powerful man, indeed. Any such society has to find a middle ground, to find a balance between these two extremes of abuse of power. The very powerful father could, in fact, not allow his children to reach their proper role in society. On the other hand, the son could become overly eager to take the place of his father and could be violent against his father. The fear of intergenerational violence in either direction is one thing that a patriarchal society has to figure some way to balance, some way to thread its way between.

The myth of the House of Atreus also speaks very clearly to Greek society's anxiety about women's trustworthiness, loyalty, and sexuality, particularly about the sexual fidelity of wives. Clytemnestra and Aerope both ruin their husbands through their infidelities. Aerope's affair with Thyestes leads to Atreus's loss of the kingship—he does get it back, but it does lead to his loss of the kingship in the first place. More clearly, Clytemnestra's infidelity with Aigisthos causes Agamemnon's death. In each case, I think it is significant that the woman's lover is a close male relative of her husband.

In at least classical Athenian society, as I talked about before, married women were kept largely sequestered. That means, among other things, that their access to potential lovers was strictly limited. But a man could not keep his wife away from every single male in his family. If you are anxious about the fidelity of your wife—and Greek culture was very anxious about wives' fidelity—then close male relatives are the most obvious source of threat. Brothers, cousins, uncles, all of those are the most obvious source of threat for infidelity of a man's wife. You might compare here Phaidra's lust for her stepson Hippolytus when we were discussing Theseus; that, I think is another manifestation of the same anxiety.

Why is it that Greek society was so anxious about women's fidelity, particularly about wives' fidelity? I think, again, this has to do with the patriarchal nature of the society. Very briefly, in a strictly patriarchal society where it is crucially important for a man to leave sons behind him, a wife's absolute fidelity also becomes crucially important. Greek men were not required to remain faithful to their wives. That was neither expected nor assumed in marriage because a Greek man could be unfaithful—to put it in our terminology—it would not even have been put that way in this society—a Greek man could have sexual relations outside of marriage and that would in no way call into question the purity of his own bloodline. If Atreus has 15 affairs with 15 other women, that does not call into question the legitimacy of Agamemnon and Menelaos. If Aerope has an affair with someone else, that does call into question the legitimacy of any children she may bear. Given that knowing the sons he was bringing up in his household were his own sons was crucially important for a Greek man, the fidelity of the wife becomes equally crucially important. Since there is no way—in a culture before the times of bloodtyping and DNA testing, there is no way—to find out who is the father of a particular child, the only way to assume that a man is the father is to make sure that his wife is absolutely, utterly faithful. Therefore, strong anxiety about women's fidelity and sexuality, which is assumed to be very strong and very ungoverned, runs throughout Greek myth.

These themes, the fear of intergenerational violence and the anxiety about female fidelity and sexuality, make the House of Atreus myth particularly resonant in Greek culture. It addresses some of the most deep-seated anxieties that Greek culture seems to reflect, and it also makes it particularly suited to the genre of tragedy, which, among other things, looks at those anxieties. All three of the great Greek tragedians wrote plays on aspects of the myth of the House of Atreus. What we will do in the next lecture is to look at the most important treatment in tragedy of the myth of the House of Atreus, namely the great trilogy the *Oresteia*, by the tragedian Aeschylus.

Blood Vengeance, Justice, and the Furies
Lecture 19

Since tragedy was performed at a festival in honor of Dionysos, it was a public occasion, and it was a time when a large proportion of the Athenian citizen body would be gathered together. The tragedians very frequently used their plays to discuss or foreground important social issues of their own day.

In this lecture, we continue our examination of the curse of the House of Atreus. The lecture focuses on Aeschylus's *Oresteia* and the ways in which the tragedian reshaped and refocused the traditional myth. Accordingly, we begin with a brief discussion of Greek tragedy's form and function in Athenian society. We then examine the specific uses Aeschylus made of the myth in his trilogy to explore issues of justice and of gender roles and discuss some of the implications for our understanding of both the myth itself and Aeschylus's drama.

The genre of tragedy developed in Athens in the 5th century B.C., where playwrights entered tragedies into competition at the annual festivals of Dionysos. Three tragedians would each enter a group of three tragedies, followed by a "satyr play." This group of three interrelated plays is called a trilogy. Aeschylus's *Oresteia* (performed in 458 B.C.) is our only surviving trilogy. Even it lacks its satyr play. The subject matter of tragedy was always drawn from myth or (very rarely) recent history. The tragedians did not make up their stories. The author's originality lay in the use he made of the myth, the way he slanted the story, not in creating a new story. We can safely assume that the audience knew the basic outlines of the story, so background exposition is minimal. At the same time, the playwright could and did add or subtract details of the story to serve his dramatic needs.

Aeschylus uses the myth of the House of Atreus to explore issues of justice, revenge, and personal responsibility. At the same time, he reshapes it to provide an aetiology for the court system of Athens. The problem of irreconcilable moral duties is one of the main themes of the *Oresteia*. In *Agamemnon*, this theme is expressed through both Agamemnon and Clytemnestra. In

Libation Bearers, the theme is expressed through Orestes. In *Eumenides*, the irreconcilable duties of the earlier plays are finally mediated by Athena, who sets up the first court in Athens. Aeschylus's Agamemnon is faced with an insoluble moral dilemma: He must lead his army to Troy, but he must not kill his daughter. In this version, Artemis's anger is not Agamemnon's fault; Artemis is angry because of an omen the army had seen, in which two eagles devour a pregnant rabbit. The meaning of this omen seems to be that Artemis is angry over what Agamemnon *will do* in Troy, not over anything that he has already done. In this situation, Agamemnon is an innocent man forced into the position of making an unbearable choice. His innocence, however, does not spare him from the consequences of his actions. The theme of irreconcilable duties is repeated in Clytemnestra. As a wife, she should remain loyal to her husband, but she is also a mother whose daughter was brutally murdered. These earlier examples set up Orestes's dilemma. He has an absolute duty to kill his father's killer, but also an absolute duty not to kill his mother.

In *Libation Bearers,* we learn that Orestes journeyed to Delphi to ask Apollo what he should do. The god answered that he must avenge his father's death. Orestes accepts the god's word and returns home, where he indeed kills Clytemnestra and Aigisthos with the help of his sister, Electra. Almost immediately after he does so, the Furies begin to pursue him. Thus Orestes's dilemma is played out on the divine level as well as in his own mind: Apollo orders him to kill Clytemnestra, but the Furies forbid it. In Homer's *Odyssey*, Orestes's killing of Aigisthos and Clytemnestra is mentioned approvingly over and over and is apparently considered unproblematic. The picture of a man caught between two mutually exclusive absolutes is Aeschylus's interpretation: Orestes absolutely must avenge his father but can only do so by killing his mother. Aeschylus helps establish this dilemma by making Clytemnestra the actual killer of Agamemnon.

The final play of the *Oresteia* provides a reconciliation for Orestes's torment and for the wider issues of the contradictions inherent in a system of blood vengeance. In *Eumenides*, Orestes appears as a defendant on a murder charge in a trial held in Athens. Apollo is, in effect, his defense lawyer, the Furies are the prosecution, and Athena serves as judge. Athena appoints a jury of Athenian citizens to hear the case. There are two separate interpretations of how the jurors voted. The first interpretation is that the jurors' votes are tied; Athena breaks the tie and acquits Orestes. The second interpretation is that the jurors vote seven to six to convict Orestes, and Athena's vote makes the tie. In either case, Athena casts the deciding vote. With Orestes's acquittal, the curse on the House of Atreus is lifted. Orestes leaves to live a normal life. He marries his cousin and has children. This trial and acquittal also apparently brings an end to the Age of Heroes; Orestes and his descendants fade into normality.

In Aeschylus's hands, the myth of the House of Atreus becomes a means to discuss methods of justice and the value of a court system. The system of blood vengeance breaks down in Orestes, who is the son of both the murdered man and the murderous woman. Orestes's dilemma is insoluble according to a system of individual justice; the only way out is through the invention of a new system of public justice. The duty of exacting vengeance must be removed from the victim's heirs and handed over to society in general. A court system must be inaugurated. Aeschylus uses the myth both to describe and to demonstrate the value of the Athenian court system, under which the state tries cases of murder rather than leaving vengeance to the victim's family.

Aeschylus's treatment of these issues is linked to a particular political development of his own day. In the 5th century B.C., Athens had a system of trial by jury, which had been in place since the early 6th century B.C. Aeschylus backdates a fairly recent development into mythic time. This is a deliberately "literary" use of myth; Aeschylus and his audience must have known that the court system did not really stretch back to the Age of Heroes. In *Eumenides*, Aeschylus situates Orestes's trial on the Areopagus, the "hill of Ares," in Athens. This was the site of an actual council whose powers were important in the 6th century but decreased in the 5th. In 462, just four years before the performance of the *Oresteia*, the powers of the Areopagus council were radically decreased. Before this time, the council had dominated most areas of Athenian government. Now its areas of authority were reduced to trying cases of homicide, arson, and malicious wounding. In the *Eumenides*, then, Aeschylus seems to be responding to these reforms of 462. He may be chiding the reformers for showing disrespect to an ancient institution. He may be reminding the members of the Areopagus council that they still have a crucial role to play in Athens.

The *Oresteia* also has a great deal to say about gender issues. The conflict throughout is largely cast in terms of shifting power between the sexes. Clytemnestra is called a man-like woman and wields power like a man. However, her motivation for killing Agamemnon is maternal love. In *Eumenides*, the conflict between the Furies and Apollo is portrayed as a conflict between older female goddesses and a younger male god. The Furies embody the principal of blood vengeance and represent wildness, ferocity, and irrationality. Apollo embodies the rationality of patriarchal society in his claim that a woman's life cannot count for as much as a man's. The gender issues come to a head in Apollo's famous argument that Orestes did not in fact kill a blood relative when he killed his mother. Apollo's argument is that the mother is not a blood relative of her child; rather, she acts as a host, preserving the child of a guest-friend (*xenos*). This was a current scientific theory of Aeschylus's day, however counterintuitive it seems. The woman was analogous to the soil where the male seed was planted. This theory does not persuade the jury; the votes are tied. Athena is the perfect solver of this dilemma. She is female but her characteristics and outlook are noticeably male. She breaks the tie vote and reconciles the two sides.

The *Oresteia* is unquestionably one of the greatest works of world literature.

The *Oresteia* is unquestionably one of the greatest works of world literature. But where does the myth end and Aeschylus's genius begin? This trilogy is a perfect example of the difficulties of trying to access classical myth through its literature. It is fairly safe to say that Aeschylus invented the trial of Orestes or at least its details. But the basic situation is built into the myth. The gender issues are even more entangled. Aeschylus puts the words into his characters' mouths, so Apollo's argument about the mechanics of conception is Aeschylus's idea. But the conflict of genders is there in the myth, and in other myths, all the way back to Hesiod. In studying classical myth, we can never disentangle the myth from the particular version of whichever author we're reading. The greater the author, the more difficult the problem. ∎

Aeschylus, *Oresteia.*

Conacher, *Aeschylus' Oresteia: A Literary Commentary.*

Goldhill, *Aeschylus: The Oresteia.*

Graf, *Greek Mythology*, pp. 142–168.

Tyrrell and Brown, *Athenian Myths and Institutions*, pp. 120–132.

Zeitlin, "Motif of Corrupted Sacrifice."

1. Can you think of any modern analogues for Aeschylus's use of myth to explore serious social issues?

2. The jurors' votes to convict and to acquit Orestes may have been evenly tied, or they may have been seven (or six) to convict and six (or five) to acquit. Does it make a difference which interpretation we take? Is anything implied about the human view of justice by either or both interpretations?

Blood Vengeance, Justice, and the Furies
Lecture 19—Transcript

In the previous lecture, we examined the myth of the House of Atreus and talked a bit about how that myth reflected some of the deep-seated anxieties of Greek culture, particularly about intergenerational violence and the control of female sexuality. In this lecture, we are going to look at the use the playwright Aeschylus made of the House of Atreus in his trilogy of tragedies, the *Oresteia*.

I want to start with a very brief description of how the genre of tragedy operated in Athens, what was different about theatre in Athens from our modern day conception of theatre. Tragedy developed as an Athenian art form in the fifth century B.C., and the playwrights entered tragedies into competition at the annual festivals held in honor of Dionysos. Three tragedians each would enter a group of three interrelated plays called a "trilogy" into the competition. Rather than entering just one play into the competition, each dramatist entered three plays. These three tragedies were followed by a very brief comic play called a "satyr play," after the mythical followers of Dionysos. The group of three interrelated tragedies is called a "trilogy." Sometimes as is the case in the *Oresteia*, the trilogy tells one unified story. Other times, the three plays are linked thematically, rather than being episodes in one overall story. Now, Aeschylus's *Oresteia*, which was performed in 458 B.C. just two years before Aeschylus's death, is our only surviving trilogy. It is the only surviving example we have from ancient Greek tragedy of three plays written to be performed together as a unified whole, and even it lacks its satyr play, so it is not entirely complete.

A sideline here: people often think that Sophocles's three plays about Oedipus and his family were a trilogy as well. They are often miscalled the Theban Trilogy (*Oedipus the King, Antigone*, and *Oedipus at Colonus*), but actually those three plays were written at three widely different times; *Antigone* first, *Oedipus the King* some 15 to 20 years later and *Oedipus at Colonus* at the very end of Sophocles's life—over 20 years after *Oedipus the King*. So those are not a trilogy in the sense that I am using the term here.

Another important thing to realize about tragedy is that the subject matter of Greek tragedy was always drawn from myth or, very rarely, from recent history. In other words, the tragedians did not invent or make up their stories. They used traditional myth to write the plays that they presented in the festival of Dionysos. Their originality, their creativity, lay in the use they made of the myths—the way they slanted the stories, the points they brought out by stressing them, and the points they overlooked in the original story— rather than what we would think of as creativity, creating a new story. We can safely assume, therefore, that the audience of a tragedy knew the basic outlines of the story before coming to the theatre. And, so, in the *Oresteia* for instance, Aeschylus does not give any kind of background exposition of the whole story of the House of Atreus. He assumes his audience already knows that. He can refer to the slaughter of children by Atreus or by Tantalos and know that his audience knows what he is talking about.

The playwright could, and did, add and subtract certain details of the story to serve his dramatic needs. Since tragedy was performed at a festival in honor of Dionysos, it was a public occasion, and it was a time when a large proportion of the Athenian citizen body would be gathered together. The tragedians very frequently used their plays to discuss or foreground important social issues of their own day. Let's turn now to looking at the particular uses that Aeschylus made of the myth of the House of Atreus in his trilogy, the *Oresteia*.

This trilogy consists of three plays, tragedies. The first one is *Agamemnon*, the second is called *Libation Bearers*—women carrying libations—and the third one is called *Eumenides*. In this trilogy, Aeschylus uses the story of the House of Atreus to explore issues of justice, revenge, and personal individual responsibility. He highlights these issues throughout the trilogy. At the same time, he reshapes the traditional myth, as we will see, to provide an aetiology for the Athenian court system, a very interesting use to make of the story of this particularly hideous, dysfunctional family.

As a means of looking at personal responsibility and issues of justice, one of the main themes Aeschylus highlights in his treatment of the myth is his treatment of human beings caught between irreconcilable moral duties. He hammers this idea home again and again in all three plays. In *Agamemnon*, this theme is expressed through the characters of both Agamemnon and Clytemnestra. We see both of them caught between two opposing and irreconcilable duties. In

Libation Bearers, the second play of the trilogy, Aeschylus looks at Orestes facing the same kind of dilemma, being caught between two moral duties that are in direct conflict with one another. In the third play, *Eumenides,* the irreconcilable duties of the earlier plays are finally mediated by Athena, through the setting up of a court system, the first court in Athens.

In the first play of the trilogy, Agamemnon is a man faced with an absolutely insoluble moral dilemma. We talked in the last two lectures, in fact, about Agamemnon's sacrifice of his daughter Iphigeneia. As Aeschylus presents the story, Agamemnon is really on the horns of an absolutely unbearable dilemma. He must lead his army to Troy, and Aeschylus leaves us in no doubt that that is an imperative duty for Agamemnon to do. Aeschylus says in the play, has the chorus of the play say, that Zeus the great guest-god, the god who stands behind *xenia,* the guest-host relationship, ordered the fleet to go to Troy. So, Agamemnon is, in effect, under direct orders from Zeus to lead his fleet to Troy. But when the wind will not blow, and they can't sail, he is told that in order to lead his fleet to Troy, he must kill his own daughter. As a father, he is under an absolute moral obligation not to kill his own child. So Agamemnon is caught in about the most horrific dilemma that one can imagine. On the one hand, his duty as a king and the leader of his people, and the eldest male of his family, to avenge the wrong that Paris has done to them by abducting Helen; on the other hand, his duty as a father not to slaughter his child.

Aeschylus hones the painfulness of Agamemnon's dilemma by making it quite clear in his version that Artemis's anger, requiring the sacrifice of Iphigeneia, is due to no wrongdoing on Agamemnon's part whatsoever. In some versions of the story, particularly in versions given by the playwright Euripides, Artemis is angry at Agamemnon because Agamemnon shot a deer that was sacred to Artemis. Now, demanding the life of a human girl in recompense for a deer is still very harsh, but in that version, Agamemnon has directly angered Artemis. Aeschylus makes it quite clear that this is not the case. In Aeschylus's version, the prophet Calchas, when he tells Agamemnon that Agamemnon must sacrifice his daughter, says that Artemis is angry because of an omen the army has seen at Aulis, at the port where they are waiting to sail. Two eagles have killed and eaten a pregnant rabbit, a rabbit and her unborn young. This, says Calchas, is why Artemis is angry; this is why Artemis demands the sacrifice of Iphigeneia, because two eagles killed a rabbit.

What seems to be going on here is that Artemis is angry at what the omen signifies. The omen signifies the Sack of Troy; the rabbit with its unborn young signifies the walled city of Troy, with the innocent women and children inside it. As we talked about before, the Greeks go way overboard during the Sack of Troy; they commit all sorts of outrages. They do things that they should never have done. In other words, Aeschylus makes it pretty clear that Artemis is angry not at anything Agamemnon has done; rather she is angry at what Agamemnon will do. She is punishing him for actions he has not yet taken. This makes Agamemnon, in the moment when he has to decide whether to become a deserter and disband the army or whether to kill his daughter—in that moment, he is a completely innocent man, caught between two choices neither one of which he has caused. He did not abduct Helen; he did not kill this rabbit who is an omen for Troy; and yet he has to choose one course or the other. So, Agamemnon is forced into an agonizing choice, makes what seems to him the choice to take the lesser of two evils, sacrifices Iphigeneia and the army goes to Troy. Of course, he does then commit the outrages that Artemis is angry about in prospect. Agamemnon's innocence obviously doesn't spare him from the consequences of his actions any more than does his membership in a cursed family let him off the hook for his actions. He suffers because he has killed Iphigeneia, despite the fact that he is forced into a position where any course he takes will be wrong.

Clytemnestra, though less obviously, can also been seen in the play *Agamemnon* as caught between two irreconcilable moral duties. As a wife, she should remain loyal to her husband, as we have discussed before; but as a mother, she feels a duty to avenge her dead daughter. So, when Agamemnon returns home, Clytemnestra murders him to take vengeance for the murder of Iphigeneia. In Aeschylus's version, that is Clytemnestra's main motivation. Again, other authors slant the story differently, but Aeschylus makes it quite clear that Clytemnestra murders Agamemnon to avenge her daughter Iphigeneia.

These earlier examples set up Orestes's dilemma; and the trilogy is, after all, called the *Oresteia*. He is the main focal point of it; it is "the trilogy about Orestes." He has an absolute duty to avenge his father's death. A son whose father has been murdered must kill the murderer; that is an absolute given of this culture that the myth reflects. But a son has no less absolute a duty not to kill either of his parents, not to kill his mother. So there Orestes is, caught between two duties that are irreconcilable if ever two duties were. He must avenge his father; he must not kill his mother; but his mother is the person who killed his father. By the time we get into the second play, *Libation Bearers*, Orestes's dilemma is set up by the foreshadowing of Agamemnon and Clytemnestra, just as the familial curse is set up generation through generation.

In the second play, *Libation Bearers,* we learn that Orestes, recognizing the very difficult position he is in, has traveled to Delphi to ask Apollo what he should do. Apollo has told him that avenging his father takes precedence over protecting his mother; that therefore, he must kill his mother to take vengeance for his father. So, in *Libation Bearers,* this is what Orestes does. He accepts the word of the god Apollo, returns home to Mycenae, and with the help of his sister, Electra, kills Clytemnestra and her lover, Aigisthos.

Now, almost immediately after Orestes commits these murders, the Furies— the spirits who take vengeance on those who have harmed kin and particularly vengeance on children who have harmed their parents—the Furies begin to pursue Orestes. Like his father Agamemnon before him, Orestes has his dilemma played out on the divine level, as well as in his own mind. Apollo directly orders him to kill Clytemnestra, just as Zeus had directly ordered Agamemnon to go to Troy. The Furies see this as a forbidden action and punish it, despite the fact that it was ordered by Apollo. So, Orestes is caught not just between two irreconcilable moral duties, but between two conflicting deities or groups of deities as well.

Aeschylus's treatment of Orestes is an excellent example of how an individual author can shape the traditional myth to serve the points that he wants to emphasize. In Homer's *Odyssey*, characters talk about Orestes killing the murderer of his father, killing Aigisthos and his mother Clytemnestra. Over and over and over again characters discuss that in the *Odyssey*, and in the *Odyssey* it seems to be utterly unproblematic. Every time it is brought up, it is used as an example of a good son doing what he ought to do. Particularly, it is offered as an example for Odysseus's son Telemachus of how a good son takes care of his father's honor in his father's absence. Homer, in other words, doesn't seem to have seen any problem whatsoever in what Orestes did. The picture of a man caught between two mutually exclusive absolutes is

Aeschylus's own interpretation of the myth. The idea that Orestes absolutely must avenge his father but can only do so by killing his mother, and that this is a conflict, is Aeschylus's interpretation of the story. Aeschylus helps establish this dilemma by changing one crucial detail. In the *Odyssey,* we are told that Aigisthos killed Agamemnon, and Clytemnestra was his accomplice and helped him. In Aeschylus's version, Clytemnestra is the one who strikes the blow, and it is a very distressing blow that she strikes, indeed. She kills Agamemnon when he is in his bath, naked, vulnerable; that is when she kills him, and Aigisthos is only an accomplice who comes in after the fact and tries to claim some of the credit. So, Aeschylus focuses in on Orestes as someone caught between two irreconcilable duties by making Clytemnestra the actual killer of Agamemnon.

The final play of the *Oresteia,* the *Eumenides*, provides a reconciliation for Orestes's torment, and wider issues that Aeschylus is addressing here, of the contradictions that are inherent in a system of blood vengeance. Let's look first at what happens in the play, and then I will look at some of the implications of it. In the *Eumenides,* Orestes appears as a defendant on a murder charge at a trial held in Athens. The *Eumenides* is actually the first courtroom drama. In it, in effect, Apollo acts as defense lawyer, the Furies are the prosecution, Orestes is the defendant, Athena is the judge and Athena appoints a jury of Athenian citizens. The text does not tell us exactly how many were in the jury, probably 12, perhaps 13, perhaps more than that. Clearly, the jury, of whatever number, is appointed by Athena. The jurors vote in a way that leads to Orestes's acquittal.

Now, here, the text is maddeningly ambiguous. There are two separate interpretations of how it is that the jurors voted. The first interpretation is that the jurors' votes are tied, because there are 12 jurors; they vote six to acquit, six to convict, and Athena then casts a vote which breaks the tie and acquits Orestes. The other interpretation is that the jurors' votes are actually split seven to convict and six to acquit, and that Athena casts the vote that makes the tie. Either way you interpret it, Athena casts the deciding vote, and incidentally, here Aeschylus provides an aetiology for a reality of Athenian law. In an Athenian law case, when the votes were evenly tied in a murder case, the defendant was acquitted. If half the jurors vote to acquit, half to convict, and the votes were evenly tied, the defendant was acquitted. This can be seen as indicating that Athena is there in the background casting a deciding vote for the defendant as she did for Orestes.

With Orestes's acquittal in the *Eumenides*, not only are all the issues of the trilogy laid to rest, but also the curse on the House of Atreus is lifted. Orestes leaves, after a speech of great thanksgiving, and walks out of myth and into history. What I mean by that is he leaves to lead a completely normal human life. He marries his cousin, who is the daughter of Menelaos and Helen, and they have children, but those children have absolutely no stories connected with them. The family fades into obscurity. As I said in the last couple of lectures, the Trojan War is the dividing line, according to Greek myth, between the Age of Heroes and what Hesiod calls "The Iron Age,"our own time. But it is really in the generation after the Trojan War that the mythic world actually ends, and the world of normal human experience begins. We can, if we like, see the acquittal of Orestes as the precise moment at which that transition happens.

In Aeschylus's hands, the myth of the House of Atreus becomes a means not just to examine individual responsibility as I have been talking about so far, but also to look at systems of justice, and why it is that a court system works better than a system of individual justice. In the Homeric poems, in the *Iliad* and the *Odyssey*, and supposedly, or at least presumably, in archaic Greek society as well, justice was an individual matter. Families took justice into their own hands. If I killed my neighbor, the neighbor's family would kill me. Then my family would kill the neighbors, and so on, and so on. It is an open-ended system, but it works pretty well as long as people don't mind it being an open-ended system and as long as murderer and victim are not members of the same family.

This system of private blood vengeance breaks down in Orestes. It is a system that cannot accommodate someone for whom both the murderer and the murder victim are members of his family. Aeschylus hones in on that to show the difficulties of a system of private vengeance, because this is the one time when it simply cannot work. Orestes's dilemma is insoluble under the traditional system of individual justice. This is a system that is reflected in all the myths that we know of; all the myths of Greek culture assume individual blood vengeance. Aeschylus, however, takes one of those myths and uses it to examine the value of a court system, which is an extraordinarily brilliant thing to do with such a myth. Orestes's dilemma can only be solved through the invention of a system of public justice, a new system of justice in which the duty of exacting vengeance is taken away from the individual's family members and handed over to society at large. In other words, it can only be solved by the inauguration of the court system. That is what Aeschylus shows us in the third play of the trilogy, in the *Eumenides.*

Why were these issues so crucial in Aeschylus's mind, why was he concerned with talking about the Athenian court system in this particular trilogy, in this particular time (remember the trilogy was performed in 458 B.C.)? In the *Oresteia*, we have an all-too-rare opportunity to set a literary work—and in this case, a literary work using the traditional myth—directly into its political context, because we happen to know about certain political events in Athens of this time period, and we can see to which political event it was that Aeschylus was directly responding in the *Oresteia.* In other words, the *Oresteia* is tied into a particular political development of Aeschylus's own day.

A little bit of background information here. In the fifth century B.C., Athens definitely did have a system of trial by jury. That system of trial by jury, which is reflected in the *Eumenides* and given an aetiology in the *Eumenides,* had been in place probably since the early sixth century B.C., for about one and a half centuries when Aeschylus wrote. Now, Aeschylus backdates the development of the court system to the end of the mythic age. He backdates it to the time right after the Trojan War. He and his audience must have known perfectly well that their court system had been developed a few generations before them. In other words, what Aeschylus is doing here is making what I call a consciously "literary" use of myth. He is using the myth of the House of Atreus in way that he and his audience must have known the traditional myth did not support. Everyone knew their Homer; everyone knew that in Homer, individual blood vengeance is the way justice operates. The Athenians must have had some vague sense of when their court system developed; they may not have know precisely how many years previously, but they certainly knew it did not date back to the time of the Trojan War.

Yet, Aeschylus makes it date back to the time of the Trojan War, or at least the time right after the Trojan War, and has the court system inaugurated by no less a figure than Athena herself, the patron goddess of Athens. Why is he doing this? In the *Eumenides*, one clue as to why he is doing this is the location of Orestes's trial. Aeschylus situates the court that tries Orestes on the hill called the "Areopagus," that means the hill of Ares. It is a hill that is still very visible in Athens. You can climb up it and get wonderful views of the Acropolis from it. It is also, of course, the hill on which St. Paul supposedly preached his first speech to the Athenians. More importantly for our purposes, it was actually the hill on which a particular council, government body, met in Athens from well before the fifth century into the fifth century B.C. This council, often called the "Areopagus Council"—or just the "Areopagus" for short, named after the hill on which they met—before the fifth century B.C., had a great many very important powers. It was one of the foremost governing bodies during the sixth century B.C.; it had the power to pass laws, had a great deal of control over Athenian society. In 462 B.C., just four years before the *Oresteia* was performed, the powers of the Areopagus Council were severely limited. This was one of the major political reforms in Athens of the fifth century, which lead to, or helped pave the way for, the flowering of democracy under Pericles.

Among the only powers that were left to the Areopagus after the reforms of 462 B.C. were that it could try cases of homicide, arson and malicious wounding, what we would call assault. So, a body, council, government entity that had, up to this time, very widespread powers, had been one of the major government entities in Athens, was suddenly reduced to being basically a homicide court. What does Aeschylus do in the *Oresteia*? He talks to us about the importance of a homicide court. Aeschylus is pretty clearly, in the *Oresteia,* responding to these reforms of 462 B.C. As is so frequently the case in discussing classical literature, modern scholars disagree on exactly what his response is. Some of us think that Aeschylus is chiding the reformers, that Aeschylus is a traditionalist who is telling the reformers that they have done a dreadful thing by restricting the powers of so ancient and venerable an institution, and thereby showing disrespect to it. Others among us think that Aeschylus is trying to remind the members of the Areopagus Council, who were not at all happy to have their powers restricted, that they still have a very important role to play, that he is saying, "Look how important homicide trials are. They can be seen as one of the qualifying elements of civilization, one of the things that makes us who we are as a people." Either way you read it, however, pretty clearly the *Eumenides* is written in response to the reforms of 462 B.C.

All of these issues I have been talking about having to do with individual responsibility, justice and so forth, are far from the only topics Aeschylus brings up in the *Oresteia*. It is one of the most amazingly dense and rich works of ancient literature. Among the other issues it addresses, the *Oresteia* has a great deal to say about gender conflict and gender issues. Throughout the trilogy, the conflict is largely cast in terms of shifting power between the sexes. Just to give one example, Clytemnestra is often referred to as "a woman like a man" in *Agamemnon*. She is called a "woman with a man's mind," "a woman who thinks like a man." Her motivation for killing Agamemnon, as we saw, is maternal love. So, she is like a man, but she also still has feminine characteristics. In the *Eumenides*, the conflict between the Furies and Apollo is very definitely cast as a conflict between older female goddesses and a younger male Olympian god—the same conflict we saw all the way back in Hesiod, and have talked about a bit since then. The Furies not only embody the principal of blood vengeance, they also represent wildness, ferocity, irrationality, connection with the earth, all of those things. Apollo embodies rationality, at least, rationality as his patriarchal society sees it, in his claim that the life of a woman should always count less than the life of a man, and that is one of his main claims for why Orestes should be acquitted.

The gender issues come to a head in Apollo's famous argument about the mechanics of conception. The crowning point of Apollo's speech for the defense is his claim that the Furies have no jurisdiction here because Orestes did in fact not kill a blood relative—because, says Apollo, the mother is not a blood relative of her own child. In other words, he tries to get Orestes off on a technicality. Apollo says that when a woman is pregnant with a child, what she is actually doing is acting as a host, nourishing the child of a guest friend. In other words, he puts pregnancy in the context of *xenia*. As bizarre as this sounds to us, and infuriating as many of my female students find it, this was a current scientific theory during Aeschylus's day. The idea was that what happened in conception was that the male provided a fully formed tiny little embryo. The woman was analogous to soil. Just as in plants, the seed falls into the soil and develops, is nourished by the soil, so supposedly in animal and human reproduction, the male plants the seed and the female soil then nourishes it.

It is not as bizarre an idea as it may sound, particularly in a culture that considers fathers much more important socially than mothers. In conception, animal or human, the contribution of the male is visible. The ovum, the female contribution, is invisible, could not be seen until the invention of the microscope. Arguing by analogy from plant reproduction is not as far-fetched as it might sound. On the other hand, this is completely counterintuitive. Anyone who has ever witnessed a birth, or seen a mother cradling a newborn baby in her arms, would find it awfully hard to say there is no blood relationship between those two. That is the primary blood relationship of the human family. It is worth noting that Apollo's argument, at best, persuades only half the jury. It does not by any means persuade all of them.

Athena is the perfect solver of this dilemma. She is female, but many of her characteristics and outlook are noticeably male, and her role in Athens as a goddess of justice, just war, wisdom—all of those are male attributes. She is really the one and only figure in Greek myth who could mediate between the Furies and Apollo, between female and male, and work out a compromise by which both sides can, at least, be more or less satisfied.

The *Oresteia* is unquestionably one of the greatest works of world literature. But where does the myth end and Aeschylus's genius begin? This trilogy is a perfect example of the difficulties we encounter when we try to access classical myth through literature. It is safe to say that Aeschylus invented the trial scene. No other version of the myth said Orestes was actually put on trial in Athens in front of a jury. Aeschylus invented that; the basic situation which allows him to invent that is there in the myth, built into the story already. Where does the myth end and Aeschylus begin?

The gender issues are perhaps even more entangled. Aeschylus gives his characters the words they say, so Apollo's argument about conception is Aeschylus's own idea, contribution. As we have already seen, the gender issues, the conflict of older female gods, younger male gods, all those things are there throughout Greek myth, from Hesiod on. So, this problem that I have talked about a bit before, of disentangling the myth from the author who tells us the myth, becomes all the more complicated the greater the author we are dealing with. It is complicated enough in the *Oresteia*. In the next lecture, we will turn to looking at what many people consider the greatest Greek tragedy of all, *Oedipus the King* and at how Sophocles manipulated that myth.

The Tragedies of King Oedipus
Lecture 20

The story of Oedipus has become, in this century, probably the single most famous individual Greek myth of all, due largely to the influence of Sigmund Freud and his use of the Oedipus myth in his psychological theory.

The basic outline of the Oedipus story as it appears in various ancient sources shows many motifs from the familiar test-and-quest pattern. The hero's birth and conception are surrounded by difficulty. Oedipus's parents know that their son will kill his father, Laios, either because of an oracle or because Laios was cursed by Pelops, whose son he had raped. An elaboration of the story adds that the oracle says Oedipus will also marry his mother, Jocasta. The infant Oedipus is exposed and expected to die—in the cultural norms of the time—but is instead rescued and brought up by foster parents. He grows up in Corinth, ignorant of his true identity. The young man performs exceptional feats of strength, cleverness, or both. These often involve encounters with monsters. Oedipus shows exceptional strength when he kills Laios and all Laios's attendants. He shows exceptional cleverness when he solves the riddle of the Sphinx, a monster that terrorizes Thebes. Successfully completing these "tests" gains the young man a bride. When Oedipus solves the Sphinx's riddle, he is granted the hand of the Queen of Thebes in marriage. Unfortunately, she is his mother. Oedipus's discovery of the truth of his actions leads to Jocasta's death and his own self-blinding.

We are most familiar with this story through Sophocles's great play, *Oedipus the King.* Two of this century's most influential theorists of myth, Freud and Lévi-Strauss, have interpreted the Oedipus myth, and other scholars have followed in their tracks. Freud assumes that Sophocles's play represents the desires of the unconscious; thus, it appeals to modern audiences no less than to ancient ones as a kind of wish-fulfillment fantasy. Scholars often object that Oedipus's ignorance of his parentage is crucial to the myth and that if Oedipus felt Oedipal desires, he would have felt them toward his adoptive mother, not Jocasta. Freud's theory of the Oedipus complex, whether correct or not, does not tell us much about the myth itself, but offers a reason for its appeal. The second main objection is the one we discussed as an objection to psychological theories of myth in general: Freud assumes that the unconscious operates the same way cross-culturally and through time. Levi-Strauss reads the myth as mediating between the two conflicting accounts of human origin, autochthony ("coming from the earth") and sexual reproduction. The riddle of the Sphinx and Oedipus's uncertainty about his parentage both concern the essential nature of being human: What are human beings and where do they come from? Lévi-Strauss finds traces of autochthony in the "lameness" characteristic of Oedipus's family—very often in autochthonic stories, the people who emerge from the earth are lame. The myth, which is about the origins of Oedipus, mediates between the theory of autochthonous human creation and the observed reality of sexual reproduction. Few classicists have been persuaded by this reading of the myth. Other scholars connect the Oedipus myth with initiation rites, which sometimes include symbolic killing of the father.

Freud assumes that the unconscious operates the same way cross-culturally and through time.

The most common reading of Sophocles's play (if not of the underlying myth) among literary critics and classicists is that its main topic is the conflict between fate and free will. The actions taken by Laios, Jocasta, and Oedipus himself all lead to the inexorable working out of fate. By trying to avoid fate, these characters guarantee its fulfillment. They are fated to commit the deeds they commit, but this fate works through their own freely chosen actions. Some scholars object that this is an anachronistic reading. The conflict that moderns find between the idea of fate and free will does not seem to have troubled the Greeks. Classical Greek, in fact, has no term for "free will."

Another way to look at the play is to see Oedipus as the paradigm of a rationalist intellectual, seeking to establish truth through the use of his own intellect, rather than through relying on the gods' oracles. Modern critics often assume that this is a good thing and see Oedipus as a kind of humanist hero, battling for truth for its own sake. In the context of 5th-century Athens, however, most people would probably have seen such intellectual independence as a bad thing. Sophocles is drawing on one of the most controversial movements of his day, the teachings of the "Sophists." Among other subjects, the Sophists, itinerant teachers, taught rhetoric and techniques of argumentation. The most famous Sophist was Protagoras, best remembered for his dictum "man is the measure of all things." They questioned the validity of oracles, which implies questioning the existence or relevance of the gods. Their opponents accused them of corrupting morals and weakening religious beliefs. Socrates was executed on just such grounds, although he vehemently denied being a Sophist. In this context, Oedipus becomes an example of a Sophist. His refusal to accept the oracle and the words of the prophet Teiresias shows the distrust of religious traditions that was characteristic of the Sophists. He is also like a Sophist in his insistence on using his own intelligence and his determination to reason out the puzzles of his own origin and of who killed Laios. Sophocles's play seems to indicate that the human intellect alone is not sufficient for understanding the world, that the gods' oracles are valid, and that the gods must be taken into account.

All these readings show the difficulty in separating the Oedipus myth from Sophocles's particular telling of it. The text of *Oedipus the King* has become so central in Western literature that it has even overshadowed Sophocles's retelling of the aftermath of Oedipus's story in his last play, *Oedipus at Colonos.* Can we cut through the later interpretations and around Sophocles's hegemony to try to uncover the original significance of the myth?

The most unusual thing about this myth is its association of parricide and incest, two elements that are not normally part of the same classical myth. Many Greek myths can be found about sons killing or almost killing fathers and vice versa. Parricide, and even lesser violence against fathers, was regarded with absolute horror as the worst imaginable crime. We tend to see the incest with Jocasta as a worse crime than the killing of Laios, but this may be anachronistic. Jan Bremmer suggests that the incest was added to the story to underline the horror of the parricide. Parricide, cannibalism, and incest are the worst imaginable transgressions. Cannibalism does not appear in Oedipus's story (unless we see it as displaced onto the Sphinx), but the incest here functions as the cannibalism does in the House of Atreus: to underline the horror of the murder. As Bremmer puts it, "the monstrosity of the transgression is commented upon by letting the protagonist commit a further monstrosity." Oedipus's eventual heroization at Colonos is a reminder that heroes, in the sense of guardian spirits, were not necessarily noted for good deeds. Oedipus's crimes mark him as different from the rest of humankind. This difference qualifies him to be a hero. In this context, it is interesting to consider Burkert's reading of the myth. Burkert connects the myth with the scapegoat or *pharmakos*, a person who is driven out of a city to free it from some disaster, such as a plague. The *pharmakos* must be disgusting or foul in some way; this quality enables him able to divert the disaster from the city. In this regard, Oedipus's pollution enables him both to lift the plague from Thebes and to protect Athens. ■

Essential Reading

Sophocles, *Oedipus the King.*

Supplementary Reading

Bremmer, "Oedipus and the Greek Oedipus Complex."

Burkert, *Structure and History*, pp. 64–72.

Dodds, "On Misunderstanding the *Oedipus Rex.*"

Freud, "The Oedipus Complex."

Knox, *Oedipus at Thebes*, especially Ch. 3.

———, "Oedipus the King: Introduction."

Leach, *Lévi-Strauss*, Ch. 4, pp. 63–86.

Lévi-Strauss, "The Structural Study of Myth."

Vellacott, "The Guilt of Oedipus."

1. Lévi-Strauss holds that all variants of a myth are part of the myth; thus, Freud's Oedipus complex is as much a part of the Oedipus myth as are Sophocles's plays. Do you agree or disagree with this view? What are its implications for interpreting myth?

2. The Oedipus myth, at least as told by Sophocles, seems to allow for an enormous range of interpretations. Is this part of its appeal? Is the attempt to isolate one primary meaning in the myth misguided from the outset?

The Tragedies of King Oedipus
Lecture 20—Transcript

In the previous lecture, we looked at Aeschylus's use of the myth of the House of Atreus in his trilogy, the *Oresteia*. In this lecture, we are going to turn to the most famous and the greatest of all Greek tragedies, *Oedipus the King* by Sophocles, and look at how Sophocles used the underlying myth of Oedipus in that play.

Now, the story of Oedipus has become, in this century, probably the single most famous individual Greek myth of all, due largely to the influence of Sigmund Freud and his use of the Oedipus myth in his psychological theory. The basic outline of the story, as it appears in various ancient authors, includes several elements from the now familiar test-and-quest pattern. The first of these is that there is some difficulty or problematic circumstance surrounding the conception and/or the birth of the hero in this kind of story. In Oedipus's case, of course, the problem has to do not with his parents wanting to conceive him, but with their knowledge that after they bear a son, he is going to do some truly terrible things. Oedipus's parents, in all versions of the story, know that their son will grow up to kill his father Laios. They know that, either because of an oracle that they have been given, or because Laios was cursed by Pelops, in an interesting connection with the House of Atreus story. According to some versions, Laios kidnapped and raped one of Pelops's sons—not one of his daughters, but one of his sons—and Pelops cursed Laios because of that action.

Either way, Oedipus's parents know that Oedipus will grow up to kill his father, and in some versions of his story, that is all that they know. Other authors elaborate the story and add the detail that Oedipus will also grow up to marry his mother Jocasta. So, Oedipus, it is safe to say, is not a wanted child. His parents tried to get rid of him shortly after his birth by exposing him in the wilderness. Infant exposure, by the way, was accepted in Greek society, so far as we can tell. It was probably never terribly widespread, but it was an accepted way of getting rid of an unwanted or defective child, to leave the infant in the wilderness to die. By leaving their son Oedipus exposed, Laios and Jocasta are not committing any kind of transgression against their culture's norms. They are perfectly within their rights to do so.

However, this being a myth, the child is rescued and brought up by strangers. He is brought up by the king and queen of Corinth. So Oedipus grows up in ignorance of who he really is, thinking that he is a prince of Corinth, rather than the son of Laios and Jocasta, king and queen of Thebes.

Another aspect of the traditional kind of test-and-quest story that we see in the story of Oedipus is that the young man performs feats of exceptional strength and bravery, exceptional cleverness, or both. We saw that in the stories of Theseus and Heracles both. In Oedipus's case, he performs a feat of exceptional strength; he does actually, in fact, kill his father Laios. This happens after Oedipus has gone to Delphi, according to Sophocles's version, to ask the god Apollo who he is. The god tells him, "You will kill your father and marry your mother." Oedipus assumes this means he will kill his adoptive parents (who he thinks are his real parents) and vows never to return back to Corinth, takes off in another direction—as it happens, he is heading toward Thebes—and on his way there, at a crossroads, meets an old man with a great many attendants. This old man is, of course, Laios, though neither Oedipus nor Laios know who the other one is. They quarrel over who has the right of way on the road, and in the ensuing mêlée, Oedipus kills King Laios and all his attendants except one. That is a feat of exceptional strength, for one man to kill many men. It also, of course, is the working out of Oedipus's fate, since he has just killed his father, though he doesn't know it for some years afterwards.

Oedipus also shows exceptional cleverness when he solves the famous riddle of the Sphinx. The Sphinx was a female monster who was terrorizing the town of Thebes. She asked everyone who passed by her a riddle, and those who could not answer her riddle she killed and ate. Oedipus is the only one who is able to answer the riddle; therefore, in distress over his conquest of her, the Sphinx kills herself and Oedipus frees Thebes from this malign influence of the Sphinx. So, that is his exceptional cleverness; that he could solve a riddle that no one else is able to solve.

Yet another element from standard folktale motifs of this type of story; the successful completion of these tests—whether strength, courage, or whatever—is often the granting of a bride to the young man in question. And so is the case with Oedipus. Because he solves the riddle of the Sphinx, and frees Thebes from her torment, Oedipus is granted the hand of the recently widowed queen of Thebes in marriage. Unfortunately, this is Jocasta, his mother, though neither of them knows it. Oedipus has fulfilled his fate of killing his father and marrying his mother. His discovery of the truth of his actions leads to Jocasta's death, to his mother's suicide in, I think, all of the versions of the story. At least in Sophocles's version, it leads to Oedipus's own self-blinding and exile.

We are most familiar with this story through Sophocles's version, as I have said before in this course. In the twentieth century, this myth, particularly as presented by Sophocles, has become extremely important in popular culture because of the use made of it by two of the most influential theorists of this century, Sigmund Freud and Claude Lévi-Strauss.

Freud, as we discussed in the third lecture back at the beginning of the course, assumes that the myth, as presented by Sophocles, reflects the unconscious or subconscious desires of all male children to kill their fathers, or at least supplant their fathers, and have sexual relations with their mothers. It is because of this, Freud thinks, that the play appeals no less to modern audiences than it did to ancient audiences. He reads it, in effect, as a kind of wish-fulfillment fantasy. Quite aside from the fact that this has always seemed, to me, unsatisfactory to explain why the play appeals to females as well as to males, one objection that is often made to Freud's interpretation is that within the myth, Oedipus's ignorance of his true parentage is an absolutely crucial element. He does these things without knowing who these people are. So, as many scholars have pointed out, if Oedipus felt Oedipal desires at all, he would feel them toward his adoptive mother and not toward Jocasta, because he does not know who Jocasta is. Freud's theory of the Oedipus complex, whether psychologically correct or not—according to this objection to his interpretation of the myth—Freud's theory of the Oedipus complex can't tell us much about the myth itself or how the myth works, as opposed to providing an explanation for why the myth appeals to its audience.

The second main objection to Freud's theory is one that we discussed as an objection to psychological theories of myth, in general; namely that Freud simply assumes the unconscious works, and the entire human psyche works, the same way in all cultures at all times. He assumes that the psychological impulses of small boys in fifth century B.C. Athens are the same as the psychological impulses of small boys in late nineteenth and twentieth century Europe. That is, at the very least, a questionable assumption, and one that needs to be demonstrated rather than just asserted.

The second great theorist of the twentieth century who focused on the Oedipus myth was Lévi-Strauss, the father of Structuralism. He reads the myth in all its versions, not just in Sophocles's telling of it, as mediating between two conflicting accounts of human origin, what is called "autochthony" and sexual reproduction. Now, "autochthony" is a word that simply means bringing from the earth. "Auto" means self; "chthon" means earth; so, autochthony means coming from the earth itself, and this is a theory of human origin that has left its traces in several Greek myths, usually in myths of particular cities. The Athenians, for instance, claim that they themselves were autochthonous. Others may have been, peoples may have been, created in one way or another, but the Athenians claim that they themselves sprang from the earth of Athens.

Lévi-Strauss thinks that the Oedipus myth encodes or represents a conflict between the theory of autochthony and the observed reality of sexual reproduction. In his reading of the myth, the riddle of the Sphinx and Oedipus's uncertainty about his parentage both concern the essential nature of being human. Where do human beings come from and what kind of creatures are they? The riddle of the Sphinx, which Sophocles himself does not tell us, according to other authors was just this; the Sphinx asked everyone she encountered "What kind of animal walks on four feet at morning, two feet at noon and three feet at evening?" Oedipus was the only one who was able to recognize that the answer was man, a human being, who crawls as a baby, walks erect as an adult and leans on a cane in old age.

So, the Sphinx's riddle has to do with what sort of a creature is a human being, and also lays emphasis on feet. Lévi-Strauss thought that the emphasis was laid on lameness in Oedipus's family—his grandfather Labdacos has a name that means lame one; Oedipus's name means "swollen foot" and refers to a detail of his myth that before he was exposed, his father Laios pierced the baby's ankles in order to lame him—Lévi-Strauss sees this stress on lameness as a reference to autochthony, because in stories of autochthonous origins, very frequently, humans who are born from the earth are lame or have some sort of oddity about their lower limbs, the last bit of them to emerge from the earth.

There is no doubt that the detail about the piercing of baby Oedipus's ankles is an odd detail in this story, as it has come down to us. It makes no logical sense. The infant is exposed as an infant. He can't even crawl yet. What is the point of laming him? Lévi-Strauss says that the point is simply that the myth requires this element of lameness in Oedipus, as in other members of his family. So, according to Lévi-Strauss, the myth, which is about the origins of Oedipus, mediates—remember Structuralism sees myth as mediating between oppositions—between the theory of autochthonous human creation and the observed reality of sexual reproduction, represented in Oedipus's story obviously by his union with his mother Jocasta.

I think it is fair to say that very few classicists have been persuaded by Lévi-Strauss's reading of the myth. Other scholars connect the story with initiation rites, since very frequently in initiation rites for young males there is at least some sort of symbolic killing of or setting aside of the father. As I mentioned when we were talking about the possibility that the Theseus myth reflects initiation rites, the main problem for this interpretation is that we simply have no evidence of ancient Greek initiation rites, so we just don't know if the myth reflects those or not.

Among literary critics and classicists, the most common reading of Sophocles's play, if not of the underlying myth itself, has been to see it as exploring and representing the conflict between fate and free will. This is a pretty obvious element in most modern readers' view of the play as Sophocles presents it. The actions taken by Laios, Jocasta and Oedipus himself all lead inexorably to the inexorable working out of fate. It is precisely because Laios and Jocasta choose to expose their infant son that he can grow up ignorant of who he is, and therefore, kill Laios and marry Jocasta without knowing what he is doing. If they had brought him up themselves, he would have known who they were, and it is the very fact that they try to avoid their fate, that enables their fate to be worked out. Similarly with Oedipus, if when the oracle of Delphi told him, "You will marry your mother and kill your father," if he had returned straight home to Corinth to his adoptive parents, he would have been safe. It is precisely because he tries to avoid his fate that he walks right into it. Many modern readers see the play as looking at the conflict between the fact that these characters are fated to commit the deeds that they commit, and yet it is their freely chosen actions, that they choose to do through their own free will, that lead them directly into that fate.

One objection that is often made to this interpretation is that it is basically an anachronistic reading. We moderns, people in modern American and modern Western culture, tend to see this conflict between fate and free will very clearly delineated in this play. That may be an effect of the Christian tradition, in which free will is stressed as being so crucially important to human spiritual development. Ancient Greek authors do not ever seem to have pointed to the Oedipus play as particularly involved with fate and free will. In fact, it is noteworthy that Classical Greek does not even have a term for "free will." This doesn't seem to have been a conflict that they were particularly interested in talking about. It is glaringly obvious to us, and I have spent many class hours having students talk about and work out and hash over, "How can free will exist if actions are fated to happen? Yet we see in the myth that these fated actions are played out through free-will choices." This topic, which we find endlessly fascinating, really does not seem to have engaged the ancient readers of this myth or viewers of this play to the same extent.

Another way to interpret this play, and one that I find fruitful and very useful, is to see Oedipus as the paradigm of a rationalist intellectual, someone who seeks to establish truth not through consulting the gods or through religious ceremonies and rituals, but through the questing of his own intellect, through the intelligence and rational use of his own mind. If we take this reading, we have to beware of anachronistic assumptions. Many modern readers who do see the play in this way—who see Oedipus as the paradigm of a rationalist intellectual trying to figure things out through his own intelligence—many modern critics who take that view tend to see it as an unambiguously good thin, to assume that Oedipus is thus some sort of proto-humanist hero who uses intellect, reason, and logic to get away from superstition and irrationality.

In the context of fifth-century Athens, in the context of the society for whom this play was written, and the society to which its author Sophocles belonged, most people would probably have seen such intellectual independence as a negative thing, not as a positive thing. In fact, Sophocles here is drawing on or making reference to one of the great intellectual movements and great philosophical controversies of his own day. He is casting Oedipus as a Sophist and looking at the philosophical movement that we call Sophism through his exploration of the Oedipus myth.

The Sophists were a group of itinerate teachers. They were centered in Athens, though most of them were not nativeborn Athenians. They taught a great many things, but one of their most important areas of teaching was in the field of rhetoric and argumentation. One of the reasons the Sophists were so controversial in fifth-century Athens was that they taught young men to argue both sides of a subject equally fluently. They taught what we would recognize as techniques of debate. To us, this seems utterly uncontroversial. We teach debaters in high school to argue both sides of the topic equally fluently, and probably, like our debate teachers, the Sophists meant this as a way of honing their pupils' intellect, training them in constructing logical arguments, training them in seeing what evidence will and will not support.

In fifth-century Athens, when this was done for the first time, it was seen as a very unnerving and a very dangerous thing. If the Sophists taught young men to argue falsehood as persuasively as to argue truth, then how could anyone, when confronted with a Sophist-trained person, know if that person was telling the truth? How can we trust what someone says to us if falsehood can be argued as persuasively as truth? The Sophists were often accused of training young men to make the worse argument seem better and of corrupting the morals of young men by doing so.

The most famous Sophist was Protagoras. In what we know about him, we see that it was not just rhetoric that made the Athenians, by and large, nervous about the Sophists, but their approach to the gods and to knowledge in general. Protagoras wrote several works none of which have survived. Unfortunately, we have only fragments of his work, usually single-sentence fragments. His most famous saying is usually translated: "Man is the measure of all things." I like to paraphrase that a bit as "the human intellect is the measure of all things," because I have found that very frequently modern students, when they hear "man is the measure of all things," interpret that to mean something like "man is the crowning pinnacle of creation, by which standard all other creatures are to be judged." That is not at all what Protagoras meant by it. I think he meant our own minds, intellects, are the only measuring stick we have for us to judge the rest of the world. Our intelligence is our only measuring stick.

In another sentence that probably opened one of his books, Protagoras says, "About the gods I know nothing, whether they exist or not; and therefore, I will not speak of them." That encapsulates what scared the Athenians, and worried the Athenians, about the Sophists. Protagoras is not an atheist, though he was accused of being one. He is not saying there are no gods. He is saying "I don't know if there are no gods." More than that, he is implying gods are irrelevant: "I am not going to talk about them. I am not interested in them. I am interested in the human mind, human intellect, and what it can do."

Obviously, if gods are irrelevant, the validity of oracles is called into question. As we talked about when discussing Apollo and the oracle at Delphi, oracles were an extremely serious matter in Greek society. They were taken seriously. They were trusted. They were believed in. A group of people who intentionally and directly question the validity of oracles are not going to be very popular among Greek traditionalists. The Sophists, indeed, were not very popular. This was all taken extremely seriously, by the way. The most famous indication of how seriously the Sophists were regarded and what a threat they were seen as being is that Socrates was executed in 399 B.C., largely on charges of being a Sophist. He said he was not. He said his teachings were very different from Sophism, but the charges against Socrates, the charges that lead to his execution, were that he had corrupted the youth of Athens and that he had denied the gods of Athens—the charges made against Sophists.

So, this is a very serious subject that Sophocles addresses in *Oedipus the King*. If we look at the play as Sophocles uses it in this context, we see that Oedipus can be read as an example of, almost a paradigm of, a Sophist. He refuses to simply accept what the oracle at Delphi tells him will happen. More importantly, in the play, he refuses to accept the warnings of the prophet Teiresias, an old, blind prophet who tells him rather frequently in Sophocles's play, and pretty clearly, that he is the one who killed Laios and that he is living in an incestuous union with his mother Jocasta. Oedipus directly accuses Teiresias, a prophet of the gods, of lying. Furthermore, Oedipus is also Sophist-like in his insistence on his own intelligence and his determination to reason out for himself the puzzles of his origin and the question of who killed Laios. It is the question of who killed Laios that motivates the action of the entire play. Sophocles's version of the Oedipus story opens with Thebes suffering under a great plague. Oedipus sends a messenger to the oracle at Delphi to find out what is causing this plague. The answer comes back that the cause of this plague is that the murderer of Laios is living in Thebes, unknown and unrecognized. So Oedipus sets out to discover who it is that murdered Laios, and that leads to the entire unraveling of the whole story.

If we read Sophocles's presentation of Oedipus as a presentation of a Sophist, a kind of prototype of a Sophist, then Sophocles's play indicates pretty clearly that in the view taken by this play, the human intellect alone is not sufficient for understanding the world. I think Sophocles here is coming down on the traditionalism side saying that Sophism doesn't work. The human intellect alone cannot solve all the problems of existence. In particular, Oedipus acts throughout the play on a mistaken premise. All of his logic works perfectly well, except he begins from the mistaken premise that he is the son of Polybos and Merope of Corinth, not the son of Laios and Jocasta of Thebes. His entire intellectual structure crumbles because it is built on a faulty basis. I think that is a pretty clear warning by Sophocles of the limitations of human intellect and the mistakes to which it is liable.

Sophocles also seems pretty clearly to say the gods' oracles are indeed valid, and the gods, indeed, must be taken into account. Throughout the play, Sophocles underlines all of these ideas with a running correspondence that he makes over and over again in the play between knowledge and blindness, ignorance and sight. Teiresias the prophet is blind, but knows the truth from the beginning of the play through to the end. Oedipus, when he has his eyes, when he has those senses that are so important for intellect, for human reasoning, doesn't know the truth, who he is. While he has his sight, he is ignorant. Once he learns the truth, he blinds himself. Throughout the play, Sophocles underlines his themes by stressing the idea that in some way sight equals ignorance, blindness in some way equals knowledge.

All of these different readings of Sophocles's play indicate how very difficult it is to separate the Oedipus myth from Sophocles's particular retelling of the Oedipus myth. *Oedipus the King* has become so central a text in Western literature that it has even eclipsed Sophocles's own further telling of the story in his later play, *Oedipus at Colonus,* where he treats the death of Oedipus. In that play, Oedipus comes to Athens, to a town named Colonus, which was actually Sophocles's hometown, near Athens, dies there and becomes a protective spirit for the Athenians, a hero worshipped by the Athenians. *Oedipus at Colonus* is not nearly as well-known in general terms as *Oedipus the King.* Is it possible to cut through the later interpretations of Sophocles's play and to cut around Sophocles's hegemony over the story, and try to decipher what the myth was doing before Sophocles got his hands on it?

We can try. The most unusual thing about this myth is its association of parricide, killing a father, and incest. Right away, Sophocles's treatment of the play and our familiarity with it means that we don't see that as an unusual association. We are so accustomed to the idea that this man killed his father and married his mother, taking that almost as one unit of action, that it is perhaps a surprise to realize, in classical myth at least, that those two actions—parricide and incest—are very seldom associated with one another. There are a good many classical myths about sons killing or almost killing fathers and vice-versa; mother-son incest is almost never associated with those myths. Parricide and even lesser violence against fathers were regarded with absolute horror in ancient Greek culture, particularly in Athenian culture. In Greek comedy, one of the worst insults you can throw at someone is to call him a "father-beater." That is one of the most unimaginable crimes, and therefore, one of the worst things you can call someone. We tend to see the incest with Jocasta as the more horrifying of Oedipus's two actions. That is probably anachronistic. For Sophocles's original audience, probably the thing that raised the hair on the back of their necks and gave them goose bumps and shudders of discomfort in their seats was probably Oedipus killing Laios, more than Oedipus's marriage to his mother Jocasta.

A scholar named Jan Bremmer has suggested in his discussion of the Oedipus story that the incest was added to the story precisely to underline the horror of the parricide. Bremmer says that parricide, cannibalism, and incest are the worst imaginable transgressions in Greek society, probably in most societies. There is no cannibalism in Oedipus's story, unless we see it as displaced onto the Sphinx who does eat humans. The incest here functions, as the cannibalism does in the House of Atreus, to underline the horror of the murder. Bremmer puts it very succinctly when he says, "The monstrosity of the transgression is commented upon by letting the protagonist commit a further transgression." So, in Bremmer's view, which I think is a very persuasive one, the underlying core of the myth is the horror of parricide, a son killing his father, and the incest with the mother is tacked on as a detail to underline how dreadful that son killing his father is. Dare I remind you, as I said at the beginning of the lecture, that in some versions of the Oedipus myth, what Laios and Jocasta know about their unborn son is that he will kill his father. So that is evidence that that was the original version of this story.

Oedipus's eventual heroization at Colonus is a reminder of a point I made when I first starting talking about heroes—that heroes, in the sense of guardian spirits, were not by any means necessarily noted for good deeds. It is Oedipus's crimes that mark him out as different from the rest of humankind, and it is that difference that makes him eligible to be a hero that can protect Athens. In this context, it is interesting to close by considering Burkert's reading of this particular myth. Burkert connects the story of Oedipus with the actual Greek ritual of a scapegoat, or a *pharmakos* to use the Greek word; a person who would be driven out of a city to take some terrible disaster, such as a plague, with him.

The crucial element here is that the *pharmakos* is not a good, noble, self-sacrificing individual who volunteers to take all the sins or misdeeds of his city upon himself and thereby free it from plague. The *pharmakos* must by definition be disgusting or foul or polluted in some way. He is an object of disgust and hatred. The idea seems to be a kind of what is sometimes called "sympathetic magic"—that this most disgusting and foul of human beings draws with him, as he is driven out of the city, whatever disaster it is that is troubling the city. In that context, in this regard, it is precisely Oedipus's pollution through killing his father and through sex with his mother, it is precisely the disgust that the chorus in the play expresses toward him once they find out what he's done, that makes him able both to lift the plague from Thebes, and later, as a heroized spirit to protect Athens.

In this lecture, we have looked very quickly at interpretations both of the Oedipus myth itself and of its treatment by Sophocles. In the next lecture, we will take slightly a different approach and look at some of the anomalous and frightening female figures—Amazons, monsters and the mythic Medea—who interact with Greek heroes in various different stories.

Monstrous Females and Female Monsters
Lecture 21

In the previous lecture on Oedipus and Sophocles's treatment of the Oedipus myth, among other things, I pointed out some of the traditional folktale elements that exist in the narrative of Oedipus's birth and childhood and his ascension to the throne of Thebes. In this lecture, we are going to look at one particular narrative element that is common to many hero-stories—the idea that heroes encounter anomalous and dangerous female creatures as part of their heroic tasks.

In this lecture, we will look at some of the female figures in Greek myth who break out of women's usual roles. We will start by discussing the Amazons, a race of female warriors who fought such heroes as Achilles, Theseus, and Heracles. We will then examine another foreign woman, Medea, who is most famous for her marriage to Jason but has tangential connections to other myths as well. Finally, we will look briefly at the numerous female monsters that appear in classical myth and discuss the possible genesis of these figures in male anxieties about women's roles.

The greatest Greek heroes all had encounters with Amazons at some point in their careers.

The greatest Greek heroes all had encounters with Amazons at some point in their careers. Theseus, Heracles, and Achilles each met and defeated an Amazon in battle. Who were the Amazons, and why was encountering them a test of hero status? The Amazons were a race of warrior women who lived somewhere on the edges of the civilized world. The most common location for their homeland is near the Black Sea. Some traditions put them in Ethiopia. The location near the edge of the known world stresses their alien nature. The myth of the Amazons may have some historical basis. It is highly unlikely that a female-only society of the type depicted in the Amazon myth ever existed. However, the location of the Amazons near the Black Sea is significant, particularly the versions that put their homeland in Scythia. Ancient Scythian women, as well as men, were riders and nomads; the two sexes dressed very much alike. The Amazon myth could be based on exaggerations of reports about the Scythians. For our purposes, the most important thing to observe about the mythical Amazons is that they reverse, or invert, almost every standard assumption of Greek society about the proper roles for women. They are warriors who meet men on equal terms on the battlefield. They are sexually active outside the bounds of marriage. They prefer female children to male children; when they give birth to boys, they kill them, castrate them, or sell them into slavery. The acts of marriage for girls and battle for boys are symbolically equivalent. A girl matured when penetrated sexually; a boy, when wounded in battle. This helps to explain the Amazons' role as warriors. They reject marriage, so they must accept its equivalent, battle. Because they are also sexually active, however, they are a sort of hybrid, both male and female, and remain sexually attractive to males (including Greek heroes). As such, they are extremely disturbing.

The interactions of Greek heroes with Amazons can be seen as reasserting the "proper" order of things, because the hero always defeats the Amazon. On the simplest level, the Greek heroes always defeat the Amazons; thus, Greek defeats barbarian and male defeats female. The encounter between a Greek hero and an Amazon always entails a re-feminizing of the Amazon. Theseus marries Hippolyta. Heracles steals Hippolyta's "girdle" (or belt); "loosening the girdle" of a woman was a standard euphemism for having sexual intercourse with her. Achilles falls in love with Penthesilea as she dies from the wound he has given her.

The myth of Hippolytos, as told by Euripides, highlights several of these themes. Hippolytos is the son of Theseus and the Amazon Hippolyta. He shuns sexuality (and so incurs the anger of Aphrodite) and devotes himself to Artemis. His refusal of sex indicates a refusal of adulthood and societal responsibilities (to beget children). Artemis is the patron goddess of young unmarried girls; in his devotion to her, Hippolytos is acting like a girl. Like the Amazons, Hippolytos is a hybrid between male and female. Unlike the Amazons, who take on aspects of both genders' adulthood, Hippolytos cannot achieve adulthood in either a male or a female way. He remains frozen in a kind of pre-adolescence.

The myth of Medea highlights many of the same points as the myth of the Amazons. In many ways, Medea is a pseudo-Amazon. Like the Amazons, Medea comes from the edges of the known world, near the Black Sea. She was princess of Colchis, to which Jason sailed in search of the Golden Fleece. She helped him on the understanding that he would take her with him and marry her. Like the Amazons, Medea is an extremely powerful woman who does not hesitate to use violence against males. She is not a warrior like the Amazons; her power consists in her knowledge of magic and sorcery. When the need arises, however, she is as capable of physical violence as any warrior; when she and Jason are fleeing Colchis, she kills her younger brother Apsyrtos and cuts his body into little pieces to delay her father's pursuit. Like the Amazons, Medea is no less desirable for being frighteningly powerful; unlike them, she uses this desirability in the framework of marriage. Jason marries her. After she leaves Jason, she becomes the wife of Aigeus. When Jason takes another wife, she murders her own sons. This murder has no direct analog in Amazon behavior; in the logic of her story, Medea kills her children to make Jason suffer. This act can also be seen as reasserting her Amazon-like status; by killing her male offspring, Medea puts herself entirely outside the pale of normal behavior for a Greek female *and* follows the normal pattern for an Amazon.

We must look closely at one more category of mythic females: the large number of threatening female monsters. These occur in various types. Some are monsters that eat men. Scylla and the Sphinx are examples of this type. Others are monsters that kill men, but don't devour them. The Gorgons, specifically Medusa, come to mind here. Often these females become monsters because of an earlier sexual transgression. Scylla was loved by the sea-god Glaucus, whom the goddess Circe desired; Circe turned Scylla into a monster to punish her for attracting Glaucus. Poseidon raped Medusa in Athena's temple, and Athena cursed Medusa with snakes for hair.

We have one example of a female monster who is *not* particularly threatening, despite being associated with snakes. This is the Scythian *echidna*, or Snake-woman, as described by the historian Herodotus. Heracles encounters her as he is driving Geryon's cattle home. The Snake-woman has stolen Heracles's mares and promises to return them only if Heracles will sleep with her. She wants children from Heracles, not to destroy him. After Heracles begets her three sons, she lets him go. She parallels the dangerous females in several ways. Like Medea and the Amazons, she lives near the Black Sea. Like Scylla and Medusa, she is partly snake; Herodotus says that she is a woman from the waist up and a snake from the waist down. Her youngest son is Scythes, who becomes the ancestor of Scythians. The Scythians later mate with the Amazons to produce a tribe called the Sauromatae.

These various females—the Amazons, Medea, and the monsters—all seem to represent the Greek male's anxiety about women's power, particularly their sexual power. This theme is encapsulated in Medea's name, which means both "genitals" and "clever plans." The theme of women bearing children only to kill them reiterates the regret that women are necessary for men to reproduce. Sexual reproduction means that women control men's ability to have offspring. Mothers' killing their offspring is simply an exaggerated form of that control. This may even help to explain the frequent rape motif in Greek myth, because such rapes always result in offspring; the motif may have less to do with male sexual pleasure than with male desire to control fertility. Women's ability to deny men continuity through offspring is enlarged in these myths into a tendency on the part of females to destroy men entirely. The connection that we saw in the House of Atreus myth between illicit sexual activity and illicit eating, specifically cannibalism, appears here as well. ■

Essential Reading

Euripides, *Hippolytus*.

Euripides, *Medea*.

Supplementary Reading

DuBois, *Centaurs and Amazons*, Ch. 1 and 5.

Herodotus, *Histories*, pp. 271–274 (on the Scythian snake-woman); 306–308 (on the Scythians and the Amazons).

Vandiver, *Heroes in Herodotus*, pp. 169–181. Analyzes the story of Heracles and the viper-woman; unfortunately, the Greek is not translated.

Questions to Consider

1. It is clear by now that Greek myth reflects a great deal of anxiety about and fear of women's powers. Given what you have learned about Greek marriage and family structures, can you suggest a reason for these anxieties, beyond the obvious one that women control fertility? What else was it about women or their position in society that was so frightening?

2. Heracles meets far fewer female monsters than do other heroes (or, put another way, the stories of female monsters tend to cluster around heroes other than Heracles), and the Scythian snake-woman is relatively benign. What is it about Heracles that accounts for this?

Monstrous Females and Female Monsters
Lecture 21—Transcript

In the previous lecture on Oedipus and Sophocles's treatment of the Oedipus myth, among other things, I pointed out some of the traditional folktale elements that exist in the narrative of Oedipus's birth and childhood and his ascension to the throne of Thebes. In this lecture, we are going to look at one particular narrative element that is common to many hero-stories—the idea that heroes encounter anomalous and dangerous female creatures as part of their heroic tasks. We are going to look specifically at the Amazons, Medea, and at some of the many dangerous female monsters who appear throughout Greek myth.

The greatest Greek heroes all have an encounter with the Amazons at some point in their careers. Heracles, Achilles, and Theseus all meet with and defeat an Amazon queen in one way or another. So, who are these Amazons and why was encountering them, in some sense, a test of hero status?

The Amazons, as I have mentioned before, were a race of warrior women. They supposedly lived somewhere near the remote edges of the world. Most accounts of the Amazons put their homeland somewhere near the Black Sea, sometimes in ancient Scythia, although some traditions put them in Ethiopia instead. That seems like a remarkable divergence, near the Black Sea or Ethiopia. What those two ideas have in common is that, wherever the Amazons lived, they lived near the edge of the known world. Greek myth reflected a very strong sense that the further you got away from the center of the world (which was Greece), the stranger cultures, customs and creatures all became. By locating the Amazons' society at the very edge of the known world, whether to the north or the south, the myth stresses the idea that the Amazons are extremely peculiar creatures.

Indeed they are. There may be some historical basis to the myth of the Amazons, surprisingly enough. It is very unlikely that there was ever a female society that lived entirely self-sufficiently, with no men at all. But, many versions of the Amazon story, as I already said, placed their homeland in Scythia, an area near the Black Sea. Ancient Scythian women were part of a nomadic society in which the women as well as the men rode astride on horses, led a nomadic existence, and the two sexes in Scythian society dressed very similarly. Women in Scythian society were given a degree of autonomy and power, so far as we can tell, that was much greater than what they were given in Greek society. It is at least possible that the Amazon story reflects or incorporates travelers' tales, tales told by Greek traders who had gone to the Black Sea to buy and sell goods, about the Scythians and their extremely manlike—according to the Greek view of things—women. For our purposes, the most important thing to observe about the mythical Amazons, whether their myth reflects some memory of Scythian women or not, is that they invert, reverse, or turn upside down, just about every standard assumption that Greek society makes about proper roles for women. First, the Amazons are warriors. That is the defining characteristic of the Amazons. They are warriors who meet men on the battlefield on equal terms, and they are very good warriors. It would not be any test of heroic prowess to overcome an Amazon, if the assumption were not that most times when Amazons meet men in battle, the Amazons are triumphant. They were very good warriors, indeed.

Secondly, they are women who are sexually active outside the bounds of marriage; in fact, they are women who reject the idea of marriage entirely. The Amazons were a self-sufficient female society in Greek myth. The one thing they could not do, being human and not goddesses, was to produce children parthenogenically. So, supposedly, once a year or so, the Amazons would go around to neighboring tribes, kidnap a certain number of men, force the men to have sex with them, and once they had become pregnant, they would either kill the men, enslave them, or just let them go again. The Amazons used men for sexual purposes, but their sexuality was outside the bounds of marriage, and marriage was not part of their culture at all.

Another way in which they invert the standard assumptions of Greek society is in their preference of female children to male children. Although I have not specifically talked about this before, you know enough about Greek society as reflected in myth that it should not come as a surprise that male children were much more highly valued than female children. In the Amazon society, that picture is precisely reversed. The Amazons would sometimes bear male children, but supposedly, when they did, they either killed the baby boys, castrated them, or sold them into slavery. Male children are undervalued; female children are valued in Amazon society. This is a point-by-point reversal of all the most important Greek assumptions about women and women's roles.

Greek culture very frequently makes a symbolic equivalency between sexual defloration for a girl and a boy's first wounding in battle, as the moment of maturity for either gender. A girl becomes mature, sexually and in other ways, when she is married and has her first intercourse with her husband. A boy becomes mature, in one way of looking at it, when he is first wounded in battle. If you want to press the point, the idea seems to be that bodily penetration, sexually for a girl and by a weapon for a male, is necessary for full maturity. The Amazons pretty clearly combine elements of maturity of both sexes. Another way of putting it is that this symbolic equivalence that Greek culture sees between marriage and resulting sex for girls, and battle for boys, helps to explain why the Amazons, women who reject marriage, are conceived of as warriors. If they reject the proper maturation required for women, they have got to have some kind of maturation, so they go through the maturation required for men instead. They reject marriage; therefore, they must take part in battle. Yet, they are also sexually active, though outside of marriage, and they remain sexually attractive to Greek males, including Greek heroes. Thus, they are a kind of hybrid. They partake of characteristics of both genders, adult females and males, and this hybrid nature—the fact that they act like men but remain very sexually attractive as women—makes them extremely disturbing in Greek myth. It is hard to know how to deal with them or categorize them.

The interactions of Greek heroes with Amazons can, among other things, be seen as reasserting the proper order of things in the Greek mind. On the simplest level, when a Greek hero confronts an Amazon, the hero defeats the Amazon. This happens with Achilles; Theseus; this happens any time a major Greek hero encounters an Amazon. The Amazon is defeated. On the simplest level, this means that the Greek is defeating the barbarian foreigner. "Barbarian" in Greek was just a term for foreigner, by the way, before it had any pejorative connotations. Supposedly, the word comes from the fact that foreigners, people who can't speak good clear Greek, make sounds that sound like "bar, bar, bar, bar." So, they are called *barbaroi*, or barbarians. That supposedly is the etymology of the word. So, when a Greek defeats an

Amazon, on the simplest level the Greek is defeating the barbarian; the male is defeating the female; in both cases the proper order of things is reasserted. Here we can remember that when Theseus kidnaps the queen of the Amazons, the Amazons come and besiege Athens to get her back. Theseus and the Athenians defeat the Amazons. That is pretty clearly seen in Athenian myth as a paradigmatic, defining moment in the Athenian construction of their self-image. When they turn the Amazons back, they are both asserting the hegemony of Greek culture over foreign cultures, and they are asserting or validating the role of males in their society as superior to females.

The encounter between a Greek hero and an Amazon works on more than just the surface level of male defeating female. It also always entails a re-feminizing or re-sexualizing, in an overt way, of the Amazon. Most obviously, Theseus marries Hippolyta. He kidnaps her, takes her back to Athens and marries her. Heracles, you will remember, steals Hippolyta's "girdle," or belt. You may wonder where is the re-feminizing, where is the sexualizing of Hippolyta in that? The answer is that "to loosen a woman's girdle" in Greek mythology was a standard metaphor for having sex with the woman, just as we will use the metaphor "he slept with her" to mean that he had sex with her. Greeks would use the metaphor "he loosened her girdle," or "he took off her girdle," to mean he had sex with her. He took off her belt. The belt, or girdle, held the woman's robe closed. If you untied the belt, the robe fell open. The assumption is there is only one reason a man would open a woman's robe, and there you have the underlying reason for the metaphor. So, although the myth does not actually say that Heracles had sex with Hippolyta, just by saying Heracles took the girdle off Hippolyta, you have the implication that Heracles sexually dominated Hippolyta.

Perhaps most interesting is that, when Achilles has his encounter with an Amazon named Penthesilea—this happens supposedly right after the action of the *Iliad*—Achilles falls in love with Penthesilea as she is dying from the wound that he has inflicted on her. This shows up in various examples of ancient Greek art. Achilles stabs Penthesilea with a spear or sword; she lies dying at his feet; their eyes meet, and he is smitten by sexual passion for her. There you see pretty clearly the idea that wounding in battle, in some way, is the symbolic equivalent of sexual intercourse. Achilles wounds Penthesilea and falls in love with her at the same moment. In each of these examples,

Theseus, Heracles, and Achilles, we have the encounter with the male hero re-feminizing the Amazon and reasserting what the Greeks would see as her proper female role, to be sexually dominated by the Greek male.

The story of Hippolytus, who you will remember is the son of Theseus and the Amazon queen Hippolyta, reflects many of these same ideas in a very interesting and unusual way, since Hippolytus is in himself male. Hippolytus is the son of an Athenian father and an Amazon mother. As I mentioned briefly, when we were talking about Theseus, Hippolytus shuns sexuality. That is why Aphrodite is angry at him, and in his story, as the playwright Euripides tells it, it is the anger of Aphrodite at Hippolytus, her anger because Hippolytus does not honor her appropriately, that leads to the whole story about Hippolytus's stepmother, Phaidra, falling in love with him, and the result is the deaths of both Phaidra and Hippolytus. In the account that the playwright Euripides gives us, all of this is Aphrodite's revenge against Hippolytus because he does not honor her appropriately.

Why doesn't he honor her appropriately? Because he shuns sexuality. He refuses to take part in any sexual activity whatsoever. Instead, Hippolytus devotes himself to the goddess Artemis. To understand what is going on in the story of Hippolytus, we have to set aside any assumptions we may have about chastity, or the eschewing of sexuality being somehow purifying or ennobling or good for the soul. In classical Greek culture, a young man who eschewed sexuality would not be seen as pure or noble. He would be seen as weird. Furthermore, he would be seen as selfish, because by eschewing sexuality, by refusing to be sexually mature, Hippolytus is refusing the duties of an adult male citizen. In a society with high infant mortality, and many enemies, it was the absolute, unambiguous, unarguable duty of every male citizen to marry and beget children whether he wanted to or not. That was his duty as a Greek citizen.

When Hippolytus refuses to take part in the area supervised by Aphrodite, he is not just failing to show respect to an important goddess, he is also refusing to be an adult male. His devotion to Artemis means that he is, in effect, acting like a young girl. As you will remember, Artemis is the patron goddess of young, unmarried girls. Hippolytus, too, like the Amazons themselves, is a kind of bizarre hybrid. He is male, but he devotes himself to a goddess who is appropriate for a young, unmarried girl, and refuses to become an adult male, to take his part in society by marrying and begetting children. In his case, however, his hybrid nature seems to involve refusing to become an adult of either gender. The Amazons are hybrids who share traits of adults of both genders. Hippolytus is frozen in a kind of pre-adolescence, let alone pre-adulthood, in which he will not or cannot become an adult of either gender. He is devoted to Artemis, the goddess to whom young girls are devoted up to the time of their marriage, but he can't marry as a female. That is simply not open to him. So, he can't move beyond devotion to Artemis, and he refuses to be an adult male. Apparently, he, the offspring of an Athenian father and an Amazon mother, is a hybrid who simply cannot exist in Athenian society. There is no place for Hippolytus. He is a hybrid that simply doesn't work.

The Amazons are not the only interesting females in Greek myth who at least invert or call into question the assumptions that Greek myth makes about the proper roles of women. One of the most obvious such females in Greek myth is Medea, who is herself the subject of a play by her name, written by the same playwright Euripides who wrote *Hippolytus*. Medea in many ways parallels the Amazons. Her story highlights many of the same points we see in the story of the Amazons. In fact, she almost is a pseudo-Amazon herself in various different ways.

First of all, she comes from the same neighborhood as the Amazons. Medea comes from a town called Colchis near the Black Sea. This is where Jason sailed on the Argo to get the Golden Fleece. He got the Golden Fleece with Medea's help. As is so common in myth, she helped him on the understanding that he would marry her and take her with him when he left Colchis, Golden Fleece in hand. And so he did. Like the Amazons, Medea is an extremely powerful woman who does not hesitate to use violence against males when she needs to. She is not a warrior like the Amazons. There is no indication that Medea ever enters into battle directly. Rather, she uses magic and sorcery to assert her power. Like the Amazons, when she has to, when need arises, she is quite capable of direct, overt physical violence against males. The most obvious and horrifying example is that when she and Jason are fleeing Colchis, when they are on the Argo sailing away from Colchis, and Medea's father, the rightful owner of the Golden Fleece, is giving chase to them in his own ship. Medea delays her father by killing her little brother, Apsyrtos, cutting his body into small pieces and throwing the pieces overboard one by one. Her father has to slow down and gather up the pieces of his son, so he can give the boy a proper funeral. Medea knows that this will slow her father's progress down enough that she and Jason can get away.

So, she is perfectly capable of using horrible physical violence against males, even males of her own family, when it suits her purposes. Like the Amazons, Medea is no less sexually desirable for the fact of being frighteningly powerful and willing to use violence. Jason marries her and begets at least two children with her. After her marriage with Jason falls apart, she becomes the wife of Aigeus, as we have already discussed. You will remember that she tries to kill Theseus when Theseus first presents himself to his father Aigeus. Medea parallels the Amazons in coming from the area of the Black Sea, in being a very powerful woman who is both capable of and willing to use violence, and in being no less sexually desirable to Greek men for the fact of her power and violence.

There is one other way in which she parallels the Amazons, and that is in the fact that she kills her own sons. Her motivation for doing so, and the time at which she does so, is very different from the Amazons. You will remember that the Amazons kill their baby boys because they want daughters and not sons. They kill the boys or get rid of them as infants. Medea, at least as Euripides presents her story, wants her children and even seems to love her children, until Jason decides to leave her for another woman. It is when Jason decides to set her aside and marry a young Greek woman that Medea kills her sons. She does this, within the logic of her own story, specifically to make Jason suffer. She knows that the worst thing she can do to him is deprive him of his sons, kill his children. Despite the fact that they are also her children, the desire to make Jason suffer outweighs, in her mind, her maternal affection for her sons, so she kills the sons to make Jason suffer.

This act can also be seen as reasserting Medea's Amazon-like status. She leaves her marriage to a Greek hero, an anomalous marriage for a foreign woman, and particularly, for an Amazonian-type woman. As she leaves her marriage to the Greek Jason, Medea reasserts her Amazon-like status by doing what an Amazon mother would have done in the first place, killing her two male children. There are many ways in which Medea follows the patterns of the Amazons, and also reverses completely the pattern of a Greek woman. The most unimaginable thing a Greek woman could do would be to kill her children, particularly her male children. This puts Medea absolutely outside the pale of normal female human behavior in the Greek view of things, or we might say in anyone's view of things.

There is one more category of mythic females to look at very closely, as well as the Amazons and Medea. That is the very large number of threatening female monsters who show up in many Greek myths. I am not saying that all monsters are female; there are certainly many male monsters. You might remember triple-bodied Geryon whom Heracles had to encounter in his tenth labor. There are a lot of monsters who are female, and they seem to play some particular or specific roles associated with their female nature. There are various, different types of these monsters. The two most important types are female monsters who eat men. Scylla, whom Odysseus encounters during his wanderings, would be an example of this. Scylla is a multi-headed, multi-bodied monster. She has six heads, six upper bodies. She is a snake, or snakes, from the waist down. She lives in a cave, halfway up a cliff. When ships sail too close to her, she leans out of the cave with all six of her upper bodies, grabs men off the decks of the ship, and eats them alive in front of their comrades. She is a particularly threatening, frightening and nasty female monster. The Sphinx is another example of a female monster. She is normally shown as having the body of a lion, or some other beast sometimes, and a woman's face and upper body, sometimes wings as well. As we saw in discussing Oedipus, she kills and devours men.

There are also monsters who kill men, but don't eat them—who are not cannibalistic monsters. Medusa, encountered by the hero Perseus (whom unfortunately I have not had time to talk about in this course), is perhaps the most famous example of a monster who kills, but does not eat. Medusa is a gorgon. That is, she is one of three mythic female monsters with snakes for hair, whose gaze turns men to stone. Just looking at her face literally petrifies anyone, man or animal, who looks at her.

One very interesting point about such monsters is that very frequently they became monsters in the first place because of some kind of sexual transgression on their part, or on the part of some male who encountered them. Scylla, for example, according to Ovid, was loved by a sea-god named Glaucos. Glaucos was, in turn, the beloved of the goddess Circe, the same sorceress goddess whom Odysseus encounters in the *Odyssey*. Because Glaucus loved Scylla, Circe was jealous of Scylla, who started life as an extremely beautiful young woman. Circe therefore turns Scylla into a monster, specifically to punish her for attracting Glaucos. So Scylla's monster-hood was a result of the sexual attraction she had exerted as a young woman on the sea-god Glaucos. Perhaps even more horrifyingly, Medusa, again according to Ovid, becomes a monster because Poseidon raped Medusa in Athena's temple. Athena therefore punished Medusa, the victim of the crime, by making her a monster with snakes for hair.

In both of those stories, we see that intentions, or in this case, even actions, are irrelevant; it is the result that seems to count. Scylla did not actually do anything; she simply attracted Glaucos. Medusa certainly did not do anything; she was Poseidon's victim. Yet, both of those young women are punished by goddesses for the very fact of their sexual attractiveness. They are punished by the goddesses by being turned into monsters who kill men. I don't think we have to delve too deep into psychological theory to see a connection there between sexual attractiveness and danger, between the woman who is sexually attractive and the woman who devours. All that kind of psychological anxiety seems very clearly to be here in this story, in which innocent young women whose only crime is being beautiful become devouring monsters who literally destroy men.

There is one fascinating example of a female monster in Greek myth who is not particularly threatening, despite being associated with snakes and encountered by a hero. This is the Scythian *echidna*, a word that is often translated "viper-woman" or "snake-woman," as described by the Greek historian Herodotus. This is an unusual story in many ways, not least that it shows up in the first work of Greek history, rather than in a work having overtly to do with myth.

Heracles encounters this Snake-woman as he is driving Geryon's cattle home from the Far West. He encounters her in Scythia, which is bizarre to begin with. If Geryon is in the Far West and Heracles is driving the cattle home from the west to Greece, I have never been able to determine what he is doing in Scythia. But, there he is, up by the Black Sea. Heracles wakes up one morning and discovers that his mares are missing, the mares who have been driving his chariot. He goes looking for them and finds, living in a cave, a Snake-women, whom Herodotus says is a woman from the waist up and a snake, or snakes, from the waist down. This Snake-woman tells Heracles that she has his mares, and that she will give them back to him if he will have sex with her. The Viper-woman, Snake-woman or *echidna*, is basically benevolent—or at least not malevolent. She does not want to harm Heracles. She does not want to devour him. She wants children from him. So, Heracles sleeps with her, Herodotus says, on that understanding, and begets three sons with her. Herodotus doesn't say if they are triplets or if Heracles stays for a while. After their three sons are born, the Snake-woman agrees to let Heracles go.

This monster parallels the dangerous females in several ways. Like Medea and the Amazons, she lives near the Black Sea in Scythia. Like Scylla and Medusa, she is partly snake. She is a woman from the waist up and a snake from the waist down. Her youngest son is Scythes. Scythes becomes the ancestor of the Scythians. A fascinating little connection with the Amazons; according to Herodotus, the Scythians later mate with the Amazons, with a few Amazons who decide they want to settle down and be normal human beings. They mate with the Scythians and produce a tribe called the "Sauromatae." There is a connection between the descendants of the Snake-woman and the Amazons.

The Snake-woman is not a malevolent monster. To be honest, I don't quite know why this should be so. I am still thinking about the myth of the Snake-woman. It occurs to me, at least, that among other things that may be going on here is the idea of reversal. Just as women don't act like women at the edges of the world, perhaps female monsters don't act like female monsters at the edges of the world. Perhaps at the very far edges of the world, you get monsters who are friendly, rather than monsters who are dangerous. In any case, these various females—the Amazons, Medea, the monsters—all seem pretty clearly to represent the Greek male's anxiety about women's power, and particularly, about women's sexual power. This theme is most clearly encapsulated in Medea, whose name means both "genitals" and "clever plan." The idea that sexuality equals deceit, that sexual power involves deceit, is encapsulated in Medea's very name.

The theme of women bearing children only to kill them pretty clearly reiterates the regret that we have talked about before, the regret felt by Greek men that women are necessary for the production of offspring. The fact that women bear the children means that, in some sense, women control men's ability to have children, as we have talked about before. Mothers who kill their offspring, bear sons to their husbands only to kill those sons, are simply an exaggerated form of that control. A woman can deny a man's continuity through children, either through not bearing the children in the first place or through killing them once she has borne them. The latter is exaggerated and unlikely, but it is the same general idea and reflects the same regret, resentment, and anxiety over the fact that men can only produce children through sexual intercourse with women.

It occurs to me that this may even help to explain the very frequent rape motif in Greek myth. I am not trying to sanitize or reduce the horror of the rape motif. It comes up very frequently, and is a very disturbing element in Greek myth for modern readers. I think one way of viewing this might be to say that since such rapes always result in offspring (and they do—a raped girl in Greek myth always gets pregnant), this theme may have less to do with males seeking sexual pleasure than with males seeking control of fertility. You still have to have access to a woman to beget sons, but in a rape story, the man is forcing reproduction on the woman with the slightest contact with her possible. This may, I think, reflect the male desire to control reproduction as much as possible, more than it reflects anything about actual Greek sexual mores *per se*; though that is a tentative suggestion that I just wanted to throw out there for what it is worth.

Women's ability to deny men continuity through offspring seems to be enlarged, in these myths, into a tendency on the part of women to destroy men entirely. I think that is a fairly clear progression. A woman can destroy a man's continuity, can destroy his family if she does not bear children. It does not take much of an imaginative leap to see that is women, or females, destroying the man himself, entirely. Finally, the connection we saw in the House of Atreus myth between illicit sexuality and elicit eating, specifically cannibalism, appears here as well. Many of these female monsters who became monsters because of sexuality, now literally devour men—don't just destroy them, but actually eat them.

The heroes' successful encounters with Amazons and with female monsters, as we have seen in this lecture, seem to represent that whole nexus of male anxieties that we have talked about so much in the course—about reproduction, women, and women's potential power in society. The whole reiteration of the idea of male dominance and female submission that comes up in these myths can serve as a reminder of the way myth both reflects and constructs the society in which it originates.

In the next lecture, we will turn to looking at the other great society of classical myth, the Roman society, and see how they used and changed some of the same myths we have discussed so far.

Roman Founders, Roman Fables
Lecture 22

> Perhaps this practicality on which the Romans prided themselves expressed itself in simply adapting Greek models rather than "reinventing the wheel," so to speak.

Classical mythology is so called because the myths in question appear in both Greek and Roman literature and art. Rome took over and adapted Greek forms of art, philosophy, history, literature, drama, and so on. One of the main reasons for this adaptation can be found in the chronology of the two cultures. Rome was founded in 753 B.C., when most of the important Greek city-states were already ancient. Athens reached its zenith during the 5th century B.C.; Athens was waning in importance as Rome was rising. In the 4th century B.C., Athens and Greece came under the domination of Philip of Macedon and then of his son Alexander. Alexander's death in 323 B.C. marks the end of the "Classical" age in Greece and the beginning of the "Hellenistic" period, which lasts until 31 B.C. Greece was politically less powerful during the Hellenistic age than it had been earlier, but it was culturally prolific in this period, producing a great deal of literature and artwork. Rome's political power was growing during the 4th, 3rd, and 2nd centuries, and the two cultures naturally came into contact with one another. The many Greek colonies in southern Italy were other areas of contact. From the 8th to the 5th centuries B.C., Greece had colonized the area around and south of Naples, an area that came to be called Magna Graecia (Great Greece). Rome was never a Greek colony, but as Roman power spread in Italy in the 4th century, the Romans came into direct contact with the ethnic Greeks of Magna Graecia. In 146 B.C., Rome conquered Greece, which then became a Roman province.

All this explains how the Romans could come into contact with Greek culture, but it does not explain *why* they borrowed so much of that culture wholesale. The Romans had an image of themselves as practical, down-to-earth people; perhaps this practicality expressed itself in their adapting of Greek models. The influence of Greece on Rome has often been compared to the influence of England on America. It may simply not have occurred to the Romans *not* to mimic Greek cultural forms. Perhaps the most surprising cultural borrowing is religion and mythology. Several stories of native Italian gods survive in literature, including Janus, the two-headed god, and the household gods, the Lares and Penates. These tend to be minor, local gods. The Romans assimilated their major deities to Greek equivalents; they also adopted Greek stories about those deities.

Despite the extent of their cultural borrowings from Greece, the Romans had a strongly ambivalent attitude toward Greece and Greek culture. The Romans saw the Greeks as cultural models, as better artists, poets, rhetoricians, and so on than they themselves were. At the same time, however, they saw the Greeks as decadent and "soft," as well as treacherous, tricky, and untrustworthy. The Roman conquest of Greece in 146 B.C. only confirmed this double view of Greece. The Romans had access to more Greek art and more Greek culture than ever before. But the Greeks had been conquered, which seemed to prove their inferiority.

This double view of Greece means that the Roman appropriation of Greek myth is bound to contain some unresolved tensions. If myth is, returning to my original definition, stories that a culture tells itself about itself, then Roman culture will need to adapt Greek myths to reflect its own values. This adaptation can be seen most clearly in the Roman accounts of the Trojan War, particularly in Virgil's treatment of the Trojan War story in the *Aeneid*. The Roman tradition that Aeneas was the ancestor of their people had its origins in the *Iliad*, where Poseidon prophesies that Aeneas will survive the sack of Troy and found a new city elsewhere. As early as the 5th century B.C., Aeneas's new city had been identified with Rome by Greek writers. Virgil's treatment of this story in the *Aeneid* is both the most complete and the most influential version to survive. Aeneas, the son of the Trojan Anchises and the goddess Venus/Aphrodite, fought for the Trojans in the *Iliad*. He managed to escape from the sack of Troy, taking his son, Ascanius, and his father, Anchises, with him. Aeneas reached Italy, married the Italian princess

> **Despite the extent of their cultural borrowings from Greece, the Romans had a strongly ambivalent attitude toward Greece and Greek culture.**

349

Lavinia, and founded a city called Lavinium. His descendant, Romulus, eventually founded Rome.

The main point of interest for us here is the psychological implications of this supposed connection to Troy. As we have seen, the Romans were ambivalent about the Greeks, particularly about their own cultural relationship to Greece. Part of this ambivalence undoubtedly sprang from Rome's knowledge that it was a much younger culture than Greece. Greece had myths that linked its cities and its leading families to mythic time and gave them gods for ancestors. Roman tradition said that Rome was founded in 753 B.C. Appropriating the Greek myth of the Trojan War by identifying themselves with the Trojans gave the Romans a pedigree as ancient as the Greeks and linked them to the same nexus of mythic history. The Romans could view themselves as every bit as ancient as the Greeks. They could also view their conquest of Greece in 146 B.C. as a "second episode" in the Trojan War. This Roman reconstruction is almost undoubtedly completely ahistorical; we have no reason to think that Trojan refugees actually came to Italy.

Side by side with the Greek story of the Trojan War, the Romans also had legends about the founding of the city of Rome itself by Romulus. By making Romulus Aeneas's descendant, the myth allows for the chronological gap between the traditional date of the fall of Troy (1184 B.C.) and the traditional date of the founding of Rome (753 B.C.). Thus, the Romans were able to feel the reassurance provided by the connection with Troy and to retain their local myth about their eponymous founder.

Romulus is a typical hero in many ways; his story contains elements that we have seen in other hero myths, and he is not an entirely admirable man. Romulus and his brother, Remus, were twin sons of a princess, Rhea Silvia, and the god Mars/Ares. They lost their birthright, then regained it. At birth, the boys were set adrift in a basket on the Tiber River by their wicked, usurping uncle. After they washed ashore, they were suckled by a she-wolf. They were found and adopted by a shepherd, who raised them. After they reached adulthood, their true lineage was discovered. They restored their grandfather to the throne of Alba Longa (a city founded by Aeneas's descendants). They then decided to found a new city of their own. This new city was Rome, so named after Romulus killed Remus over a quarrel about who would name it. After founding his city, Romulus offered asylum to anyone who wished to come join him there. He soon gathered a large group of men, but they needed wives. To procure wives for themselves, the new Romans invited their neighbors, the Sabines, to a religious festival, then abducted all the young, unmarried women. Romulus began his rule over Rome by murdering his brother. He consolidated his rule by violating a religious festival through a mass abduction. Again, heroes need not be "good" men. Romulus's ambiguous nature—a violent founder—is reflected in the story of his death, of which the Roman historian Livy gives two versions. The first version says that Romulus was taken up into the clouds by the gods. The second says that the Senators tore him to pieces and hid the body.

Livy wrote in the late 1st century B.C. By this time, we see a strong rationalizing tendency in writers' treatment of myth. Unlike Greece, Rome was a literate society from its earliest times. This means that we have nothing comparable to Hesiod or Homer, who are located near the introduction of writing into Greece and, therefore, may preserve less contaminated versions of myth. The earliest Roman writers do not deal with myths. The problems of reconstructing myth through literature are even more pressing when we study Roman myths than they were with Greek myths. This problem comes to a head when we consider Ovid. ■

Essential Reading

Livy, Book I.

Ovid, *Metamorphoses*, pp. 305–324. (This passage begins with the story of the contest between Ajax and Ulysses—the Greek Odysseus—for the armor of Achilles. The depiction of Ulysses is anything but flattering.)

Virgil, *Aeneid*, Book II.

Supplementary Reading

Wiseman, *Remus*.

1. The Roman attitude toward Greece is often compared to the American attitude toward England, particularly in the 19th century. Have we "borrowed" any cultural myths from England as Rome did from Greece?

2. Why do you think Roman culture invented the ambiguous figure of Romulus as its founder? Why attribute your city's name to an act of fratricide?

Roman Founders, Roman Fables
Lecture 22—Transcript

In the previous lecture, we talked about myths dealing with anomalous females such as the Amazons, Medea, and many different monsters, and discussed how those myths reflect Greek society and helped also to construct the understanding of Greek society. In this lecture, we are going to turn from Greek culture to Roman culture and look at the uses that the Romans made of the myths they inherited, or borrowed, from the Greeks.

As I said in the very first lecture, "classical" mythology is so called because the myths appear in both Greek and Roman literature and art. Mythology was not the only borrowing that the Romans made from Greek culture. Rome took over and adapted to its own uses all sorts of Greek categories: culture, philosophy, rhetoric, history, epic, tragedy, their forms of art, their method of making statuary. In all of these areas, Rome borrowed from Greece and modified Greek originals to its own purposes. The reason for this, the reason that Rome borrowed so much and so directly from Greece, has a great deal to do, among other things, with the chronology of the two cultures. I mentioned this briefly in the very first lecture, that Greece was the first culture; Rome was the second. Greece preceded Rome as a culture of note and importance in the Mediterranean.

Rome was founded—the city of Rome, which became the center of Roman power, was founded—in 753 B.C., the eighth century B.C. At that point, most Greek city-states were already ancient. Just to put it in context, this is about the same time that Hesiod was probably writing *Theogony* and *Works and Days*, and about the same time, give or take 50 years, that the Homeric epics were probably being written down. That is the time when Rome was actually founded. Athens's zenith, the high point of Athenian culture, was during the fifth century B.C., about 300 years after the founding of Rome. This means that as Rome was gaining in importance, as Rome was coming into ascendancy in the Mediterranean culture, Athenian power was waning. So, Greek culture becomes less important politically and economically speaking, as Roman culture becomes more important.

In the fourth century B.C., after the high point of the fifth century, Athens and Greece both came under the domination of Philip, King of Macedon, and later of Philip's son Alexander, whom we know as Alexander the Great. Alexander the Great's death, in 323 B.C., is the date that historians normally point to as the end of the "classical" age in Greece. That is purely a convention to make historical periodization easier for historians. It is not a matter of everyone waking up one day in 323 B.C. and saying, "I guess the classical age is over now." But, that is the date that we fix upon to delineate the difference between classical and post-classical Greece. From 323 B.C., with the death of Alexander the Great, up to 31 B.C., we refer as to the Hellenistic age or the Hellenistic period of Greek culture. During this period of about 300 years—again, about 323 B.C. to 31 B.C. are the conventional limits of the Hellenistic age—Greece is less important politically and economically than it had been in the classical age, has less political control and domination. Hellenistic Greece was still remarkably fruitful culturally. A great deal of literature and of art was produced by Greece during the Hellenistic period. So, as Rome's political power was growing, especially in the fourth, third, and on into the second centuries B.C., the Romans would have come into contact with the Greeks of the Hellenistic age, would have interacted with them, seen their artwork, read their literature, etc.

Another point of contact between Rome and Greece, or between Roman and Greek culture, was the numerous colonies of central and southern Italy. These colonies had been founded by Greek settlers from the eighth to the fifth centuries B.C. Many Greek cities sent out colonists to this area of Italy, the area around and south of Naples. There were so many Greek cities, colonies of cities back in Greece that were founded in Italy, that this area of Italy around and south of Naples came to be called *Magna Græcia* (which in Latin means "great" or "large Greece.") So, the Romans, as they were developing in the part of Italy where Rome is located, north of Naples, would have had constant and undoubtedly very important contacts with the cities of Magna Græcia.

Rome itself was never a Greek colony. That city itself was not founded by Greek colonists. As Roman power spread in Italy, particularly in the fourth century B.C., the Romans would have interacted a great deal with the ethnically Greek, Greek-speaking, culturally Greek people of Magna Græcia.

Finally, in 146 B.C., Rome conquered Greece, and Greece became a Roman province. That means that Greece then came under direct governmental control by Rome. So, throughout this period of several centuries, as Greece is waning in political power and Rome is rising, Roman and Greek culture intermesh, interact with one another. They talk with each other and the Romans are exposed over and over again to Greek cultural forms and artifacts, such as their literature, their drama, their art, and so on.

This explains how the Romans could come into contact with Greek culture, but it doesn't explain why they borrowed so much of that culture wholesale, why they simply lifted forms of literature and of content of things, such as mythology, from Greece and adapted it into their own culture. Trying to describe why that happened, we are on uncertain ground. All I can do is offer a few possible explanations. First off, the Romans had an image of themselves as practical, down-to-earth people. Remember Ovid's description of his own people, the Romans, as descendants of the stones that Deucalion and Pyrrha threw over their shoulders. We talked before about how that implied that they were a hardy race, that people who were descended from those stones were hardy. It also probably reflects the idea that they are plain, down-to-earth, matter-of-fact, earthy, in that sense.

Perhaps this practicality on which the Romans prided themselves expressed itself in simply adapting Greek models rather than "reinventing the wheel," so to speak. Why figure out how to write epic? Greece has already done it; let's just borrow the idea. Why develop our own native dramatic tradition? Greece has already done that too. Let's just borrow the idea. And so on. Another possibility is that it simply may not have occurred to the Romans *not* to mimic Greek cultural ideas. In this regard, the influence of Greece on Rome has often been compared to the influence of England on the United States. Greece was seen as a parent culture, or a mother country in some regard, from which the Romans simply naturally took over cultural forms and means of expression. Maybe, but that is a somewhat flawed analogy because when the United States began—I am not talking here about Native American cultures, but when the United States itself began—the people in power and those writing literature weren't just borrowing from England, they were English. Naturally, the early English settlers in New England continued to use their own cultural forms rather than inventing new ones. The relationship

355

between Greece and Rome is not that simple or straightforward. We don't really know; it is an odd thing for one culture to take over most of its cultural means of expression wholesale from another one. We don't really know why the Romans decided to do this.

One of the strangest, most surprising cultural borrowings is that Rome took over a great deal of its religion, and especially its mythology, directly from Greece. There were native Italian and Roman gods and native stories about them. As far as anthropologists and historians can tell, there has never yet been a human culture that did not develop some stories about some kinds of gods or divinities. The Romans were no exception. We know that there were native Roman and Italian gods and that they did have stories attached to them. Some of those gods survived and were recorded in literature, and some of them we know about. An example would be the god Janus, god of doors and of beginnings, a god with two faces, one on either side of his head because he looks backward and forward as a door looks. It is Janus who gives us the name of the first month of our year, January. That comes from his name, a month that looks both backward and forward.

Most of the native Roman gods that we know about, however, tended to be minor, local deities. By that I mean that if people who lived in a particular little town outside of Rome had a particular god of a hill or grove or lake or stream, they probably continued to refer to that god by his Italian name and did not assimilate him to a Greek god. Furthermore, the Romans also kept their belief throughout their culture, as far as we know, in their specific household and family gods, in particular, in two different types of gods called the "Lares" and "Penates," who were seen as being protective spirits of individual families and households. In some excavated Roman households, particularly in Pompeii and in Ostia, an area near Rome, you can still see shrines set in the walls where offerings were given to the Lares and Penates.

When it comes to the major deities, the Olympians, the really main and very important gods, there the Romans assimilated their native gods to the Greek ones. By that I mean that the Romans already had, as part of their native tradition, a main god named Jupiter. As they came into contact with Greek culture, the Romans began to say to themselves something along the lines of: "What we call Jupiter the Greeks call Zeus. They have all these stories about

Zeus. Let's now take those stories and tell them about Jupiter." So, the idea is that instead of maintaining their own native original stories about their major gods and goddesses and saying, "Maybe these are the same deities the Greeks worshipped, maybe they are not," as Greece did with Egypt, the Romans assumed that their gods were the same ones Greece worshipped, but then they took over the Greek stories wholesale.

This means, for our purposes, that very frequently a particular account of a Greek god we will know through the writings of a Roman author. This is also why, if you look in a modern handbook of classical mythology, you will find listings that say things like "Zeus (Jupiter)" or "Jupiter—*see under Zeus*." We say in handbooks of mythology that Zeus and Jupiter are the same god, Hera and Juno are the same goddess, and so on. Originally they weren't. Originally, they came from these two very separate cultures, but the Romans decided that their gods were the same as the Greek gods and used the same stories about them.

Despite the extent of their cultural borrowings from Greece, the Romans had, pretty much throughout their history, a strongly ambivalent attitude toward Greece and Greek culture. On the one hand, the Romans saw the Greeks as better artists, poets, rhetoricians, than they themselves were. They saw the Greeks as being culturally superior in a great many ways. But, at the same time, along with that view of the Greeks as culturally superior, the Romans tended to view the Greeks as soft, a little effeminate, tricky, deceitful and untrustworthy. There is a real ambivalence in the Roman view of Greece and the Greeks. The Roman conquest of Greece in 146 B.C. only confirmed this ambivalent attitude and made this double view all the more noticeable. On the one hand, having conquered Greece in 146 B.C., the Romans had easier and greater access to all forms of Greek culture. At this point, we see an influx of highly-educated Greek slaves into Rome, where they work as tutors for the children of wellborn families. There was a real cachet in having a Greek philosopher tutor your sons, for instance. But, while the Romans were getting more exposure to Greek culture than ever before, at the same time, they had just conquered the Greeks, which seems to prove the Greeks' inferiority. They lost; they must be inferior. The ambivalent attitude of Rome toward Greece runs pretty much throughout Roman culture. It means, among other things, that the Roman appropriation of Greek myth is bound to contain some unresolved tensions.

If we return to the definition that I gave back at the beginning of the course, that myths are stories that a society tells itself about itself, encoding its worldview, its beliefs, aspirations, fears and so on, then we will see that Roman culture would have to adapt Greek myths to reflect its own values. Even if it takes the stories over part and parcel, it is still going to have to somehow manipulate them or mold them to reflect specifically Roman values. And, of course, this is what we see happening. The adaptation of Greek myth to reflect Roman views and values can be seen most clearly in the Roman accounts of the Trojan War, and particularly, in Virgil's treatment of the Trojan War story in his epic, the *Aeneid*.

The Roman tradition out of which the *Aeneid* grew was that Aeneas was the ancestor of the Roman people. This tradition had its beginnings in the *Iliad* where, in a rather enigmatic passage, the god Poseidon says that Aeneas cannot be killed in battle in a particular time because he is fated to survive the war, go west, and found another city somewhere else. As early as the fourth century B.C., Greek writers had identified Aeneas's new city as Rome, which makes some kind of sense. The Greeks assumed that their myths reflected the way things actually had been in the time periods in which the myths were recounted. Poseidon says that Aeneas is going to go west and found a new city somewhere; then he must have done so. What new city could he have founded? Rome was a primary candidate. So, as early as the fifth century B.C., Greek writers had said Rome must be the city that Aeneas was prophesied to found.

Virgil's treatment of this story in the *Aeneid* is both the most influential and the most complete version to survive. There are many different versions about how Aeneas got to Italy, what he did on the way there, how he founded his city and so forth. What I want to focus on here, rather than Aeneas's story, how Aeneas happened to make his way to Italy, taking his father Anchises and his son Ascanius with him, is the Roman view of what the Trojan War itself meant, and how they manipulated the Greek myth of the Trojan War to fit their own cultural needs.

The Romans were ambivalent about the Greeks and particularly ambivalent about their own cultural relationship to Greece. Greece is better than/ inferior to Rome. Part of this ambivalence undoubtedly sprang from Rome's knowledge that it was in actual fact a much younger culture than Greece. Greece had myths that stretched all the way back to the origins of time itself. The Greeks took it for granted. No one ever questioned that they had been around since the very beginning. All of the myths we have looked at, all of the stories that the Greeks told, stretched back from humankind, into the Heroic Age, back before that. So the Greeks are a very ancient culture.

The Romans knew—their own native tradition said—that their city had been founded in 753 B.C. While the Greeks have this vast pedigree stretching way back into the beginnings of time, and incidentally connecting the families of everyday modern Greece with the heroes and gods of antiquity, the Romans know that their own culture only stretches back to 753 B.C. When the Romans appropriated the Greek myth of the Trojan War, by identifying themselves with the Trojans, saying "We Romans are the descendants of Trojans," think about the implications of that. Suddenly, they have given themselves a pedigree that stretches back every bit as far as the Greek pedigree. Suddenly they have said, "Well, we were there all along, too. We are as ancient as you are; we are as admirable and venerable as you are; we are just the Trojans, not the Greeks." It is a remarkably neat way of overcoming the psychological difficulty of being the new kid on the block, so to speak, and of getting rid of the inferiority that the Romans felt toward the Greeks. It also meant that the Romans had a way of getting around the embarrassing fact that if they were the Trojans, then they lost the Trojan War. That is one problem with deciding that they were descended from the Trojans. The Greeks won that war, so that makes the Romans descended from losers. Remember, the Romans have just conquered Greece in 146 B.C. Once that happened, once Roman culture gets to that point, then that can be seen almost as a second episode in the Trojan War. "The Greeks won the first round, but we came back and beat them soundly in 146 B.C. We defeated them."

All of this Roman reconstruction of, and Roman adaptation of, the Trojan War myth is almost undoubtedly completely ahistorical. By that I mean, there is no good reason to think that any Trojan survivors actually made their way to Italy, even if we assume that the Trojan War was a historical event, as it probably was. (There probably was some kind of war between the peoples of Mycenaean Greece and people who lived at what we call Troy. I imagine it was probably over shipping rights in the Dardanelles, rather than over Helen.) If we assume that there was actually a war, there is still no reason to think, and absolutely no evidence, that survivors from that war ever made their way west to Italy. Furthermore, even if they did, so what? It would be negligible. There would be few enough of them that when they arrived in Italy, they would have been subsumed both culturally and genetically into the native Italian peoples who were there. To say that the Romans of the second and first centuries B.C. were descendants of the Trojans is wonderful psychological myth, but it is completely impossible, historically speaking. It was a very strong article of faith—hardly too strong a word to use for it—for the Romans. It was a very important part of their self-construction of their identity.

However, side by side with the Greek story of the Trojan War, the Romans also had legends about the founding of the city of Rome itself by Romulus. This was one area in which native Roman tradition remained very strong, never was overcome by Greek tradition and never went away. Built into this idea that Romulus founded Rome in 753 B.C., there is quite a strong chronological problem. The *Iliad* says that Aeneas goes west and founds another city. Greek writers, as early as the fifth century B.C., said the city Aeneas founded was Rome. But Troy fell in 1184 B.C.; Roman tradition says Romulus founded Rome in 753 B.C. We have a minor matter of some 400 years there to bridge, aside from the fact that if Romulus founded Rome, Aeneas can't also have founded Rome.

Roman adaptation of the Trojan War myth accounted for this too. We see this in Virgil's *Aeneid*. Aeneas does make his way to Italy and he becomes the ancestor of the Roman race, but he doesn't actually found the city of Rome. Romulus, the myth decides, is a descendant of Aeneas, his great-great—however many "greats" it takes—great-great-grandson. Therefore, the Romans are able to have it both ways. They are the descendants of the Trojans; their race was founded by Aeneas; but Romulus founded their actual city.

One other thing about saying that they were the descendants of Aeneas. As I said briefly in passing, by linking themselves to the Trojan War heroes, the Greek families who made this connection were able to say, "We are descended from heroes;" and, since heroes are often children of one god and one human, that means, "We are descended from gods." By picking Aeneas specifically as an ancestor, the Romans can say precisely the same thing because Aeneas is the child of Aphrodite's affair with the human Anchises. The Romans too are descended from one of the primary Olympian deities through Aeneas. This seems to have been taken pretty seriously. Julius Caesar and his entire family traced their descent back directly to Aeneas. They though that their name Julius—that was the family name in Latin—came from the name of Aeneas's son, Julus. Therefore, they were direct descendants of Aeneas and direct descendants of Venus. Ovid uses this in *Metamorphoses* in a scene where he has Venus talking to Jupiter, asking Jupiter to save her son from his assassins. The son she is talking about is Julius Caesar, who is about to be assassinated in 44 B.C. Venus calls him, in Ovid's *Metamorphoses,* her son. So, the idea that the Julius family was descended from Aeneas, and thus from Venus (Aphrodite in Greek), seems to have been at least accepted as a metaphor if not taken literally, all the way up to the first century B.C.

What about Romulus? So much for the Roman borrowing of the Trojan War myth, how does Romulus fit in? Romulus is in many ways a typical hero of the type we have seen before. His story contains many of those folktale-like elements, including the difficulty of birth, the recognition later in life after he has grown up elsewhere away from his original home, and so forth. Romulus and his twin brother, Remus, were sons of a princess, Rhea Silvia, a descendant of Aeneas and the god Mars. They were, at birth, set adrift in a basket on the Tiber River by their wicked usurping uncle. They were washed ashore, found and rescued by a she-wolf, a female wolf who suckled them as though they were cubs. They were then adopted by a shepherd who brought them up as his own sons.

When they reached adulthood, their true lineage was discovered through a series of complicated coincidences. They reinstated their grandfather on the throne of Alba Longa, the city founded by Aeneas's descendants, and decided to found their own city to rule over on their own. The city they founded, of course, was Rome. It took its name from Romulus, after a quarrel between the two brothers over which of them should have the right to name the city and which should, therefore, have the right to rule the city. The two brothers quarreled over this. Romulus killed Remus, so that Rome originates in fratricide, and Romulus gave his own name to the city. After founding his city, Romulus gathered around him a group of young men, ne'er-do-wells and refugees from other cities, and said that they would now be his citizen body. The same problem that plagued Greek men; you can't have a city without children and new generations. You can't have new generations without women. So the new Roman men needed wives. Here, Romulus is far from an admirable figure in this story, just as he is far from an admirable figure when he kills his brother, Remus. The way the Romans got their first wives was to invite a neighboring tribe called the Sabines to a religious festival. At a prearranged signal, the young Roman men abducted all the Sabine women, whom they then married and made their wives. Romulus begins his rule over Rome by murdering his brother and consolidates it by violating a religious festival through a mass abduction, reiterating once again the idea we have talked about before that heroes, even heroes who found a city, need not necessarily be "good" men in classical myth. It would be a stretch to call Romulus a good man.

Romulus's ambiguous nature—the founder of Rome, but violent and treacherous—may be reflected in the story of his death, of which the Roman historian Livy gives us two different versions. The Romulus story is told in its most complete form by Livy, by a historian writing in the first century B.C. Livy says that there are two different versions by which Romulus died. The first version given by Livy is that on a certain day, when Romulus had been talking to the Senators, a government body that he had founded, suddenly the gods lifted Romulus up bodily in a cloud and carried him up to Mount Olympus to make him a god. That is version one. Version two, Livy says, is that the Senators, at a prearranged signal, tore Romulus to shreds and hid the body.

Two very different versions, and I mention that because that gives us a good way to look at the problems that are even more pressing in studying Roman myth than in studying Greek myth—trying to figure out what the myths actually said in their pristine form through the literature that recounts them for us. Livy writes in the late first century B.C. By this time, there is a strong rationalizing tendency in Greek and Roman authors, both, in their treatment of myth. In Rome, unfortunately, unlike in Greece, we don't ever have anyone equivalent to Hesiod or Homer writing at the beginning of literacy, and perhaps preserving some fairly uncontaminated versions of the myths for us. Unlike Greece, Rome was a literate society from its very earliest days. To make the problem even worse for us, the earliest Roman writers who have survived did not write about myth. That means by the time we get our earliest Roman accounts of myth, the myth has been reworked, thought about, rationalized, played with, disbelieved, shaken up, turned around, and is in no way recognizable as a pristine, living, working myth. At least it is difficult to recognize it as such. So the problems of reconstructing myth through literature are even more pressing when we look at Roman literature than they were when we looked at Greek literature. It is even more difficult to reconstruct Roman myth from Roman literature than it was to reconstruct Greek myth.

This problem comes to a head when we turn to talking about Ovid, the author of *Metamorphoses,* and is exacerbated by the fact that Ovid is our main source for some of the most important and famous classical myths that survive. In the next lecture, we will continue our examination of the Roman use of Greek myth by looking at Ovid's *Metamorphoses,* and what he does with myth in them.

"Gods Are Useful"
Lecture 23

> *Metamorphoses* was written probably between A.D. 4 and A.D. 8. In it, Ovid takes myth as his stated subject, specifically myths about transformations; that is what "metamorphoses" means. He says in the opening lines that he is going to sing or write about bodies transformed into other shapes, about transformations such as Daphne into a laurel tree. That is the ostensible link between all the stories he tells throughout *Metamorphoses*.

Throughout the course, we have read selections from the Roman author Ovid. We will now look more closely both at Ovid's great mythological work, *Metamorphoses*, and at the poet himself, in the context of his own society. Ovid is our primary source, at times our only source, for some of the most well known classical myths, such as the stories of Apollo and Daphne, Phaethon, and Narcissus. Daphne was a nymph, the daughter of a river god. Apollo was struck with desire for her, but she had vowed to remain a virgin. To escape Apollo, she was turned by her father into a laurel tree. Apollo makes the laurel his sacred tree. Phaethon was the child of Apollo in his aspect as sun-god and the nymph Clymene. Wishing to prove his parentage, he asked Apollo to grant him one request. This request was to drive the chariot of the sun; in the attempt, Phaethon was killed. Narcissus was a youth who was too proud to yield to any lover. As a punishment, he fell in love with his own reflection in a pool. He died of starvation, unable to tear himself away from his "beloved," which he thought was a water nymph. Because *Metamorphoses* is our primary source for these and other myths, we need to have some idea of the work's overall tone and purpose. What sort of book is *Metamorphoses*?

Ovid wrote near the end of the 1st century B.C. and the beginning of the 1st century AD. This was a crucial time in Rome's political and cultural history. From about 509 B.C. on, Rome was a republic, governed by elected officials. Under the Republic, Roman power expanded from the city of Rome itself throughout Italy and into other areas. Rome came into its own as an international power after the Punic Wars, a series of three wars with Carthage.

Rome's internal situation was far from stable; in the 2nd and 1st centuries B.C., it saw a series of social upheavals, often breaking into full-scale civil war. A crisis was reached with Julius Caesar's assassination on March 15, 44 B.C. Caesar's assassins claimed that he had wanted to establish himself as king, a point still hotly debated. After Caesar's death, an open power struggle went on for many years. The struggle had two primary contenders: Marcus Antonius ("Mark Antony"), Caesar's trusted friend, who was involved and allied with Cleopatra. Octavian, Caesar's great-nephew and adopted son. Finally, in 31 B.C., Octavian defeated the combined forces of Antony and Cleopatra at the Battle of Actium. With his victory at Actium, Octavian became the sole ruler of Rome and remained so until his death in AD 14. In 27 B.C., he was awarded the title Augustus ("the revered one"), which came to function as his name. He cleverly refused to adopt the names of kingship.

For our understanding of Ovid, we must understand three crucial aspects of the new government of Augustus (which he claimed was the restitution of the old Republic). Augustus wanted to reestablish old-style religious ceremonies and reverence for the gods. He also wanted to reestablish old-style morality. In 18 B.C., Augustus passed laws regulating marriage, making adultery a criminal offense, and encouraging couples to have children. Augustus was also a patron of the arts, including poetry. During his reign, Roman literature entered its "Golden Age." Virgil and Horace were among those who received his patronage; Ovid was not.

Ovid's work could hardly have been less congenial to a regime that espoused old-fashioned moral and social values. Ovid's earlier work was focused on amatory poetry. *Amores* (c. 16 B.C.) is a collection of short love elegies to Ovid's mistress, Corinna. *Ars Amatoria* (c. 1 B.C.) contains practical advice for both men and women on how to find lovers. He is, in fact, advocating adultery, contrary to Augustus's laws. *Remedia Amoris* (between 1 B.C. and AD 2) advises the reader on how to get out of a love affair. *Metamorphoses* (written probably between AD 4 and 8) takes myth as its stated subject, specifically myths about the transformations of bodies into other forms. Even here, most of the myths Ovid recounts include a sexual element, often a very strange and outlandish sexual element. In the story of Daphne, Ovid places less emphasis on the aetiological aspects of the story and concentrates on Apollo's passion and Daphne's revulsion. In many episodes in *Metamorphoses*, the transformation seems to be added almost as an afterthought, so that Ovid will have an excuse to tell the story. The treatment of the gods and traditional myth is done humorously, scarcely calculated to please Augustus. Ovid was exiled by Augustus in 8 AD. The exact reason for this exile remains a mystery, but it had something to do with Ovid's writing. Ovid says that it was for *carmen et error*—"a poem and a mistake." The poem is probably *Ars Amatoria*. We do not know what the "mistake" was. The most common theory is that he found out something compromising about the emperor's family. In any case, Ovid died in exile.

Metamorphoses, like Ovid's other works, is a highly polished, literary, and self-consciously ironic production. These qualities have profound implications for the use of *Metamorphoses* as a source of classical myth. First, we cannot assume that Ovid is giving us the "straight" version of any myth; he may be altering myth significantly for effect. His overall tone is playful and almost always ironic. The anthropomorphism of the gods is used to comic advantage, as in the story of Phaethon. Ovid may have added some of the more unusual sexual permutations in some of the stories. Second, we cannot assume that all the myths mentioned in *Metamorphoses* were well-known or important ones. Although *Metamorphoses* contains many myths that are well attested elsewhere, Ovid did not necessarily limit himself to major or important myths. Several of the stories Ovid tells in *Metamorphoses* are obscure and may well have been included to demonstrate his erudition. Others stories, such as that of Pyramis and Thisbe, may be entirely Ovid's own invention.

Ovid's target audience was the highly educated, sophisticated elite, who would be able to read and enjoy his tales of the gods as literary stories.

In sum, Ovid's use of myth anticipates the use that later authors will make of it, when the myths survive as literary tropes but no longer as part of a belief system. Questions of an author's beliefs are very difficult to determine, but Ovid's attitude throughout *Metamorphoses* seems close to a statement he makes elsewhere, that the gods are "useful." Undoubtedly Roman society showed a whole range of beliefs, but Ovid's target audience was the highly educated, sophisticated elite, who would be able to read and enjoy his tales of the gods as literary stories. Given the separation of *Metamorphoses* from living myth, it is an ironic twist of history that it exercised an extraordinary degree of direct influence on later literature and art. ∎

Supplementary Reading

Lyne, "Augustan Poetry and Society."

Questions to Consider

1. I have assumed in this lecture that Ovid's playful and ironic tone in *Metamorphoses* must mean that he did not literally believe in the gods he described. Is this a safe assumption or is it grounded in my own preconceptions about belief and the nature of divinity?

2. Because Ovid is our only source for several of the tales in *Metamorphoses*, is it valid to call these tales "myths" at all? Is there any way for us to know if Ovid simply made them up? Does it matter?

"Gods Are Useful"
Lecture 23—Transcript

In the previous lecture, we began discussing the way Roman culture adopted and transformed Greek myth to fit its own cultural needs. In this lecture, we are going to discuss, focus directly on, the author Ovid and his work, *Metamorphoses*—to which we have referred throughout the course—and try to discover exactly what kind of work *Metamorphoses* is, and what the implications of its nature might be for our understanding of the myths Ovid recounts in it.

Metamorphoses is Ovid's great mythological work. He wrote many other books as well, but in *Metamorphoses,* he focuses on classical myth as it is inherited by the Romans from the Greeks. *Metamorphoses* is our primary source, and many times our only source, for some of the best-known, most famous classical myths. Just to give three examples, *Metamorphoses* gives us the fullest accounts that we have of the stories of Apollo and Daphne, of Phaethon, and of Narcissus.

Apollo and Daphne is a story that is frequently shown in art and that is still quite well known. Daphne was a nymph. Nymphs are beings who are intermediate between gods and humans. They personify trees, rivers or lakes, and caves or mountains. They are, if not immortal, at least very long-lived. A tree nymph or *dryad* would die when her tree was cut down, for instance. A water nymph would die if her stream dried up, and so forth. Daphne is a nymph and the daughter of a river god. Apollo is struck with desire for her when he is struck by an arrow of his younger brother, Cupid (Eros, in Greek terminology), and wants to marry her, or at least, wants to mate with her. Daphne has vowed to remain forever a virgin, Apollo chases Daphne, trying to catch her. As Daphne runs away, she prays for help to her father, the river god, and she is turned into a laurel tree. Apollo then makes the laurel his sacred tree and takes a wreath of laurel leaves to wear on his head, and that becomes one of his common attributes in art afterwards. This myth is mainly aetiological. Why does Apollo use the laurel wreath? Why is the laurel tree sacred to Apollo? Daphne in Greek just means "laurel." The point is here that Ovid is the author who gives us the fullest account of this story.

Another such story that we know of mainly from Ovid is the story of Phaethon. Phaethon was the son of Apollo, in Apollo's aspect as sun-god. By the time Ovid writes, Apollo has taken over for Helios as the god of the sun, and in his role as sun-god Ovid tends to call him Phoebus, another name for Apollo, which basically just means bright or shining. Phaethon is the son of Phoebus and a mortal mother, and Phaethon wants to find out if the sun-god really is his father. So, he journeys to the palace of the sun-god in the remote East and asks the sun-god, "If you truly are my father, promise on the River Styx that you will grant me my one request." Apollo, or Phoebus, makes the promise, and Phaethon's one request is to be allowed to drive the chariot of the sun across the sky for a single day. His father, Apollo, knows that such an attempt will be fatal. He tries to reason with the boy, tells him that not even another god, not even Jupiter himself, can drive this chariot, but Phaethon insists, and since Apollo has promised by the River Styx, he can't go back on his word. He lets the boy drive the chariot and, of course, Phaethon is killed.

A third story, very famous, that we know mainly through Ovid is the story of Narcissus. Narcissus was a youth too proud to yield to any lover. Though many people desired him, he did not think any of them were worthy of his affection or attention. As a punishment, he fell in love with his own reflection in a pool and starved to death, staring into the pool, unable to tear himself away from his beloved (whom he thought, apparently, was a water nymph) long enough even to eat. Apparently, this is where psychology gets the term "narcissism," from the name Narcissus.

Those are just three examples. There are many, many more, of myths that we know existed in Greek mythology because we have passing references to them in other authors, but it is Ovid who preserves the fullest versions of the stories that we have, that allow us to recognize the story behind the other fleeting versions. I suppose the best example of all might be Niobe, who is referred to throughout Greek literature but whose story is recounted for us in full by Ovid. Since *Metamorphoses* is our primary source for these and for several other myths, we need to have some idea of that work's overall tone and purpose before we talk about how safely we can reconstruct myth from the accounts Ovid gives in *Metamorphoses*.

What sort of book is *Metamorphoses*? What is Ovid doing in it, why did he write it? To answer that question, I need to give you some background on Ovid, and to give you some background on Ovid, I have to give you a little more background on Roman history to set everything in context. So a very brief little excursus into a little bit of Roman history.

You remember that Rome was founded, supposedly by Romulus, in 753 B.C. From about 509 B.C. onwards, Rome was a Republic governed by elected officials. For the first couple of hundred years of its existence, it was ruled by kings, but the kings were thrown out in or around 509 B.C. Rome became a Republic and was ruled by elected officials. The Romans became very suspicious of anyone who seemed to want to set himself up as a king. It was under the republican form of government that Roman power expanded from the city of Rome itself throughout Italy and into other areas, as we talked about a little bit in the previous lecture. Rome really came into its own as an international power after a series of three wars with its rival state, Carthage, situated in Africa.

While Rome was gaining external power, its internal situation was anything but stable. Particularly in the second and first centuries B.C., Rome was plagued by a series of social upheavals which often broke into full-scale civil war. The social unrest of the second and first centuries B.C. came to a crisis with the assassination of Julius Caesar on March 15, 44 B.C. Caesar's assassins claimed that Caesar wanted to establish himself as a king; historians are still hotly divided. This is still strongly debated between ancient historians, whether Caesar did or did not want to set himself up as a king. Some think yes, some think no. His assassins thought that he did, and that is why they killed him. After the death of Julius Caesar, there was an open power-struggle for many years. Ironically, Caesar was assassinated to prevent him from setting himself up as a king; yet after his death, it pretty quickly became obvious that what was going to happen to Rome was one-man rule. It was just a question of who that one man should be.

There was an open power-struggle with two primary contenders. The first was named Marcus Antonius, better known to English speakers as Marc Antony, who was Caesar's trusted friend and confidant. Marc Antony was also involved with, living with, perhaps in his own mind married to, and allied with Cleopatra, the queen of Egypt. The other major contender for power after Caesar's death was Octavian, Caesar's great-nephew and adopted son. When things came to a head in 31 B.C., at a battle called the "Battle of Actium" off the coast of Greece, Octavian defeated the combined forces of Antony and Cleopatra, and thereafter, Octavian was really established as the sole ruler of Rome. This was in 31 B.C. In 27 B.C., Octavian was awarded the title Augustus, which means "revered one." Historians usually refer to him as Octavian while he is still engaged in the power struggle with Marc Antony, and refer to him as Augustus once he has established himself as the sole ruler of Rome. In fact, most histories will refer to Augustus as the first emperor of Rome. Augustus was, in all but name, a king. He was a one-man ruler. He had supreme power in Rome, but he was very careful and very clever in not using any of the terms of kingship. We call him the first emperor, and looking back with hindsight at the system of government Rome had after Augustus, we can see that he was the first of a series of one-man rulers who might as well be called emperors. He himself said that what he wanted to do was restore the old Republic. So, he put back into place the appearance of old-style republican government.

For our understanding of Ovid, there are three crucial aspects to what Augustus did in his new government, which he claimed was the old government reconstituted. First, Augustus wanted to reestablish old-style religious ceremonies and reverence for the gods. He built new temples, he refurbished old temples, he thought that Rome needed to return to old-fashioned, old-style religion and reverence for the gods. Secondly, he also wanted to reestablish what he saw as old-style morality. He thought that Rome in his time was extremely decadent—that sexual mores, in particular, were out of control—and he thought that Rome needed to return to a more old-fashioned, old-style system of values and morality.

In 18 B.C., Augustus passed laws regulating marriage, making adultery a criminal offense, which it had never been before; it was a private matter. Now, it was a criminal offense, an offense against the state with very stiff penalties. He also passed laws that penalized men for not marrying and that penalized married couples for not having children. So, he was trying to encourage marriage and fertility. By the way, it didn't work. His laws, which are often called his "social reforms," seem to have had very little effect on either the marriage, the divorce, or the fertility rate. The point here is that this was what he wanted to do. He saw sexual immorality as a real problem for Roman culture and wanted to try to get back to old-fashioned family values (if I may call them that).

Augustus was also a patron of the arts, including poetry. During his reign, Roman literature entered into what is still referred to as its Golden Age. It was during this time that Virgil wrote the *Aeneid*, that Horace wrote his poems, that Livy wrote his *History of Rome* and so forth. Augustus was a patron of many poets, and his patronage extended to Virgil and Horace.

Ovid was very definitely not among those who received Augustus's patronage. So, what was it about Ovid and Ovid's work that kept Augustus from being his patron? Ovid's overall work could hardly have been less calculated to appeal to an emperor who wanted to encourage respect for the traditional gods and a return to traditional sexual morality. *Metamorphoses,* as I mentioned before, is the work in which Ovid pays most attention to mythology. Most of his work concentrates on amatory poetry, poetry written about love affairs. His first published work, *Amores* (that is a title that just means "loves" or "love affairs"), was published around 16 B.C., two years after Augustus had passed his moral legislation. *Amores* is a collection of short love elegies to Ovid's mistress, whom he calls Corinna. In these poems, Ovid makes it quite clear that he is not married to Corinna and has no intention or desire to marry her; he is quite happy having an affair with her.

His second work, *Ars Amatoria,* which means more or less "the art of loving," or perhaps "the seducer's art" would be a better way to translate it, was published around 1 B.C. If *Amores* was calculated to annoy Augustus, *Ars Amatoria* would have infuriated him. It contains advice for both men and women—mostly men—on how to find and attract lovers. He gives very practical advice, such as telling young men that a good way to attract a lover to go to the circus, the entertainment, and sit next to an attractive woman. While everyone else is watching the races, put your foot on top of hers and rub your knee against hers and so forth, and the rest will just happen on its own. He also advises young men specifically to have affairs with older, married women, partly because they are so grateful to you for paying them any attention and partly because they can't make a fuss when you dump them. So, in *Ars Amatoria,* Ovid is specifically advocating—although in a very ironic, playful and humorous manner—adulterous affairs of precisely the kind that Augustus has outlawed, has made criminal offenses.

Ovid's third main work on amatory matters is called *Remedia Amoris,* which means the cure of love. This was written and published probably between 1 B.C. and A.D. 2. It advises a reader on how to get out of a love affair. Once you have attracted a lover, what do you do when you are tired of him or her and want to move on to someone else? Here, his advice consists in practical suggestions, such as thinking of one of your lover's flaws. Everybody has one thing wrong with them, one flaw. Think of the flaw, concentrate on it, don't allow yourself to think of anything else and fairly soon you will find that you are not attracted to the person anymore after all. He also wrote books about makeup for women; all sorts of this kind of thing.

These, obviously, were not going to get him into the Emperor Augustus's good graces. What about *Metamorphoses* itself? *Metamorphoses* was written probably between A.D. 4 and A.D. 8. In it, Ovid takes myth as his stated subject, specifically myths about transformations; that is what "metamorphoses" means. He says in the opening lines that he is going to sing or write about bodies transformed into other shapes, about transformations such as Daphne into a laurel tree. That is the ostensible link between all the stories he tells throughout *Metamorphoses.* Every story he tells includes some sort of transformation, though some are minor transformations and are mentioned so briefly that you could almost overlook them.

Even here, even in a work of mythology, of recounting mythological stories, and of talking about transformations of bodies into other shapes, most of the stories Ovid tells contain some element of sexuality, sexual adventure, sexual perversion very frequently. Even when he is supposedly writing about myth, he is really writing about strange sexual encounters as much as he is writing about myth. In the story about Daphne, for instance, Ovid lays much less emphasis on the aetiological aspects of the story, and concentrates on Apollo's passion and Daphne's revulsion. As I already mentioned, in many of the stories of *Metamorphoses,* the transformation, change of form, seems to be added almost as an afterthought so that Ovid will have an excuse to tell the story that he wants to tell. A lot of them are pretty shocking stories, indeed.

Metamorphoses is a fascinating work. I wish we had time to spend several lectures on it alone, because it runs the whole gamut from really horrifyingly violent and grotesque stories through some of the most emotionally charming and attractive stories that have survived from classical antiquity. He runs the whole gamut of emotions and of possibilities of human interactions. In it, he includes stories of men in love with women, men in love with men, women in love with women, men in love with animals, women in love with their fathers, a man in love with a statue. Just about anything you can think of, Ovid has got somewhere in *Metamorphoses.*

The sexual side of *Metamorphoses,* the emphasis on strange sexual adventures, is one aspect that would have made it unlikely to please Augustus. Another aspect of this work that also probably annoyed Augustus is that, in it, the treatment of the gods and the traditional stories of the gods is done very humorously and anything but seriously. For instance, Ovid makes a great deal of fun of the anthropomorphism of the gods in *Metamorphoses,* as I will get back to in a few minutes.

Ovid was exiled by Augustus in 8 A.D. He was sent away from Rome to a place called Tomis on the Black Sea, a place that Ovid absolutely hated. He wrote some poetry while in exile, addressed, in part, to Augustus, begging to be allowed to come back home and, in part, to Ovid's own wife in Rome, so Ovid had married at some point. He was exiled for reasons that we do not precisely know. In the poetry he writes from exile, Ovid himself says that his banishment from Rome was for, as he puts it, *carmen et error*—"a poem and a mistake." The poem is almost undoubtedly *Ars Amatoria.* Of all his works, that one, "the seducer's art," is the one that would have been most calculated to enrage Augustus. But that poem was written in or around 1 B.C., and Ovid was not exiled until 8 A.D. There is a gap of nine years. So there was something else that happened, some catalyst for his exile. That must be what he means when he says it was an error, a mistake. About that, what it was, we simply don't know. It is one of the great, frustrating, unsolved mysteries of Roman antiquity.

Elsewhere in his poetry of exile, Ovid hints that it was because of something he saw or overheard, and the most common theory about this is that somehow Ovid became privy to some embarrassing or dangerous secret about the imperial family. He found something out about Augustus or Augustus's family, or Augustus's plans for the state or something like that, that made him dangerous to keep in Rome. We don't know, and we probably never will know unless there is some discovery of some heretofore unexpected diary that Ovid wrote or something like that, which I don't think we can really hope for. In any case, Ovid died in exile. It is a very sad ending to the story of this extremely urbane, sophisticated city person, if ever there was a city person. Ovid loved Rome, and he hated his place of exile. Even after the death of Augustus, Ovid lived another four years or so. He was still not allowed to come home. Augustus's successor, Tiberius, also did not allow Ovid to return to Rome, and he died in exile.

Like Ovid's other works, *Metamorphoses* is a highly polished, very literary and self-consciously ironic production. This has profound implications for our using *Metamorphoses* as a source of classical myth. We do this a great deal. Any time anyone teaches a course on classical mythology, or any time anyone writes about classical mythology, they very probably are using Ovid's *Metamorphoses* as a source for at least some of the myths they discuss. That is a proceeding that is absolutely fraught with danger because of the tone, the presentation, and the kind of work that *Metamorphoses* is.

First of all, we can't ever assume that Ovid is giving us the straight version of any myth, as opposed to altering the myth significantly for effect. His overall tone is playful and almost always ironic. As I mentioned a few moments ago, the anthropomorphism of the gods is pointed out and used for comic effect, or at least for the effect that making it clear that nobody could believe in such anthropomorphic gods. Let me give you just one example. In the story of Phaethon, which I already mentioned, when Phaethon is trying to drive the chariot of the sun, the horses are entirely out of control, and at one point, the chariot of the sun comes much too close to the earth, over the continent of Africa. That, Ovid says, is when the deserts appeared in Africa and when the people of Africa became dark-skinned, because the sun was so close to the Earth. But the point I want to concentrate on here is the description of Earth herself, Gaia in Hesiodic terms, Terra in Latin. We are told that she, Earth herself, looks up toward Jupiter and, shading her brow with her hand, cries out to Jupiter and asks why she is being burned to death, what she has ever done to deserve so terrible a fate.

When we were discussing Hesiod, I talked about the problems of trying to picture Gaia, the problem with having an entity that is the great mother goddess, who gives birth to other gods but is at the same time the ground that we walk on. I talked about the fact that it is difficult to say Gaia is either one or the other; she is both. Yes, Hesiod says she has a body, she has bodily parts, bodily appetites and so forth. But Hesiod does not force you to contemplate the implications of that in as direct a sense as Ovid does. Hesiod does not talk about Gaia's hands. Hesiod doesn't talk about Gaia raising her hand to shade her forehead from the light of the sun. When Ovid does this, I think he is intentionally forcing his readers to look at anthropomorphism and see how silly a concept, or how unworkable a concept, it is when you are talking about actual, sublime gods. Or, "forcing his readers" sounds like his readers didn't want to do this. Perhaps asking his readers to share the joke would be a better way to put it, assuming that his readers are witty and sophisticated and urbane as he is, and will agree that these traditional stories of the gods are there to have fun with, more than to show respect and belief to.

Another problem with using the myths in *Metamorphoses* is, as I have already mentioned, that there are many unusual sexual permutations throughout them. Ovid may have added some of those for his own purposes. When we have no other version to compare with, we can't ever be sure what Ovid has put into the story and what was there in the story to begin with. Secondly, we can't assume that all of the myths Ovid mentions in *Metamorphoses* were well-known or important myths. Some of them were. Niobe is an example. We can be pretty sure that the myth of Niobe was quite important because her name pops up and little snippets of her myth are mentioned in so many ancient Greek writers. But while there are many myths like the myth of Niobe in *Metamorphoses*, myths that are tested elsewhere and that we can vouch for from elsewhere, there are also several myths that are attested in only one or two other places, and therefore may not have been terribly important, or are attested only in Ovid.

For example, the story of Pyramis and Thisbe, that sort of proto-Romeo and Juliet story that I mentioned a few lectures back, in which the two young lovers are forbidden to marry by their parents. They run away together, Pyramis thinks that his beloved Thisbe is dead, and kills himself. Thisbe comes back, finds Pyramis's body and kills herself. (And by the way, the metamorphoses in that story is tacked on at the very end. They kill themselves under a mulberry tree, their blood splashes up onto the berries, and the berries that had always previously been white turn purple and stay that way for ever after).

Pyramis and Thisbe is not attested anywhere else in classical literature before Ovid. It is mentioned a few times after Ovid but that doesn't prove anything, because those references could simply be references to Ovid himself. It is mentioned nowhere else. Ovid could very well have invented it. He says that it is a Babylonian story, but there is no evidence to think that it is. The names certainly are not Babylonian. So we simply don't know. Is Pyramis and Thisbe actually a traditional myth, or is it a nice little story that Ovid made up and put into the book for his own purposes and his own reasons?

Some of the stories Ovid tells in *Metamorphoses*, that are very obscure, are probably included to demonstrate just how well read and erudite he is. Just as I mentioned in his creation story, his story of the creation of the world, Ovid runs through just about every scientific, philosophical, and religious theory of his time, I think in part to demonstrate that he knows them all; so he may include some very obscure little known myths, both to entertain his readers and to demonstrate just how widely read and knowledgeable he himself is. In sum, Ovid's use of myth anticipates, in many ways, the use that later authors will make of classical myth, when the myths themselves survive as literary tropes but no longer as part of an active belief system. We can see that process beginning in Ovid's own work. The myths are now being used as literary devices, as entertainment value stories, but are not—at least I think for Ovid—part of a living belief system.

Here I am treading on some extremely dangerous ground, because the question of what a particular author does or does not believe, as determined from the work that the author has written, is a notoriously dangerous and difficult question to try to determine. It is very, very problematic to take the words of an author's written text as evidence for that author's own personal belief system. But, as far as I can read or judge it, Ovid's attitude throughout *Metamorphoses* seems close to a statement he makes in one of his other works, where he says, "Gods are useful. And since they are useful, let's say they exist." That is a kind of cynical and detached attitude toward using gods as a literary device. That is not the statement of someone who has any kind of living religious belief; rather, referring to the gods simply as useful for our purposes in this particular work. It is useful to have gods, so let's say we have them.

Undoubtedly, Roman society, like any other society, showed a whole range of beliefs and degrees of belief. I would imagine if we could transport ourselves back to first century B.C. Rome and talk to various people on the street, we would probably find a whole range of religious beliefs, from people who took every word of the traditional myths literally, all the way up to flat-out atheists. Where any particular person, including Ovid, falls in that continuum is not easy to determine. But it seems fairly clear that Ovid's target audience was the highly educated, very sophisticated Roman elite who would be able to read and enjoy his tales of the gods as literary stories. In other words, Ovid was writing for a target audience who, it is probably safe to assume, did not believe in these gods in any literal sense, and may not have believed in them even as representations of a more sublime kind of god.

Given the separation of *Metamorphoses* from living myth, the fact that *Metamorphoses* is our source for a great many myths, but is also, as we have just seen, very definitely separated from myth as a living and believed-in force, it is a very ironic twist of history (as ironic as anything Ovid could have though up, in fact) that *Metamorphoses* could have exercised an extraordinary degree of direct influence on later European literature and art. It is to that influence of *Metamorphoses* on later European culture that we will turn in our final lecture.

From Ovid to the Stars
Lecture 24

Remember back in the early lectures of the course I said that the allegorical interpretation of myth has had a very long run for its money? It has been a very popular interpretation of myth from antiquity onwards. Certainly, this is what we see with the treatment of *Metamorphoses* in the Middle Ages and the Renaissance. In fact, by the fourteenth century A.D., the allegorical use of Ovid reached its high point in an anonymous French verse poem of 70,000 verses entitled *Ovide Moralisé* ("Ovid interpreted as moral exemplar," more or less).

In this final lecture, we consider the enormous influence Ovid had on later European culture, especially on English literature and culture through Shakespeare. We then discuss the influence of classical mythology in general, an influence that continues in literature and art to the present day. Finally, the lecture concludes by suggesting that the prevalence of stories about extraterrestrials in our own society is a reflection of the myth-making impulse and that the particular form of our most popular science fiction stories reflects the ongoing influence of classical mythology.

Classical mythology permeates our culture's literature, art, and language.

Classical civilization gave way over time to Christianity, but beginning in the late 11ᵗʰ century, classical literature was resurrected. Ovid's influence on European culture from the late 11ᵗʰ century onward was significant. The 12ᵗʰ century has been called the *aetas ovidiana*, the "Ovidian Age." The growth of cathedral schools increased knowledge of Ovid's work. Medieval writers interpreted *Metamorphoses* as a collection of allegories, both moral and specifically Christian. By the 14ᵗʰ century, the allegorical use of Ovid reached its highpoint in an anonymous poem of 70,000 verses entitled *Ovide moralisé*. In this work, the flight of Daidalos and his son Icaros was interpreted as representing the soul's flight toward God. Daphne was interpreted as representing the Virgin Mary. By the 14ᵗʰ century, Ovid was also becoming well known in England. William Caxton published the first English translation of *Metamorphoses* in 1480. Caxton worked from a French translation and included explanations of the "morals" or allegorical interpretations behind Ovid's stories.

For English literature and culture, the crucial point is Ovid's influence on Shakespeare. Shakespeare clearly knew *Metamorphoses* very well indeed. We do not know the details of Shakespeare's education, but if he studied at the Stratford Grammar School,

William Caxton published the first English translation of Ovid's *Metamorphoses* in 1480.

he would have read Ovid in the original Latin. He probably also used Golding's 1567 translation of *Metamorphoses*. *Metamorphoses* permeates Shakespeare's works to an extraordinary extent. When Shakespeare wants a point of comparison, Ovid seems to be the first example that springs into his mind. These allusions are part of what makes Shakespeare difficult for modern readers. Because Shakespeare's influence on English literature is incalculably great, it is fair to say that Ovid, too, has had an incalculably great influence.

Ovid is only one author, but he can stand as a representative of the enormous influence classical mythology has had and continues to have on later Western civilization. Authors have taken and continue to take themes, images, plots, and points of comparison from Homer, Virgil, Ovid, the tragedians, and many other classical authors. Because these ancient authors' subject matter was largely based in myth, the modern authors who use them as sources reflect classical myth. Sometimes the author makes the connection obvious through the title of a work; examples would be Joyce's *Ulysses* or O'Neill's *Mourning Becomes Electra*. Other authors do not indicate their intentions so clearly; an example is Charles Frazier's novel *Cold Mountain*, which owes not just much of its plot but many of its episodes and images to the *Odyssey*.

Classical mythology permeates our culture's literature, art, and language. Is this the only reason why it is still important to us? Most of the theorists we surveyed at the beginning of the course would say that myth is important to us for deeper reasons than merely its influence on our culture. These theorists may well be right that myth taps into some deep structure or psychological tendency in the human mind. But this leaves unanswered the question of why *classical* myth, in particular, is so congenial to us. Its continuing use in our literature and art explains its familiarity, but does not seem adequate to explain its appeal. I think the reason for this is that classical myth's presence in our culture represents more than just a borrowed set of literary and artistic tropes and images. In the stories of Greco-Roman antiquity, we have inherited a whole cast of mind. Literature does more than entertain; it interacts with other areas of human endeavor to shape our worldview.

Finally, the question remains of where the myth-making impulse has turned in our own society. As I said in the first lecture, all cultures have myths; however, identifying and analyzing these myths from within a culture can be very difficult. If myths are stories a culture tells itself that encode its aspirations, anxieties, beliefs, and fears, then I think we can identify at least one strong mythic tendency in modern American culture: the whole complex of stories, word-of-mouth accounts, and widespread belief in visitors from extraterrestrial cultures. We can no longer place our monsters and our bizarre creatures at the edges of our own world; we know what is there. The impulse that put the Amazons in Scythia and triple-bodied Geryon in the far west now puts savage monsters in outer space. We can no longer place our Age of Heroes in the remote past; history and archaeology have made that impossible. Instead, we put them in the remote future. And, of course, in our culture, we find these stories not in books, but in film and television. Popular television programs and movies, such as the *Star Trek* series, reflect the same theme as Hesiod's "Race of Heroes." However, the pattern is now inverted chronologically. We tell stories about a race of people greater, stronger, and more capable than we, who are in some sense related to us, but these people are our descendants, not our ancestors. Hesiod's pessimism is not lacking; many of our "futuristic" movies portray a dark and horrible future.

Even there, though, a hero figure is usually present, who overcomes great difficulties, such as in the *Road Warrior* and *Terminator* movies.

What is the explanation for these recognizable mythic themes in modern entertainment? Psychological theorists, of course, would say that the stories of fantasy and science fiction are reflections of the mythic impulse welling up from the subconscious and that the oddly familiar characters we find there are archetypes. In my opinion, it is more likely that these stories are an indication of the degree to which the patterns of classical mythology have permeated our culture. These stories are appealing because 25 centuries of repetition have made them familiar and have built them into the texture of our minds. ■

Supplementary Reading

Lerner, "Ovid and the Elizabethans."

Questions to Consider

1. Most modern readers would reject allegorical readings of *Metamorphoses* that find a specifically Christian message in it, because Ovid died before the development of Christianity. Are other allegorical interpretations of *Metamorphoses* valid? For instance, can we read the story of Phaethon as a warning against pride, or does Ovid's ironic tone preclude such interpretations?

2. I have suggested that the modern genre of science fiction owes a great deal to classical mythology. Can you think of any other modern genres of entertainment that reflect some of the narrative patterns (such as the test-and-quest pattern) that we have discussed in this course?

From Ovid to the Stars
Lecture 24—Transcript

In the previous lecture, we talked about Ovid's place in Roman history and his use of myth in *Metamorphoses*, the type of work it is, and what Ovid was doing with myth. In this last lecture, I want to look at the enormous influence that Ovid's work exercised on later European culture from about the eleventh century A.D. onward.

To get from Ovid to the eleventh century A.D., we need to do a little recapping of history from the period on which the Roman Empire became Christian onward. Classical civilization, the belief in the classical gods, like the Minoan and Mycenean civilizations before it did not simply disappear all of the sudden. It waned over a period of time, with the growing influence of Christianity playing a very strong role in that waning. In the fourth century A.D., with the conversion of the emperor Constantine, often called Constantine the Great, Christianity became the primary religion of the Roman Empire. From that time onward, belief in the pagan gods began to disappear from European culture. It is impossible to tell when the final transition came, when no one any longer believed in the traditional gods of Greece and Rome. We know that after Constantine's conversion to Christianity, there was a later emperor called Julian the Apostate who reigned from 361 to 363 A.D., who tried to return the Roman Empire to the traditional pagan gods. Julian supposedly was the last person ever to receive an oracle from Apollo's oracle at Delphi. Julian sent to Delphi and got the answer that said, "Tell the king," to the messengers Julian had sent, "that Apollo's hall has fallen. The sacred spring speaks no longer. He has no prophetic laurel any longer." There is no one here, in other words. Julian was not successful in returning Roman culture to the pagan gods, and Christianity remained the primary religion of Roman culture.

Between the fourth century (the time of Constantine and Julian) and the eleventh century A.D., and later on, Latin was the main language of communication in Western Europe. Literary evidence for these centuries is relatively sparse, and most literature that does survive this time period is specifically Christian-oriented, is specifically about church matters, lives of saints, that sort of thing. It is in the late eleventh century and onward, in the high Middle Ages and the Renaissance, that we see classical literature, and particularly Ovid, coming back into play as major influences on European culture. Ovid's influence (or I should say the influence of *Metamorphoses,* because his amatory poetry was much less important) on European culture from the late eleventh century onward was surprisingly large. In fact, the twelfth century A.D. has even been called by some scholars an *aetas ovidiana* or Ovidian age, an age that models itself on Ovid.

Why should *Metamorphoses* have suddenly become so important a model text in the twelfth century in Western Europe? There are a few reasons. First, the growth of cathedral schools in this time period increased the knowledge of Ovid's work. Classical literature, in general, survived—after the conversion of classical civilization to Christianity, classical literature survived mainly in copies held in the libraries of monasteries, convents, and great churches. Classical literature, like all literature before the invention of the printing press, was preserved by being copied laboriously by hand, manuscript to manuscript. Many works were lost in this time period, these centuries, from the fourth century onward, not out of any malicious intent, but simply because the labor required to copy works that were no longer considered important was too great to justify. But primary classical works— Virgil, Ovid, the historian Livy and so forth—were copied and continued to exist, therefore, in monastery, convent and cathedral libraries. Thus, when cathedral schools became a force to be reckoned with in the twelvth century A.D., in particular, more people were able to gain knowledge of Ovid's work. Those who attended those schools would encounter Ovid, along with other classical and ecclesiastical works that they would find in the libraries associated with their schools. This, of course, doesn't explain why Ovid, more than Virgil or any other classical writer, was popular. The answer to that question seems to be, very surprisingly, that medieval writers interpreted *Metamorphoses* as a collection of allegories, both moral allegories in general, and specifically Christian allegories.

Remember back in the early lectures of the course I said that the allegorical interpretation of myth has had a very long run for its money? It has been a very popular interpretation of myth from antiquity onwards. Certainly, this is what we see with the treatment of *Metamorphoses* in the Middle Ages and the Renaissance. In fact, by the fourteenth century A.D., the allegorical use of Ovid reached its high point in an anonymous French verse poem of 70,000 verses entitled *Ovide Moralisé* ("Ovid interpreted as moral exemplar," more or less).

In this work, the flight of Daidalos and his son Icaros was interpreted as representing the soul's flight toward god. Daidalos, you will remember, was the great artisan, the craftsman who constructed the Labyrinth in which the Minotaur was kept imprisoned. Later in his story, Daidalos himself and his son Icaros were imprisoned by Minos, and made their escape by making wings for themselves and flying away from the island of Crete. Daidalos fashioned these wings by gathering feathers from seabirds, making wax forms that he fitted to his own and to his son's arms, warming the wax and pressing the feathers into it. Then he and Icaros could fly. Daidalos warned his son not to fly too near to the Sun or the heat would melt the wax and the feathers would drop off his arms; not to fly too low or the moisture from the sea would make the feathers too heavy and pull him down; but to fly in the middle path. Icaros flew too near to the sun, the wax melted, he fell into the sea and was drowned.

There are undoubtedly many allegorical ways to interpret that myth. I suppose the most obvious one is that it is a representation of the Delphic maxim, "Nothing in excess;" keep to the middle way. In the book *Ovide Moralisé,* in the fourteenth century, it was seen as representing the soul's flight toward God. Perhaps even more surprisingly, and more specifically Christian in allegory, was the way this work read the tale of Daphne and Apollo. Daphne was seen in her purity, her rejection of sexuality, as representing the Virgin Mary. Ovid was used, in this time period, as a source of allegory that was seen as being specifically Christian most of the time, and the rest of the time at least very moral. An odd twist of fate for Ovid, who, as we saw in the last lecture, was so ironic and urbane and sophisticated a writer, that he should be used as a source of completely un-ironic allegory, as a source of instruction for youth; but that is how he was used.

By the fourteenth century, when *Ovide Moralisé* was written, Ovid was also becoming well known in England in his Latin original. Students who went to grammar schools in England learned to read Latin; that is why grammar schools were called "grammar" schools, because that is where students studied Latin grammar. When we move on into the fifteenth century, William

Caxton published the first English translation of *Metamorphoses* in 1480. Caxton worked from a French translation and from the Latin, and he included morals, or allegorical interpretations, and explanations of the stories in Ovid. Caxton's translation was really a translation plus commentary, and reflected the same assumption that we saw earlier in the *Ovide Moralisé,* that Ovid's main use is as a source of morals and allegories, and that interpreting those is part of what the translator should do for his audience. With Caxton's translation, obviously, Ovid became available to more English readers, because now even those who did not know Latin could read Ovid in English.

For English literature and culture, however, the crucial point about Ovid is reached with Ovid's influence on Shakespeare. Shakespeare clearly knew *Metamorphoses* very well, indeed. He knew it backwards and forwards. It permeates Shakespeare's work to an extent that can hardly be exaggerated. We do not know the details of Shakespeare's education. We know very little about Shakespeare's life. But if he studied at the Stratford Grammar School—there was a grammar school at Stratford—he would have read Ovid in the original Latin as a schoolboy. He probably also used, as a grown man, the translation of 1567 done by Golding, which was a very popular book in England in the late sixteenth century.

Whether Shakespeare took his Ovid directly from the Latin or whether he worked mostly or entirely from Golding's translation, *Metamorphoses* permeates Shakespeare's works to an absolutely extraordinary extent. It is almost as though *Metamorphoses* is the text lying behind Shakespeare on just about every page of just about every play. When Shakespeare wants a point of comparison, when he wants something to use as a metaphor or a simile or a more general kind of comparison, one of Ovid's stories in *Metamorphoses* seems to be the first thing that springs to his mind in a very great number of cases. It has always seemed to me, particularly in teaching modern American college students, that this is a large part of what makes Shakespeare difficult for modern readers. People often think that the difficulty of Shakespeare lies in his language. I don't think so; the archaic language is fairly easy to get past. I think the difficulty of Shakespeare lies in the fact that he makes so many allusions to things that are meaningless to modern readers.

I can give you one example to serve for all of the examples in Shakespeare. In her great second balcony speech, when Juliet is waiting for Romeo to come join her for their wedding night, she opens the speech with a mythological reference. Just to remind you where we are in the play at this point, Romeo and Juliet have secretly been married. Romeo has murdered Juliet's cousin Tybalt, and therefore has been banished from Verona. Juliet is waiting for him to come join her for what they know will probably be their one and only night together, and she is standing on her balcony waiting for night to fall. This is what she says, "Gallop apace, ye fiery-footed steeds, / Towards Phoebus' lodging: such a wagoner / As Phaethon would whip you to the west, / And bring in cloudy night immediately." When I teach mythology to college students, I always recite that speech the first day of class and ask them if they know what it means. Almost without exception, they haven't a clue what it means. I might as well be saying, "Blah, blah, blah." Then, tell them the story of Phaethon and watch their faces light up and their heads nod in understanding when I recite Juliet's lines again. If you know the story of Phaethon, you realize that Juliet is saying, in effect, that she does not care if the entire world is destroyed; she does not care if every other living creature dies that very night; she wants Romeo and she wants him as soon as possible.

Of course, there is more at work in this image even than that. There is a resonance of Juliet referring to the eager, passionate, ardent, young, doomed teenager Phaethon, when she herself is an eager, passionate, ardent, young, doomed teenager. The death of Phaethon—that anyone who has read Ovid knows is inevitable in the story of the wagoner Phaethon whipping the horses to the west—the death of Phaethon prefigures the deaths of Romeo and Juliet themselves. It is an image that works on all sorts of levels, and it is an extraordinarily powerful way for Juliet to begin her speech describing her desire for night to come in immediately and bring her Romeo. If you haven't read Ovid or if you haven't read classical myth, it falls about as flat as anything possibly could fall. This is just one example out of Shakespeare; there are many, many others. Since Shakespeare's influence on English literature is incalculably great, I think it is fair to say that Ovid's influence on English literature through Shakespeare is also incalculably great.

Ovid is only one author, granted, but he can stand as a representative of the enormous influence that classical mythology, in general, has had and continues to have on later Western civilization, both European and American. Authors have taken and continued to take themes, images, plots, characters, points of comparison from Homer, Virgil, the tragedians, from many other classical authors, as well as from Ovid. Since these ancient authors' subject matter was, as we have seen throughout this course, if not directly myth, then at least permeated with myth, that means later authors who draw upon the ancient authors are inevitably drawing upon those same myths for their plots, characters, points of comparison.

Sometimes a modern author will make this obvious through the title of a work. When James Joyce calls his novel *Ulysses*, he is giving a clue that it is, in some way, a reworking of the story of Odysseus, whose name in Latin was Ulysses. When Eugene O'Neill writes a play that he entitles *Mourning Becomes Electra,* he is telling us through that title what he doesn't tell us overtly in the play itself, that it is in some way a reworking of the myth of the House of Atreus. Obviously, in both cases, those authors simply assume that their audiences are familiar enough with classical mythology that they will understand the point of the reference in the title. Other modern authors don't indicate their intentions so clearly, but that does not make their debt to classical mythology necessarily any less. An example of what I mean here would be Charles Frazier's marvelous novel *Cold Mountain* that came out a couple of years ago, which owes not just much of its plot, but many of its specific episodes and many of its imagery, to *The Odyssey*. It is a story about a Civil War soldier walking home to rejoin his fiancée, and it would hardly be an exaggeration to say that it is a reworking of *The Odyssey* set in the post-Civil War American South, though with some remarkable changes from *The Odyssey* as well.

Classical mythology clearly permeates our culture's literature. It also permeates our culture's art. Not so much in modern art as in art from the Middle Ages up through the last century or so, but anyone who has ever gone to a great art museum will remember that when you look at paintings in any of the great art museums in Europe or America, a great many of them have their subject matter taken either directly from the Bible or directly from classical mythology. Classical mythology also is in our language. I have mentioned some examples already in the course: tantalize, narcissism, that sort of thing.

Are these the only reasons it is still important to us, that we find it as images in our literature and our art, and as the occasional metaphor in our language? Most of the theorists we surveyed at the beginning of this course would say that myth is important to use for deeper reasons than merely its influence on our culture. They would say that myth taps into some deep structure or some psychological tendency in the human mind—to mediate binary oppositions, to express our repressed desires, to link us to the archetypes. They may be right about that. I don't claim to know whether they are or not. But this will leave unanswered the question of why *classical* myth, in particular, is so congenial to us. That perhaps requires a little bit of explanation. In my experience and in the experience of most people I have talked to, classical myth is congenial in a way that the myths of many other cultures aren't. People who have turned from reading classical myth to reading the myth of Navaho or ancient African cultures, or many other cultures, find that there is a kind of familiarity to classical myth that makes it immediately congenial in a way that the myths of other cultures are not.

To some extent that may be a matter of familiarity; these stories are common in our culture, we already know them, we recognize them as familiar. That does not seem to me to be quite adequate to explain not just the appeal of classical myth, but also the alien-feeling nature of myths from other cultures. I think what is going on here is that classical myth's presence in our culture represents much more than just a borrowed set of literary and artistic tropes and images. I think, and perhaps here I am agreeing more than I realize with the psychological theorists, that classical myth resonates for us on a deeper level than simply being a convenient set of metaphors that we plug in whenever we need a comparison.

In the stories of Greco-Roman antiquity, I think we have inherited not just stories, but a whole caste of mind. I am certainly not trying to say that we agree with those cultures in every particular. We quite obviously don't. But I think we do have access in their myths to an entire caste of mind, worldview, that perhaps has more influence on us still than we often realize. I think furthermore that literature—and when I say literature here, I am including other forms of entertainment that have to some extent superceded books in our culture, such as movies and television—does much more than merely entertain us. I think it is more important than that; that it interacts with other areas of human endeavor to shape our entire worldview, and that, therefore, classical myth has to some extent helped in shaping our worldview, in shaping our culture, just as it helped in shaping the cultures that developed it.

One final question that I would like to address in this lecture, before we leave classical mythology and mythology in general, is to look at the question of where the myth-making impulse has turned in our own society. If classical myth still serves us as a set of traditional stories that we can draw upon, what about the myth-making impulse, what about the impulse that creates myth in any culture? What about the traditional stories that we developed ourselves, rather than the ones that we inherited from another culture?

As I said in the very first lecture, all cultures have myths, but it can be very difficult to analyze and identify myths from within a culture. I even suggested that myth is a category that really only exists when you are outside a culture looking in; that when you are inside the culture, myth tends to be seen as true descriptions of the way things really are. I still stand by that statement. But, if myths are stories a culture tells itself that encode its aspirations, anxieties, beliefs and fears, as I have suggested as a working definition of myth, then I think we can identify at least one strong mythic tendency in modern American culture. Even if this does not yet have the full status of myth in the senses we have looked at in this course, I think we can identify one strong tendency toward what may yet become myth, one strong myth-making tendency.

What I think this is, is the whole complex of stories, word-of-mouth accounts, and widespread beliefs in visitors from extraterrestrial cultures that we see in modern American society. I think there are several reasons why those stories are so common now, not just in word-of-mouth accounts, but also in our entertainment; why so many movies, in particular, deal with space travel, aliens, the whole genre that we call rather misleadingly, science fiction.

Why would those appeal to us so greatly? We can no longer place our monsters and our bizarre creatures at the edges of our own world. We know what is at the edges of our known world. We know that our world has no edges. We have seen pictures of our world from outer space; we know what is here. We can't any longer put monsters at the far-lying reaches, where nobody knows what is located there really. So, what do we do with them? We put them in outer space. The same impulse that put the Amazons in Scythia, and triple-bodied Geryon in the Far West, now puts savage monsters beyond the solar system. I think it really is precisely the same impulse, just as medieval mapmakers, when they got to the edge of the known world, would write in the white space beyond it, "Here are monsters," so we when we get to the edge of the solar system write in the space beyond it: "Here are monsters." We locate it there because we can't locate them any more on Earth.

Similarly, and here I think there is a very interesting correspondence indeed, we can no longer place our age of heroes in the remote past. History and archaeology have made that impossible. We know too much about what happened in the past to say that there was a Golden Age, to say that there were people who were greater, more culturally developed, more technologically advanced than we are living in the remote past. What do we do with them? What do we do with that impulse? We put them in the remote future. We have all sorts of stories about people who are greater than we, more technologically advanced than we, and yet somehow connected to us, and we place them several centuries in the future, rather than in the past.

In our culture, we are probably more likely to find these stories in film and television than in books. I don't think that matters at all for the point I am trying to make here. Popular television programs and movies, such as the *Star Trek* series, I think reflect precisely the same impulse we see played out in Hesiod in his account of the Age of Heroes. The pattern is inverted chronologically. This race of people greater, stronger, and more capable than we, are still in some sense related to us, but they are not our ancestors; they are our descendants. Over and again in the *Star Trek* series, some character will find a photograph or talk about or tell a story about an ancestor who lived in America in the twentieth century, or an ancestor from the nineteenth century. The writers of that series very much make the point that these people are our descendants.

Even Hesiod's pessimism is not entirely lacking. In *Star Trek* it is, but in other science fiction it is not. Many of our "futuristic" movies portray a future that is dark and horrible, that seems to agree with Hesiod's description of The Iron Race, that things were going to go from bad to worse. But even in those—and this is something I find especially fascinating—those particularly nihilistic and distressing futures, there is usually some figure, strong and powerful and brave figure, who overcomes grave affliction—such as in the *Terminator* movies or the *Road Warrior* movies—there is some figure who arises to try to overcome the difficulties of the extremely negatively-pictured future.

What is the explanation for all of this, for what I have identified as the myth-making impulse moving toward science fiction and toward setting up our myths in the future rather than in the past? What is the explanation for the recognizable mythic themes that I think I have identified in modern entertainment? Again, psychological theorists would say that the stories of fantasy and science fiction are reflections of the mythic impulse welling up through our subconscious minds; that, in them, we see characters who are oddly familiar and situations that are oddly familiar, because they are reflecting the archetypes, or our subconscious desires, or the inevitable binary working of our opposition-moded minds. That may well be part of the answer.

In my opinion, it is very likely that these stories and their popularity are an indication, not so much of immutable realities in the human psyche, as the degree to which the patterns of classical mythology have permeated our culture. I think that these stories and others like them tend to be appealing to us, not simply because they reflect archetypes, or patterns, of human thought that would be the same in any culture of any time. Rather, I think a great deal of the reason for their appeal to us lies in the familiarity that comes to us, because of the repetition through 2500 years of the stories of classical myth. Those 25 centuries of repetition, I think, have made the patterns of these particular stories familiar to us and, in fact, have built those story patterns into the textures of our minds. Just as the Athenian myths of Theseus and his encounters with the Minotaur preserved some memory of Minoan culture, despite the fact the Athenians did not know that that was what they were doing, so too I think many of the stories that we tell ourselves as a society— the stories that encode our hopes, aspirations and fears—preserve the traces of classical culture and myth and are part of our classical legacy.

Timeline

c. 7000–c. 2000 B.C.E. .... The "Pre-Palatial" period of Minoan civilization on Crete. Knossos was colonized around 7000, possibly by settlers from southwest Anatolia.

c. 3000–c. 1000 .... Successive cities occupy Hisarlik in northwestern Turkey; one of them may have been "Homer's Troy."

c. 2200–c. 2000 .... Probable timeframe for arrival in Greece of speakers of an Indo-European language, the ancestor of Greek.

c. 2000–c. 1470 .... The "Palatial" period of Minoan civilization in Crete and Thera, which was the culture's high point.

c. 1575–c. 1450 .... The "formative period" of Mycenaean culture in Greece.

c. 1470–1100 .... The "Post-Palatial" period of Minoan civilization. After 1100, the Minoans disappear as a cultural presence on Crete and Thera.

c. 1450–c. 1200 .... The "Palatial" period of Mycenaean culture. The civilization's highpoint, during which it gained control over Minoan culture.

c. 1200–c. 1050/1000	The "Post-Palatial" period of Mycenaean civilization in Greece, after which culture in Greece reverted to a pre-Mycenaean level.
c. 1184	The most commonly accepted traditional date for the Fall of Troy.
c. 1100–c. 776	The "Dark Ages" in Greece; 776, the traditional ending date of the Dark Ages, is the traditional date of the first Olympic Games.
c. 800?–780	The alphabet introduced into Greece.
753	Traditional date of the founding of Rome.
c. 750?–700	The *Iliad* and *Odyssey* are perhaps transcribed into writing.
c. 700?	Hesiod writes *Theogony* and *Works and Days*.
c. 525	Birth of Aeschylus, author of *The Oresteia* and other works.
496	Birth of Sophocles, author of *Oedipus the King*, *Oedipus at Colonos*, and other works.
480	Birth of Euripides, author of *Bacchae*, *Hippolytos*, *Medea*, and other works.
458	*The Oresteia* performed in Athens.
456	Death of Aeschylus.

Timeline

431–405 .... The Peloponnesian War (between Sparta and Athens and their respective allies).

429 .... Probable date of performance of *Oedipus the King*.

c. 420 .... Herodotus publishes his *Historia* (or *Inquiry*), which includes many references to the heroes of mythology.

406 .... Deaths of Sophocles and Euripides.

405 .... Posthumous performance of Euripides's *The Bacchae*.

401 .... Posthumous performance of Sophocles's *Oedipus at Colonos*.

399 .... The execution of Socrates.

c. 380 .... Plato writes *Republic*, which includes the "Myth of Er."

264–241 .... First Punic War between Rome and Carthage; this war and the two succeeding Punic wars establish Rome's hegemony over the Mediterranean.

218–202 .... Second Punic War.

151–146 .... Third Punic War; final defeat of Carthage. Corinth is captured this same year.

44 B.C. .... Assassination of Julius Caesar on March 15.

43 B.C. .... Birth of Ovid.

31 B.C. .... Battle of Actium; Augustus's victory here marks the end of the Roman Republic and the beginning of the Roman Empire.

29?–19 B.C. .... Virgil writes the *Aeneid*, modeled on the Homeric epics but taking the viewpoint of the Trojans (whom the Romans considered their ancestors). Book II of the *Aeneid* gives the fullest extant account of the Sack of Troy. The *Aeneid* was left incomplete when Virgil died in 19 B.C.

c. AD 4? .... Ovid writes *Metamorphoses*.

8 .... Ovid exiled to Tomis on the Black Sea.

14 .... Death of Augustus.

17 .... Death of Ovid, still in exile.

1st–2nd centuries .... Probable period of composition of Apollodorus's *Library of Greek Mythology*.

312 .... Constantine converts to Christianity after his victory at the Battle of the Milvian Bridge.

361–363 .... Reign of the Roman emperor Julian "the Apostate," who briefly re-established paganism as the official religion of the Empire. Supposedly received the last oracle ever given by Delphi.

1054 AD .... Permanent break between Roman Catholic and Greek Orthodox churches leads to rapid loss of knowledge concerning Greek language and literature in the West.

c. 1313–1321 .... Dante writes *The Divine Comedy*.

1396 .... Manuel Chrysoloras offers classes in Greek in Florence. This begins the revival of interest in Greek literature in Europe.

14th century .... Publication of Ovide moralisé.

1453 .... The Sack of Constantinople by the Ottomans. A great many Greek scholars flee to Italy, bringing manuscripts with them. The study of Greek becomes important in Europe.

1480 .... William Caxton publishes *Ovyde Hys Booke of Methamorphose*, the first English translation of *Metamorphoses*.

1495 .... Aldus Manutius founds the Aldine Press in Venice and begins printing editions of Greek classics.

1498 .... Erasmus begins teaching Greek at Oxford. He becomes professor of Greek at Cambridge in 1511.

1567 .... Arthur Golding publishes his translation of *Metamorphoses*, which Shakespeare probably used.

1626	George Sandys publishes his *Ovid's Metamorphoses Englished.*
1870–1873	Heinrich Schliemann conducts his first excavations at Hisarlik. He finds the "Treasure of Priam" in 1873 and continues to excavate sporadically until his death in 1890.
1890	Sir James Frazer publishes the first edition of *The Golden Bough* in two volumes.
1900	Freud publishes *The Interpretation of Dreams*, which includes his theory of the Oedipus complex.
1900	Sir Arthur Evans excavates at Knossos on Crete. He finds the remnants of a great prehistoric civilization that he calls "Minoan."
1903	Jane Harrison publishes *Prolegomena to the Study of Greek Religion.*
1906–1915	Third edition of *The Golden Bough*, expanded to eleven volumes.
1912	Jane Harrison publishes *Themis.*
1913	Freud publishes *Totem and Taboo*, which suggests that myths are the wish-dreams of a culture and defines the Oedipus myth as a memory of an actual occurrence in the "primal horde."

Timeline

1926.. Bronislaw Malinowski publishes "Myth in Primitive Psychology."

1928.. Vladimir Propp publishes *Morfologija skaski* (*Morphology of the Folktale*); the first English translation was published in 1958.

1941.. Carl Jung publishes *Einfuhrung in das Wesen der Mythologie* (translated into English in 1949 as *Essays on a Science of Mythology*), in collaboration with Karl Kerenyi.

1949.. Joseph Campbell publishes *The Hero with a Thousand Faces*.

1959–1967...................................... Joseph Campbell publishes *The Masks of God* (four volumes).

1964–1968...................................... Claude Lévi-Strauss publishes *Mythologiques* (English: *Mythologies*); the first volume is *Le cru et le cuit* (*The Raw and the Cooked*).

Glossary

aetiological myths: Myths that provide an explanation ("aetiology") for how something came into existence. The myth of Persephone is an aetiology for the existence of the seasons.

ambrosia: The food of the gods. In the *Iliad*, the gods anoint the dead bodies of Patroklos and Hector with ambrosia to protect them from corruption. See **nectar**.

anthropomorphism: The representation of non-human entities in human form and with human emotions.

Areopagos: The "Hill of Ares" in Athens; meeting site of the Areopagos council, whose powers were restricted in 462 B.C. to hearing cases of murder, arson, and malicious wounding. In Aeschylus's *Eumenides*, it is the site of Orestes's trial for the murder of Clytemnestra.

athanatoi: "Deathless ones." A term used to refer to the gods, particularly as contrasted to mortals, or *thnêtoi*.

charter myths: Myths that provide a justification for a social institution or custom. The term is Malinowski's.

dactylic hexameter: The meter of epic. It is constructed of six "feet," each consisting of *either* a dactyl (one long syllable followed by two short syllables) or a spondee (two long syllables). The resulting line is flexible and varied in Greek, though it tends to sound pedestrian in English.

Colchis: Town on the Black Sea where the Golden Fleece was kept. Jason sailed there in search of the Fleece, which Medea, daughter of the King of Colchis, helped him to steal.

Delphi: Site of Apollo's most important oracle and the temple complex associated with it. Oracles at Delphi were spoken by the Pythia, a priestess supposedly inspired with prophetic powers by the god.

Eleusinian Mysteries: Religious ceremonies held at Eleusis in honor of Demeter. The term "mysteries" means "secrets"; the ceremonies were open only to initiates, who were bound by an oath not to divulge what was done in the rites. Our knowledge of the Eleusinian Mysteries is tantalizingly imprecise; however, it seems clear that the rites promised that initiates would have a better status in the afterlife than non-initiates. Initiation was open to males and females and to slaves as well as free people. The Mysteries fell into disuse around 400 AD.

Epic Cycle: A series of epics, no longer extant, which told the story of those episodes of the Trojan War not contained in the *Iliad* and the *Odyssey*.

Euhemerism: The theory that all myths are misunderstood history; named for Euhemeros, who said that the Olympian gods had originally been great kings whose stories were exaggerated over time.

herm: A stylized representation of Hermes, used to guard houses and mark boundaries. Herms were pillars topped with a bearded man's head; they were otherwise featureless except for an erect phallus.

Homeric Hymns: A collection of poems in dactylic hexameter in honor of various gods and goddesses; they range from a very few lines to several hundred lines in length. The longest and most important ones were probably written between 650 and 400 B.C.; the others were probably written later, though the exact dates are uncertain.

Indo-European: The prehistoric parent language of Greek, Latin, Sanskrit, most modern languages of Europe, and many modern languages of India. Indo-European was never written down, but scholars have made hypothetical reconstructions of some of its words and forms by comparative study of the languages that descended from it. The people who spoke this language are referred to as "Indo-Europeans."

Hisarlik or **Hissarlik**: The flat-topped hill in the Troad where Schliemann located the prehistoric ruins of Troy.

Knossos: Ancient city on Crete; Sir Arthur Evans uncovered its ruins in 1900.

Linear B: Mycenaean syllabic writing system; Michael Ventris's decipherment of it in 1952 proved that the Mycenaeans spoke Greek.

mêtis: Wisdom, skill, cunning, craftiness. In Hesiod's *Theogony*, personified as a goddess with whom Zeus mates.

Minoan culture: Pre-Hellenic culture of Crete and Santorini (Thera); discovered by Sir Arthur Evans and named "Minoan" after King Minos of myth. Minoan culture flourished from c. 2000 to c. 1470 B.C., after which time it came under the influence of Mycenaean culture and eventually vanished.

Mycenaean culture: The name given by archaeologists to the prehistoric Bronze Age culture discovered in Greece by 19th-century archaeologists. The Mycenaeans were descended from Indo-European speakers and spoke an archaic form of Greek; their cities figure prominently in Greek myth.

nectar: The drink of the gods. See also **ambrosia**.

pharmakos: A "scapegoat"; a human being driven out of his own city during a crisis, such as a plague, on the assumption that he would somehow take the contagion or other crisis with him.

potnia theron: "Mistress of Beasts"; a phrase used by Homer to describe Artemis.

psyche: Often translated as "soul," this word originally seems to have meant "breath." It is what leaves the body at death. Though it survives in some sense in Hades, its existence there is vague and shadowy.

satyr play: A short, comic or satirical play performed after a trilogy of tragedies.

synoikistes: A unifier; used of Theseus as the supposed unifier of Attica under Athenian rule.

thnêtoi: "The dying ones." A term used to refer to human beings, particularly as contrasted to the immortal gods, or *athanatoi*.

transliteration: The system of representing the sounds of one language (e.g., Greek) in the alphabet of another (e.g., English).

xenia: The "guest/host relationship." Our term "hospitality" does not convey the seriousness of the concept. *Xenia* was protected by Zeus and covers the whole range of obligations that guests and hosts (*xenoi*, singular *xenos*) have to one another. Violations of these obligations bring dire consequences: Paris's theft of Helen was, among other things, a violation of *xenia*.

xenos: A guest, host, friend, stranger, or foreigner (cf. *xenophobia*). The range of this word's meanings reflects the essential nature of *xenia* (see previous entry), which does not depend on prior acquaintance but operates between strangers. Once two men have entered into a relationship of *xenia*, when one of them stays in the other's house, they are "guest-friends" and have obligations to one another.

Biographical Notes

I. Real People

Aeschylus (525–458 B.C.). The first and oldest of the three great Athenian tragedians. He wrote about ninety tragedies, of which seven are extant: *Persians, Prometheus Bound* (some scholars doubt that Aeschylus wrote this), *Seven Against Thebes, Suppliant Women*, and the trilogy *The Oresteia* (composed of the plays *Agamemnon, Libation Bearers*, and *Eumenides*).

Augustus (Gaius Julius Caesar Octavianus; 63 B.C.–AD 14). Great-nephew and adopted son of Julius Caesar. After Caesar's assassination, Octavian (as he was then called) became an obvious contender for power; his main rival was Mark Antony. Octavian defeated the combined forces of Antony and Cleopatra at the Battle of Actium in 31 B.C. and became the uncontested head of the Roman state. In 27 B.C., he was granted the title Augustus, under which name he is usually identified as the first emperor of Rome.

Caesar, Gaius Julius (100–44 B.C.). General, politician, and author. His assassination in 44 B.C. was motivated by the belief of many senators that he was planning to establish himself as king. The aftermath of his assassination led to the establishment of the Roman Empire or Principate by his adopted son and great-nephew, Augustus.

Burkert, Walter (1931–). Great scholar of Greek religion and myth. Sometimes called a neo-ritualist. His work incorporates many of the strategies of structuralism; his main contribution is to trace ritual behaviors and mythic patterns to biological causes.

Campbell, Joseph (1904–1987). Popular author and lecturer on myth, who argued that all myth functions the same way in all cultures and is a necessary component of spiritual and psychological health.

Euhemerus (c. 300 B.C.). Ancient theorist of myth, who thought that all myths were misunderstood history. Zeus and the other gods had originally been great kings, whose stories were exaggerated and misremembered over time.

Euripides (480–06 B.C.). The third and youngest of the three great Athenian tragedians. His tragedies include *The Bacchae*, *Hippolytos*, and *Iphigeneia at Aulis*.

Evans, Sir Arthur (1851–1941). Excavator of Knossos on Crete; uncovered evidence of Minoan civilization (which he named after the mythical King Minos). He purchased the site of Knossos in 1899 and dug there for the next twenty-five years. His partial reconstructions of the palatial buildings at Knossos are criticized by modern archaeologists, but there is no doubt that he was a pioneer in his field and made discoveries of enormous value.

Frazer, Sir James George (1854–1941). Author of *The Golden Bough*; anthropological pioneer. His theory that myth is traceable to rituals in honor of the Dying Year God has fallen out of favor, but he is an important figure in the history of thought about myth.

Freud, Sigmund (1856–1939). The father of psychoanalysis. His Oedipus complex may be the most famous modern interpretation of any classical myth.

Gimbutas, Marija (1921–1994). Professor of European Archaeology, University of California, Los Angeles. Her publications argue for the existence of a "great mother goddess" in prehistoric European society and have been profoundly influential on the modern "Goddess movement."

Harrison, Jane (1850–1928). Primary member of the "Cambridge Ritualist School." Her most famous publication, *Themis*, argued for a ritual theory of myth's function.

Hesiod (c. 700 B.C.?). Poet; author of *Theogony* and *Works and Days*, two of the oldest surviving works of Greek literature (the *Iliad* and the *Odyssey* are generally considered to be older, but even this is not certain). He was probably a farmer and shepherd, according to details he himself mentions in his poems.

Homer (c. 750 B.C.?). The name traditionally given to the bard of the *Iliad* and the *Odyssey*. Scholars do not agree about when or where such a person lived or even if it is reasonable to refer to one bard for the epics at all.

Jung, Carl (1875–1961). Founder of analytic psychology and theorist of myth. His most important contribution to the study of myth is his theory of the collective unconscious and the archetypes.

Lang, Andrew (1844–1912). Opponent of Müller's solar mythology; he thought that all myths were aetiological, a form of proto-science.

Lévi-Strauss, Claude (1908–). Founder and major proponent of structuralism. His theory holds that myths serve to mediate binary contradictions present in all human cultures and societies.

Livy (Titus Livius; 59 B.C.–AD 17). Roman historian whose great work *Ab urbe condita libri* (*Books from the Foundation of the City*) covered the history of Rome up to 9 B.C. Of the 142 original volumes, only 35 survive. The first book includes the story of Romulus and Remus, as well as other legendary episodes of Roman history, such as the abduction of the Sabine women.

Malinowski, Bronislaw (1884–1942). Anthropologist whose work among the Trobriand islanders led him to formulate the "functionalist" theory of myth, according to which myth serves to justify, or provide "charters" for, societal institutions and customs.

Mark Antony (Marcus Antonius; 86 or 83–30 B.C.). Friend and supporter of Julius Caesar; main rival of Octavian for primary power after Caesar's assassination. His liaison with Cleopatra was very unpopular in Rome. Octavian defeated Antony and Cleopatra at the Battle of Actium (31 B.C.), and they both committed suicide the next year. Antony's suicide was motivated by a false rumor that Cleopatra was dead.

Müller, Max (1823–1900). Indo-European linguist and theorist of myth; proponent of the "Solar Myth" theory, in which all myths are viewed as stories about the battle between sunlight and darkness. He is famous for saying that mythology is a "disease of language."

Ovid (Publius Ovidius Naso; 43 B.C.–AD 17). Roman poet, author of *Metamorphoses*. His other works include *Amores*, *Ars amatoria*, and *Remedia amoris*, all of which are concerned with sex and love affairs. He was exiled from Rome by Augustus in AD 8, for *carmen et error* ("a poem and a mistake"). The poem was probably *Ars amatoria*; the "mistake" remains a mystery.

Propp, Vladimir (1895–1970). Russian folklorist. His *Morphology of the Folktale*, published in Russian in 1928, began the "formalist" approach to myth. The book became very influential after its translation into English in 1958.

Protagoras (c. 490–c. 420 B.C.). The most famous of the Sophists; best known for his saying "Man is the measure of all things."

Pythagoras (c. 550–? B.C.). A philosopher, mathematician, and mystic, Pythagoras founded a religious sect (Pythagoreanism) that believed in reincarnation. It is very difficult to determine which of the doctrines attributed to him were actually his and which were later developments from his teachings.

Pythia. The title of Apollo's priestess at Delphi who spoke the god's oracles. She was an unmarried woman over the age of fifty.

Schliemann, Heinrich (1822–1890). German archaeologist; the "discoverer of Troy" and excavator of Mycenae. He began excavations at Hisarlik in 1871 and discovered the "Treasure of Priam" in 1873. From 1874 to 1876, he ran excavations in Greece, notably at Mycenae and Orchomenos, and returned to Troy in April 1876. Though he did not understand the complexity or age of the ruins he excavated, misidentifying Troy II (c. 2200 B.C.) as Homer's Troy, Schliemann deserves great credit for his pioneering work.

Sophocles (496–406 B.C.). Second of the great Athenian tragedians. He wrote perhaps as many as 120 plays, of which only 7 survive: *Ajax, Antigone, Electra, Oedipus the King, Oedipus at Colonus, Philoctetes*, and *Trachiniae*. There is a tradition, probably trustworthy, that after his death he was worshipped as a hero under the name "Dexion."

Ventris, Michael (1922–1956). The decipherer of Linear B. In 1952, he discovered that the language of the Linear B tablets was a form of Greek.

Virgil (Publius Vergilius Maro; 70–19 B.C.). Born near Mantua. Author of the *Eclogues,* the *Georgics,* and the *Aeneid*; generally recognized as the greatest Roman poet. Friend of Horace and Maecenas. The *Aeneid* was incomplete when he died; supposedly, he asked on his deathbed for it to be burned.

II. Mythological Characters: Humans, Monsters, and Gods

Note on transliteration of names: There is no easy way to handle the question of how to transliterate Greek names into the Roman alphabet. The old Latinized system (in which Greek *kappa* becomes *c*, the ending *-os* becomes *-us*, *iota* on the end of diphthongs becomes *e*, and so on) is the most familiar, but it is inaccurate in many ways. The more accurate system is jarring to English readers' eyes and often renders familiar names unrecognizable (Oedipus becomes Oidipous, Ajax becomes Aias, Jocasta becomes Iokaste, and so on).

For ease of reference, I have followed the intermediate system adopted in R. Hard's translation of Apollodorus's *Library*, because I recommend that text. This system uses *c* instead of *k*, but preserves the Greek vowels (Cronos, not Kronos or Cronus). Like Hard, I have departed from that system for names that are extremely familiar in their Latinized forms (e.g., Oedipus). Finally, for names that we encounter only in Ovid, I have used the Latin spellings (e.g., Narcissus, not Narkissos).

Achilles. Greatest Greek warrior in the Trojan War, main character of the *Iliad*. Son of the goddess Thetis and a human father, Peleus.

Actaeon. Man who inadvertently saw Artemis nude. As punishment, she turned him into a stag, but left his mind aware of who he was. He was torn apart by his own hounds.

Adonis. Beautiful youth beloved by Aphrodite. He was killed while hunting.

Aerope. Wife of Atreus, mother of Agamemnon and Menelaos. She gave the golden ram on which the kingship of Mycenae depended to Atreus's brother Thyestes, with whom she was having an affair.

Aeneas. Son of the goddess Aphrodite (Venus) and the Trojan Anchises; husband of Creusa and later of Lavinia; father of Iülus. A member of a collateral branch of the Trojan royal family; the main character of the *Aeneid*.

Agamemnon. Commander-in-chief of the Greek forces at Troy. Brother of Menelaos; husband of Clytemnestra. He sacrifices his daughter Iphigeneia to receive a fair wind for Troy. On his return, Clytemnestra kills him; she is later killed by their son Orestes to avenge Agamemnon's death. These events form the plot of Aeschylus's trilogy *The Oresteia*.

Aigeus. King of Athens; father of Theseus by the Troezenian princess Aithra. Briefly married to Medea.

Aigisthos. Cousin of Agamemnon and Menelaos, who seduces Clytemnestra while Agamemnon is away at war. He murders Agamemnon upon his return from Troy and is himself killed by Agamemnon's son Orestes. This story is frequently cited in the *Odyssey* as a parallel to Odysseus's family situation.

Aithra. Princess of Troezen; mother of Theseus, by either Aigeus or Poseidon.

Alcestis. Wife of Admetos; she agreed to die in his place so that he could continue to live. Heracles wrestled Death and defeated him, thus bringing Alcestis back from the dead.

Alcmene. Wife of Amphitryon; mother of Heracles and Iphicles. Heracles's father was Zeus, while Iphicles's father was Amphitryon.

Amazons. A race of warrior-women who lived at the edges of the world, commonly thought to be somewhere near the Black Sea. The theme of fighting an Amazon recurs in the stories of various heroes, including Heracles, Theseus, and Achilles.

Amphitryon. Alcmene's husband; father of Iphicles; stepfather of Heracles.

Anchises. A member of the Trojan royal family who had an affair with Aphrodite. Their son was Aeneas, the title character of Virgil's *Aeneid.*

Antiope. See **Hippolyta**.

Anush. Hurrian god corresponding to Ouranos.

Aphrodite (Roman Venus). Goddess of sexual passion. According to *Theogony*, she was born from Ouranos's severed genitals; according to the *Iliad*, she was the daughter of Zeus and Dione. Wife of Hephaistos; mother (by the mortal Anchises) of the Trojan Aeneas; lover of Ares.

Apollo: Son of Zeus and Leto, twin brother of Artemis. In the *Iliad*, he appears mainly as the god of prophecy and as the bringer of plague and sudden death. Later authors would stress his association with reason, healing, and music. His identification with the sun is much later than Homer. He is also called Phoebus.

Apsyrtos. Medea's younger brother, whom she kills, chops into pieces, and throws overboard to slow down her father's pursuit of the Argo.

Ares (Roman Mars). Son of Zeus and Hera; god of war; particularly associated with the physical, bloody, distressing aspects of war (cf. **Athena**).

Argo. The ship on which Jason sailed to Colchis in search of the Golden Fleece. All the greatest heroes of his day sailed with him.

Argonauts. The sailors on the Argo.

Ariadne. Daughter of Minos and Pasiphae of Crete (and, thus, half-sister of the Minotaur). She helps Theseus to kill the Minotaur by giving him a ball of thread to guide him out of the Labyrinth. He takes her with him when he leaves Crete, but abandons her on the island of Naxos.

Artemis (Roman Diana). Daughter of Zeus and Leto; twin sister of Apollo. A virgin goddess. She is the patron of hunters, wild animals, and girls before their marriages. She brings sudden death to women. Her identification with the moon is later than Homer.

Athena (Roman Minerva). Daughter of Zeus, who sprang from his brow fully grown and wearing armor; according to *Theogony*, Zeus had previously swallowed her mother, Metis ("wisdom" or "cleverness"). Athena is the goddess of warfare in its nobler aspects (cf. **Ares**). A virgin goddess, she is associated with wisdom, cleverness, and weaving.

Atlas. Son of Iapetos, brother of Prometheus and Epimetheus. He holds the sky upon his shoulders.

Atreus. Grandson of Tantalos, son of Pelops, father of Agamemnon and Menelaos. After his brother Thyestes seduced Atreus's wife, Aerope, Atreus took revenge by killing Thyestes's sons and serving their flesh to him at a banquet.

Augean Stables. Heracles's fifth labor involved cleaning these stables, which had never been cleaned. He accomplished the task by diverting two rivers to run through them.

Calchas. Agamemnon's seer during the Trojan War. He interpreted the omens to tell Agamemnon that Artemis demanded the sacrifice of Iphigeneia.

Cassandra. Daughter of Priam and Hecabe; sister of Hector and Paris. During the Sack of Troy, Aias the Lesser rapes her in the temple of Athena. This outrage motivates the goddess's anger at the Greeks.

Centaur. Creature with the body of a horse and the torso and head of a man. Centaurs are almost always violent, sexually aggressive, and dangerous.

Cerberos. The three-headed (or fifty-headed) hound of Tartaros. Heracles's final labor was to capture him and lead him to the world of the living.

Ceres. See **Demeter**.

Cerynian Hind. Capturing this golden-horned deer was Heracles's third labor.

Chaos. According to Hesiod, the primordial "gap" from which, or after which, Gaia, Tartaros, and Eros came into being.

Clytemnestra/Clytaimestra. Wife of Agamemnon, mother of Orestes, half-sister of Helen. She takes Aigisthos as her lover while Agamemnon is away at Troy and assists Aigisthos in murdering Agamemnon upon his return.

Cronos (Roman Saturn). Youngest son of Gaia and Ouranos, with whom Gaia plots against Ouranos. Cronos castrates his father with the help of a sickle that Gaia makes him, whereupon Ouranos retreats to his proper place as the sky and all of Gaia's children can be born.

Cretan Bull. Capturing this ferocious Bull was Heracles's sixth labor.

Cupid. See **Eros**.

Cybele. A Phrygian "great mother" goddess. Artemis at Ephesus has some characteristics in common with her, as does Demeter.

Daidalos. Great craftsman and artisan. He made the wooden cow that enabled Pasiphaë to mate with the bull and conceive the Minotaur; he also, at Minos's command, constructed the Labyrinth in which the Minotaur was kept.

Daphne. Nymph, sworn to chastity, whom Apollo desires and chases. She calls out for help to her father, a river god, and is turned into a laurel tree.

Deianeira. Heracles's wife. Her use of the blood of the centaur Nessos, which she thinks is a love-charm, leads to Heracles's death.

Demeter (Roman Ceres). One of Zeus's five siblings; goddess of grain and agriculture. Her quest for her daughter Persephone, who was kidnapped by Hades, is recounted in the *Homeric Hymn to Demeter*. The Eleusinian Mysteries, celebrated in her honor, were one of the most important religious festivals of ancient Greece.

Demophoön. Son of Metaneira. Demeter serves as his nanny and tries to immortalize him; Metaneira's interference angers the goddess and ends the attempt. Demophoön probably dies shortly afterward.

Deucalion. With his wife, Pyrrha, the only survivor of the Great Flood (at least according to Ovid). They repopulate the world by throwing stones over their shoulders.

Diana. See **Artemis**.

Diomedes. King of Thrace, who had a pair of man-eating mares. Taming these mares and driving them back to Greece was Heracles's seventh labor. According to some authors, he fed their master to the mares.

Dionysos (Roman Bacchus). Son of Zeus and the mortal woman Semele. After Semele's incineration, Dionysos was incubated in Zeus's thigh. He is the god of wine, intoxication, frenzy, and drama; also associated with rapidly growing plants, such as vine and ivy. Euripides's *Bacchae* is our fullest extant description of him.

Echidna. One of the many female monsters of Greek mythology; her body is partly in the form of a snake.

Electra. Agamemnon and Clytemnestra's daughter, who helped her brother Orestes avenge their father's death.

Epimetheus. Son of Iapetos, brother of Prometheus. In Hesiod's *Works and Days*, he receives the gift of Pandora.

Erebos. One of the earliest gods, according to *Theogony*; the child of Chaos. Erebos embodies the gloomy darkness of Tartaros.

Eris. Goddess of strife or discord. Angry over not being invited to the wedding feast of Peleus and Thetis, she threw an apple marked "For the fairest" onto the banquet table. This Apple of Discord began a chain of events that led to the Trojan War.

Eros. God of sexual desire. Hesiod lists him as one of the three deities to appear first after Chaos; in other versions, he is the son of Aphrodite.

Erymanthian Boar. Heracles's fourth labor was to bring this beast to Eurystheus.

Eumenides. A euphemistic term for the Furies; literally means "Kindly Ones."

Eurydice. Wife of Orpheus; after her untimely death, he journeyed to Tartaros to beg for her return. His singing was so beautiful that Hades and Persephone agreed to let her return to life; however, Orpheus was ordered not to look back at her until they had reached the upper world. He did look back, and she vanished into Tartaros.

Eurystheus. King of Tiryns, whom Heracles served for twelve years, probably as expiation for killing his wife, Megara, and their children.

Furies. Spirits of blood vengeance who avenge violence against kin and especially violence of children against their parents. According to *Theogony*, they were born from the drops of blood that fell from Ouranos's severed genitals. In Aeschylus's *Eumenides*, they torment Orestes for killing his mother, Clytemnestra.

Gaia/Ge. The earth; according to Hesiod's *Theogony*, one of the three primordial deities who came after Chaos (the others are Tartaros and Eros).

Geryon. Triple-bodied monster who lives in the remote West. Stealing his cattle and driving them back to Greece was Heracles's tenth labor.

Gilgamesh. One of the very few heroes who features in Mesopotamian myth. His adventures are recounted in the fragmentary "Epic of Gilgamesh." He has some characteristics in common with both Heracles and Achilles.

Gorgons. Three monstrous sisters, mentioned in *Theogony* and elsewhere. They have snakes for hair and their gaze turns living creatures to stone. One of the sisters, Medusa, is mortal; the hero Perseus beheads her and uses her severed head as a weapon to petrify his enemies.

Hades (Roman Pluto). Brother of Zeus, husband of Persephone. Ruler of the Underworld (Tartaros), which comes to be called Hades after him.

Hebe. Daughter of Zeus and Hera; her name means "youthful bloom." Wife of the deified Heracles.

Hecabe. Queen of Troy, wife of Priam, mother of Hector, Paris, and Cassandra. (May be more familiar in the Latinized spelling of her name, "Hecuba.")

Hector. Crown prince of Troy, son of Priam and Hecabe, husband of Andromache, father of Astyanax. He was killed by Achilles.

Helen. Daughter of Zeus and Leda, sister of Clytemnestra, wife of Menelaos; the most beautiful woman in the world. Her seduction (or kidnapping?) by Paris was the cause of the Trojan War.

Helios. A Titan; god of the sun.

Hephaistos (Roman Vulcan). Son of Zeus and Hera or, perhaps, of Hera alone. In the *Iliad*, he is married to Charis; in the *Odyssey*, to Aphrodite. He is lame and ugly. The smith-god who, to some extent, represents fire itself.

Hera (Roman Juno). Wife and sister of Zeus, mother of Hephaistos and Ares. She is the patron goddess of marriage and married women. In the *Iliad*, she hates the Trojans and favors the Greeks.

Heracles (Roman Hercules). Greatest Greek hero, son of Zeus and the mortal woman Alcmene. He lived (probably) two generations before the Trojan War. He is cited as a paradigm of the hero throughout both epics; Odysseus speaks to his spirit in the Underworld (*Od.* XI).

Hermes (Roman Mercury). Often identified as the "messenger of the gods," his role is actually far more complex. He is a god of boundaries and transitions and of exchange and commerce. He serves as the patron for travelers, merchants, thieves, heralds, and messengers. In his role as *Psychopompos*, he escorts the souls of the dead to Tartaros.

Hesperides. Three nymphs who live on an island in the far West. They guard a tree with three golden apples (a wedding present from Gaia to Hera). Heracles's eleventh labor is to get these apples; he accomplishes this with the help of Atlas, for whom he holds the sky temporarily.

Hestia (Roman Vesta). Goddess of the hearth; sister of Zeus.

Hippodameia. Daughter of Oinamaos of Pisa; any suitor who wants to marry her must first defeat Oinamaos in a chariot race. Pelops does so by treachery, bribing Oinamaos's slave Myrtilos to remove the linchpins from Oinamaos's chariot. Oinamaos is killed, and Pelops marries Hippodameia. Their children include Atreus and Thyestes.

Hippolyta. Amazon queen; Heracles's ninth labor was to fetch her belt (or "girdle"). She may be the same queen (often called Antiope) whom Theseus married.

Hippolytos. Son of Theseus and Hippolyta (or Antiope), the Amazon queen. His devotion to Artemis and scorn for Aphrodite and its consequences are the subject of Euripides's play *Hippolytos*.

Hydra. See **Lernaian Hydra**.

Iapetos. A Titan; father of Prometheus and Epimetheus.

Iolaos. Heracles's nephew who served as his charioteer and helped him in some of his labors.

Iphicles. Heracles's twin and half-brother; Heracles was fathered by Zeus, and Iphicles was fathered the next night by Alcmene's husband, Amphitryon.

Iphigeneia. Daughter of Agamemnon and Clytemnestra. Agamemnon sacrificed her to gain a fair wind to sail to Troy.

Jason. Leader of the Argonauts who sailed to Colchis on the Black Sea in search of the Golden Fleece. He married the Colchian princess Medea, whose magic helped him get the Fleece. Years later, when he wanted to divorce her to marry a Greek princess, Medea retaliated by killing their sons.

Jocasta. Wife of Laios; wife and mother of Oedipus; mother (and grandmother) of Antigone, Ismene, Polyneices, and Eteocles.

Juno. See **Hera.**

Jupiter. See **Zeus.**

Kumarbi. Hurrian god, equivalent to Cronos.

Laios. King of Thebes, husband of Jocasta, father of Oedipus. Because he received an oracle telling him that any son he had with Jocasta would kill him, Laios exposed the baby Oedipus on a mountain. Years later, Laios was indeed killed by Oedipus, who did not know that Laios was his father.

Leda. Wife of Tyndareus, mother of Clytemnestra and Helen (as well as of two sons, Castor and Pollux). Zeus appeared to Leda in the form of a swan, and Helen was hatched from an egg.

Lernaian Hydra. Snake-like creature with nine heads, one of which was immortal. Killing it was Heracles's second labor, which he accomplished with Iolaos's help. Whenever a head was cut off, two grew in its place; Iolaos cauterized the stumps as Heracles cut off the heads. Heracles buried the immortal head under a boulder.

Leto (Roman Latona). Mother of Apollo and Artemis.

Maenads. Female followers of Dionysos; in myth, they have extraordinary powers, such as the abilities to make wine or milk flow from the ground, to handle snakes, and to tear animals apart with their bare hands.

Mars. See **Ares**.

Medea. Princess of Colchis, daughter of Aiëtes, and granddaughter of the sun god Helios. She was skilled in sorcery and magic. She helped Jason obtain the Golden Fleece and returned with him as his wife to Greece, where she bore him two sons. When Jason wanted to divorce her to marry the princess of Corinth, Medea retaliated by killing her own children. She then escaped on a dragon-drawn chariot sent to her by Helios and went to Athens, where she married Aigeus and bore him a son. However, she was exiled from Athens for trying to kill Aigeus's son Theseus.

Medusa. A Gorgon; the only mortal one of the three sisters. According to Ovid, she was originally very beautiful; Poseidon raped her in Athena's temple, and Athena cursed Medusa with snakes for hair. Most other authors say that all three Gorgons had snakes instead of hair.

Megara. Heracles's first wife. In a fit of madness sent by Hera, he killed their children (varying in number from three to eight, depending on the source) and perhaps Megara as well. Those versions in which he does not kill Megara say that he gave her to Iolaos after killing the children.

Metis. Zeus's first wife, whom he swallowed when she was pregnant with Athena. Her name means "wisdom" or "cleverness."

Menelaos. Brother of Agamemnon, husband of Helen.

Metaneira. Queen of Eleusis; hired the disguised Demeter to be a nanny for her baby son, Demophoön. When Demeter tried to immortalize Demophoön, Metaneira's horrified interference stopped the process.

Minerva. See **Athena**.

Minos. King of Crete; husband of Pasiphae, father of Ariadne and Phaedra. He hired Daedalos to construct the Labyrinth in which the Minotaur was confined.

Minotaur. Man-eating monster, half-human and half-bull. He was conceived when Pasiphae mated with a bull. Kept in the Labyrinth; each year seven young men and seven young women from Athens were fed to him. He was killed by Theseus with the help of Ariadne.

Myrtilos. Charioteer whom Pelops bribed to help him win Hippodameia. Myrtilos removed the linchpins from Oinomaos's chariot wheels, so that the wheels fell off and Oinomaos was killed. Myrtilos was later killed by Pelops for trying to rape Hippodameia.

Narcissus. Beautiful youth who fell in love with his own reflection and pined away.

Nemean Lion. Heracles's first labor was to kill this beast. He wore its skin as a cloak forever after.

Nessos. Centaur who tried to rape Heracles's wife, Deianeira. Heracles shot him; as he was dying, Nessos told Deianeira to save some of his blood as a love-charm in case Heracles ever lost interest in her. She did so, but when she used the "charm" years later, it burned Heracles's flesh and caused him such agony that he killed himself.

Niobe. Queen of Thebes, sister of Tantalos. She boasted that she was better than Leto, because Leto had only two children but she, Niobe, had fourteen. Apollo and Artemis killed all Niobe's children. Some authors say she turned into a cliff with water running down it continually to represent her tears.

Oceanos. Titan; the river that flows around the edges of Gaia (the earth).

Odysseus. Cleverest and craftiest of the Greeks; the Trojan Horse was his idea. Main character of the *Odyssey*.

Oedipus. Son of Laios and Jocasta. Exposed on a mountain as an infant, because Laios had received an oracle that any child of his and Jocasta's would grow up to kill him. Not knowing who his true parents were, Oedipus did indeed kill Laios and marry Jocasta. Sophocles's *Oedipus the King* is the most famous account of this myth.

Olympians. These originally included Zeus, his five siblings, and eight of his children: Zeus, Poseidon, Hades, Hestia, Demeter, Hera, Athena, Apollo, Artemis, Ares, Hephaistos, Aphrodite, Hermes, and Dionysos. Later, the number twelve became canonical, and Hades and Hestia were omitted.

Orestes. Son of Agamemnon and Clytemnestra. He avenges his father's murder by killing Aigisthos and Clytemnestra. This story is frequently cited in the *Odyssey* as a parallel to Odysseus's family situation.

Orpheus. The greatest bard who ever lived. When his wife, Eurydice, was killed, he journeyed to Tartaros to beg for her return. His singing was so beautiful that Hades and Persephone agreed to let her return to life; however, Orpheus was ordered not to look back at Eurydice until they had reached the upper world. He did look back, and she vanished into Tartaros.

Ouranos. Son and husband of Gaia; his name means "Sky." When he would not allow Gaia's children to be born, she enlisted the help of her youngest son, Cronos, who castrated Ouranos with a sickle. Ouranos retreated to his position as sky, Gaia's children were freed, and Cronos took over the rule.

Pandora. The first woman. Unnamed in *Theogony*, in *Works and Days* she is sent as a gift from the gods to Epimetheus. Her jar contained all the evils of the world, plus hope; she opened the jar and released the evils.

Paris. Son of Priam and Hecabe, brother of Hector; prince of Troy. His abduction or, perhaps, seduction of Helen from her husband, Menelaos, motivated the Trojan War.

Pasiphaë. Wife of Minos; mother of Ariadne, Phaidra, and the Minotaur. She conceived the latter child through an unnatural passion for a bull; Daidalos built a wooden cow into which Pasiphaë crawled to mate with the bull.

Peleus. Achilles's father; mortal husband of Thetis.

Pelops. Son of Tantalos, whom Tantalos butchered to feed to the gods. He was resurrected and given an ivory shoulder to replace the shoulder Demeter ate. His sons were Atreus and Thyestes.

Pentheus. Young king of Thebes; his refusal to believe in the divinity of Dionysos led to his terrible death at the hands of his own mother and aunts. Euripides's *Bacchae* tells the story of these events.

Persephone (Roman Proserpina). Wife of Hades; daughter of Demeter; queen of the Underworld. The *Homeric Hymn to Demeter* recounts the story of her abduction by Hades and Demeter's search for her.

Phaethon. Mortal son of the Sun God, who begs the favor of driving the chariot of the sun for a single day. He is killed in the attempt.

Phaidra. Daughter of Minos and Pasiphaë; sister of Ariadne and the Minotaur; wife of Theseus. Her passion for her stepson Hippolytos leads to her own and Hippolytos's death. Euripides's *Hippolytos* tells the story.

Phoebus. See **Apollo**.

Pirithous. Friend of Theseus; they went together to Tartaros to try to kidnap Persephone to be Pirithous's wife. Theseus was trapped there for many years until he was freed by Heracles; Pirithous was trapped forever.

Polyxena. Young daughter of Priam and Hecabe, whom the Greeks sacrificed to the ghost of Achilles as they left Troy.

Pontos. Son of Gaia; the personification of the Mediterranean Sea.

Poseidon (Roman Neptune). Brother of Zeus, god of the sea. One of the twelve Olympians.

Priam. King of Troy. During the Sack of Troy, he was slain at his own household altar.

Procrustes. One of the brigands whom Theseus met and killed on his way from Troezen to Athens. Famous for his bed, which he made every traveler fit.

Prometheus. Son of Iapetos; benefactor of mankind. In *Theogony*, he tried to trick Zeus into accepting the worse portion of the first sacrifice. Zeus responded by hiding fire, which Prometheus then stole for humans. His punishment was to be tied to a crag in the Caucasus and have his liver eaten every day by an eagle. He was eventually freed by Heracles.

Pyramus. In Ovid's *Metamorphoses*, a young man who commits suicide when he thinks his beloved Thisbe is dead.

Pyrrha. Wife of Deucalion. After the Great Flood, she and Deucalion repopulated the world by throwing stones over their shoulders.

Remus. Twin brother of Romulus.

Rheia. Titan; daughter of Ouranos and Gaia; wife of Cronos; mother of Zeus and his five siblings.

Romulus. Founder of Rome. He and his brother Remus were set afloat on the Tiber River in a basket; they were found and nursed by a she-wolf. After they grew up and decided to found their own city, Romulus killed Remus in a quarrel over the naming of the city.

Satyrs. Mythical male followers of Dionysos. Usually shown in art as snub-nosed men with animal-like ears and horses' tails. Extremely sexually aggressive.

Scylla. A female monster, with snakes for legs and six heads and torsos. She eats men.

Semele. Princess of Thebes; mother of Dionysos. Hera tricked Semele into making Zeus promise to show himself to her in his full glory. When he did so, Semele was incinerated; Zeus rescued her son Dionysos from her womb and sewed him into his own thigh.

Sinis. One of the brigands Theseus killed on his way to Athens; he tied travelers to two bent-over pine trees, then released the trees.

Sisyphos. One of the "cardinal sinners" in Tartaros; he had tried to avoid dying by imprisoning Death in chains. His punishment is to roll a stone uphill continuously, only to have it roll back down as he reaches the summit.

Sphinx. A female monster that was devastating Thebes by eating anyone who could not answer her riddle. Oedipus solved the riddle and the Sphinx killed herself.

Stymphalian Birds. These birds had arrow-tipped feathers that they could shoot at will. Heracles's sixth labor was to kill them.

Tantalos. One of the "cardinal sinners" in Tartaros. He tried to trick the gods into eating the flesh of his own son, Pelops. His punishment is to stand forever in a river of water with fruit trees over his head; he is eternally hungry and thirsty, but when he tries to drink, the water flows away and when he tries to eat, the fruit blows out of his reach.

Tartaros. The Underworld, the land of the dead; the realm of Hades. According to Hesiod, one of the three primordial gods (with Gaia and Eros).

Teiresias. Great Theban seer; a character in Sophocles's *Oedipus the King* and *Antigone* and in Euripides's *Bacchae*.

Teshub. Hurrian storm-god; equivalent of Zeus.

Theseus. Athenian hero and legendary king of Athens. His most famous exploit was fighting and killing the Cretan Minotaur.

Themis. Goddess whose name means "right order." She was Zeus's second wife, after Metis; her children included Justice and Peace.

Thetis. Sea-goddess; mother of Achilles; wife of Peleus.

Thisbe. In Ovid's *Metamorphoses*, a young girl who commits suicide in despair over the death of her beloved Pyramus.

Thyestes. Grandson of Tantalos, son of Pelops, father of Aigisthos, brother of Atreus. After Thyestes seduced Atreus's wife, Aerope, Atreus took revenge by killing Thyestes's sons and serving their flesh to him at a banquet.

Titans. The children of Gaia and Ouranos; Cronos and his siblings. After Zeus overthrew Cronos, the two generations engaged in a "Battle of the Gods and Titans," which ended in victory for Zeus and his fellow Olympians.

Tithonos. Trojan man, beloved of the dawn goddess Eos. She gives him eternal life, but forgets to ask for eternal youth. Thus, Tithonos is doomed to grow older and older forever.

Tityos. One of the "cardinal sinners" in Tartaros. His crime was the attempted rape of Leto; his punishment is to have his liver continuously devoured by a vulture.

Tyndareus. King of Sparta; husband of Leda; father of Clytemnestra; stepfather of Helen.

Venus. See **Aphrodite**.

Zeus (Roman Jupiter). The ruler of the Olympian gods. Brother and husband of Hera; brother of Hades and Poseidon; father of Aphrodite, Apollo, Ares, Artemis, Athena, and perhaps Hephaistos. Originally a sky-god, he controls thunder and lightning. The patron of justice, suppliants, and *xenia*.

Bibliography

Essential Readings:

(Note: Most of the Greek and Roman texts cited are available in many different translations. The editions listed here reflect my own preferences and an attempt to offer a balance in different translating styles.)

Aeschylus. *Aeschylus I. Agamemnon, The Libation Bearers, The Eumenides*, trans. Richmond Lattimore. Chicago: University of Chicago Press, 1953. This poetic translation succeeds in conveying the flavor of Aeschylus's Greek.

Apollodorus. *The Library of Greek Mythology*. Trans. Robert Hard. Oxford, New York: Oxford University Press, 1997. A clear and readable translation; includes very useful genealogical tables.

Euripides. *Euripides I*. Includes *Medea*, trans. Rex Warner, and *Hippolytus*, trans. David Grene. In *The Complete Greek Tragedies*, D. Grene and R. Lattimore, eds. Chicago: The University of Chicago Press, 1955. Clear, readable translations.

————. *Euripides V*. Includes. *The Bacchae*, trans. William Arrowsmith. In *The Complete Greek Tragedies*, D. Grene and R. Lattimore, eds. Chicago: University of Chicago Press, 1959. Excellent, highly readable translation.

Hesiod. *Theogony, Works and Days, Shield*. Trans. Apostolos N. Athanassakis. Baltimore, London: The Johns Hopkins University Press, 1983. Excellent translation with thorough and helpful notes.

The Homeric Hymns. Trans. Apostolos N. Athanassakis. Baltimore, London: The Johns Hopkins University Press, 1976. Clear, readable translation with useful notes.

Kirk, G. S. *The Nature of Greek Myths*. London, New York: Penguin Books, 1974. A clear, concise introduction for the general reader. Contains chapters on definitions of myth, approaches to myth, the appearances of Greek myths in literature, and the nature of Greek heroes. An excellent place to begin any study of classical myth or of theories about myth in general.

Livy. *The Early History of Rome*. Trans. Aubrey de Sélincourt. London, New York: Penguin Books, 1960. Translates the first five books of Livy's great work; includes an account of Romulus and Remus. Excellent introduction.

Ovid, *Metamorphoses*. Trans. Rolfe Humphries. Bloomington, Indiana: Indiana University Press, 1983. Fast-paced, readable translation; very free at times, but good at capturing Ovid's "tone."

The Oxford Classical Dictionary. 3rd ed. Simon Hornblower and Anthony Spawforth, eds. Oxford and New York: Oxford University Press, 1996. The standard one-volume reference work on Greek and Roman antiquity.

Segal, Robert A. "Joseph Campbell's Theory of Myth," in Alan Dundes, ed., *Sacred Narrative: Readings in the Theory of Myth*. Berkeley, Los Angeles, London: University of California Press, 1984, pp. 256–269. A succinct, clear exposition of the objections many scholars have to Campbell's theory.

Sophocles, *The Three Theban Plays: Antigone, Oedipus the King, Oedipus at Colonus*. Trans. Robert Fagles. New York, London: Penguin Books, 1982. This edition is particularly useful for the introduction and notes by Bernard Knox.

Virgil, *The Aeneid*. Trans. Robert Fitzgerald. New York: Vintage Books, 1984. This is probably the most frequently used translation in college literature courses. It translates Virgil's hexameters into quick moving, fluid, and very readable lines of iambic pentameter. The line numbers of the original are given at the foot of each page, which is helpful to the student who is reading supplementary materials that include line references.

Supplementary Readings:

(Note: In recent decades, a vast amount has been written on classical mythology and myth in general. I have tried to winnow out a representative selection of useful and interesting studies while avoiding books that assume knowledge of complicated modern theoretical approaches. I have also included several works that disagree, at least to some extent, with my own views of what myth is, how it works, and the interpretation of individual classical myths, so that students may gain some sense of the immense complexity of these topics. Finally, I have tried to favor works that have good bibliographies to aid students who wish to continue their investigations into mythology.)

Arthur, Marilyn. "Politics and Pomegranates: An Interpretation of the *Homeric Hymn to Demeter*," in Foley, *Homeric Hymn,* pp. 211–242. A literary analysis based on Freudian theory; the author seeks to "elucidate a common structure underlying both the ancient text and the modern theory" (p. 211).

Bascom, William. "The Forms of Folklore: Prose Narratives." In Dundes, *Sacred Narrative,* pp. 5–29. A survey of various definitions of the terms "myth," "legend," and "folktale."

Berkowitz, Luci, and Theodore F. Brunner, eds. *Oedipus Tyrannus.* Norton Critical Edition. New York, London: W. W. Norton and Company, 1970. Includes a translation of the play, passages from ancient authors, and a collection of critical and interpretative essays.

Boardman, John, Jasper Griffin, and Oswyn Murray, eds. *The Oxford History of the Roman World.* Oxford and New York: Oxford University Press, 1991. A very useful collection of essays, written with the non-specialist in mind.

Bremmer, Jan. *The Early Greek Concept of the Soul.* Princeton, NJ: Princeton University Press, 1983. Argues that Greek culture originally recognized two types of soul, the "free soul," which represented a person's individual essence, and the "body soul," which endowed the body with consciousness and motion. Chapter 3, on the soul after death, is particularly useful.

————, ed. *Interpretations of Greek Mythology*. London and Sydney: Croom Helm, 1987. A useful collection of essays; topics range from the definition of myth to studies of individual myths and characters.

————. "Oedipus and the Greek Oedipus Complex," in Bremmer, *Interpretations*, pp. 41–59. Examines and critiques various interpretations of the Oedipus myth; concludes that the main point of the incest is to underline the horror of the parricide.

————. "What is a Greek Myth?," in Bremmer, *Interpretations*, pp. 1–9. Surveys several definitions of myth and the difficulties with each.

Burkert, Walter. *Ancient Mystery Cults*. Cambridge, MA, London: Harvard University Press, 1987. A succinct, readable discussion of ancient mystery cults and their appeal to their adherents.

————. *Creation of the Sacred: Tracks of Biology in Early Religions*. Cambridge, MA, London: Harvard University Press, 1996. A fascinating and controversial exploration of the idea that sacrifice and religion in general may have a biological basis. The author draws on non-classical and classical material.

————. *Greek Religion*. Trans. John Raffan. Cambridge, MA: Harvard University Press, 1985. Standard text for understanding Greek rites and rituals. Contains useful sections on individual gods and heroes. Good notes and bibliography.

————. *Structure and History in Greek Mythology and Ritual*. Berkeley, Los Angeles, London: University of California Press, 1979. An engrossing examination of the interaction of myth and ritual; pays particular attention to scapegoat and "master of animal" myths. Incorporates much structuralist methodology.

Caldwell, Richard. *The Origin of the Gods: A Psychoanalytic Study of Greek Theogonic Myth*. New York, Oxford: Oxford University Press, 1989. A reading of Hesiod's *Theogony* in light of Freudian theory.

———. "The Psychoanalytical Interpretation of Greek Myth," in Edmunds, *Approaches*, pp. 344–389. A clear, well-written description of Freudian theory as applied to myth; contains interesting interpretations of individual myths.

Conacher, D. J. *Aeschylus' Oresteia: A Literary Commentary*. Toronto, Buffalo: University of Toronto Press, 1987. A clear, informative introduction for the general reader, organized scene by scene.

Dodds, E. R. "On Misunderstanding the *Oedipus Rex*," in Berkowitz and Brunner, *Oedipus Tyrannus*, pp. 218–229. An influential article that locates the main point of Sophocles's play in Oedipus's role as an intelligent questioner. Argues against earlier interpretations that stress fate or Oedipus's guilt.

DuBois, Page. *Centaurs and Amazons: Women and the Pre-History of the Great Chain of Being*. Ann Arbor: The University of Michigan Press, 1982. Examines the function of anomalous creatures, such as Centaurs (half-man, half-animal) and Amazons (women who act like males), in Athenian thought and culture; particular emphasis on the growth of philosophical thought in the late 5th and early 4th centuries B.C.

Dundes, Alan, ed. *Sacred Narrative: Readings in the Theory of Myth*. Berkeley, Los Angeles, London: University of California Press, 1984. A valuable collection of critical essays, covering the history and development of theories about myth in the 19th and 20th centuries.

Edmunds, Lowell, ed. *Approaches to Greek Myth*. Baltimore, London: The Johns Hopkins University Press, 1990. Useful collection of essays by top theorist, describing and critiquing various approaches to the study of myth.

Fitton, J. Lesley. *The Discovery of the Greek Bronze Age*. Cambridge: Harvard University Press, 1996. A readable and entertaining account of the pioneering archaeologists who excavated the most important Bronze Age sites.

Foley, Helene P., ed. *The Homeric Hymn to Demeter: Translation, Commentary, and Interpretive Essays.* Princeton: Princeton University Press, 1994. An invaluable book, combining a good translation with extensive notes and explanatory essays. Also reprints several useful articles by other scholars.

Fontenrose, Joseph. *The Delphic Oracle.* Berkeley, Los Angeles: University of California Press, 1978. Examines the evidence for the nature and workings of the oracle. Argues against the idea that the oracle was intentionally ambiguous.

Freud, Sigmund. "The Oedipus Complex," in Berkowitz and Brunner, *Oedipus Tyrannus*, pp. 69–72. Freud's original statement, from *The Interpretation of Dreams*, of what he later called the Oedipus complex. It is well worth reading what he actually says about the myth and its implications for human psychological development.

Galinsky, G. Karl. *The Herakles Theme: The Adaptation of the Hero in Literature from Homer to the Twentieth Century.* Oxford: Blackwell, 1972. A comprehensive examination of Heracles's appearance in literature.

Gantz, Timothy. *Early Greek Myth: A Guide to Literary and Artistic Sources.* 2 vols. Baltimore, London: Johns Hopkins University Press, 1993. An extremely detailed survey of all the sources of traditional Greek myths.

Gimbutas, Marija. *The Living Goddesses.* Miriam Robbins Dexter, ed. Berkeley, Los Angeles, London: The University of California Press, 1999. Gimbutas is often called the "mother" of the goddess movement. This is her final book, edited after her death. It contains, according to the editor, "a synthesis of her earlier work and the addition of new research" (p. xv).

Goldhill, Simon. *Aeschylus: The Oresteia.* Cambridge: Cambridge University Press, 1992. A thought-provoking introduction to the trilogy, arranged thematically rather than scene-by-scene. Pays particular attention to gender issues and to the human-divine relationship.

Goodison, Lucy, and Christine Morris. *Ancient Goddesses: The Myths and the Evidence.* Madison: University of Wisconsin Press, 1999. A collection of essays evaluating the evidence for prehistoric goddess worship in ancient Mediterranean cultures. Balanced, scholarly, and very readable.

————. "Beyond the 'Great Mother': The Sacred World of the Minoans," in Goodison and Morris, *Ancient Goddesses*, pp. 113–132. Discusses the limitations in the archaeological evidence for Minoan religion and the difficulties involved in interpreting it.

Graf, Fritz. *Greek Mythology: An Introduction.* Trans. Thomas Marier. Baltimore and London: The Johns Hopkins University Press, 1993. Very readable and lucid introduction to theories of myth and to Greek myth's appearance in epic, tragedy, and elsewhere.

Herodotus. *The Histories.* Trans. Aubrey de Sélincourt. London, New York, Ringwood, Toronto: Penguin Books, 1972. The first Greek example of the genre that would later come to be called history. Includes a great deal of mythic material and many references to such heroes as Heracles and Perseus. The section on Heracles's encounter with a snake-woman in Scythia is intriguing.

Jung, C. G. "The Psychology of the Child Archetype," in Dundes, *Sacred Narrative*, pp. 244–255. This article, reprinted from the *Journal of the American Academy of Religion* 44 (1978), gives a brief, clear exposition of Jung's theory of the collective unconscious and the archetypes, with special reference to the "child archetype."

Kirk, G. S. "Aetiology, Ritual, Charter: Three Equivocal Terms in the Study of Myths," in *Yale Classical Studies*, vol. 22, pp. 83–102. A thorough, enlightening discussion of these three terms and their limitations.

————. *Myth: Its Meaning and Function in Ancient and Other Cultures.* Cambridge: University of Cambridge Press; Berkeley and Los Angeles: University of California Press, 1970. Well-written, clear discussion surveying various theories of myth. Includes material on South American and

Mesopotamian myth, as well as Greek myth. Argues that myth has different characteristics and functions in different cultures.

————. "On Defining Myths." In Dundes, *Sacred Narrative*, pp. 53–61. A discussion of the difficulties inherent in attempts to arrive at any single theory of what myth is; suggests that the only safe definition is "traditional oral tale."

Knox, Bernard. *Oedipus at Thebes: Sophocles' Tragic Hero and His Time*, new ed. New Haven and London: Yale University Press, 1998. A reissue of a groundbreaking study that first appeared in 1957. Considers Sophocles's Oedipus in the political and intellectual context of Athens in the 5th century. Particularly useful in setting the play in the context of Sophist thought in 5th-century Athens.

————. "Oedipus the King: Introduction," in Sophocles, *The Three Theban Plays*, pp. 131–153. A brilliant and succinct essay surveying various interpretations of the play.

Leach, Edmund. *Claude Lévi-Strauss*. New York: Viking Press, 1974. An introduction to Lévi-Strauss and social anthropology, geared to the general reader. Chapter 4 is particularly useful on Lévi-Strauss's theory of myth and on its application to Oedipus in particular.

Lerner, Laurence. "Ovid and the Elizabethans," in Martindale, *Ovid Renewed*, pp. 121–135. Examines the influence of *Amores* and especially *Metamorphoses* on Elizabethan poets, including Marlowe and Shakespeare.

Lévi-Strauss, Claude. *The Raw and the Cooked: Introduction to a Science of Mythology*. Trans. John and Doreen Weightman. New York and Evanston: Harper & Row, Publishers, 1969. First volume of the multi-volume *Introduction to a Science of Mythology*. Lévi-Strauss's own exposition of his theory of myth.

————. "The Structural Study of Myth," repr. in Thomas A. Sebeok, *Myth: A Symposium*, Bloomington, Indiana: Indiana University Press,

1971, pp. 81–106. Presents Lévi-Strauss's much discussed analysis of the Oedipus myth.

Lyne, R. O. A. M. "Augustan Poetry and Society," in Boardman et al., *Oxford History*, pp. 215–244. A clear, concise account of poetic patronage in Augustan Rome and of poets who were Ovid's contemporaries.

Lyons, Deborah. *Gender and Immortality: Heroines in Ancient Greek Myth and Cult*. Princeton: Princeton University Press, 1997. A groundbreaking study of the role of female heroes. Contains much useful information on goddesses and heroines and the interaction of both with men.

Malinowski, Bronislaw. "Myth in Primitive Psychology," in *Magic, Science, and Religion and Other Essays*. Garden City, NJ: Doubleday, 1955, pp. 93–148. This essay, first published 1926, is perhaps Malinowski's most frequently cited work and the clearest exposition of his views on the relationship between myth and the organization of society.

Martindale, Charles. *Ovid Renewed: Ovidian Influences on Literature and Art from the Middle Ages to the Twentieth Century*. Cambridge, New York, Port Chester, Melbourne, Sydney: Cambridge University Press, 1988. A collection of several essays demonstrating the depth and range of Ovid's influence.

Penglase, Charles. *Greek Myths and Mesopotamia: Parallels and Influence in the Homeric Hymns and Hesiod*. Groundbreaking study of the relationship between the myths of Mesopotamia and those preserved in archaic Greek literature.

Peradotto, John. *Classical Mythology: An Annotated Bibliographical Survey*. Boulder, CO: The American Philological Association, 1977. A thorough and helpful bibliography of materials available at its time of publication. Contains a useful discussion of different theoretical approaches to myth.

Pomeroy, Sarah B. *Goddesses, Whores, Wives, and Slaves: Women in Classical Antiquity*. New York: Schocken Books, 1975. When it appeared, this book was pioneering, one of the first studies to systematically examine women's roles and lives in classical culture. Although dated in some respects, it remains a very useful and readable source of information.

Powell, Barry B. *Classical Myth*. Englewood Cliffs, NJ: Prentice Hall, 1995. The best college-level textbook on classical myth available. Includes many selections from ancient texts, good discussion, and helpful bibliography.

Propp, Vladimir J. *Morphology of the Folktale*. Trans. Laurence Scott. Bloomington, Indiana: University of Indiana Press, 1958. Analyzes Russian "quest" folktales according to a set pattern of thirty-one "functions." This book was not known outside Russia until the 1950s, when it became influential.

Sale, William. "The Psychoanalysis of Pentheus in the *Bacchae* of Euripides," in *Yale Classical Studies*, vol. 22, pp. 63–82. A thought-provoking analysis of Pentheus's resistance to Dionysos in psychological terms.

Sappho. "Hymn to Aphrodite," trans. E. Vandiver. A translation of Sappho's one surviving complete poem that attempts to retain the metrical pattern of the original. Found on the following Web site: Diotima: Materials for the Study of Women in the Ancient World (http://www.uky.edu/AS/Classics/vandiver.html).

Segal, Robert A. *Joseph Campbell: An Introduction*. New York and London: Garland Publishing, Inc., 1987. A clear, helpful introduction to and critique of Campbell's method and conclusions, written for the general reader.

Sienkewicz, Thomas J. *Theories of Myth: An Annotated Bibliography*. Lanham, MD, and London: The Scarecrow Press, Inc; Pasadena, CA, and Englewood Cliffs, NJ: Salem Press, 1997. This bibliography is an invaluable aid to those who wish to pursue the theoretical study of myth.

Tringham, Ruth, and Margaret Conkey. "Rethinking Figurines: A Critical View from Archaeology of Gimbutas, the 'Goddess' and Popular Culture," in Goodison and Morris, *Ancient Goddesses*, pp. 22–45. Discusses the difficulties involved in trying to extrapolate cultural beliefs and practices from figurines.

Tyrrell, William Blake, and Frieda S. Brown. *Athenian Myths and Institutions: Words in Action.* New York, Oxford: Oxford University Press, 1991. A wide-ranging examination of the interaction between myth and Athenian cultural institutions, such as tragedy, funeral orations, and sculpture.

Vandiver, Elizabeth. *Heroes in Herodotus: The Interaction of Myth and History.* Studien zur klassischen Philologie 56. Frankfurt: Peter Lang, 1991. Examines the function of mythological heroes in the *Histories* of Herodotus. Unfortunately, Greek and other foreign languages are left untranslated (if I had it to do over again, I would change this), but the recommended section does not depend on the Greek to be comprehensible.

Vellacott, P. H. "The Guilt of Oedipus," in Berkowitz and Brunner, *Oedipus Tyrannus,* pp. 207–218. A provocative article that goes against most interpretations of the play by arguing that Oedipus actually knew Laius was his father and Jocasta, his mother.

Vermeule, Emily. *Aspects of Death in Early Greek Art and Poetry.* Berkeley: The University of California Press, 1975. Surveys the evidence for the way the Greeks viewed death. Discusses mourning and burial rituals, as well as conceptions of the Underworld. Well-written and interesting.

Walker, Henry J. *Theseus and Athens.* New York, Oxford: Oxford University Press, 1995. An examination of Theseus's role as "culture hero" for the Athenians. Traces Theseus's development from a relatively minor hero to an idealized ruler of all Attica.

Wender, Dorothea. "The Myth of Washington," in Dundes, *Sacred Narrative,* pp. 336–342. A wonderfully witty spoof that applies several theories of myth to "prove" that George Washington is a purely mythical character who never existed at all. Entertaining and thought-provoking.

Wiseman, T. P. *Remus: A Roman Myth.* Cambridge: Cambridge University Press, 1995. A thorough, very readable, and fascinating exploration of the function of Remus in Roman myth and of the Romulus and Remus story overall. Includes an appendix giving various ancient versions of Rome's foundation story.

Wood, Michael. *In Search of the Trojan War*. Berkeley: University of California Press, 1998. A fascinating, well-written, and well-documented examination of the evidence for the historicity of the Trojan War. Includes many illustrations, maps, and other aids.

Woodford, Susan. *The Trojan War in Ancient Art*. Ithaca: Cornell University Press, 1993. A useful summary of the mythical background to the Trojan War, with illustrations from ancient art.

Yale Classical Studies, vol. 22: "Studies in Fifth-Century Thought and Literature," Adam Parry, ed. Cambridge: Cambridge University Press, 1972. One of the premier annuals in the field of classical studies; collects essays by leading scholars, including Kirk on myth and Sale on Dionysos and Pentheus.

Zeitlin, Froma. "The Motif of the Corrupted Sacrifice in Aeschylus' *Oresteia*," *Transactions of the American Philological Association* 96 (1965): 463–508. A groundbreaking essay that examines human and animal sacrifice in the *Oresteia*.

Notes

Notes

Notes

Notes

Notes

Notes